Otomen

Story & Art by
Aya Kanno

Volume
ELEVEN

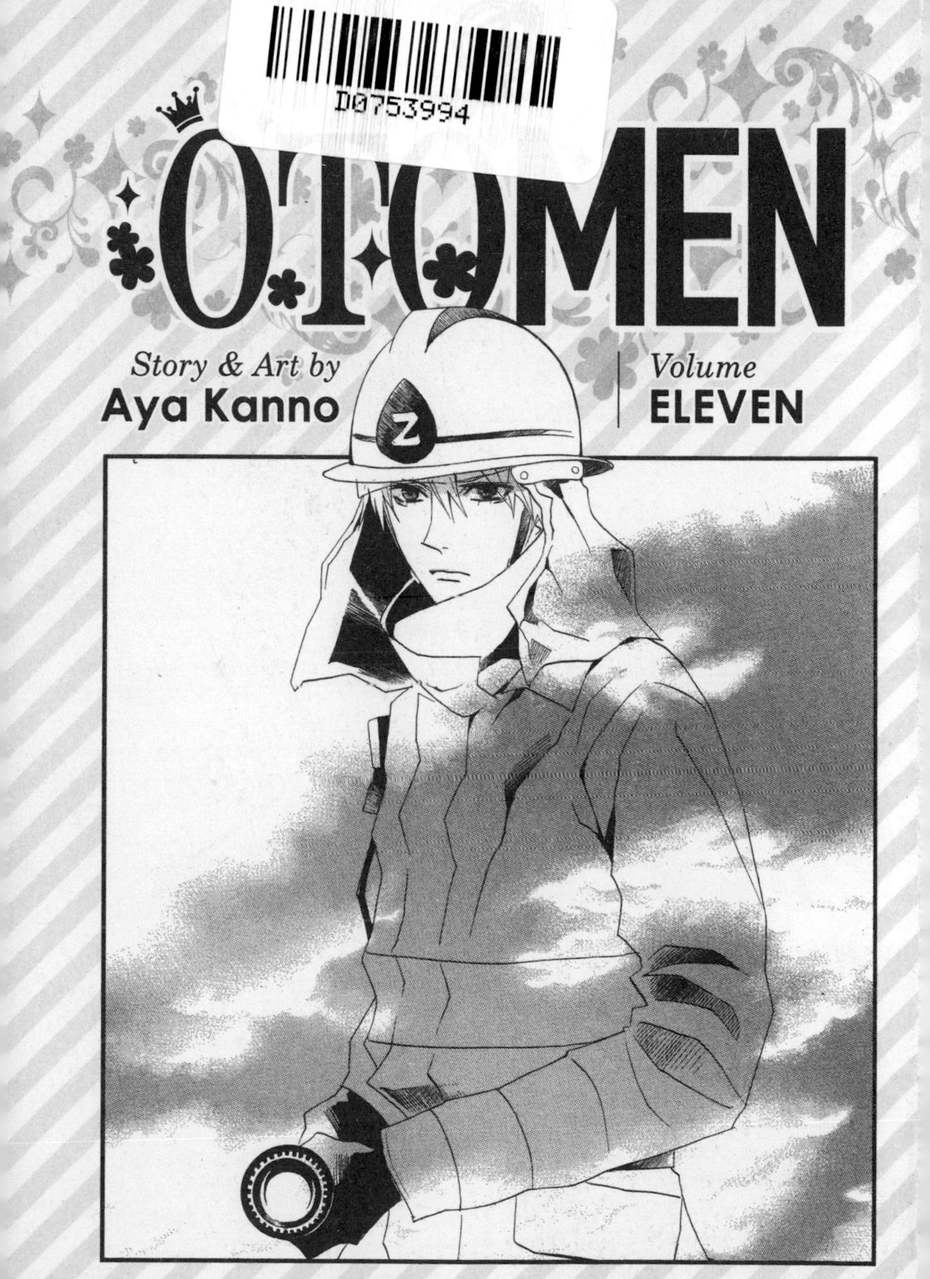

Z

OTOMEN Characters & Story

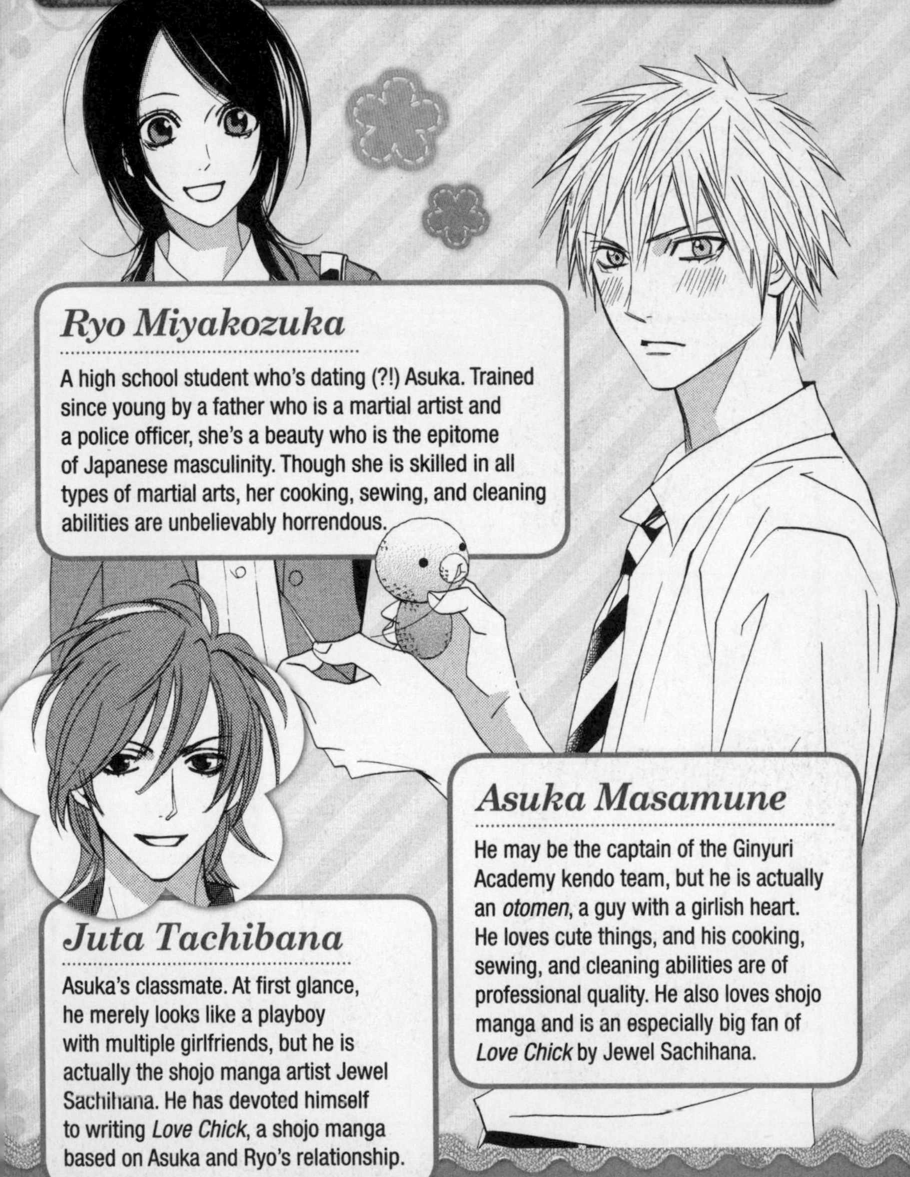

Ryo Miyakozuka

A high school student who's dating (?!) Asuka. Trained since young by a father who is a martial artist and a police officer, she's a beauty who is the epitome of Japanese masculinity. Though she is skilled in all types of martial arts, her cooking, sewing, and cleaning abilities are unbelievably horrendous.

Asuka Masamune

He may be the captain of the Ginyuri Academy kendo team, but he is actually an *otomen*, a guy with a girlish heart. He loves cute things, and his cooking, sewing, and cleaning abilities are of professional quality. He also loves shojo manga and is an especially big fan of *Love Chick* by Jewel Sachihana.

Juta Tachibana

Asuka's classmate. At first glance, he merely looks like a playboy with multiple girlfriends, but he is actually the shojo manga artist Jewel Sachihana. He has devoted himself to writing *Love Chick*, a shojo manga based on Asuka and Ryo's relationship.

STORY

Asuka's cousin Kasuga brings special teachers to Ginyuri Academy in order to rid it of *otomen*. One of them, Mifune Naito (a foreigner), teaches Japanese history and is a samurai fanatic. He takes Asuka and his friends on a school trip where they are forced to live like samurai.

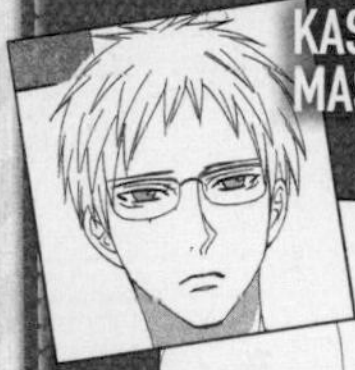

KASUGA MASAMUNE

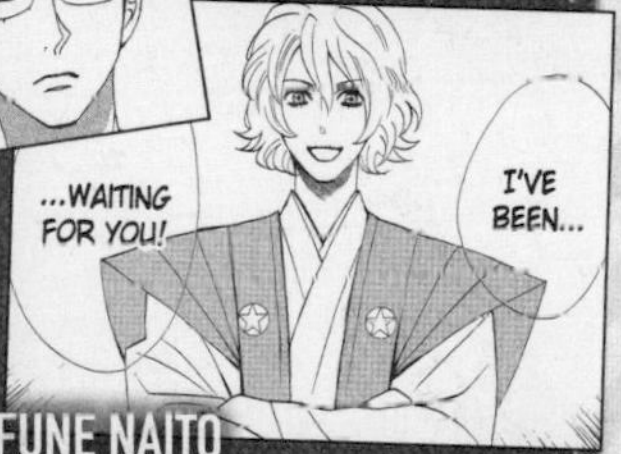
I'VE BEEN...
...WAITING FOR YOU!

MIFUNE NAITO

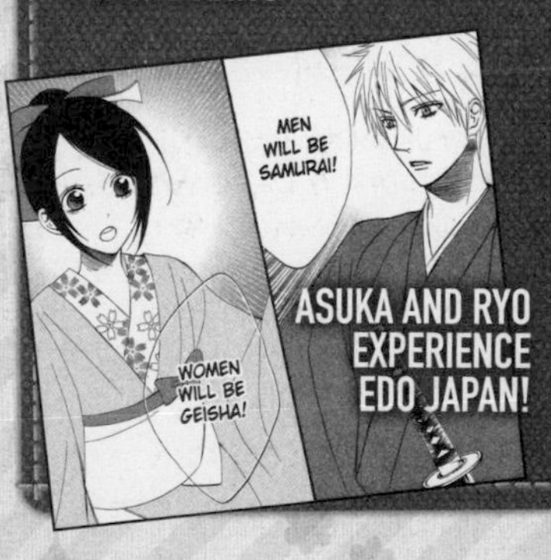
MEN WILL BE SAMURAI!
WOMEN WILL BE GEISHA!

ASUKA AND RYO EXPERIENCE EDO JAPAN!

OTHER OTOMEN

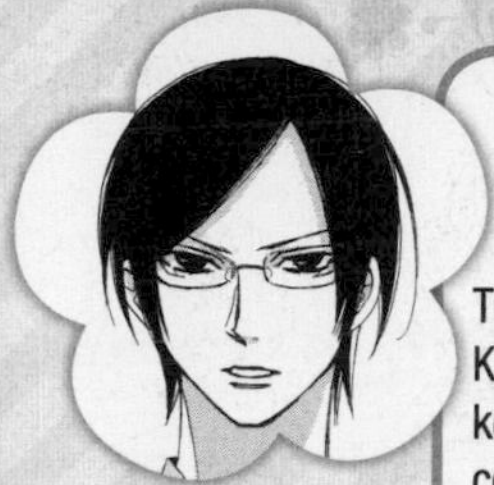

Hajime Tonomine

The captain of the Kinbara High School kendo team, he considers Asuka his sworn rival. He is actually an *otomen* who is good with cosmetics.

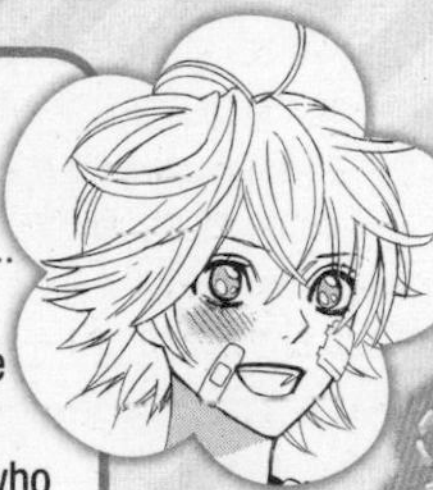

Yamato Ariake

He is younger than Asuka and looks like a cute girl. He is a delusional *otomen* who admires manliness.

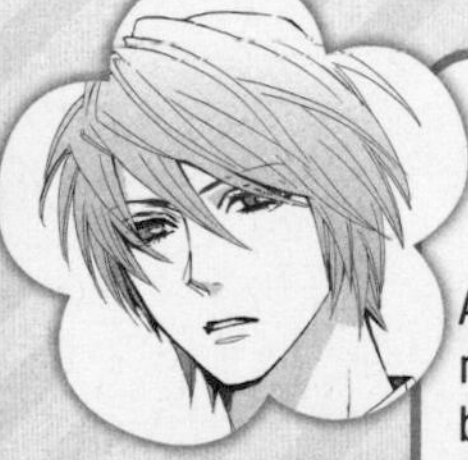

Kitora Kurokawa

Asuka's classmate. A man who is captivated by the beauty of flowers. He is an obsessed *otomen* who wants to cover the world in flowers.

OTOMEN
volume 11
CONTENTS

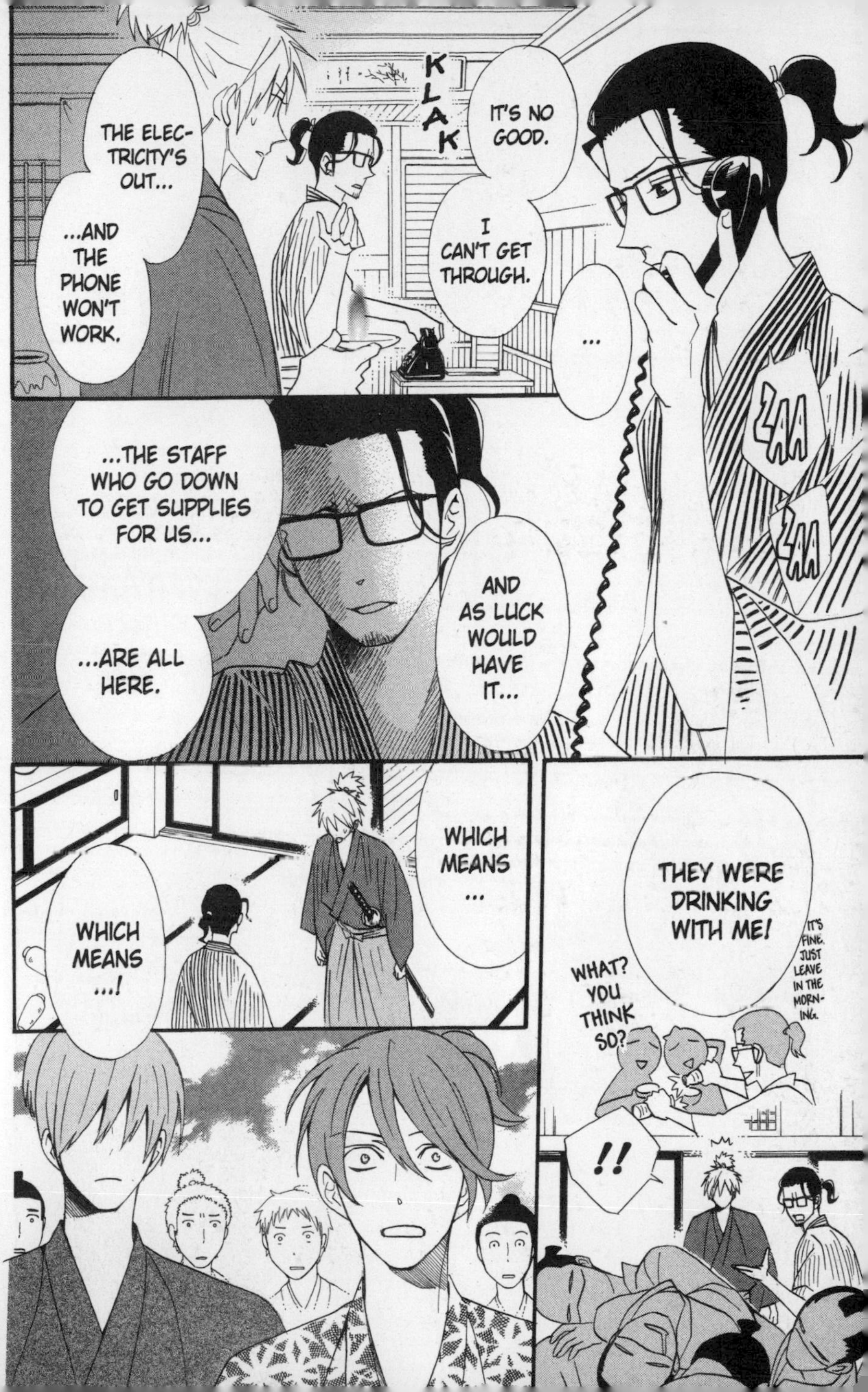
...
ZAA
ZAA
KLAK
IT'S NO GOOD.
I CAN'T GET THROUGH.
THE ELEC-TRICITY'S OUT...
...AND THE PHONE WON'T WORK.
AND AS LUCK WOULD HAVE IT...
...THE STAFF WHO GO DOWN TO GET SUPPLIES FOR US...
...ARE ALL HERE.
THEY WERE DRINKING WITH ME!
IT'S FINE. JUST LEAVE IN THE MORN-ING.
WHAT? YOU THINK SO?
WHICH MEANS...
WHICH MEANS...!
!!

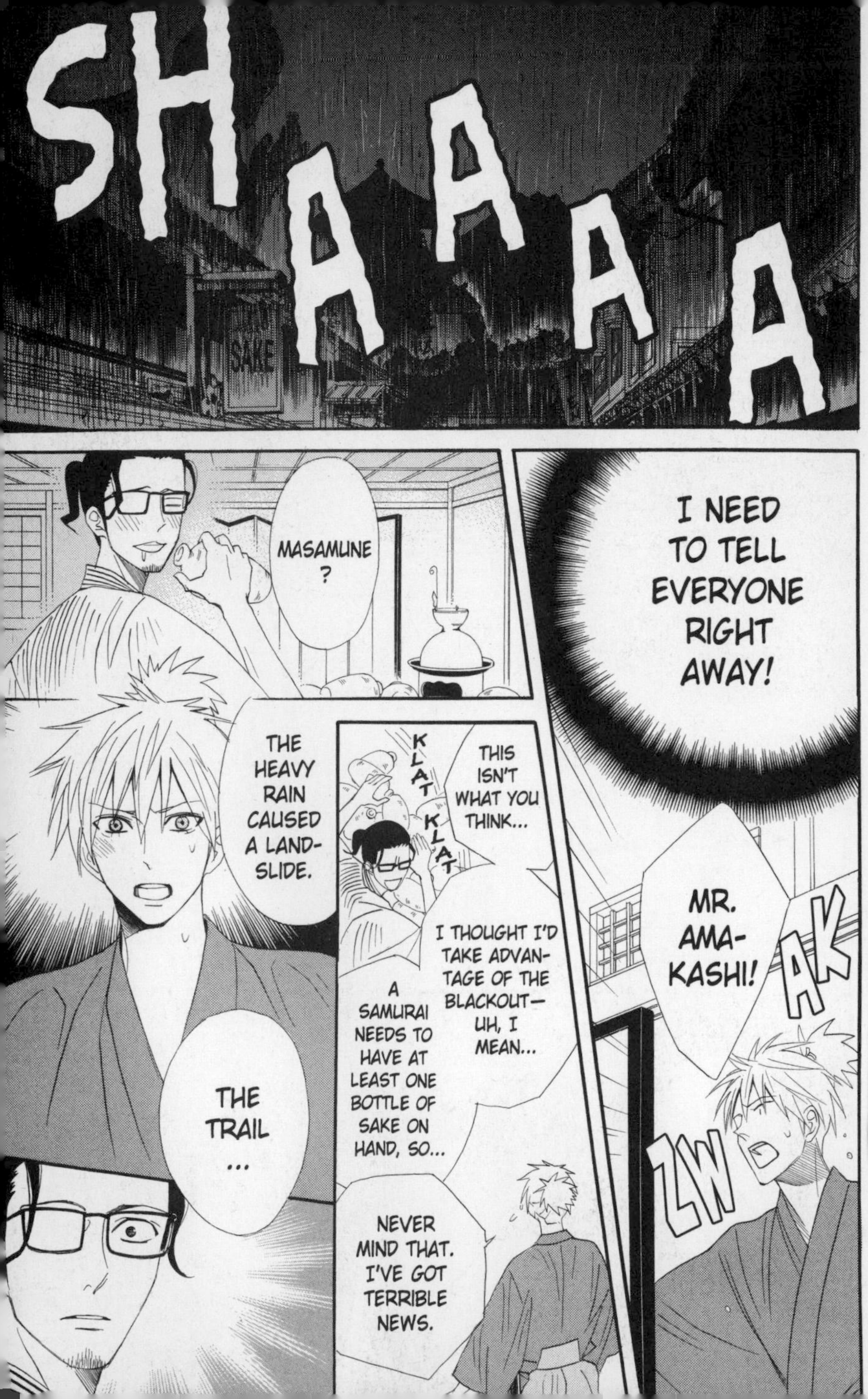
SHAAAAA
SAKE
I NEED TO TELL EVERYONE RIGHT AWAY!
MASAMUNE?
ZW
AK
MR. AMA-KASHI!
THIS ISN'T WHAT YOU THINK...
KLAT KLAT
I THOUGHT I'D TAKE ADVAN-TAGE OF THE BLACKOUT— UH, I MEAN...
A SAMURAI NEEDS TO HAVE AT LEAST ONE BOTTLE OF SAKE ON HAND, SO...
NEVER MIND THAT. I'VE GOT TERRIBLE NEWS.
THE HEAVY RAIN CAUSED A LAND-SLIDE.
THE TRAIL...

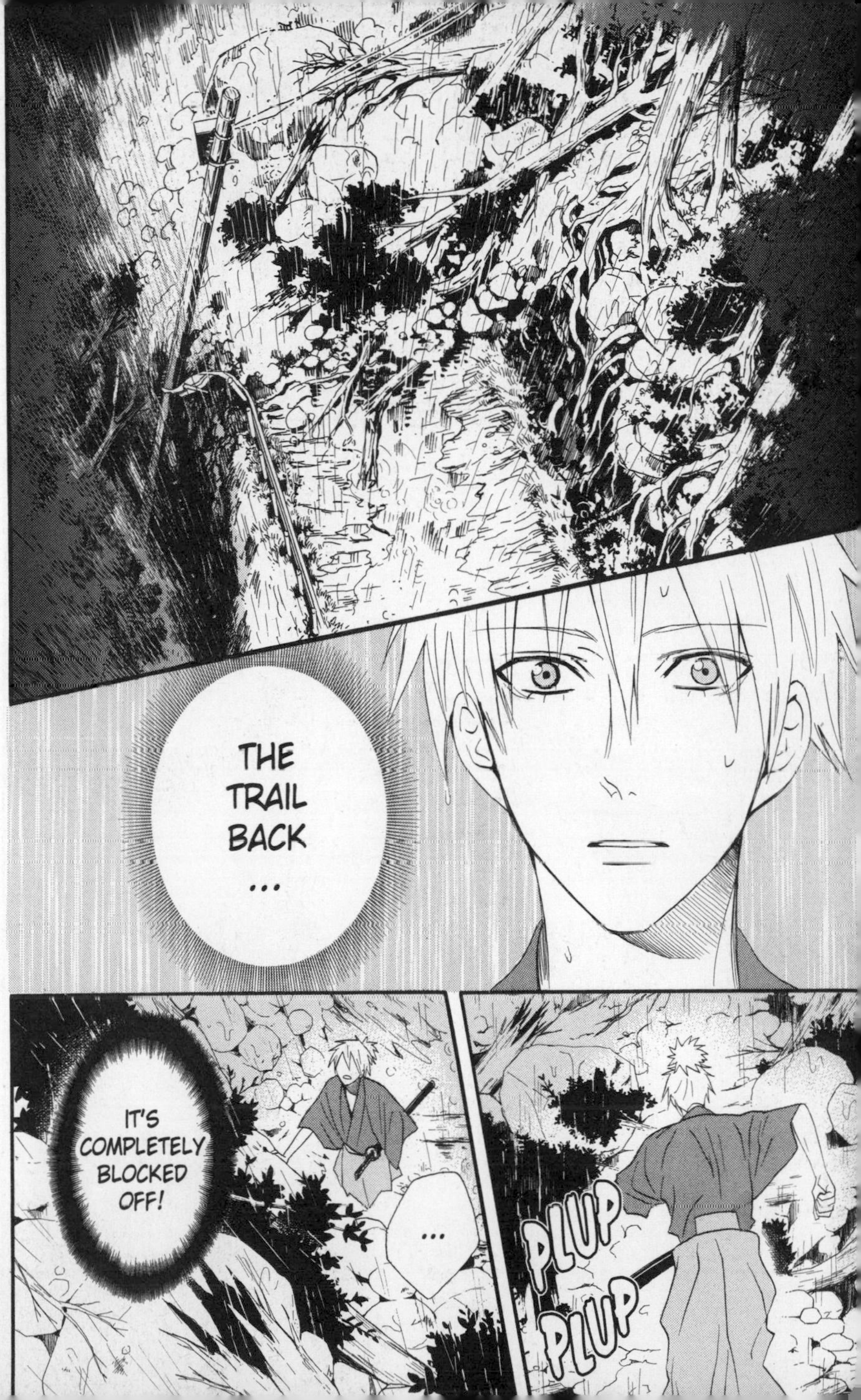
THE TRAIL BACK ...
PLUP PLUP
...
IT'S COMPLETELY BLOCKED OFF!

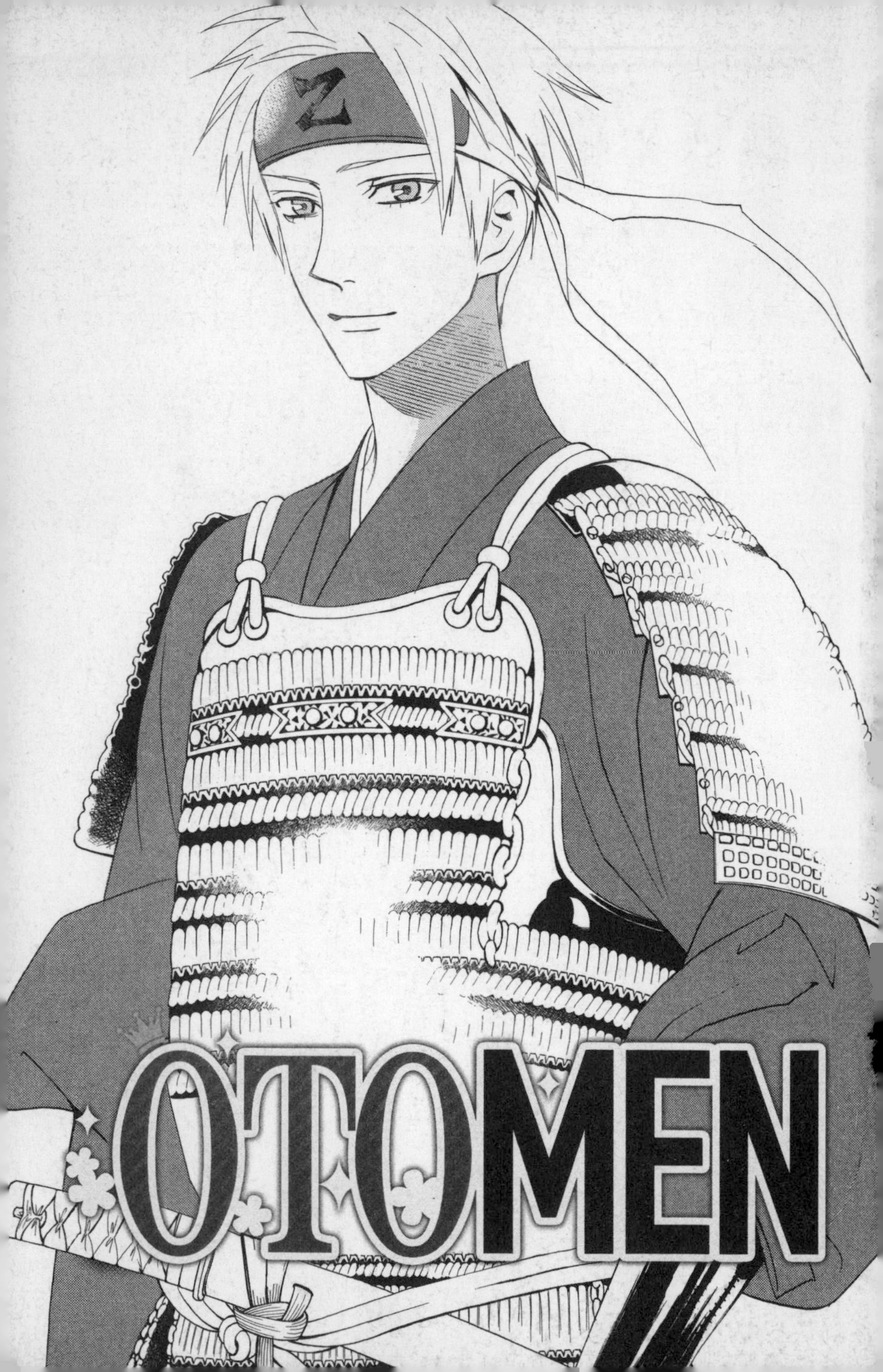
OTOMEN

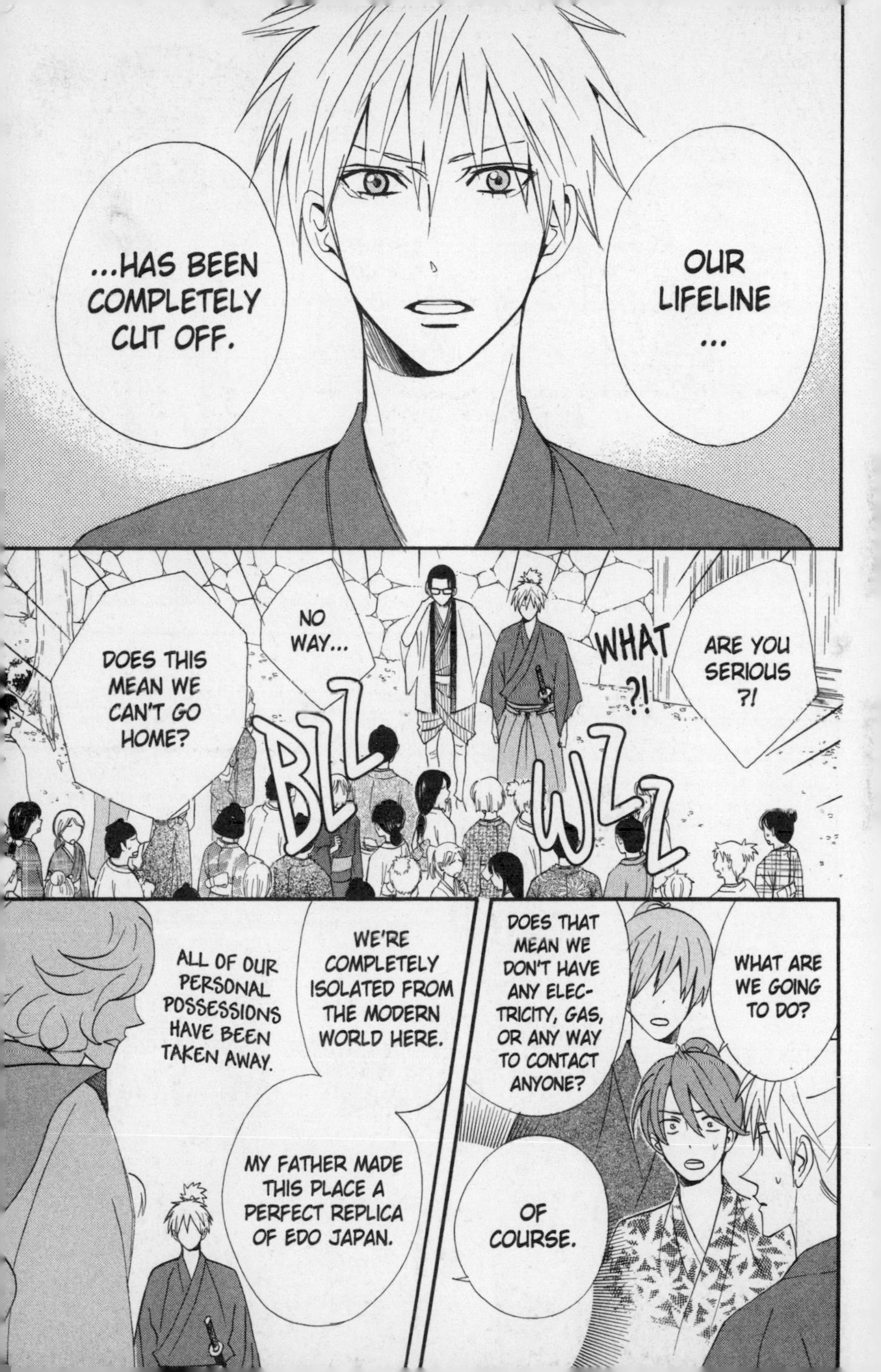
OUR LIFELINE ...
...HAS BEEN COMPLETELY CUT OFF.
ARE YOU SERIOUS ?!
WHAT ?!
NO WAY...
DOES THIS MEAN WE CAN'T GO HOME?
WHAT ARE WE GOING TO DO?
DOES THAT MEAN WE DON'T HAVE ANY ELECTRICITY, GAS, OR ANY WAY TO CONTACT ANYONE?
OF COURSE.
WE'RE COMPLETELY ISOLATED FROM THE MODERN WORLD HERE.
ALL OF OUR PERSONAL POSSESSIONS HAVE BEEN TAKEN AWAY.
MY FATHER MADE THIS PLACE A PERFECT REPLICA OF EDO JAPAN.

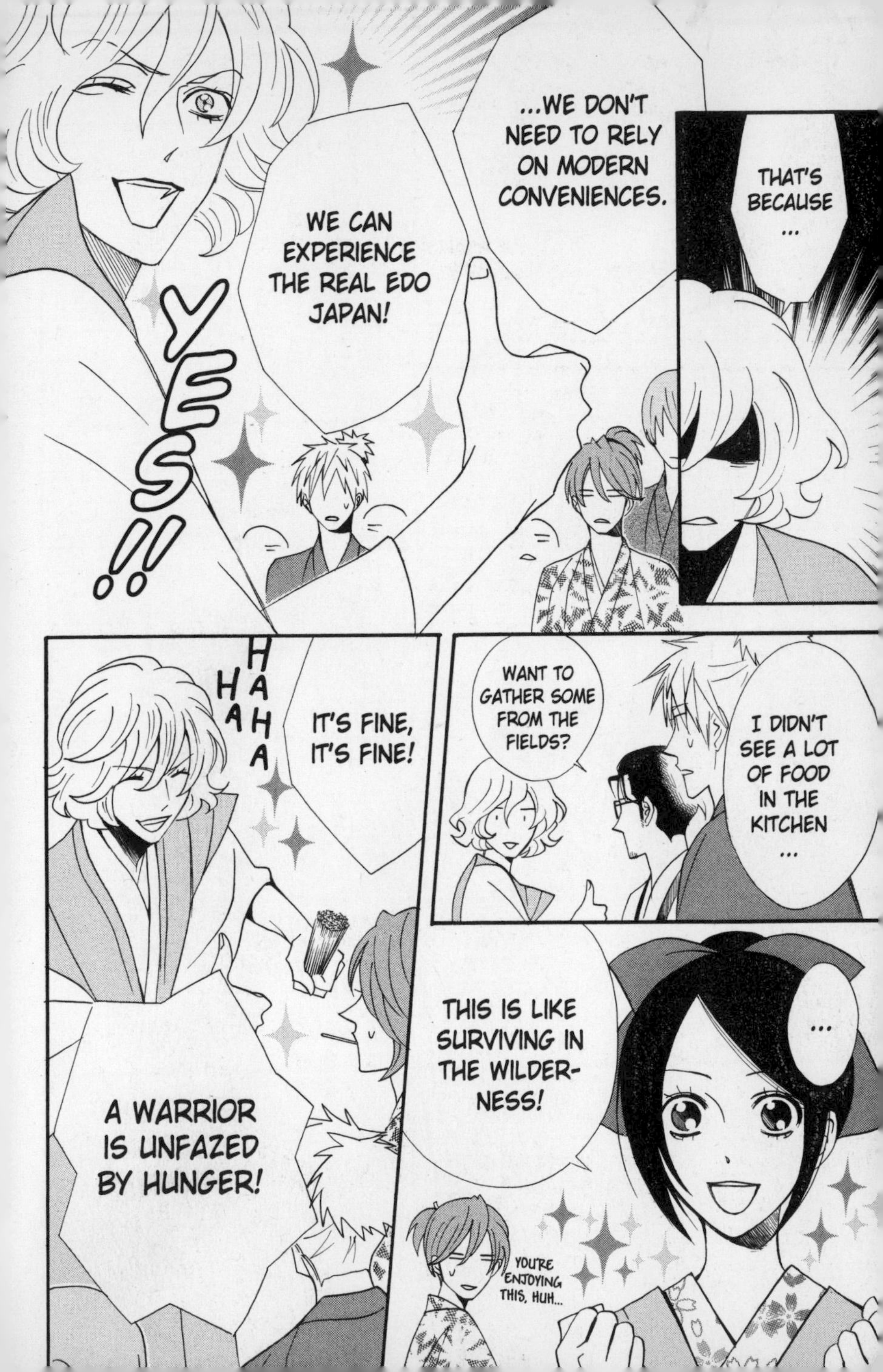
THAT'S BECAUSE ...
...WE DON'T NEED TO RELY ON MODERN CONVENIENCES.
WE CAN EXPERIENCE THE REAL EDO JAPAN!
YES!!
I DIDN'T SEE A LOT OF FOOD IN THE KITCHEN ...
WANT TO GATHER SOME FROM THE FIELDS?
...
THIS IS LIKE SURVIVING IN THE WILDER-NESS!
YOU'RE ENJOYING THIS, HUH...
HA HA HA HA
IT'S FINE, IT'S FINE!
A WARRIOR IS UNFAZED BY HUNGER!

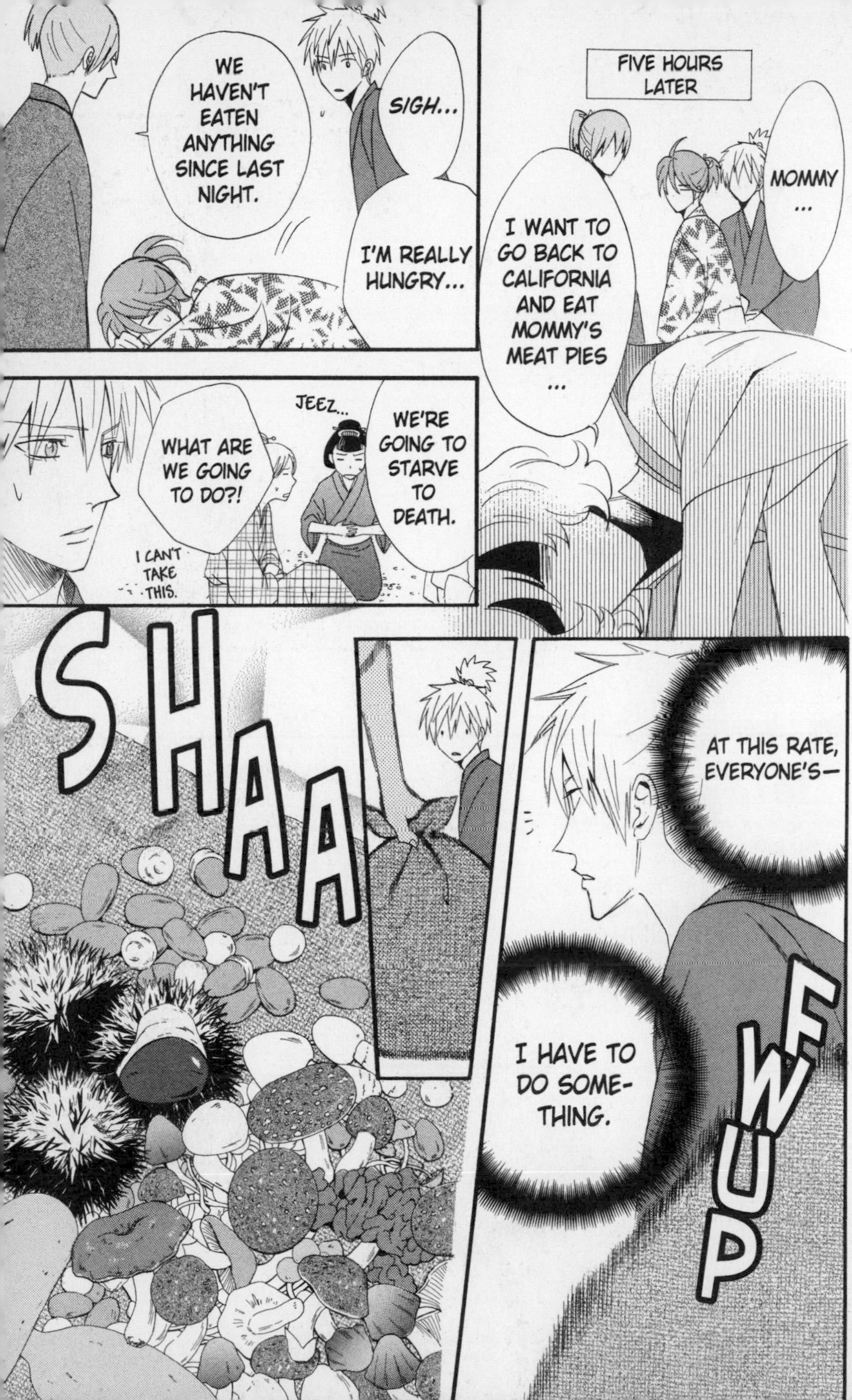
FIVE HOURS LATER
MOMMY ...
I WANT TO GO BACK TO CALIFORNIA AND EAT MOMMY'S MEAT PIES ...
SIGH...
WE HAVEN'T EATEN ANYTHING SINCE LAST NIGHT.
I'M REALLY HUNGRY...
WE'RE GOING TO STARVE TO DEATH.
JEEZ...
WHAT ARE WE GOING TO DO?!
I CAN'T TAKE THIS.
AT THIS RATE, EVERYONE'S—
I HAVE TO DO SOME-THING.
FWUP
SHAA

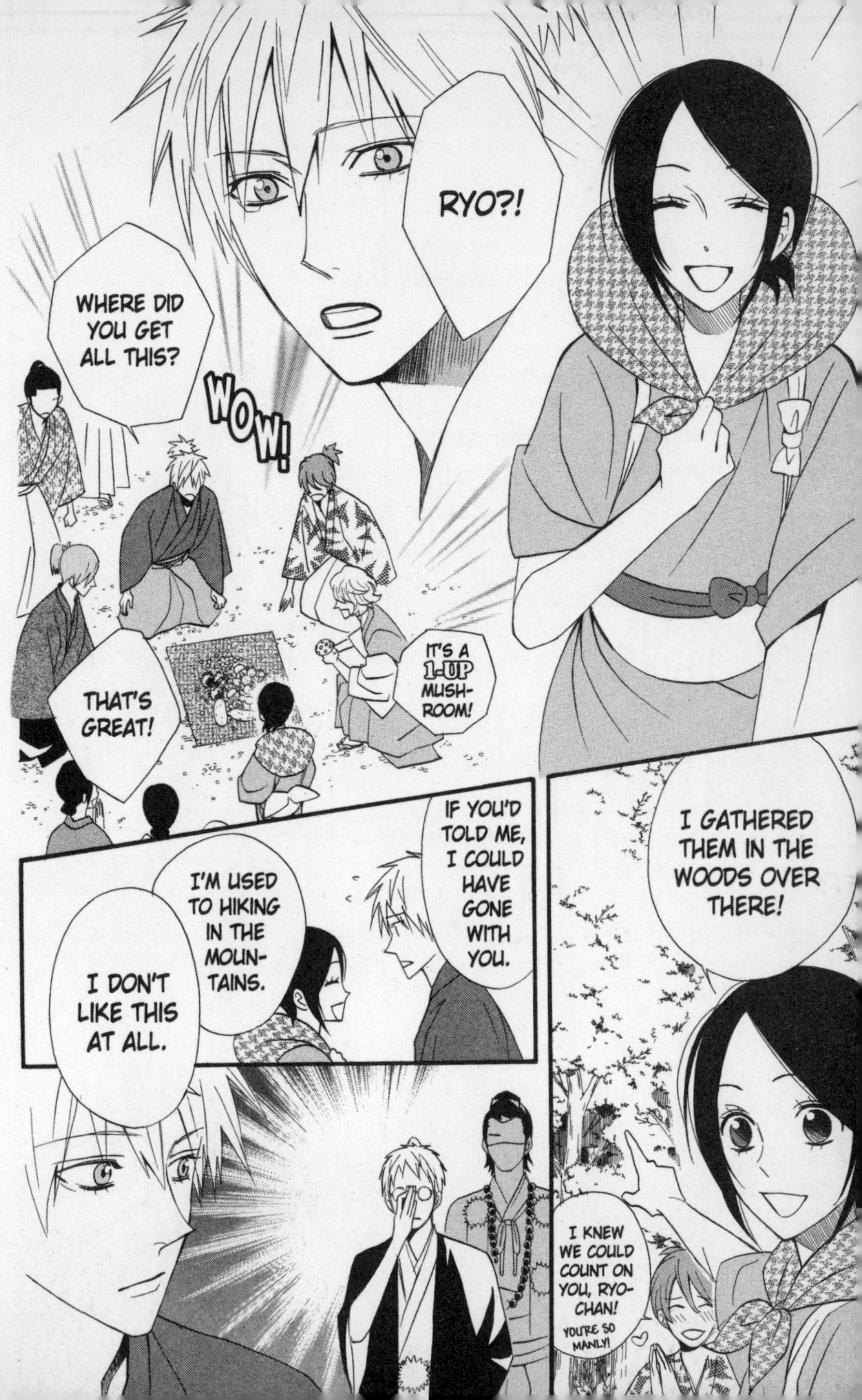
RYO?!
WHERE DID YOU GET ALL THIS?
WOW!
IT'S A 1-UP MUSHROOM!
THAT'S GREAT!
I GATHERED THEM IN THE WOODS OVER THERE!
I KNEW WE COULD COUNT ON YOU, RYO-CHAN!
YOU'RE SO MANLY!
IF YOU'D TOLD ME, I COULD HAVE GONE WITH YOU.
I'M USED TO HIKING IN THE MOUNTAINS.
I DON'T LIKE THIS AT ALL.

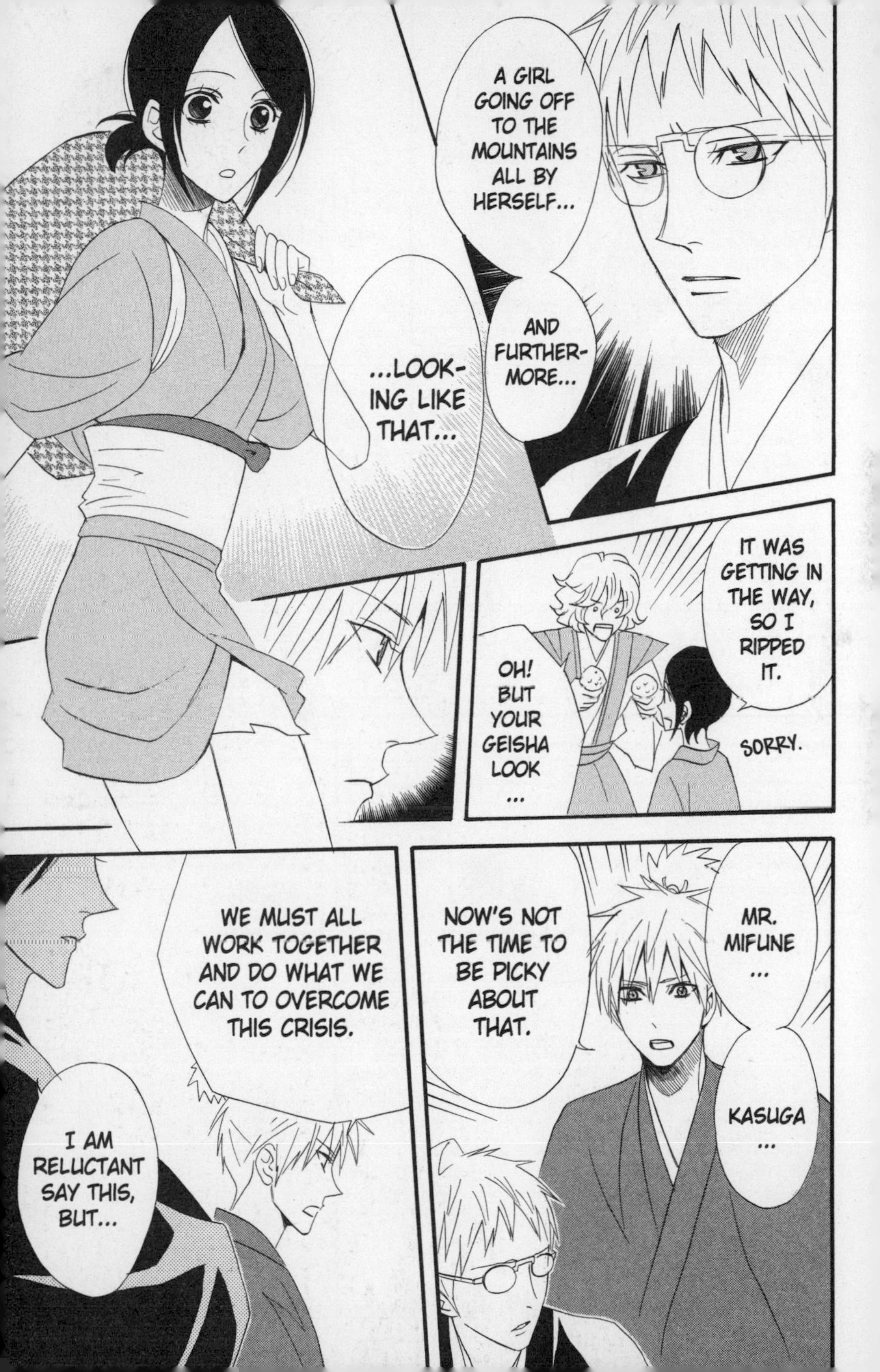
A GIRL GOING OFF TO THE MOUNTAINS ALL BY HERSELF...
AND FURTHER-MORE...
...LOOK-ING LIKE THAT...
IT WAS GETTING IN THE WAY, SO I RIPPED IT.
SORRY.
OH! BUT YOUR GEISHA LOOK ...
MR. MIFUNE ...
KASUGA ...
NOW'S NOT THE TIME TO BE PICKY ABOUT THAT.
WE MUST ALL WORK TOGETHER AND DO WHAT WE CAN TO OVERCOME THIS CRISIS.
I AM RELUCTANT SAY THIS, BUT...

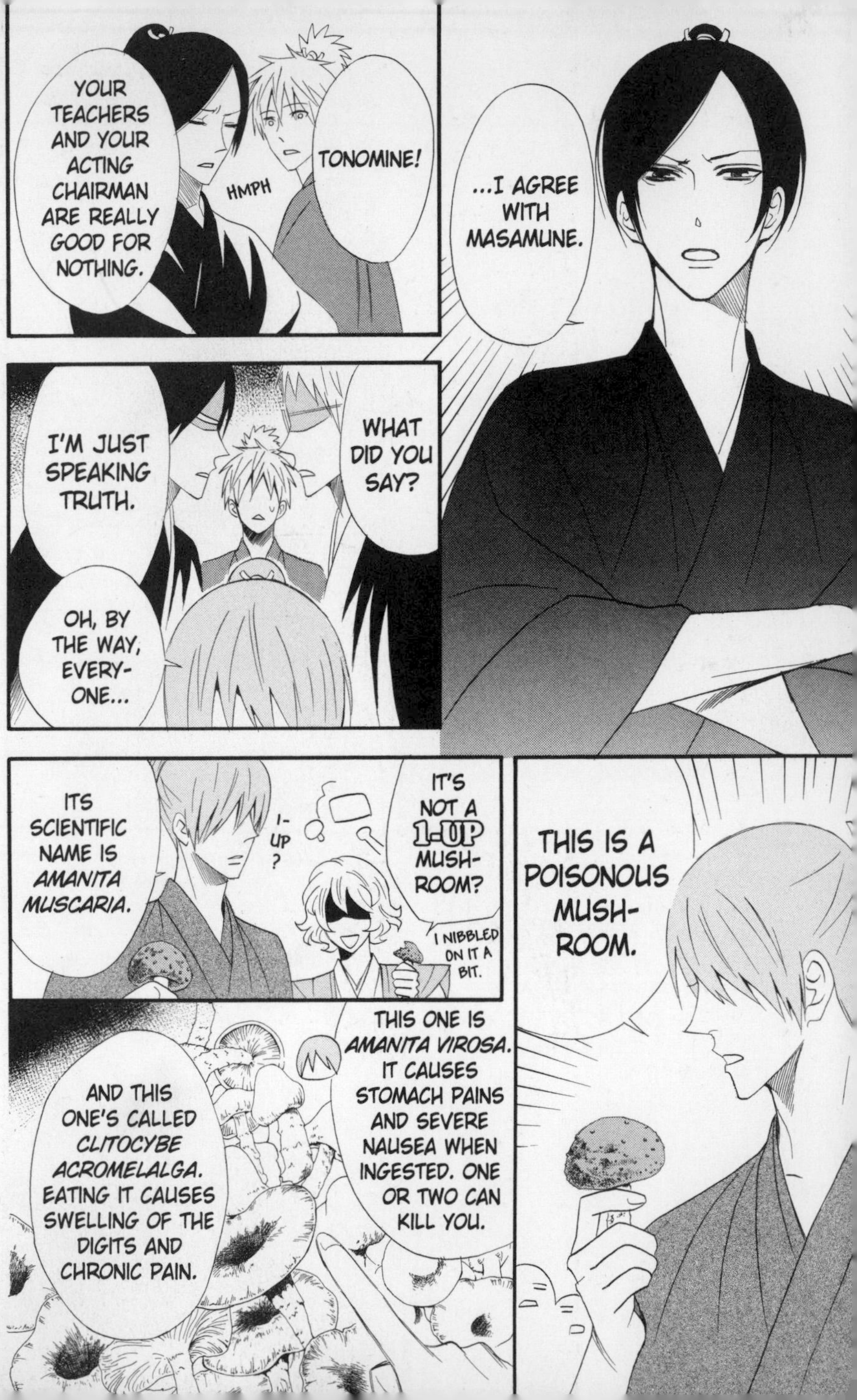
...I AGREE WITH MASAMUNE.
TONOMINE!
YOUR TEACHERS AND YOUR ACTING CHAIRMAN ARE REALLY GOOD FOR NOTHING.
HMPH
WHAT DID YOU SAY?
I'M JUST SPEAKING TRUTH.
OH, BY THE WAY, EVERY-ONE...
THIS IS A POISONOUS MUSH-ROOM.
IT'S NOT A 1-UP MUSH-ROOM?
I NIBBLED ON IT A BIT.
1-UP?
ITS SCIENTIFIC NAME IS *AMANITA MUSCARIA*.
THIS ONE IS *AMANITA VIROSA*. IT CAUSES STOMACH PAINS AND SEVERE NAUSEA WHEN INGESTED. ONE OR TWO CAN KILL YOU.
AND THIS ONE'S CALLED *CLITOCYBE ACROMELALGA*. EATING IT CAUSES SWELLING OF THE DIGITS AND CHRONIC PAIN.

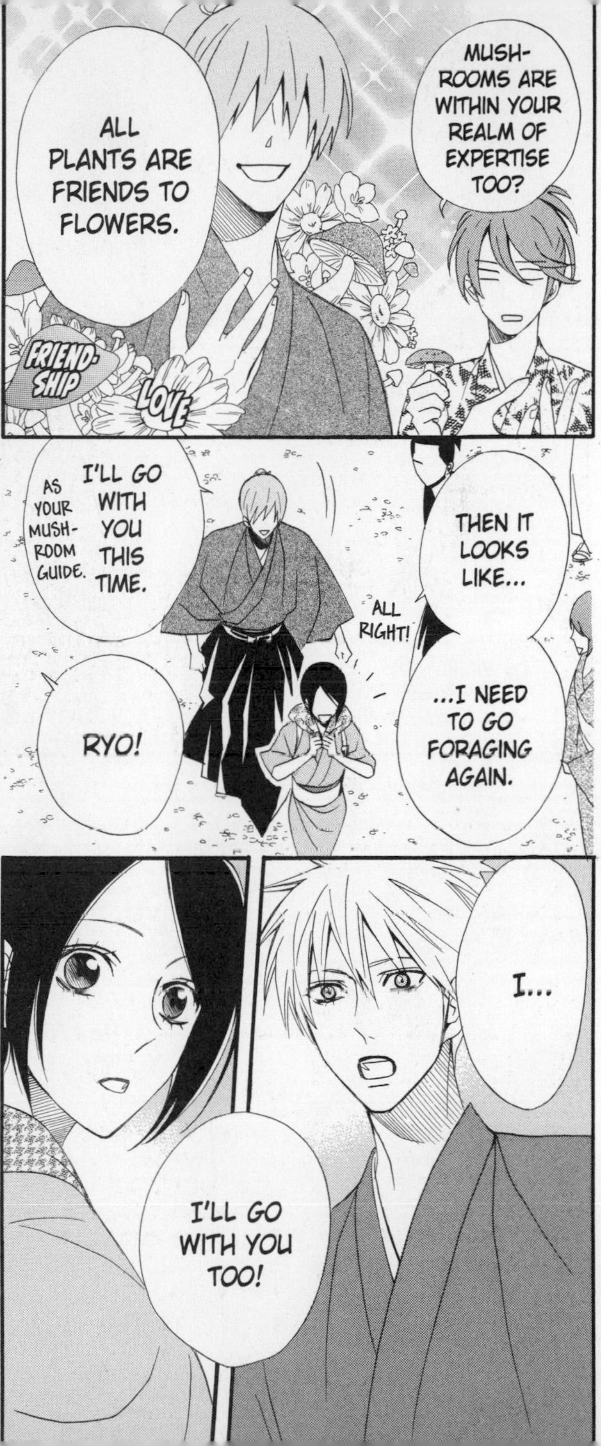
MUSH-ROOMS ARE WITHIN YOUR REALM OF EXPERTISE TOO?
ALL PLANTS ARE FRIENDS TO FLOWERS.
FRIEND-SHIP
LOVE
THEN IT LOOKS LIKE...
...I NEED TO GO FORAGING AGAIN.
ALL RIGHT!
I'LL GO WITH YOU THIS TIME.
AS YOUR MUSH-ROOM GUIDE.
RYO!
I...
I'LL GO WITH YOU TOO!

It's Volume 11! Hello.

Writing this chapter reminded me that writing period pieces is fun.
After this chapter went to print, I took two breaks. I tried to bring that old *Otomen* feeling back in the following story. The short story I wrote in between was very serious, so I remember feeling how pleasant it was to do *Otomen* again.
This series is the longest I've ever done, so I feel like it's a big part of me.

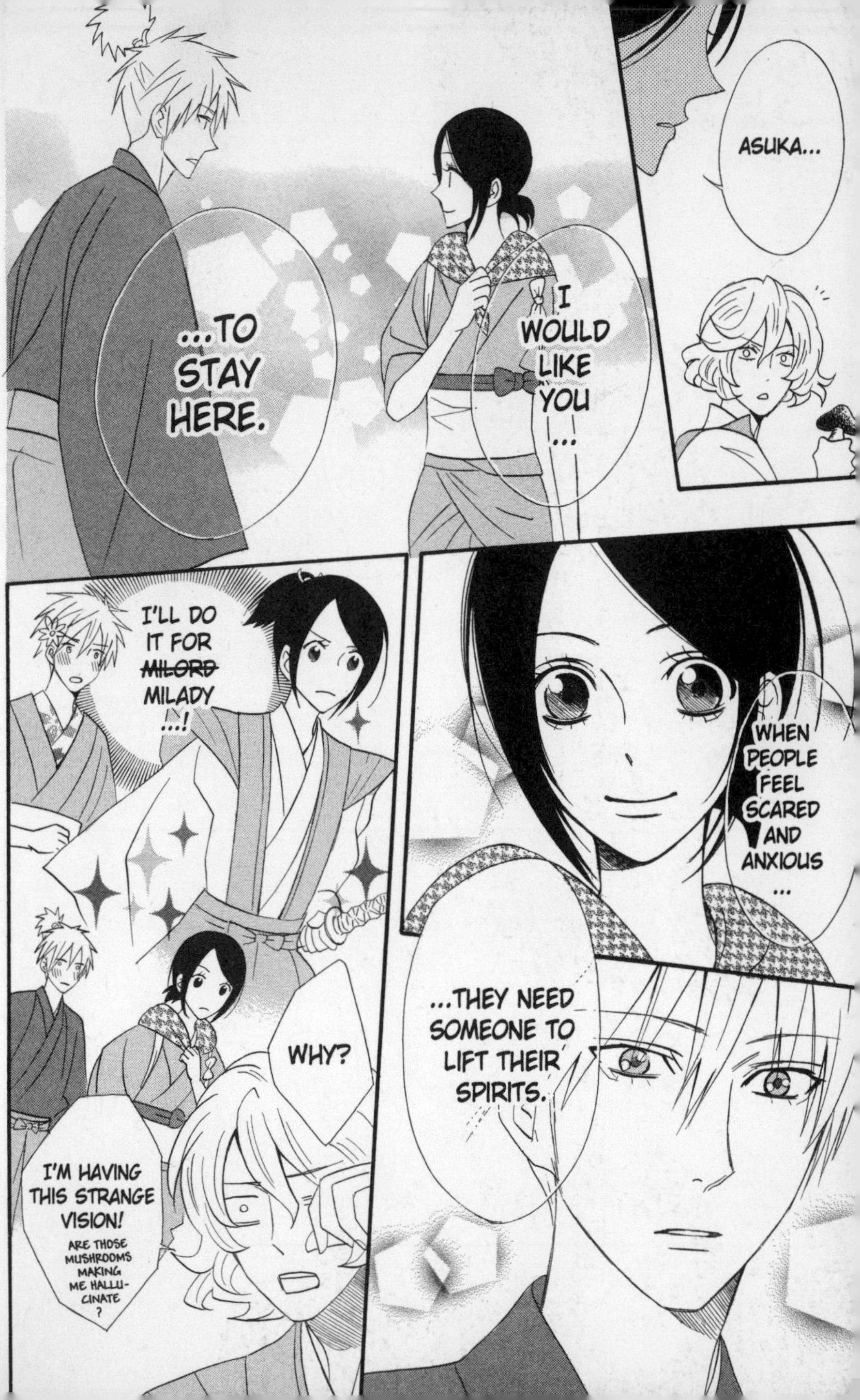
ASUKA...
I WOULD LIKE YOU...
...TO STAY HERE.
WHEN PEOPLE FEEL SCARED AND ANXIOUS...
...THEY NEED SOMEONE TO LIFT THEIR SPIRITS.
I'LL DO IT FOR ~~MILORD~~ MILADY...!
WHY?
I'M HAVING THIS STRANGE VISION!
ARE THOSE MUSHROOMS MAKING ME HALLUCINATE?

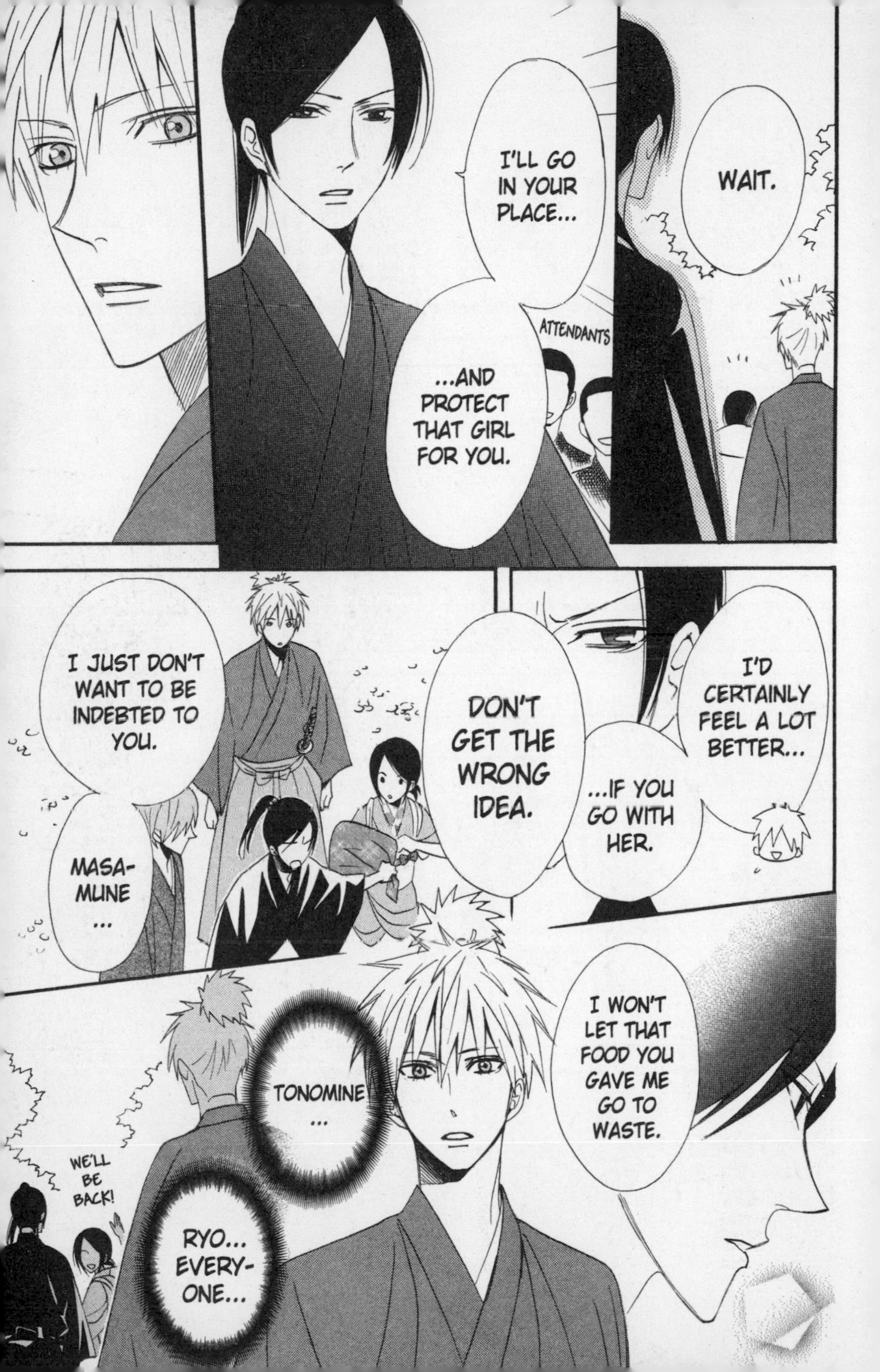
WAIT.
I'LL GO IN YOUR PLACE...
...AND PROTECT THAT GIRL FOR YOU.
ATTENDANTS
I'D CERTAINLY FEEL A LOT BETTER...
...IF YOU GO WITH HER.
DON'T GET THE WRONG IDEA.
I JUST DON'T WANT TO BE INDEBTED TO YOU.
MASA-MUNE ...
I WON'T LET THAT FOOD YOU GAVE ME GO TO WASTE.
TONOMINE ...
RYO... EVERY-ONE...
WE'LL BE BACK!

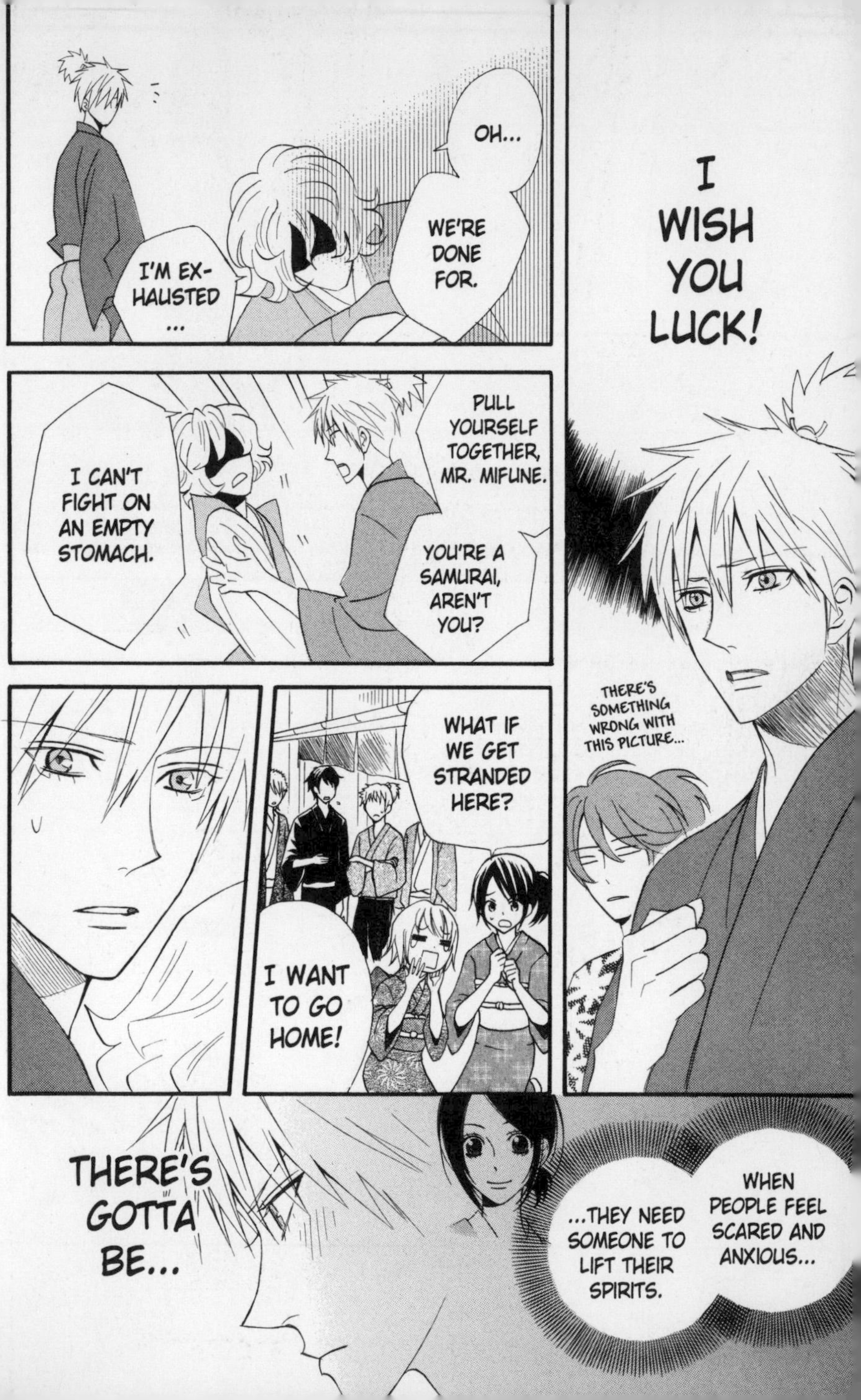
I WISH YOU LUCK!
THERE'S SOMETHING WRONG WITH THIS PICTURE...
OH...
WE'RE DONE FOR.
I'M EX-HAUSTED ...
PULL YOURSELF TOGETHER, MR. MIFUNE.
YOU'RE A SAMURAI, AREN'T YOU?
I CAN'T FIGHT ON AN EMPTY STOMACH.
WHAT IF WE GET STRANDED HERE?
I WANT TO GO HOME!
WHEN PEOPLE FEEL SCARED AND ANXIOUS...
...THEY NEED SOMEONE TO LIFT THEIR SPIRITS.
THERE'S GOTTA BE...

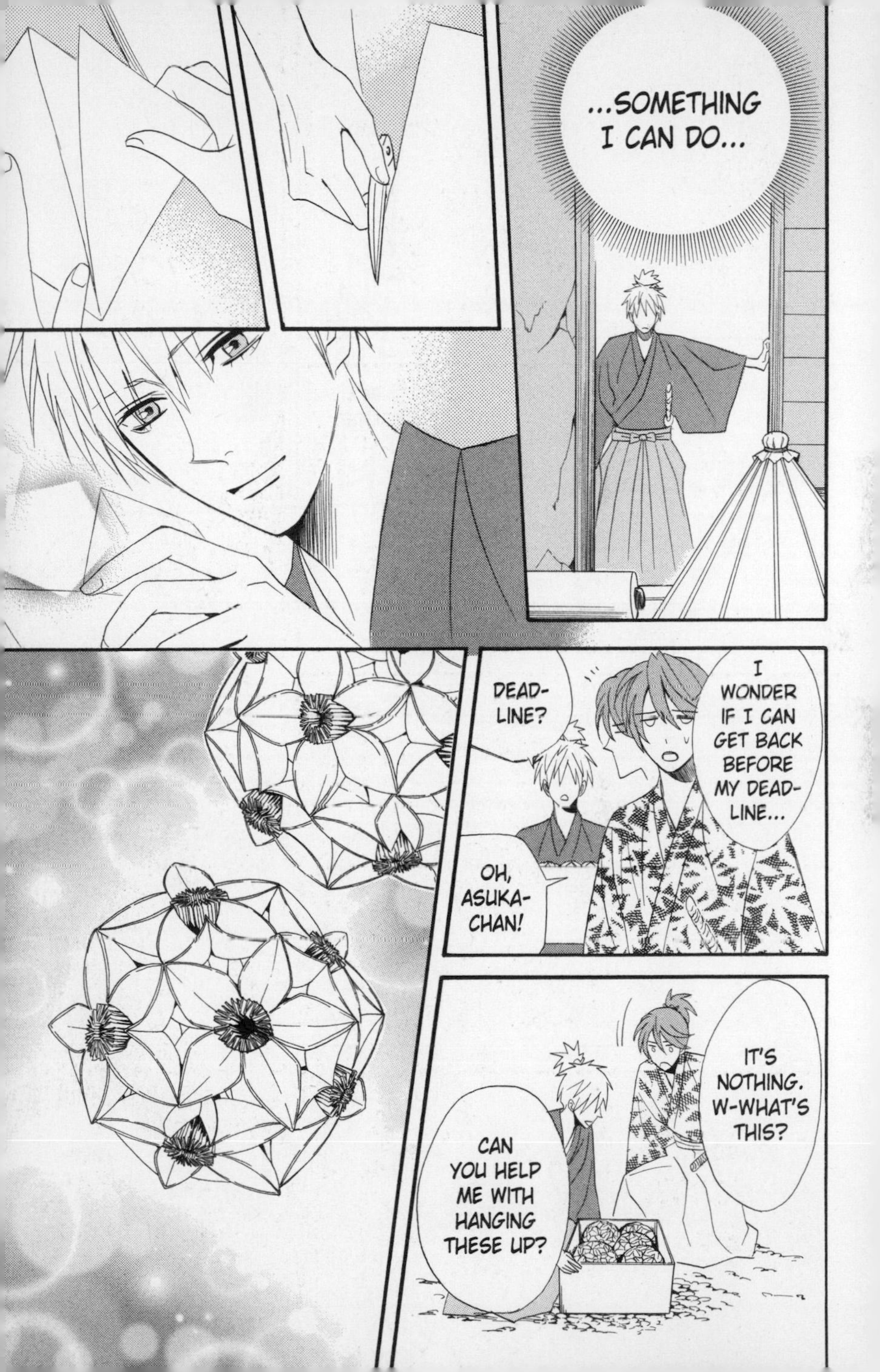
...SOMETHING I CAN DO...
I WONDER IF I CAN GET BACK BEFORE MY DEAD-LINE...
DEAD-LINE?
OH, ASUKA-CHAN!
IT'S NOTHING. W-WHAT'S THIS?
CAN YOU HELP ME WITH HANGING THESE UP?

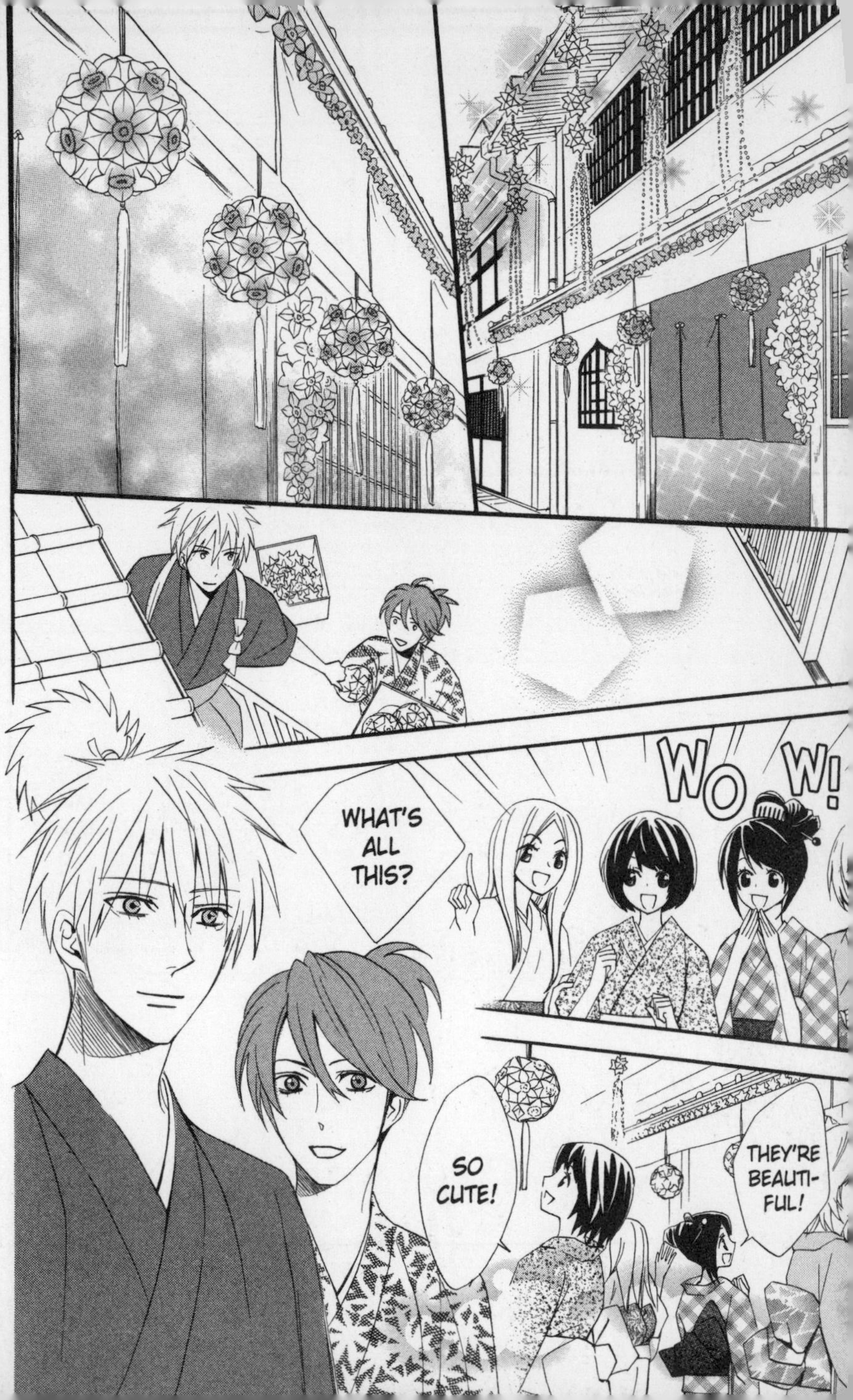
WOW!
WHAT'S ALL THIS?
THEY'RE BEAUTI-FUL!
SO CUTE!

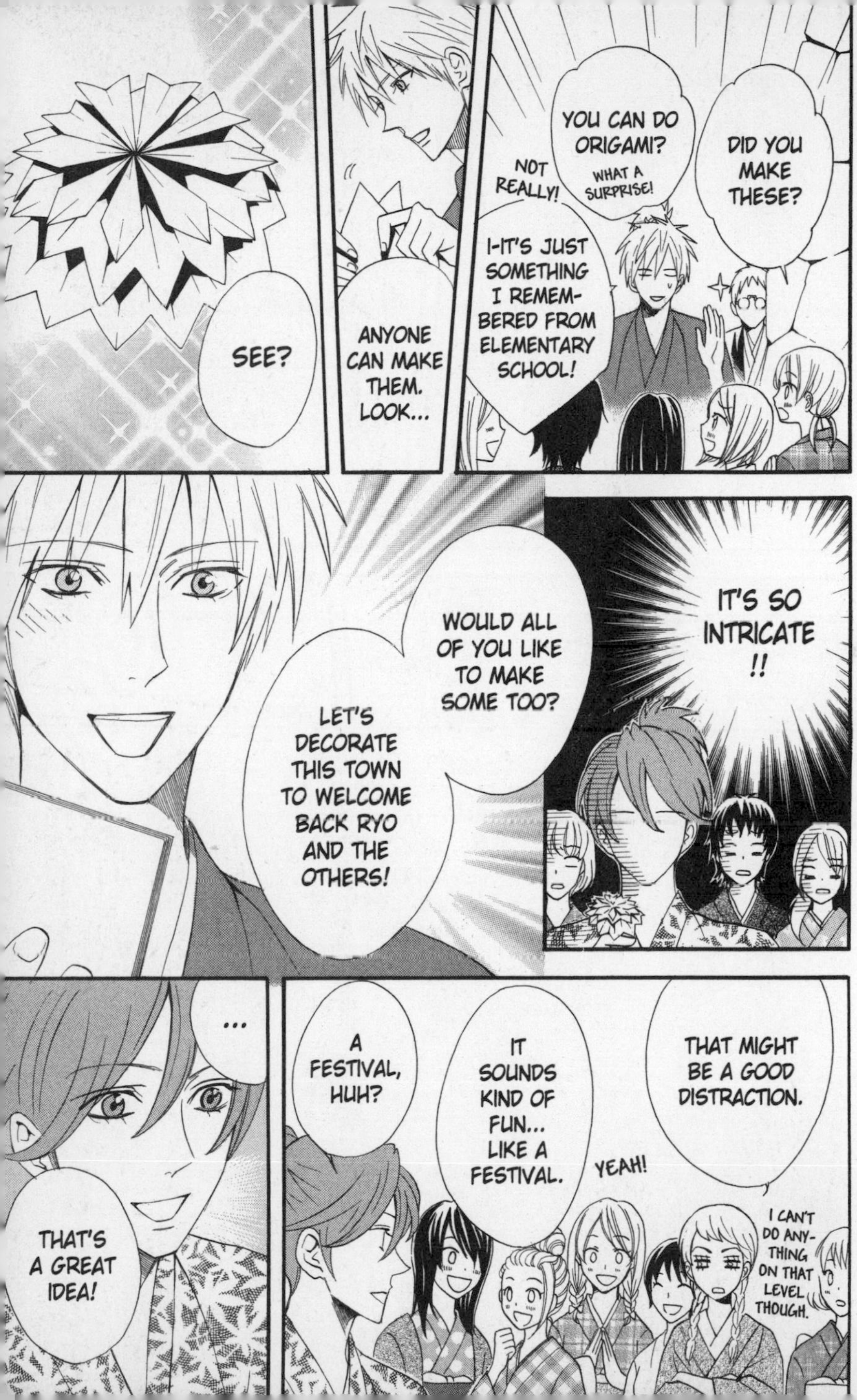
DID YOU MAKE THESE?
YOU CAN DO ORIGAMI?
WHAT A SURPRISE!
NOT REALLY!
I-IT'S JUST SOMETHING I REMEMBERED FROM ELEMENTARY SCHOOL!
ANYONE CAN MAKE THEM. LOOK...
SEE?
IT'S SO INTRICATE !!
WOULD ALL OF YOU LIKE TO MAKE SOME TOO?
LET'S DECORATE THIS TOWN TO WELCOME BACK RYO AND THE OTHERS!
THAT MIGHT BE A GOOD DISTRACTION.
I CAN'T DO ANYTHING ON THAT LEVEL THOUGH.
IT SOUNDS KIND OF FUN... LIKE A FESTIVAL.
YEAH!
A FESTIVAL, HUH?
...
THAT'S A GREAT IDEA!

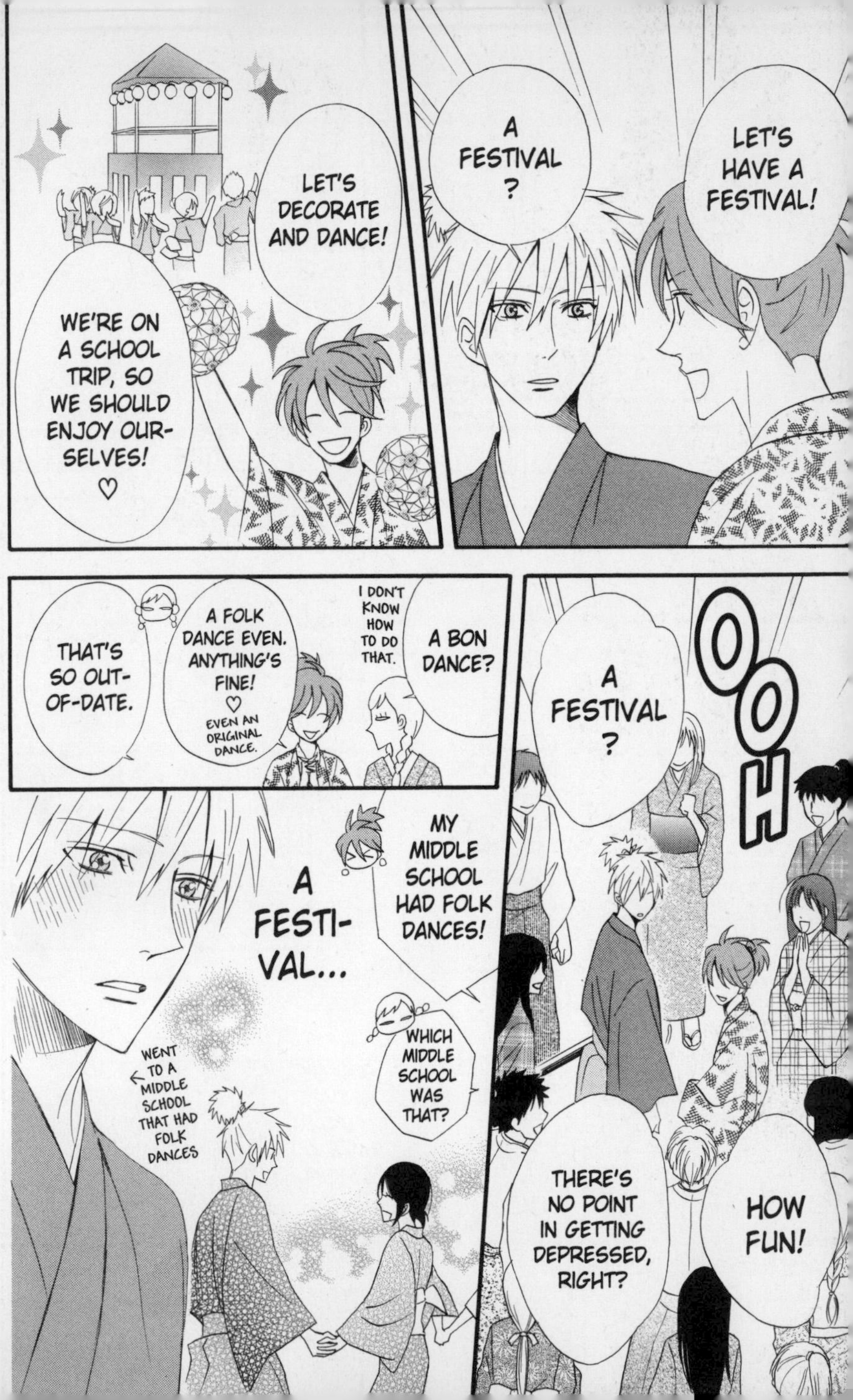
LET'S HAVE A FESTIVAL!
A FESTIVAL?
LET'S DECORATE AND DANCE!
WE'RE ON A SCHOOL TRIP, SO WE SHOULD ENJOY OURSELVES! ♡
A FESTIVAL?
OOOH
HOW FUN!
THERE'S NO POINT IN GETTING DEPRESSED, RIGHT?
A BON DANCE?
I DON'T KNOW HOW TO DO THAT.
A FOLK DANCE EVEN. ANYTHING'S FINE! ♡
EVEN AN ORIGINAL DANCE.
THAT'S SO OUT-OF-DATE.
MY MIDDLE SCHOOL HAD FOLK DANCES!
A FESTIVAL...
WHICH MIDDLE SCHOOL WAS THAT?
← WENT TO A MIDDLE SCHOOL THAT HAD FOLK DANCES

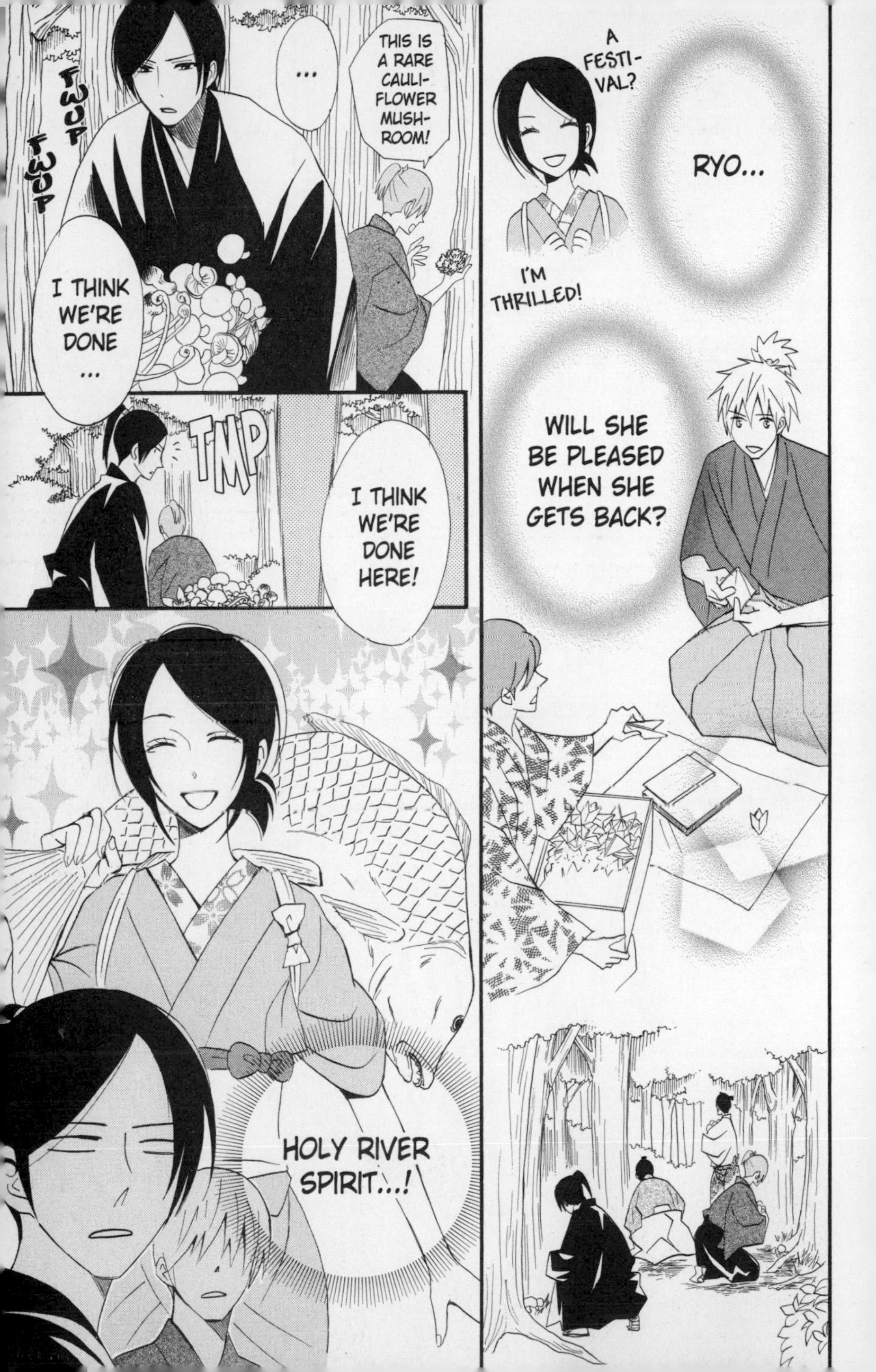
A FESTIVAL?
I'M THRILLED!
RYO...
WILL SHE BE PLEASED WHEN SHE GETS BACK?
THIS IS A RARE CAULIFLOWER MUSHROOM!
...
FWUP FWUP
I THINK WE'RE DONE ...
TMP
I THINK WE'RE DONE HERE!
HOLY RIVER SPIRIT...!

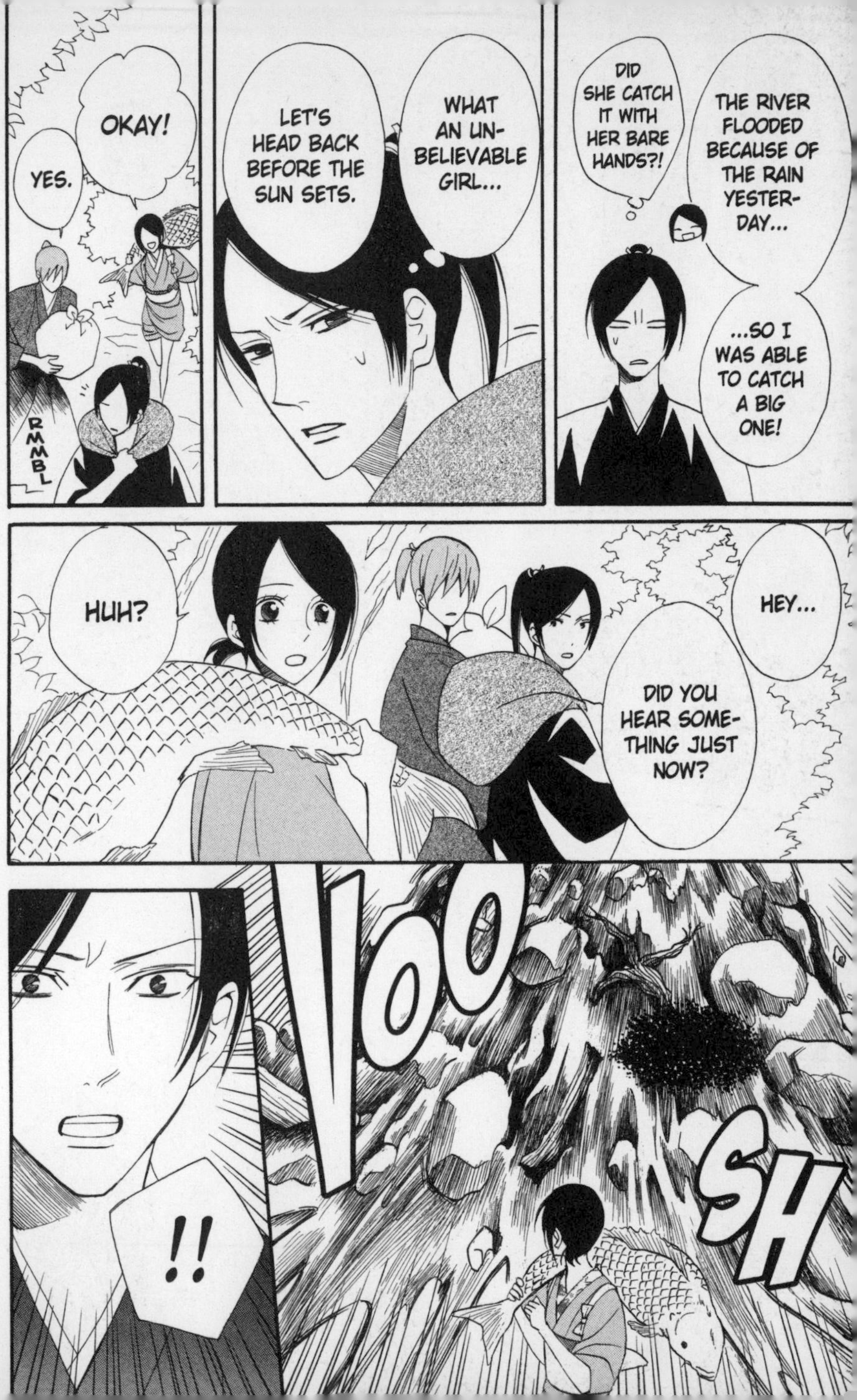
THE RIVER FLOODED BECAUSE OF THE RAIN YESTER-DAY...
DID SHE CATCH IT WITH HER BARE HANDS?!
...SO I WAS ABLE TO CATCH A BIG ONE!
WHAT AN UN-BELIEVABLE GIRL...
LET'S HEAD BACK BEFORE THE SUN SETS.
OKAY!
YES.
RMMBL
HEY...
DID YOU HEAR SOME-THING JUST NOW?
HUH?
VOO
SH
!!

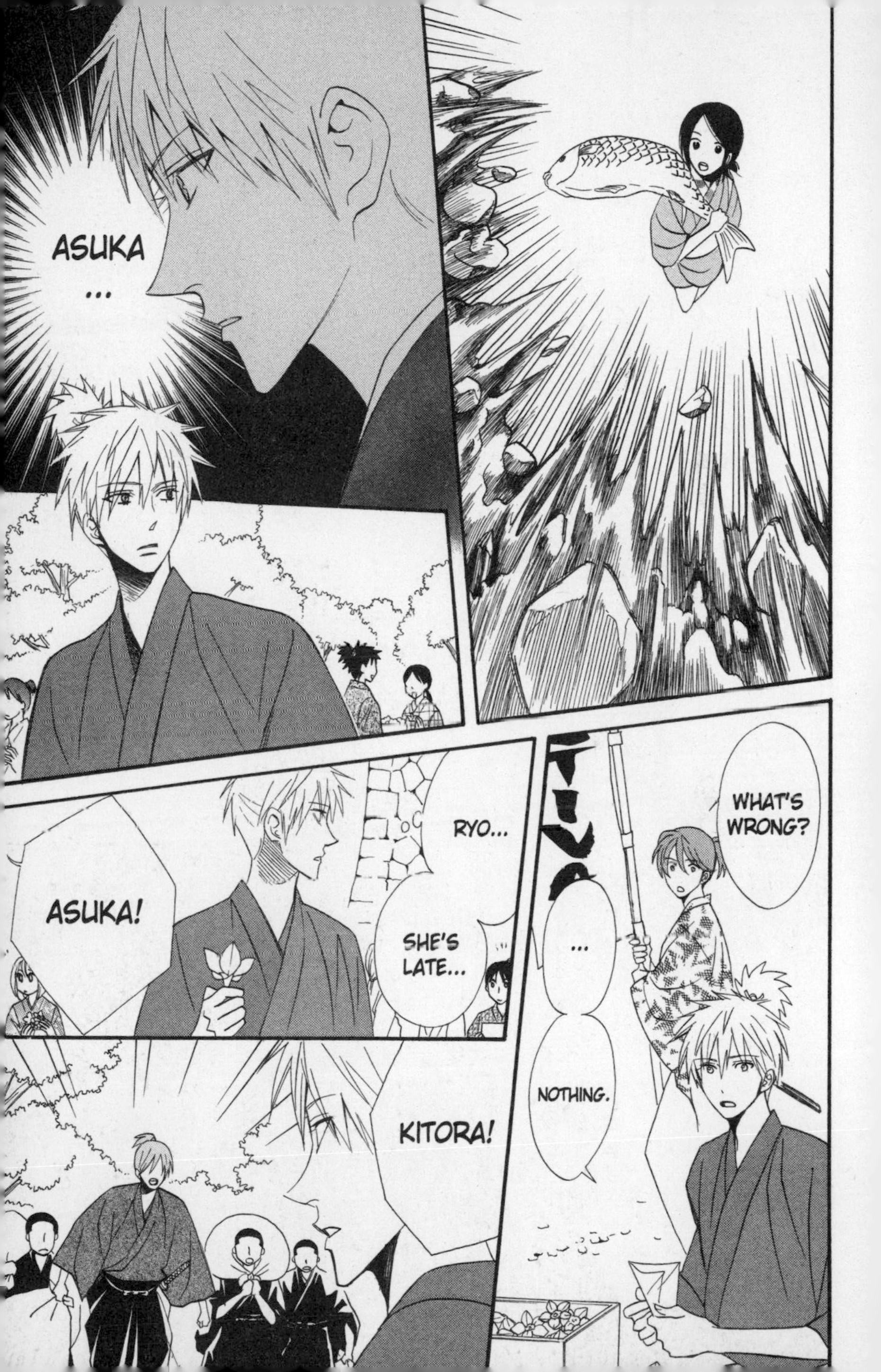
ASUKA
...
WHAT'S WRONG?
...
NOTHING.
RYO...
ASUKA!
SHE'S LATE...
KITORA!

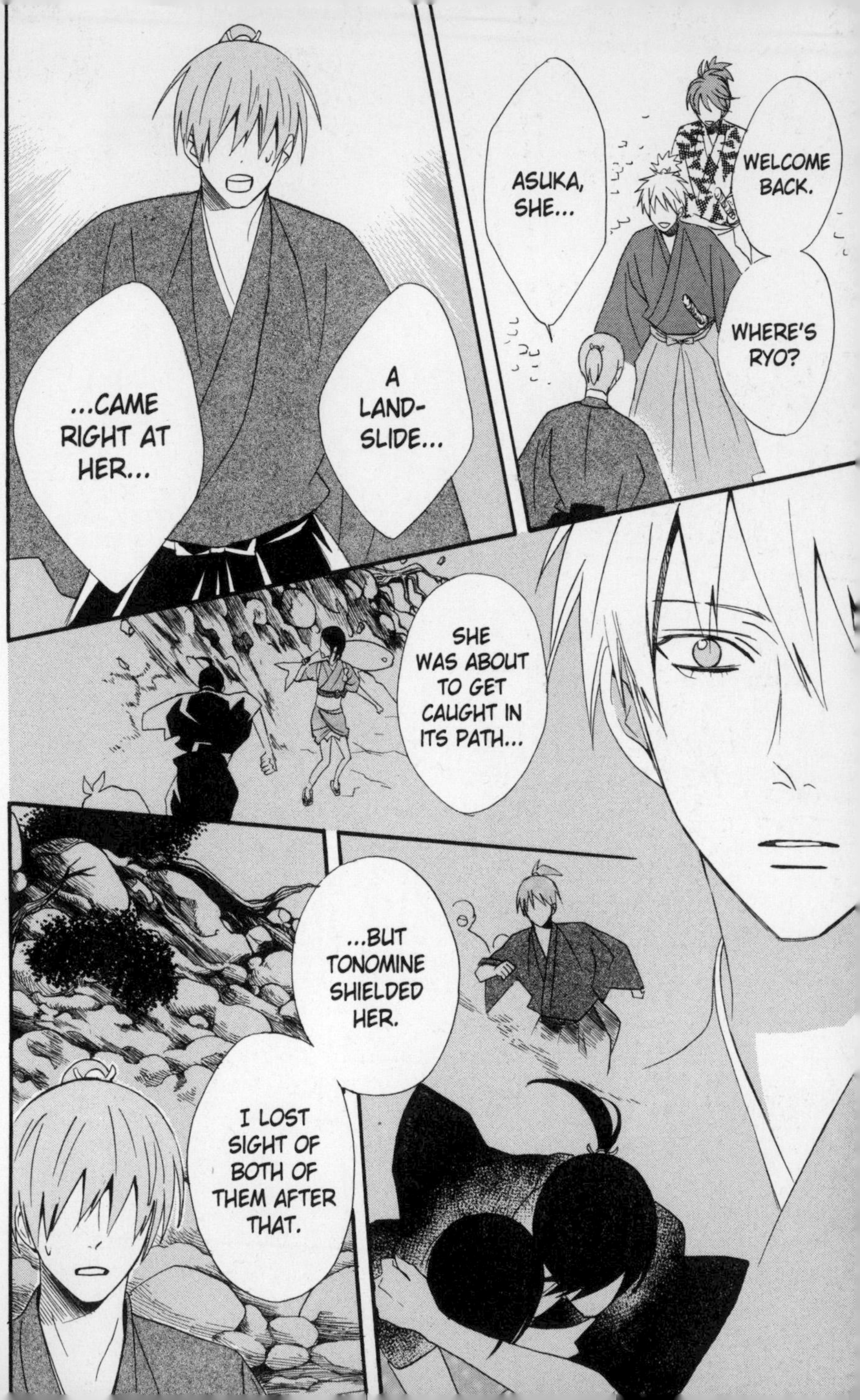
WELCOME BACK.
WHERE'S RYO?
ASUKA, SHE...
A LAND-SLIDE...
...CAME RIGHT AT HER...
SHE WAS ABOUT TO GET CAUGHT IN ITS PATH...
...BUT TONOMINE SHIELDED HER.
I LOST SIGHT OF BOTH OF THEM AFTER THAT.

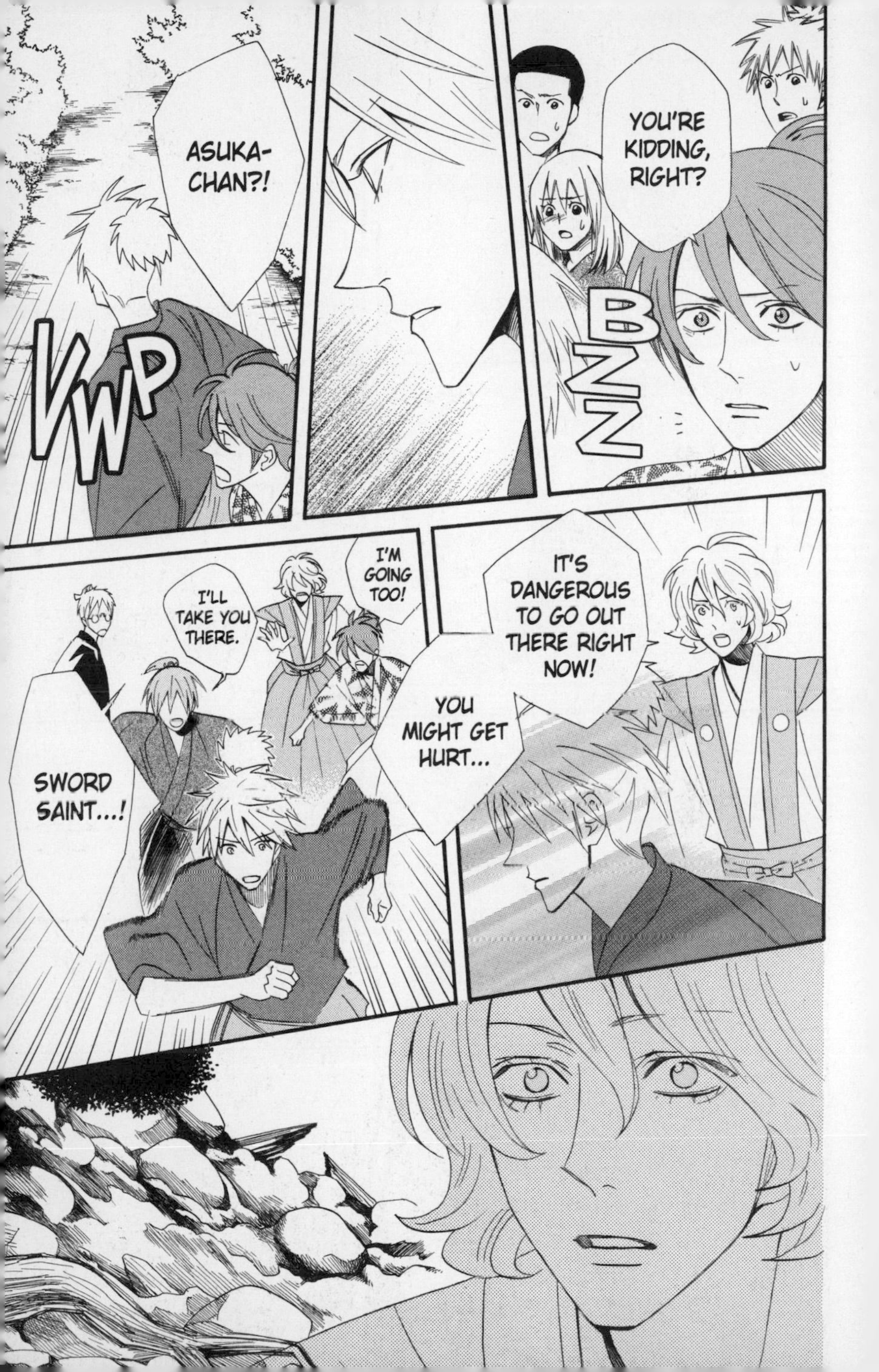
YOU'RE KIDDING, RIGHT?
BZZ
ASUKA-CHAN?!
VWP
IT'S DANGEROUS TO GO OUT THERE RIGHT NOW!
YOU MIGHT GET HURT...
I'M GOING TOO!
I'LL TAKE YOU THERE.
SWORD SAINT...!

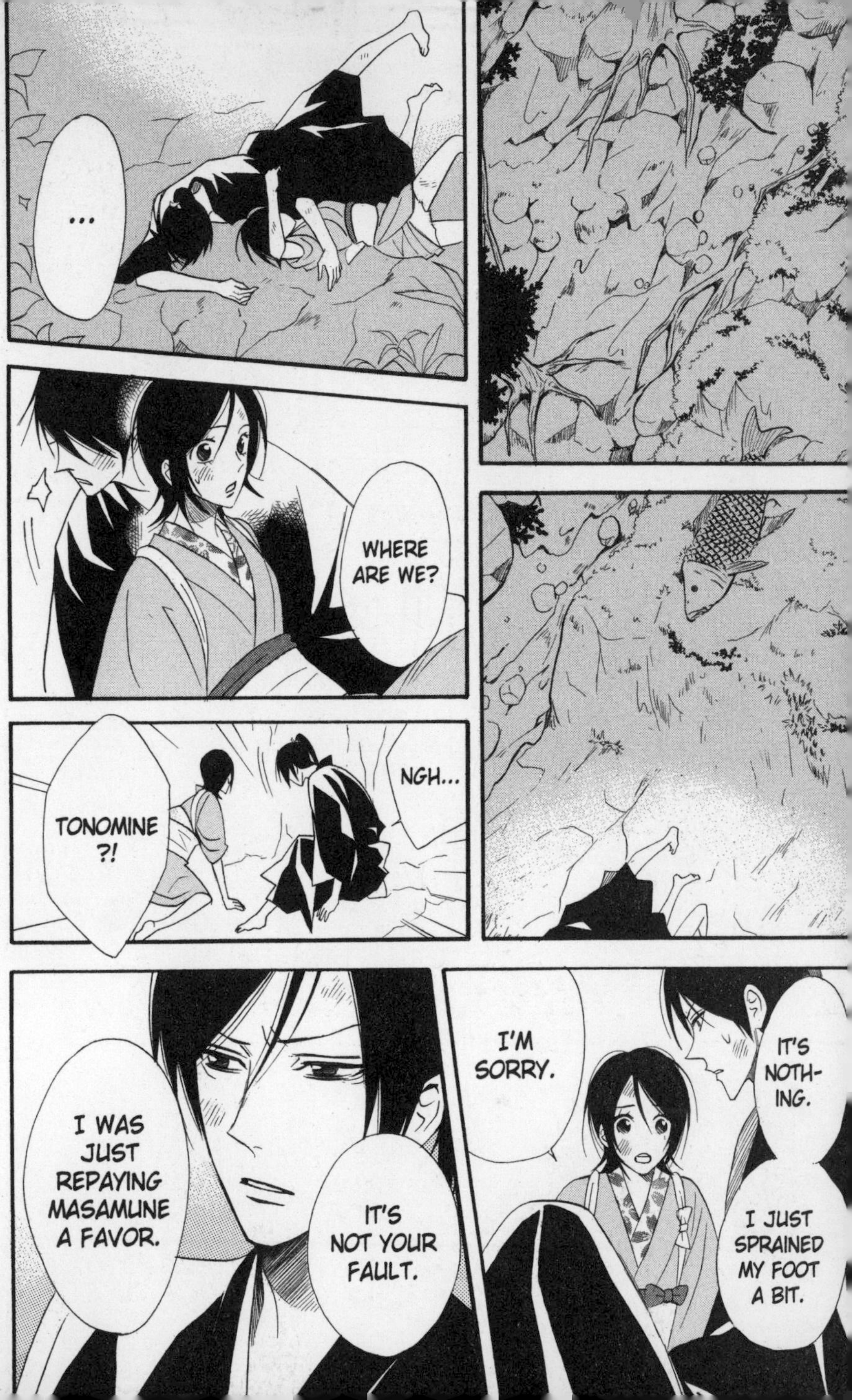
...
WHERE ARE WE?
NGH...
TONOMINE ?!
I'M SORRY.
IT'S NOTH-ING.
I JUST SPRAINED MY FOOT A BIT.
IT'S NOT YOUR FAULT.
I WAS JUST REPAYING MASAMUNE A FAVOR.

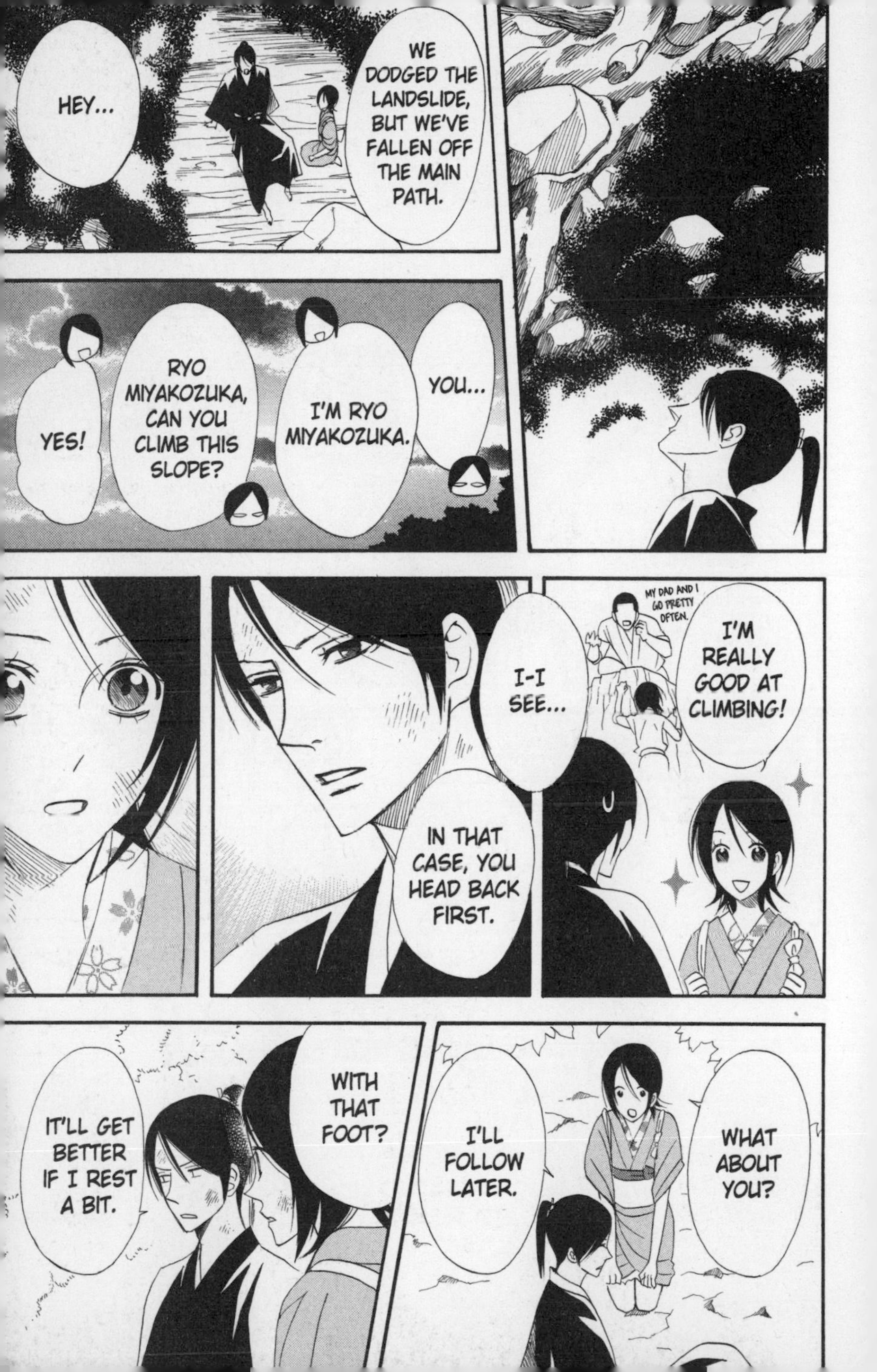
WE DODGED THE LANDSLIDE, BUT WE'VE FALLEN OFF THE MAIN PATH.
HEY...
YOU...
I'M RYO MIYAKOZUKA.
RYO MIYAKOZUKA, CAN YOU CLIMB THIS SLOPE?
YES!
I'M REALLY GOOD AT CLIMBING!
MY DAD AND I GO PRETTY OFTEN.
I-I SEE...
IN THAT CASE, YOU HEAD BACK FIRST.
WHAT ABOUT YOU?
I'LL FOLLOW LATER.
WITH THAT FOOT?
IT'LL GET BETTER IF I REST A BIT.

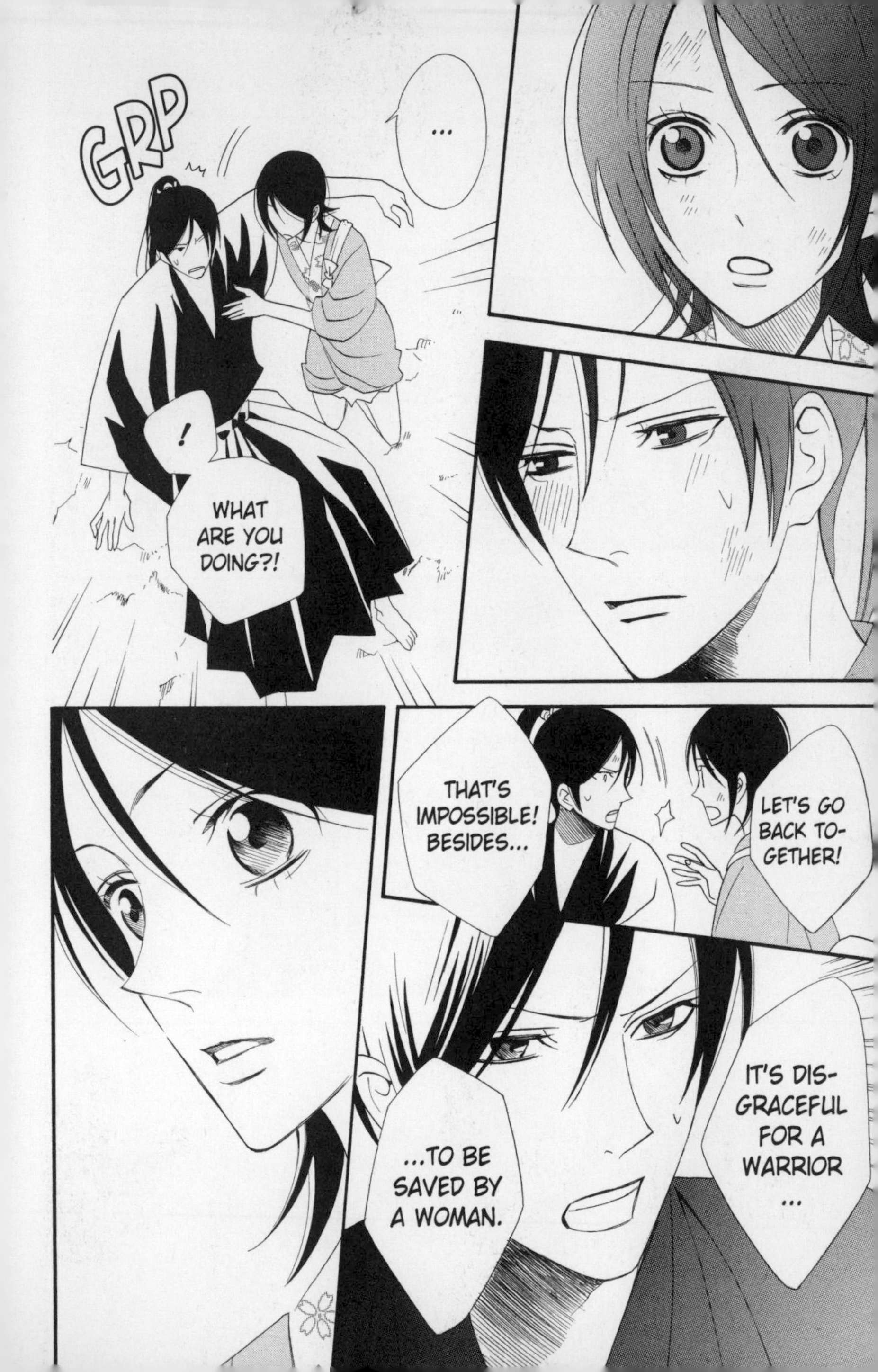
...
GRP
!
WHAT ARE YOU DOING?!
LET'S GO BACK TO-GETHER!
THAT'S IMPOSSIBLE! BESIDES...
IT'S DIS-GRACEFUL FOR A WARRIOR ...
...TO BE SAVED BY A WOMAN.

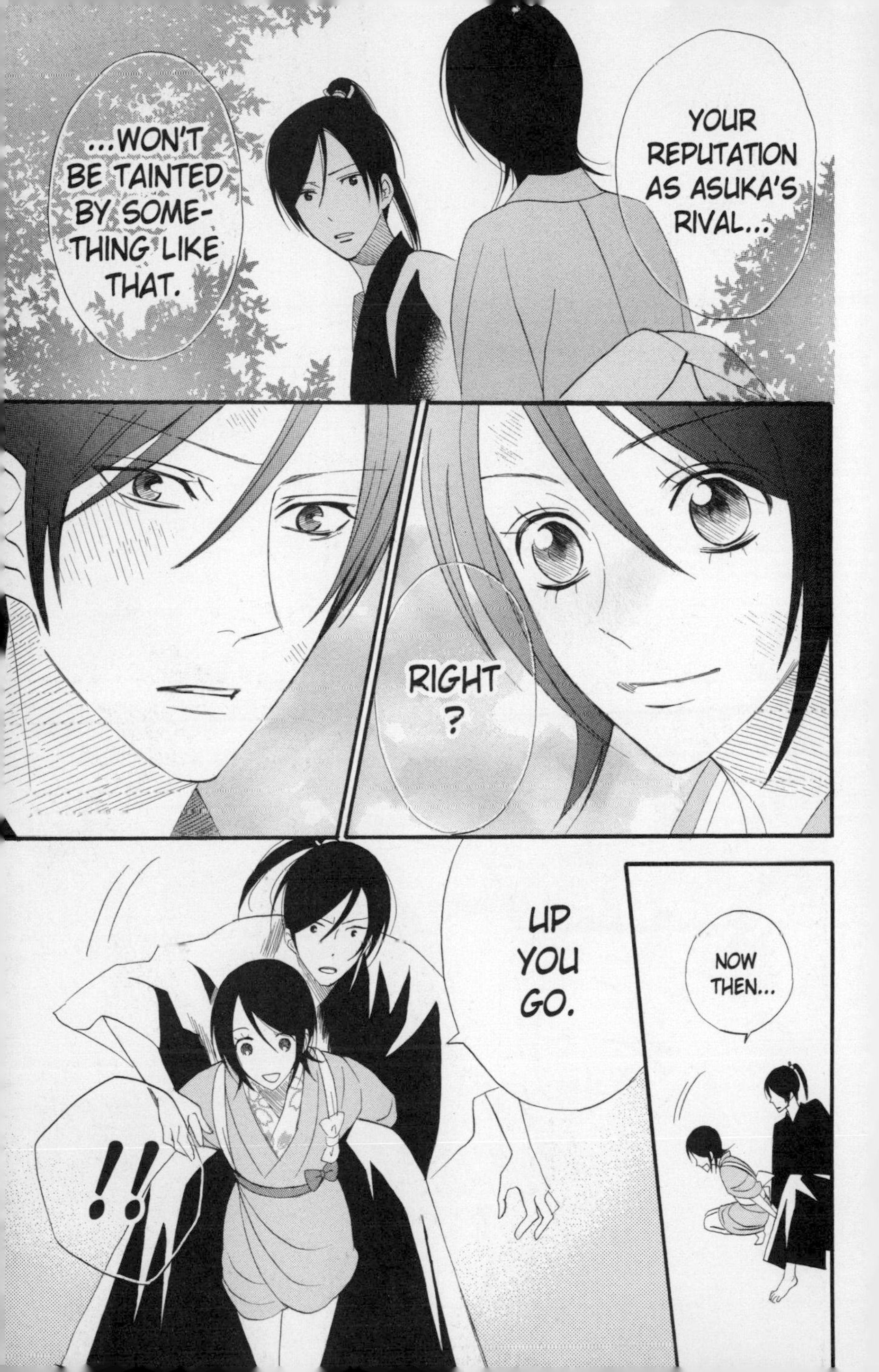
YOUR REPUTATION AS ASUKA'S RIVAL...
...WON'T BE TAINTED BY SOME-THING LIKE THAT.
RIGHT?
NOW THEN...
UP YOU GO.
!!

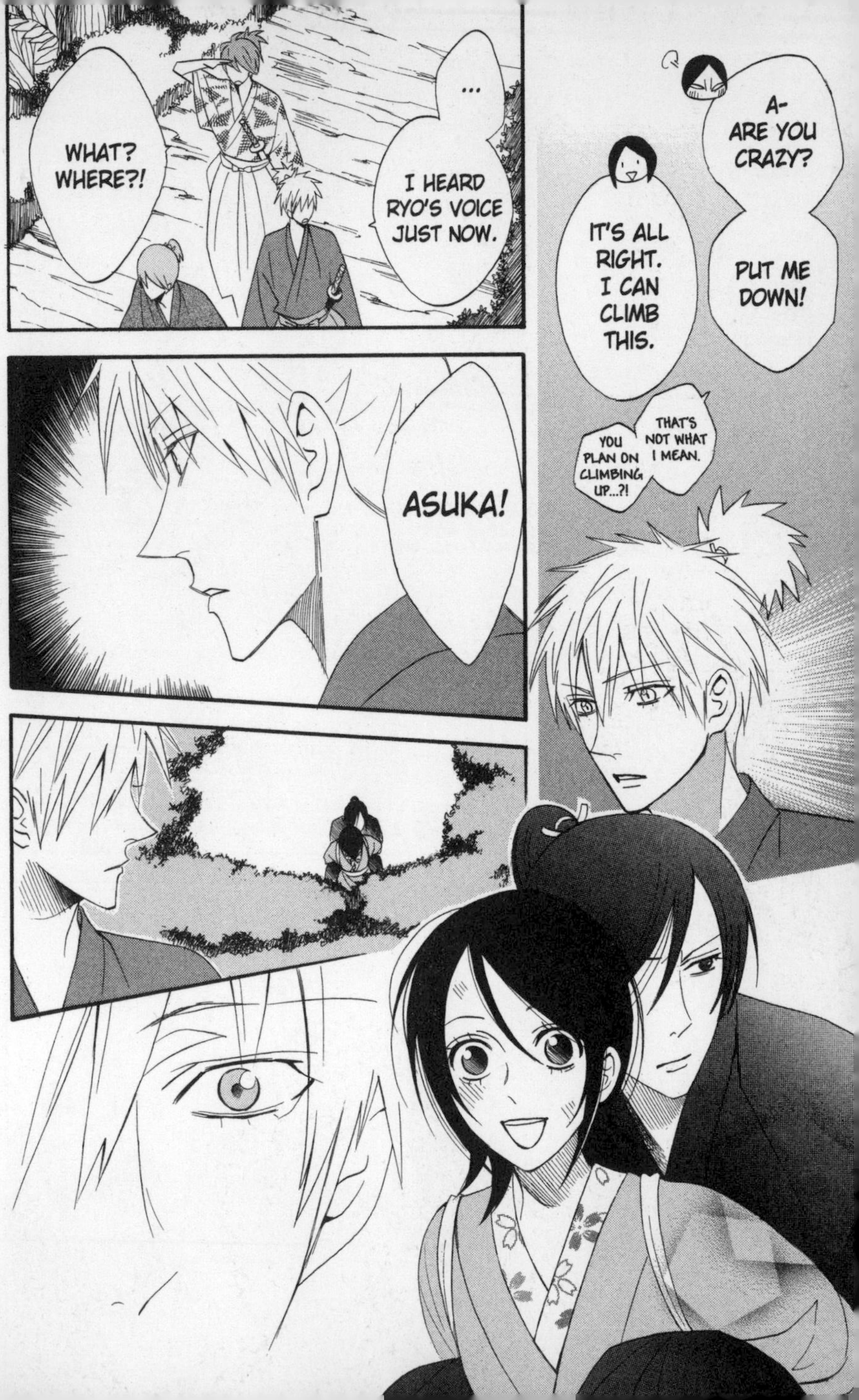
A- ARE YOU CRAZY?
PUT ME DOWN!
IT'S ALL RIGHT. I CAN CLIMB THIS.
THAT'S NOT WHAT I MEAN.
YOU PLAN ON CLIMBING UP...?!
...
I HEARD RYO'S VOICE JUST NOW.
WHAT? WHERE?!
ASUKA!

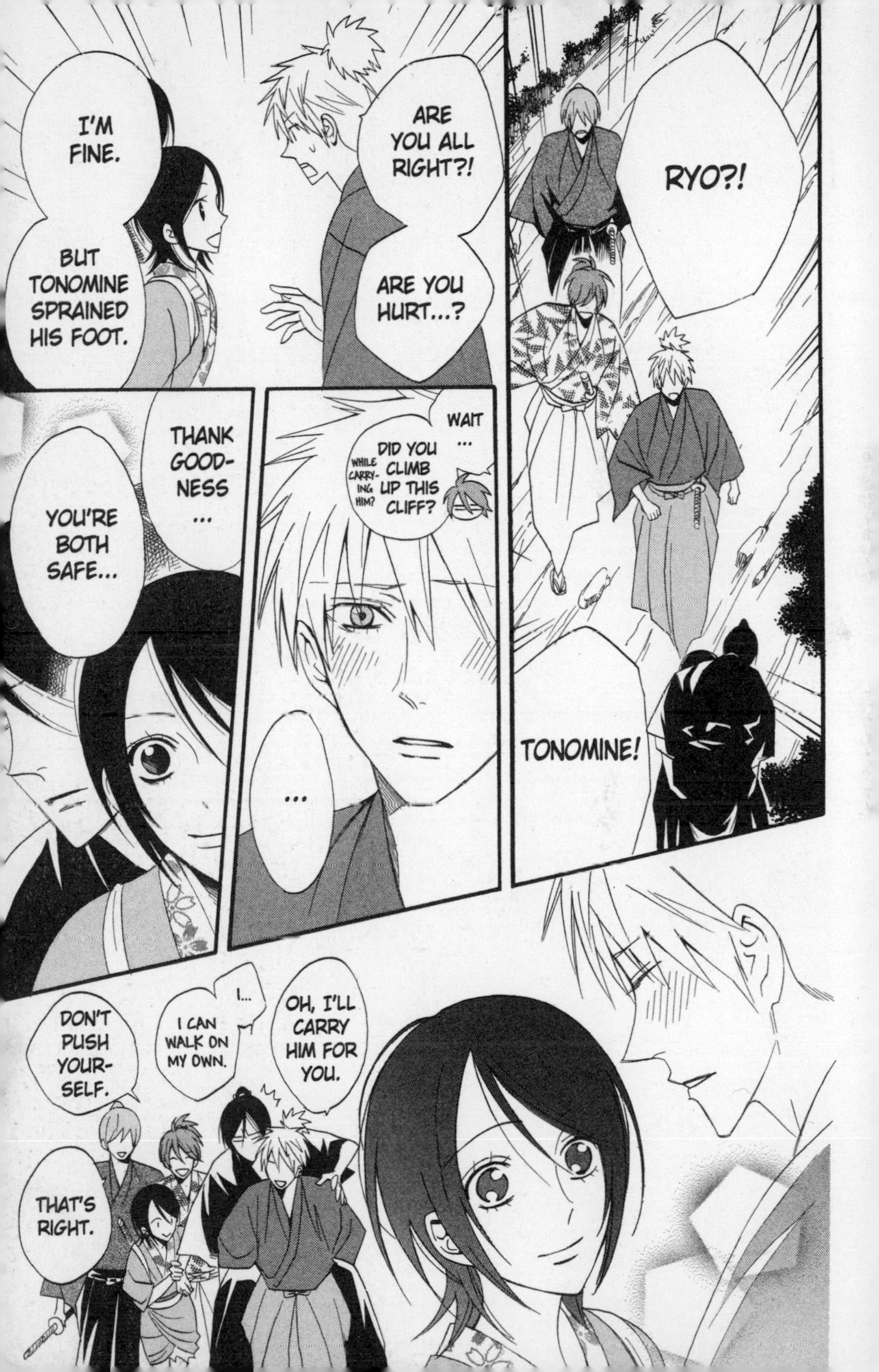
RYO?!
TONOMINE!
ARE YOU ALL RIGHT?!
ARE YOU HURT...?
I'M FINE.
BUT TONOMINE SPRAINED HIS FOOT.
WAIT ...
DID YOU CLIMB UP THIS CLIFF?
WHILE CARRY-ING HIM?
...
THANK GOODNESS ...
YOU'RE BOTH SAFE...
OH, I'LL CARRY HIM FOR YOU.
I...
I CAN WALK ON MY OWN.
DON'T PUSH YOUR-SELF.
THAT'S RIGHT.

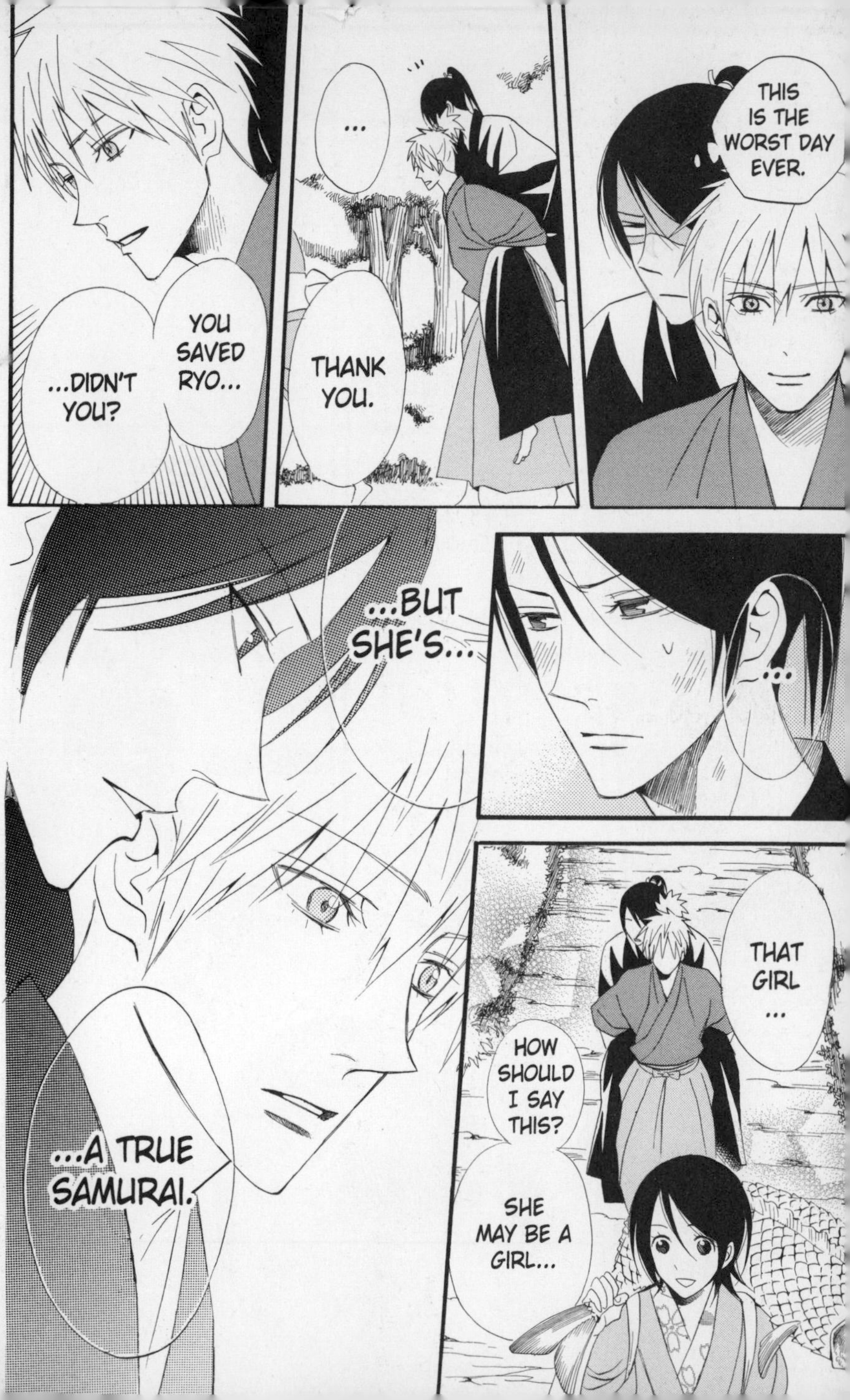
THIS IS THE WORST DAY EVER.
...
THANK YOU.
YOU SAVED RYO...
...DIDN'T YOU?
...
THAT GIRL ...
HOW SHOULD I SAY THIS?
SHE MAY BE A GIRL...
...BUT SHE'S...
...A TRUE SAMURAI.

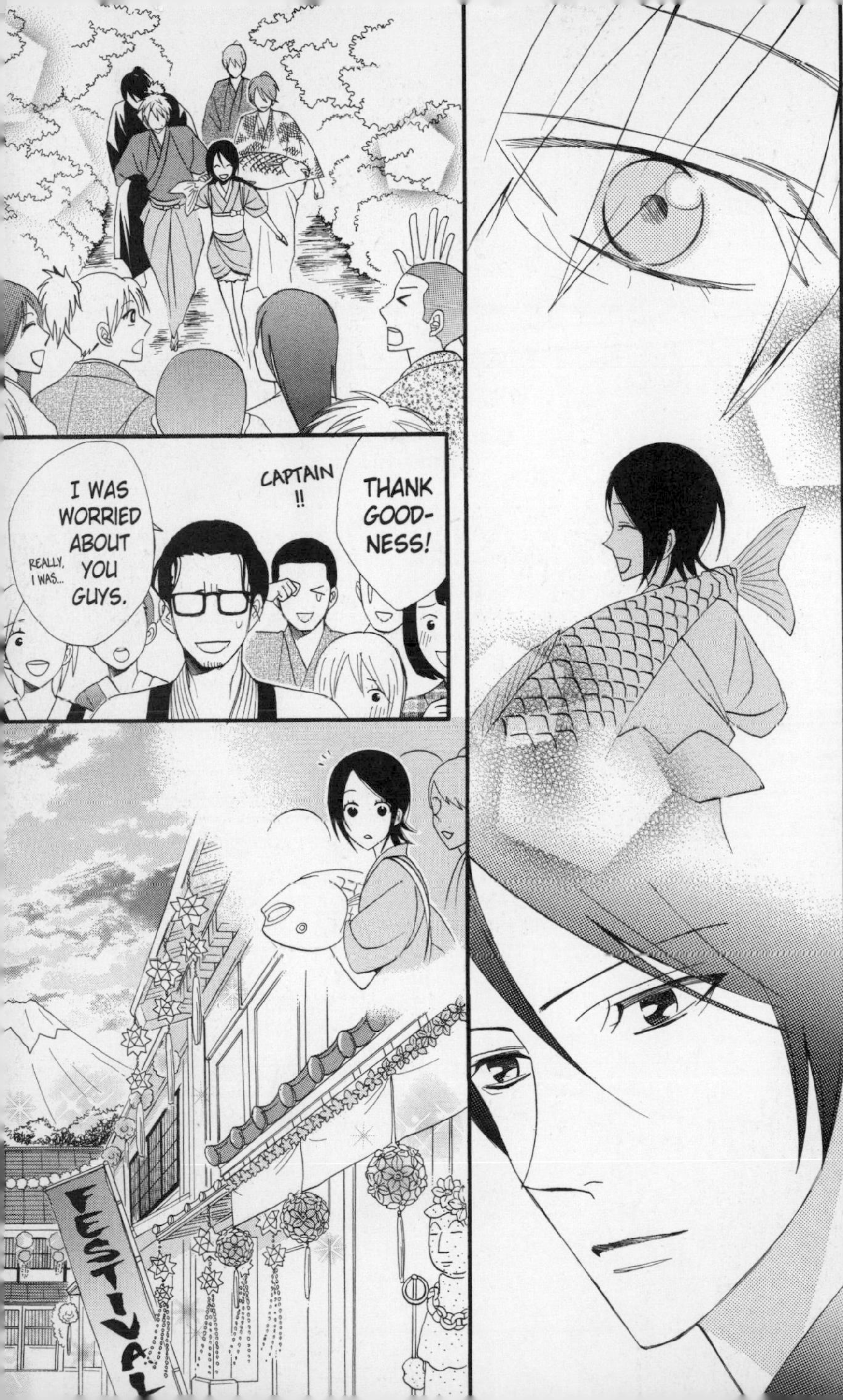
THANK GOODNESS!
CAPTAIN !!
I WAS WORRIED ABOUT YOU GUYS.
REALLY, I WAS...
FESTIVAL

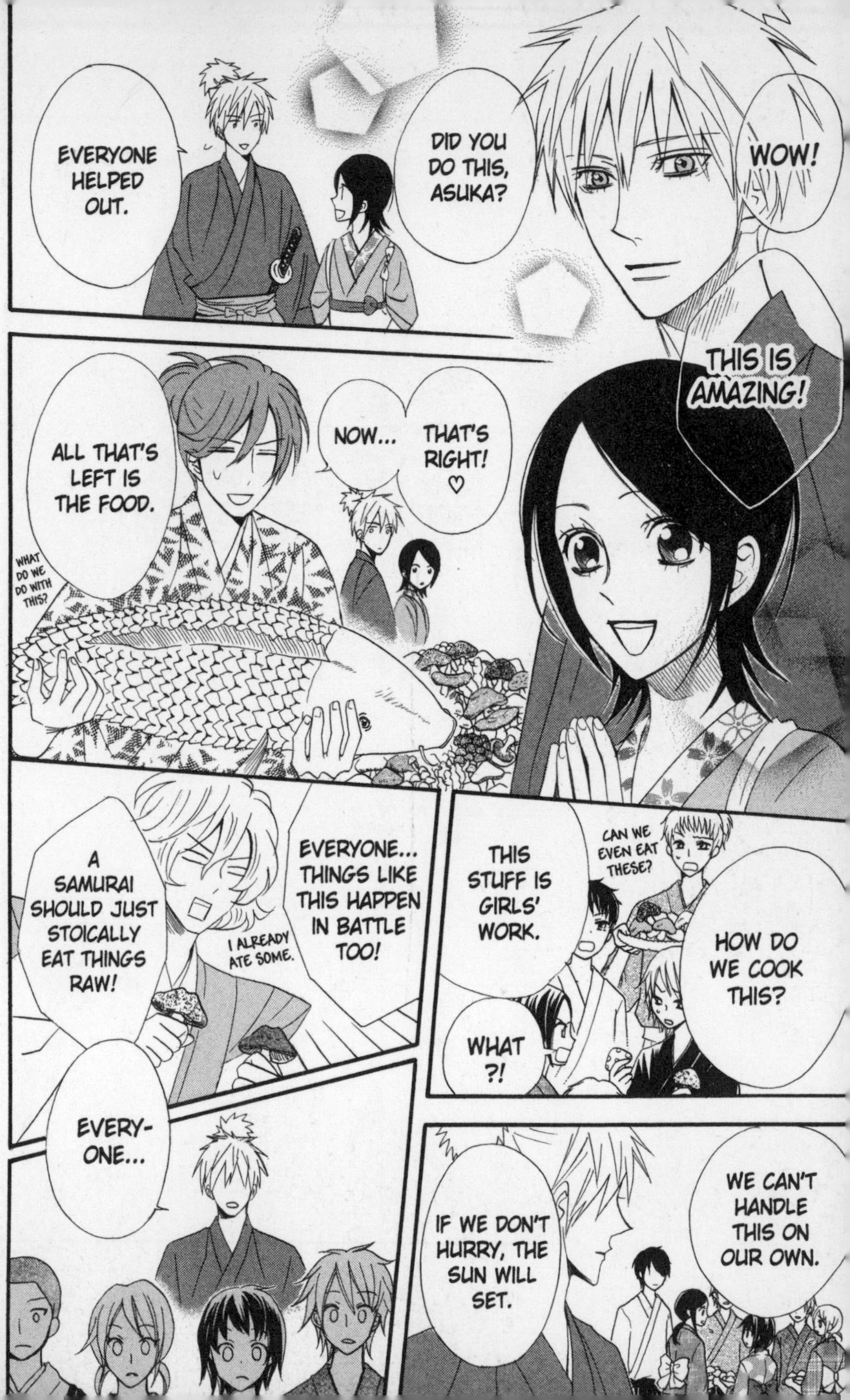
WOW!
DID YOU DO THIS, ASUKA?
EVERYONE HELPED OUT.
THIS IS AMAZING!
THAT'S RIGHT! ♡
NOW...
ALL THAT'S LEFT IS THE FOOD.
WHAT DO WE DO WITH THIS?
HOW DO WE COOK THIS?
CAN WE EVEN EAT THESE?
THIS STUFF IS GIRLS' WORK.
WHAT ?!
EVERYONE... THINGS LIKE THIS HAPPEN IN BATTLE TOO!
I ALREADY ATE SOME.
A SAMURAI SHOULD JUST STOICALLY EAT THINGS RAW!
WE CAN'T HANDLE THIS ON OUR OWN.
IF WE DON'T HURRY, THE SUN WILL SET.
EVERY-ONE...

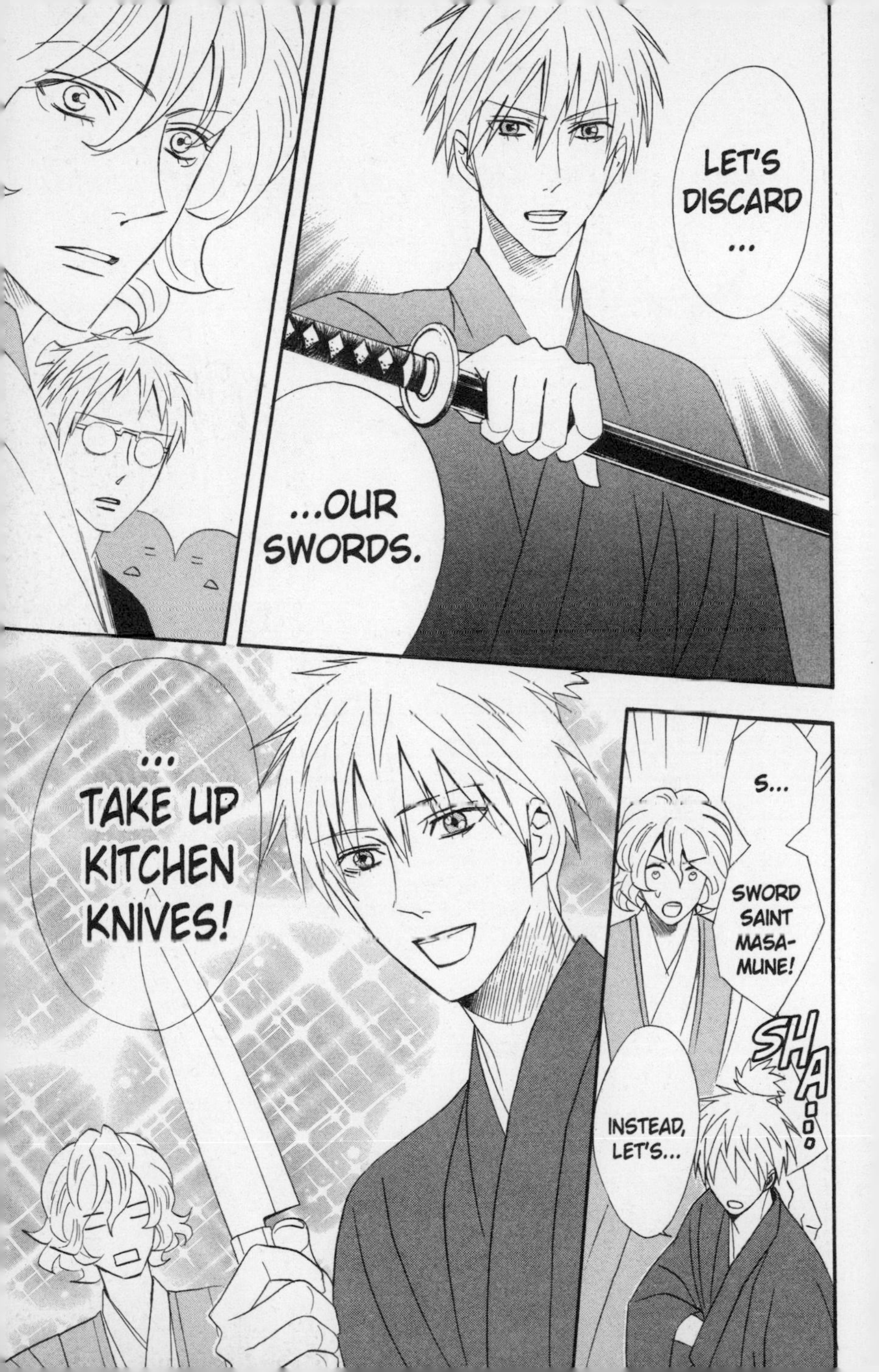
LET'S DISCARD ...
...OUR SWORDS.
S...
SWORD SAINT MASA-MUNE!
SHA...
INSTEAD, LET'S...
... TAKE UP KITCHEN KNIVES!

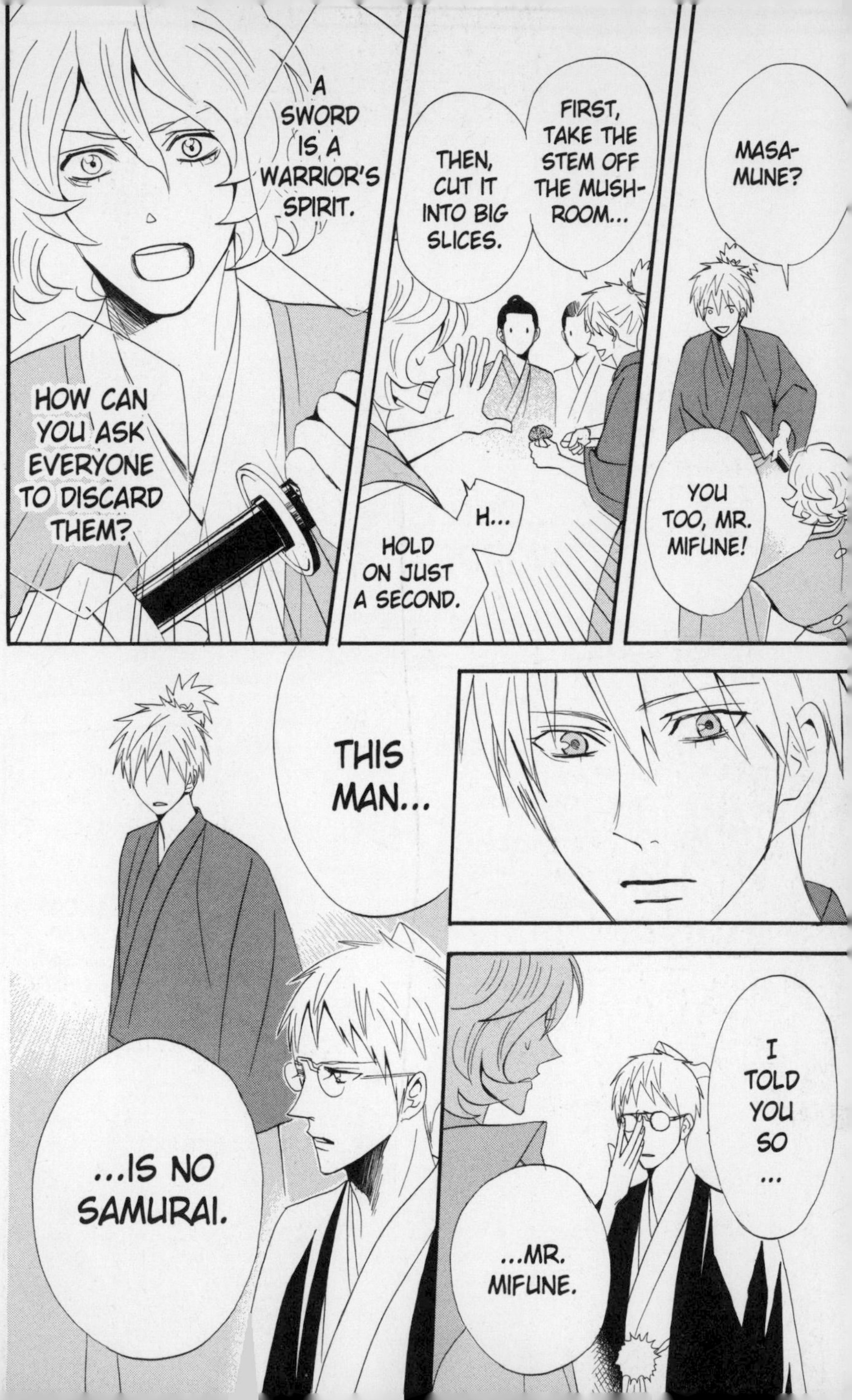
MASA-MUNE?
YOU TOO, MR. MIFUNE!
FIRST, TAKE THE STEM OFF THE MUSH-ROOM...
THEN, CUT IT INTO BIG SLICES.
H...
HOLD ON JUST A SECOND.
A SWORD IS A WARRIOR'S SPIRIT.
HOW CAN YOU ASK EVERYONE TO DISCARD THEM?
THIS MAN...
I TOLD YOU SO ...
...MR. MIFUNE.
...IS NO SAMURAI.

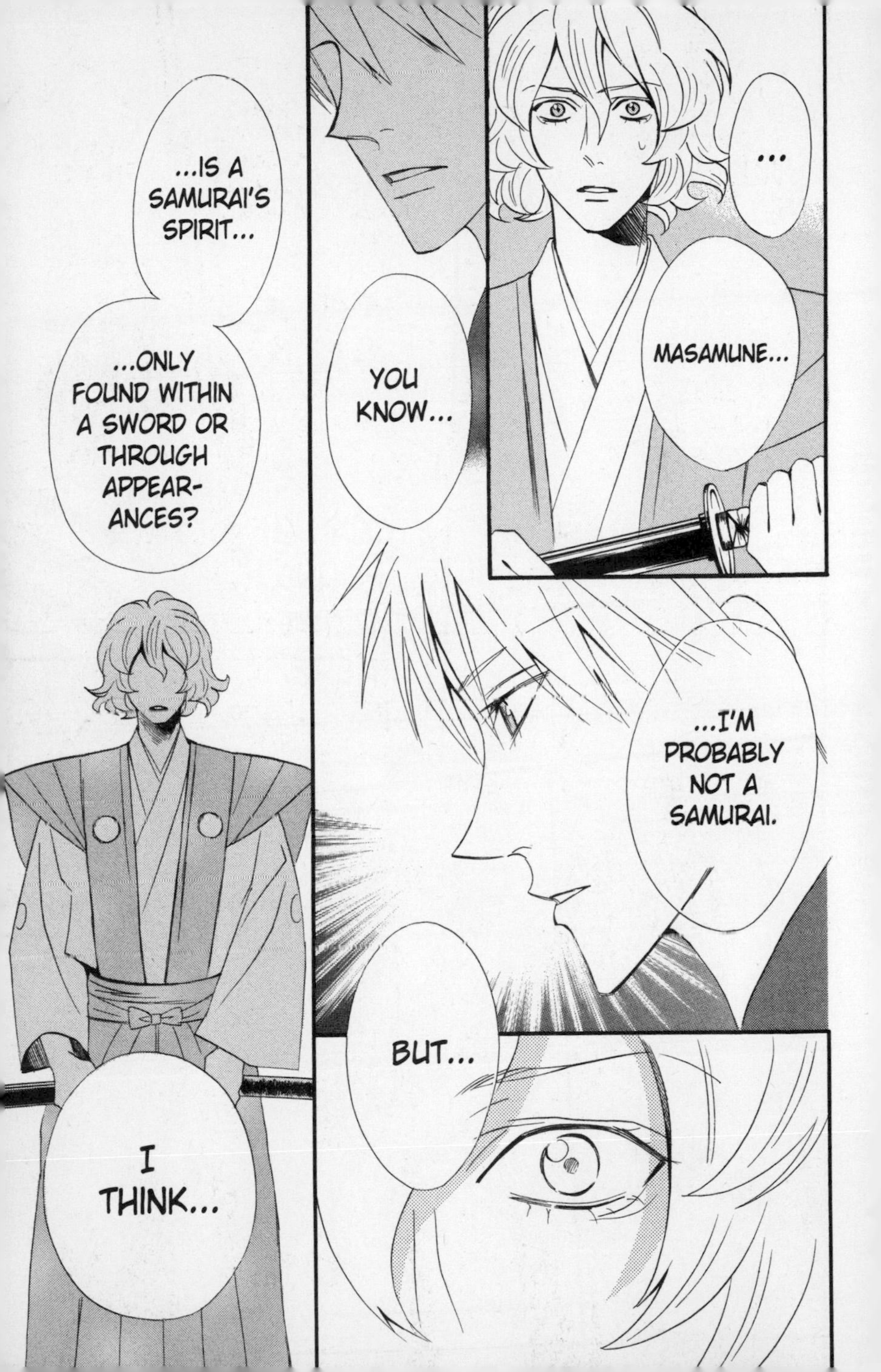
...
MASAMUNE...
YOU KNOW...
...I'M PROBABLY NOT A SAMURAI.
BUT...
...IS A SAMURAI'S SPIRIT...
...ONLY FOUND WITHIN A SWORD OR THROUGH APPEAR- ANCES?
I THINK...

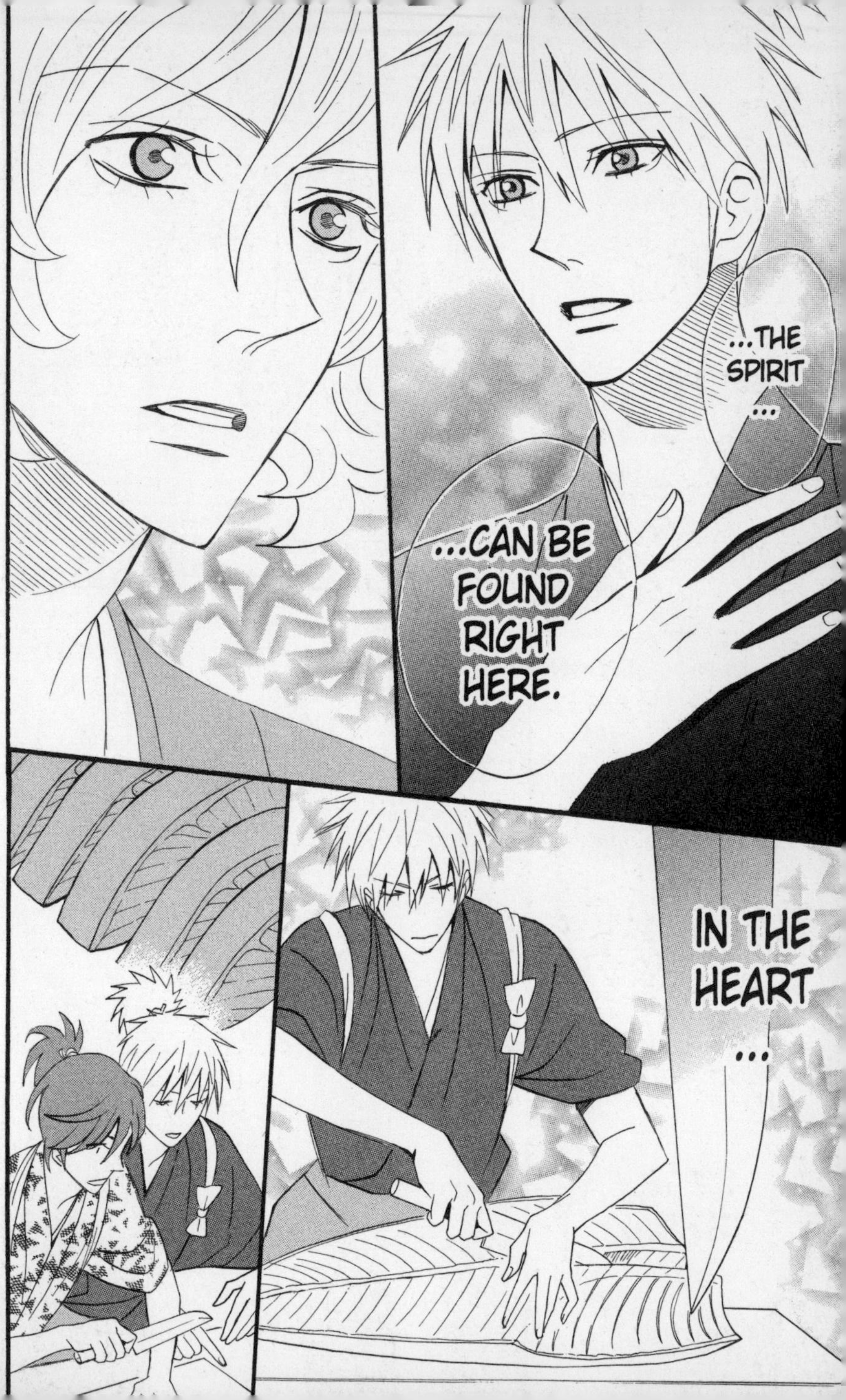
...THE SPIRIT ...
...CAN BE FOUND RIGHT HERE.
IN THE HEART ...

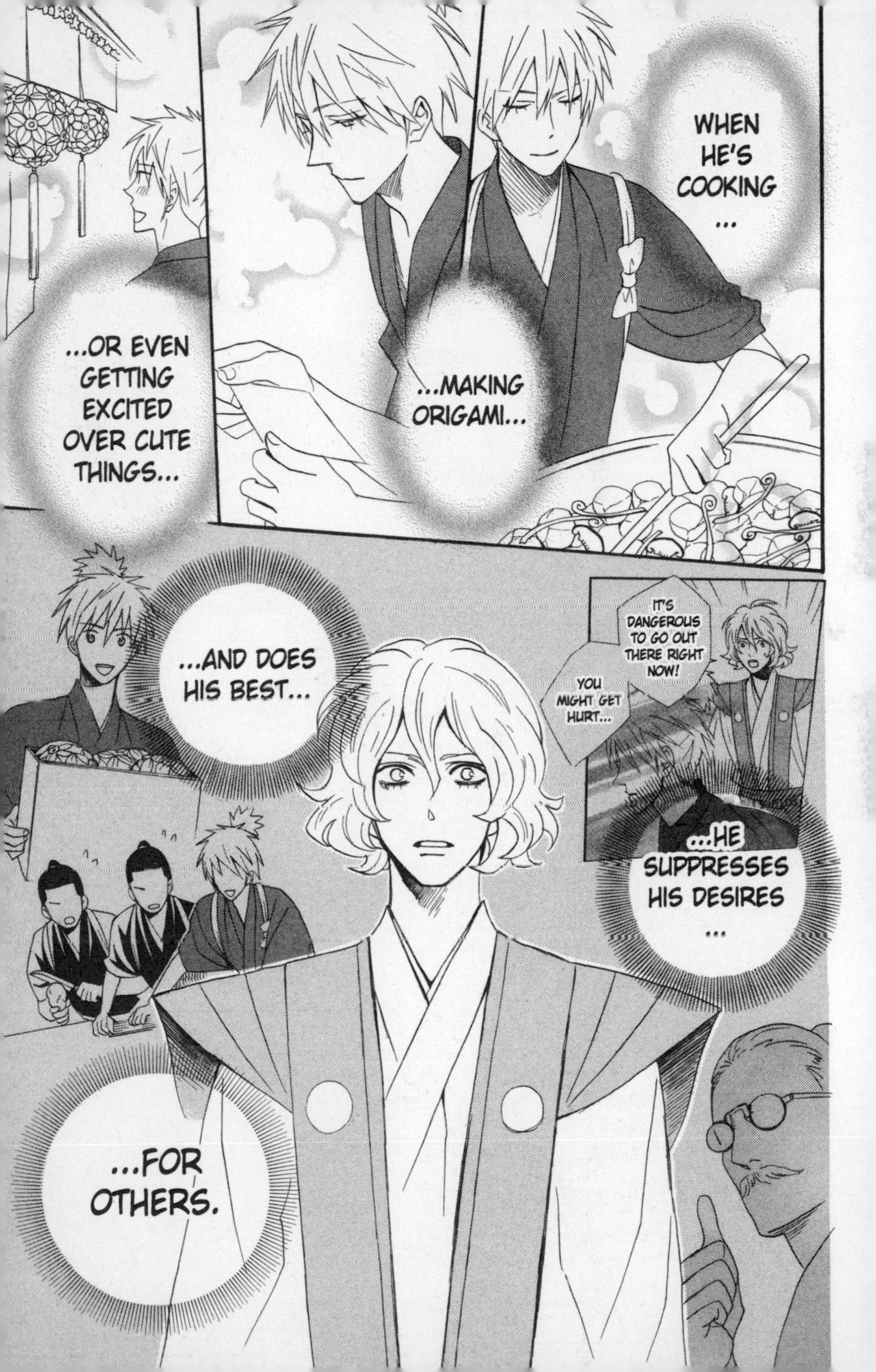
WHEN HE'S COOKING ...
...MAKING ORIGAMI...
...OR EVEN GETTING EXCITED OVER CUTE THINGS...
IT'S DANGEROUS TO GO OUT THERE RIGHT NOW!
YOU MIGHT GET HURT...
...HE SUPPRESSES HIS DESIRES ...
...AND DOES HIS BEST...
...FOR OTHERS.

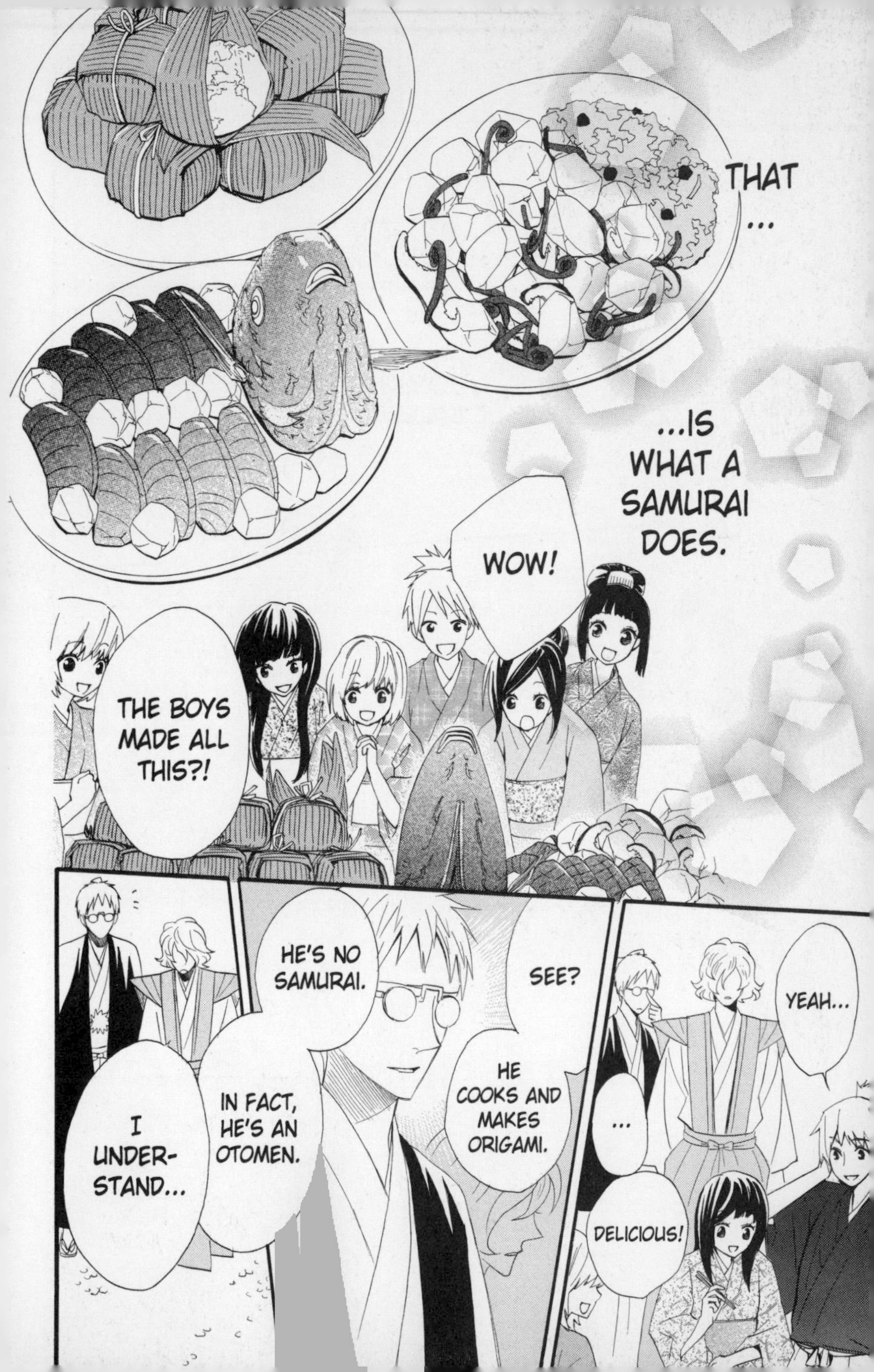
THAT...
...IS WHAT A SAMURAI DOES.
WOW!
THE BOYS MADE ALL THIS?!
YEAH...
...
DELICIOUS!
SEE?
HE COOKS AND MAKES ORIGAMI.
HE'S NO SAMURAI.
IN FACT, HE'S AN OTOMEN.
I UNDER-STAND...

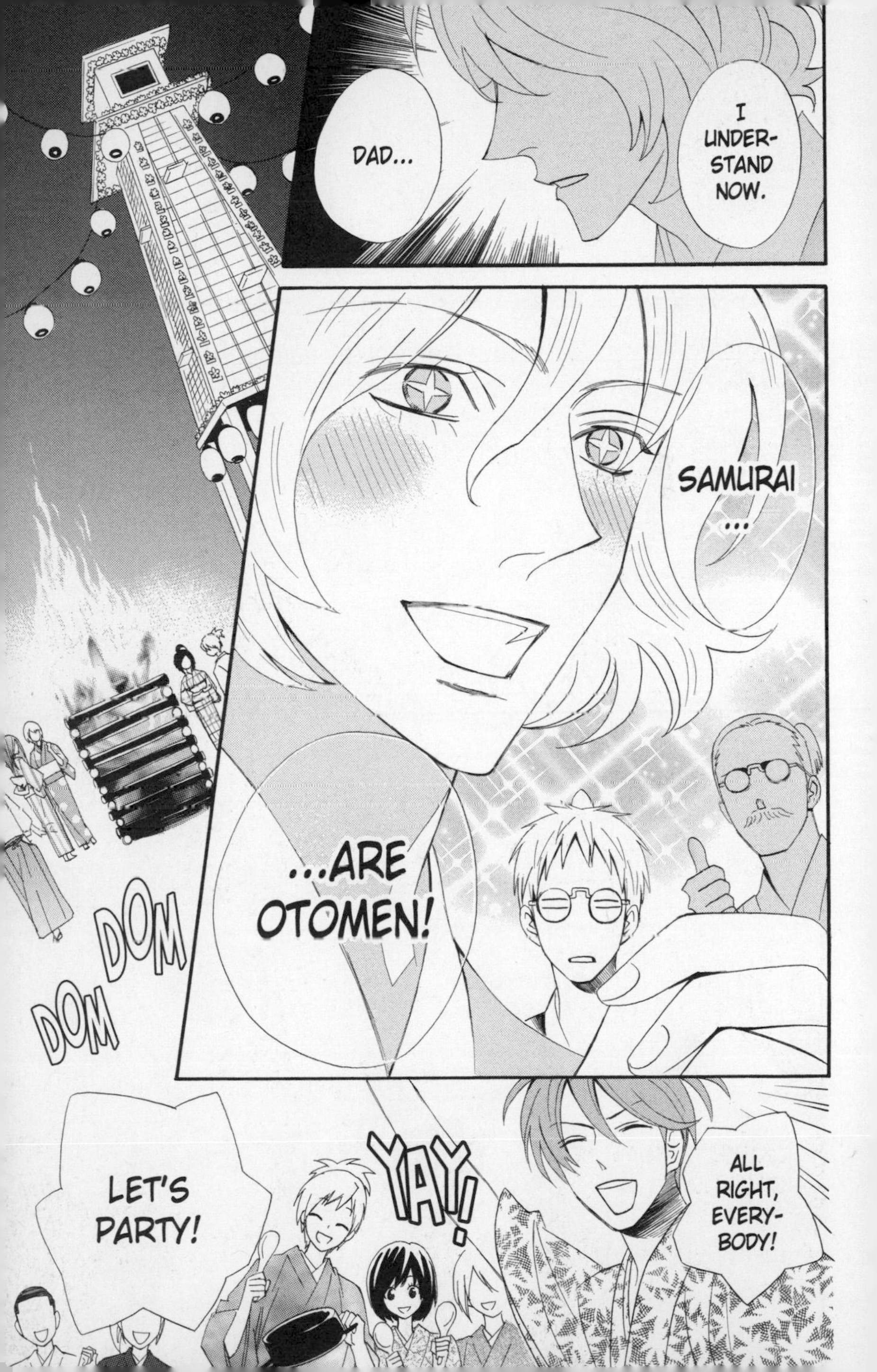
I UNDER-STAND NOW.
DAD...
SAMURAI ...
...ARE OTOMEN!
DOM DOM DOM
ALL RIGHT, EVERY-BODY!
YAY!
LET'S PARTY!

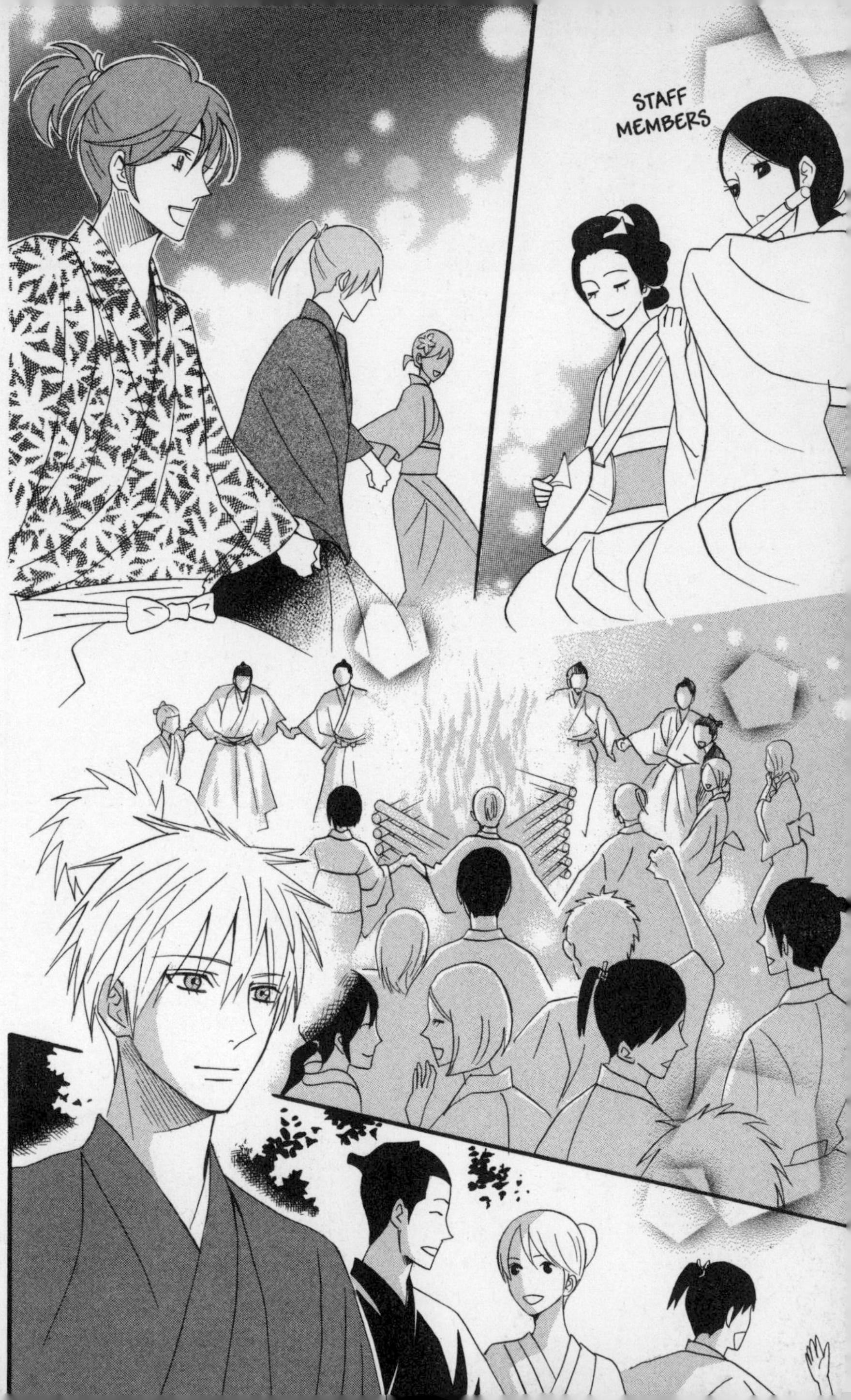
STAFF MEMBERS

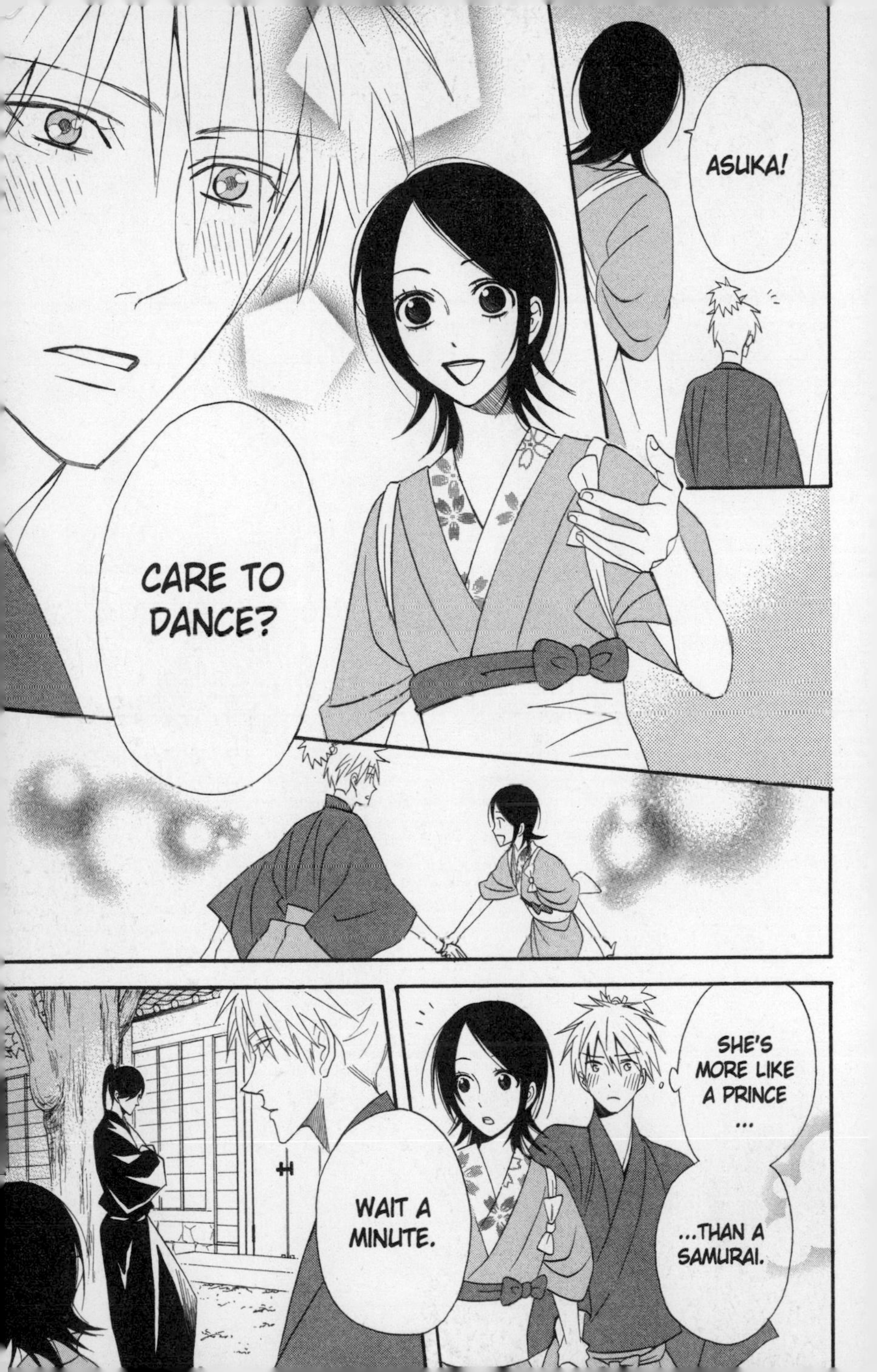
ASUKA!
CARE TO DANCE?
SHE'S MORE LIKE A PRINCE ...
...THAN A SAMURAI.
WAIT A MINUTE.

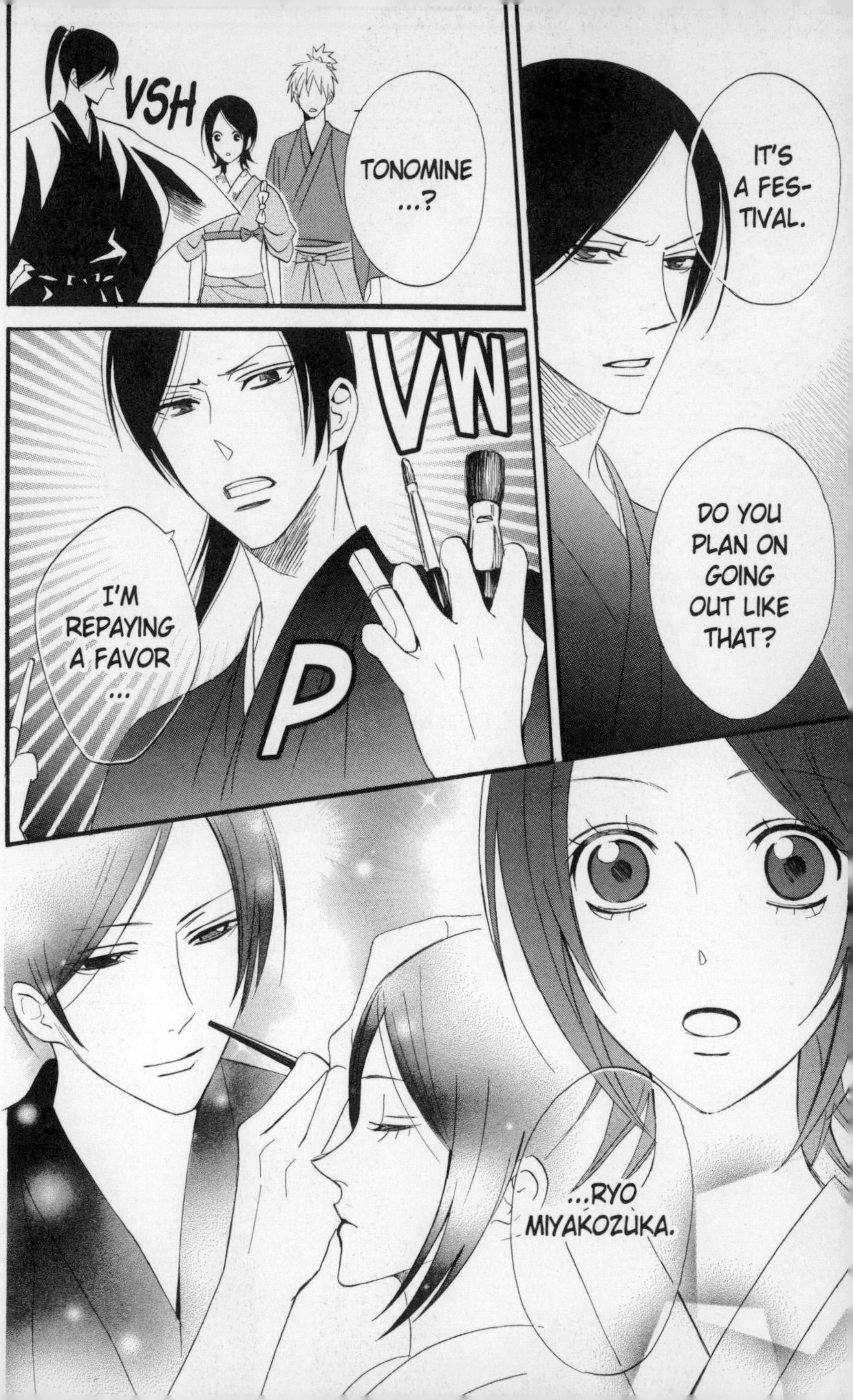
IT'S A FES-TIVAL.
DO YOU PLAN ON GOING OUT LIKE THAT?
VSH
TONOMINE ...?
VW
I'M REPAYING A FAVOR ...
P
...RYO MIYAKOZUKA.

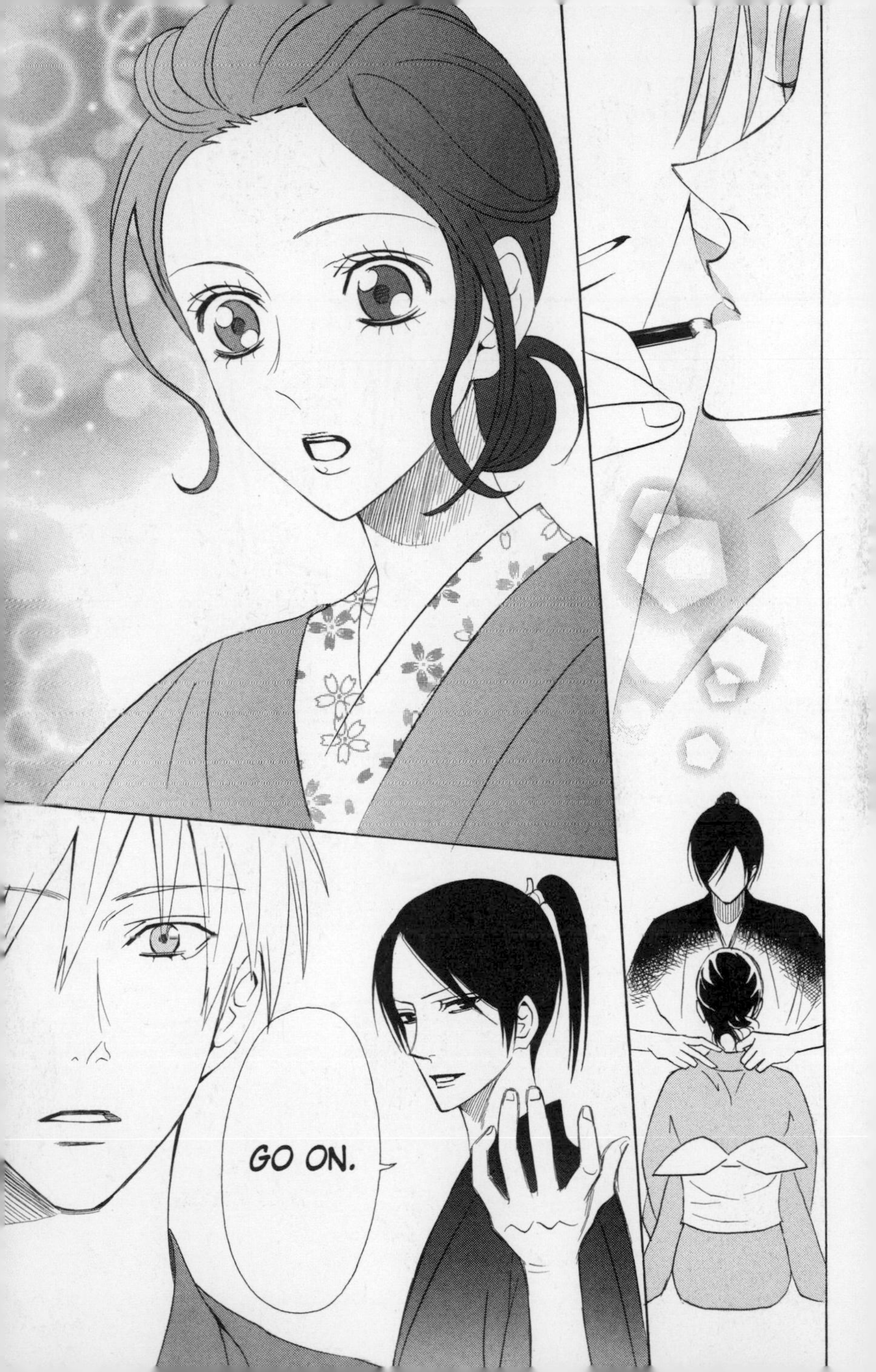
GO ON.

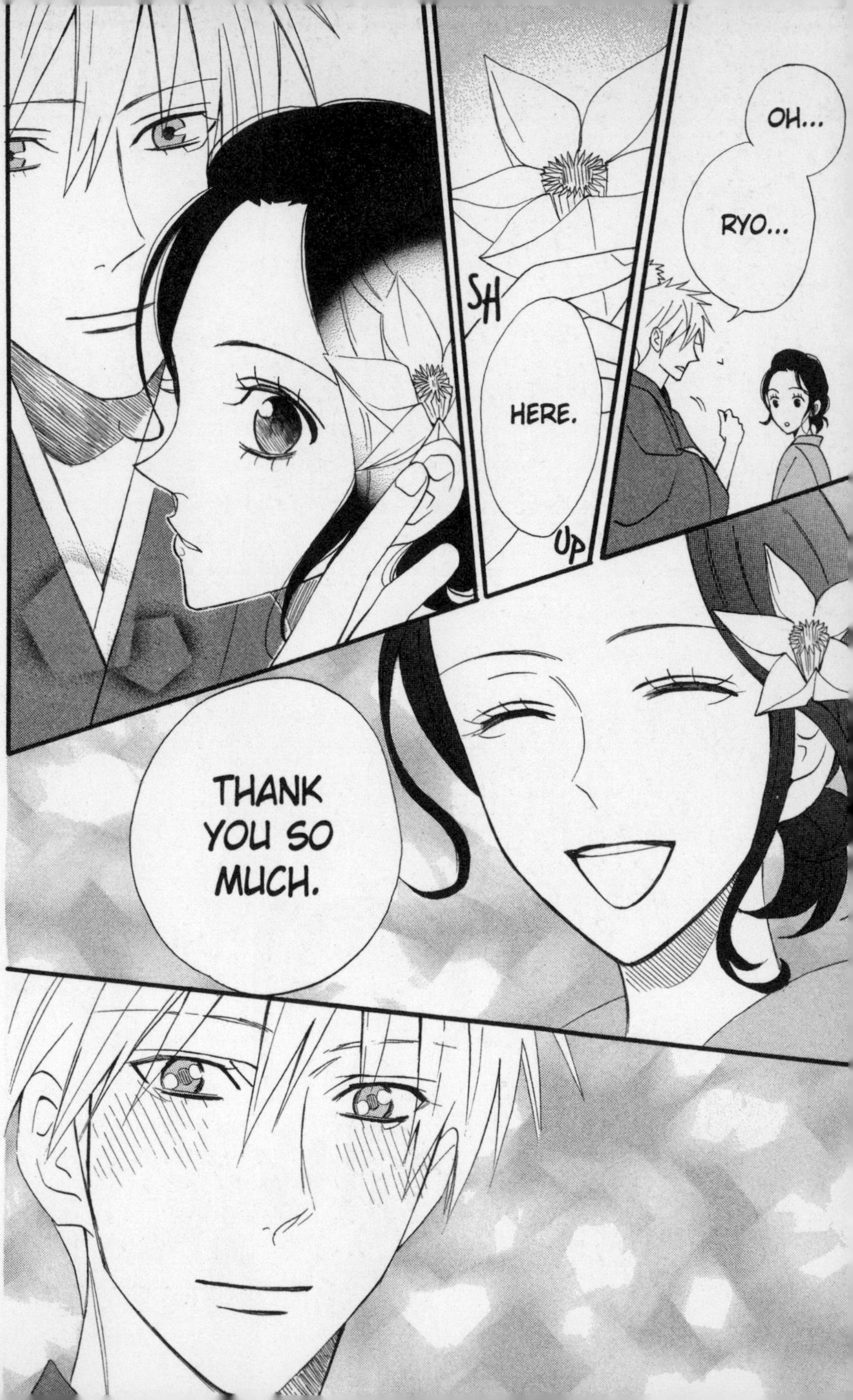
OH...
RYO...
SH
HERE.
UP
THANK YOU SO MUCH.

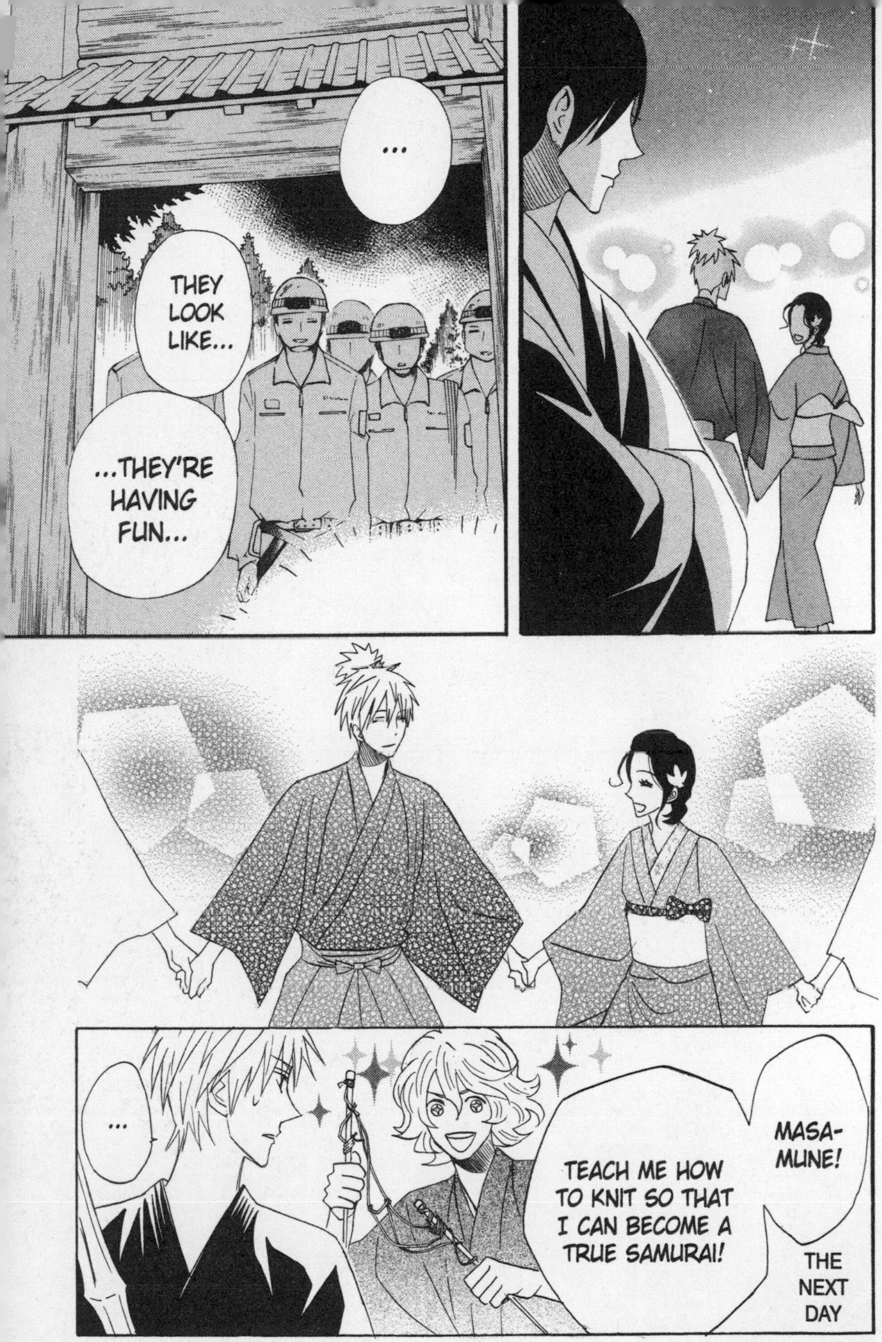
...
THEY LOOK LIKE...
...THEY'RE HAVING FUN...
MASA-MUNE!
THE NEXT DAY
TEACH ME HOW TO KNIT SO THAT I CAN BECOME A TRUE SAMURAI!
...

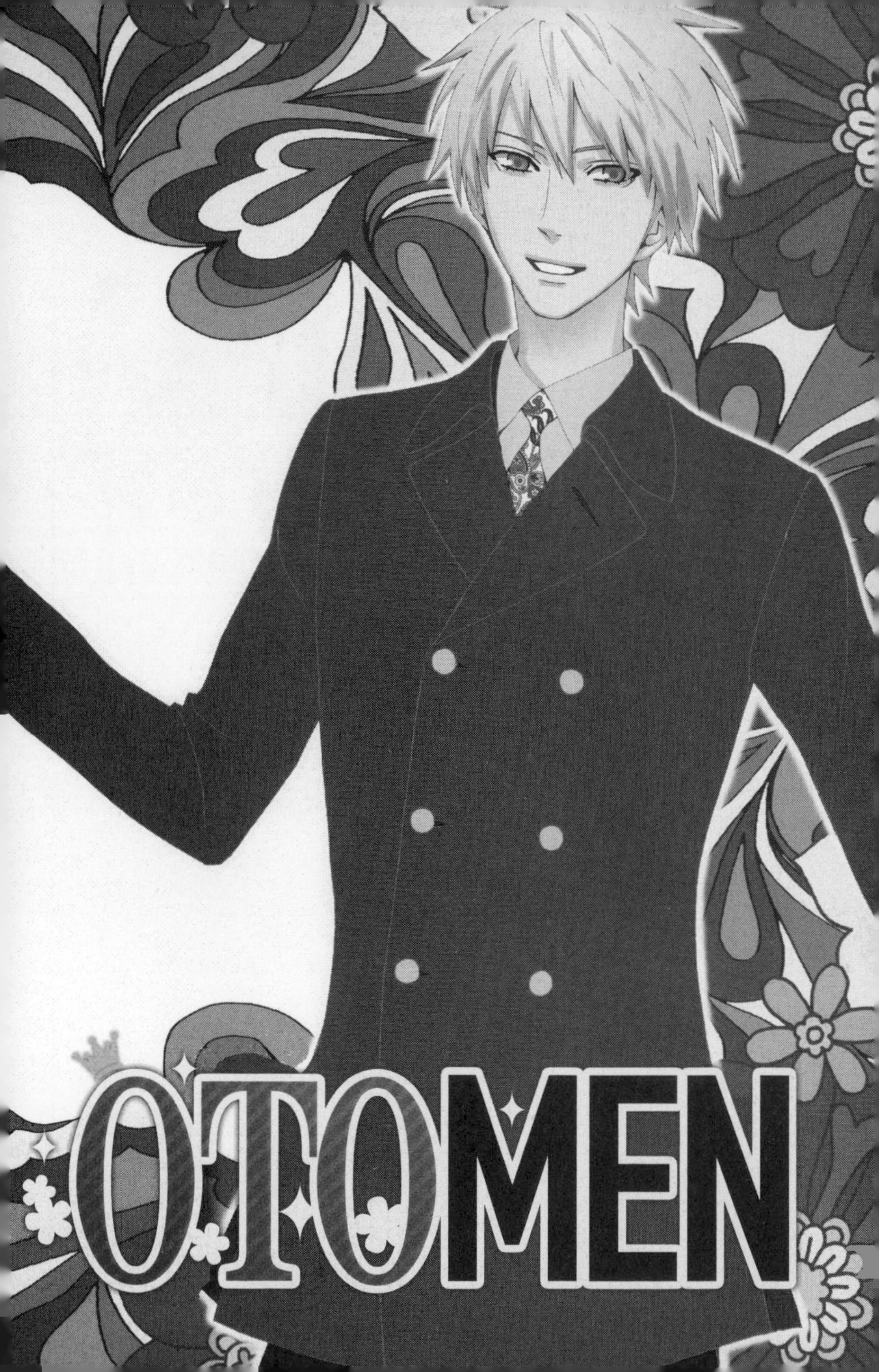
OTOMEN

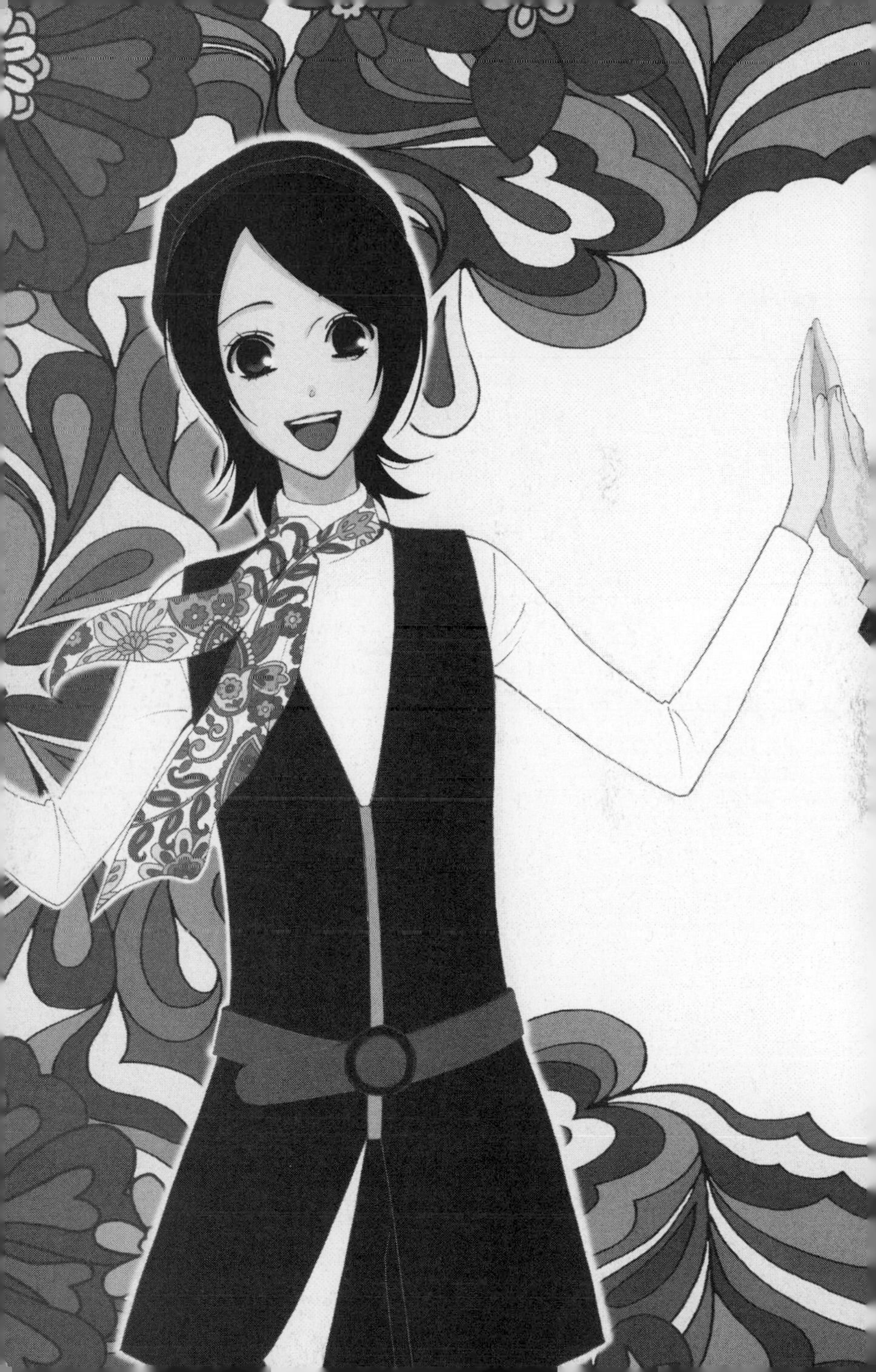

OTOMEN

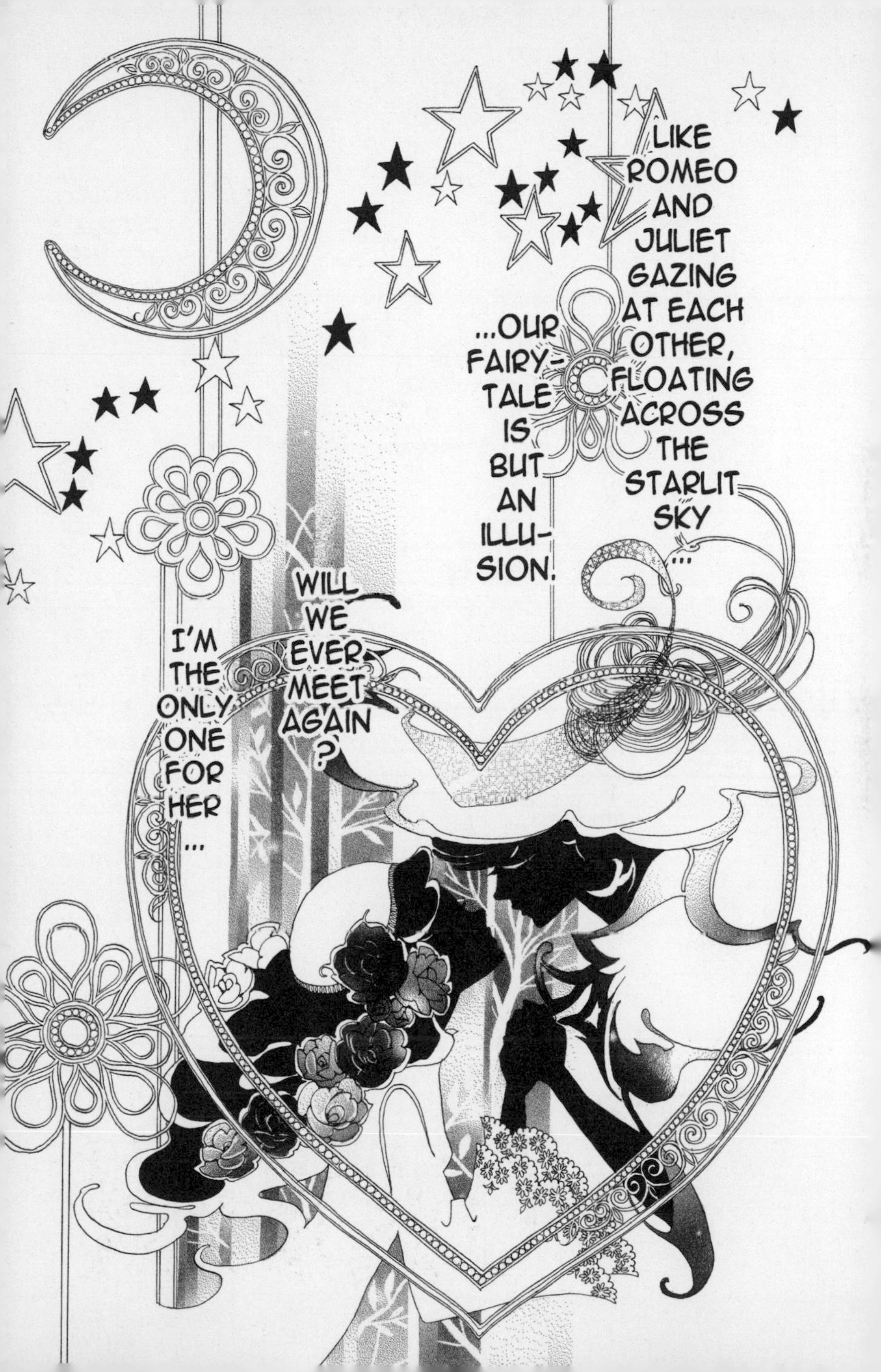
LIKE ROMEO AND JULIET GAZING AT EACH OTHER, FLOATING ACROSS THE STARLIT SKY...
...OUR FAIRY-TALE IS BUT AN ILLUSION.
WILL WE EVER MEET AGAIN?
I'M THE ONLY ONE FOR HER...

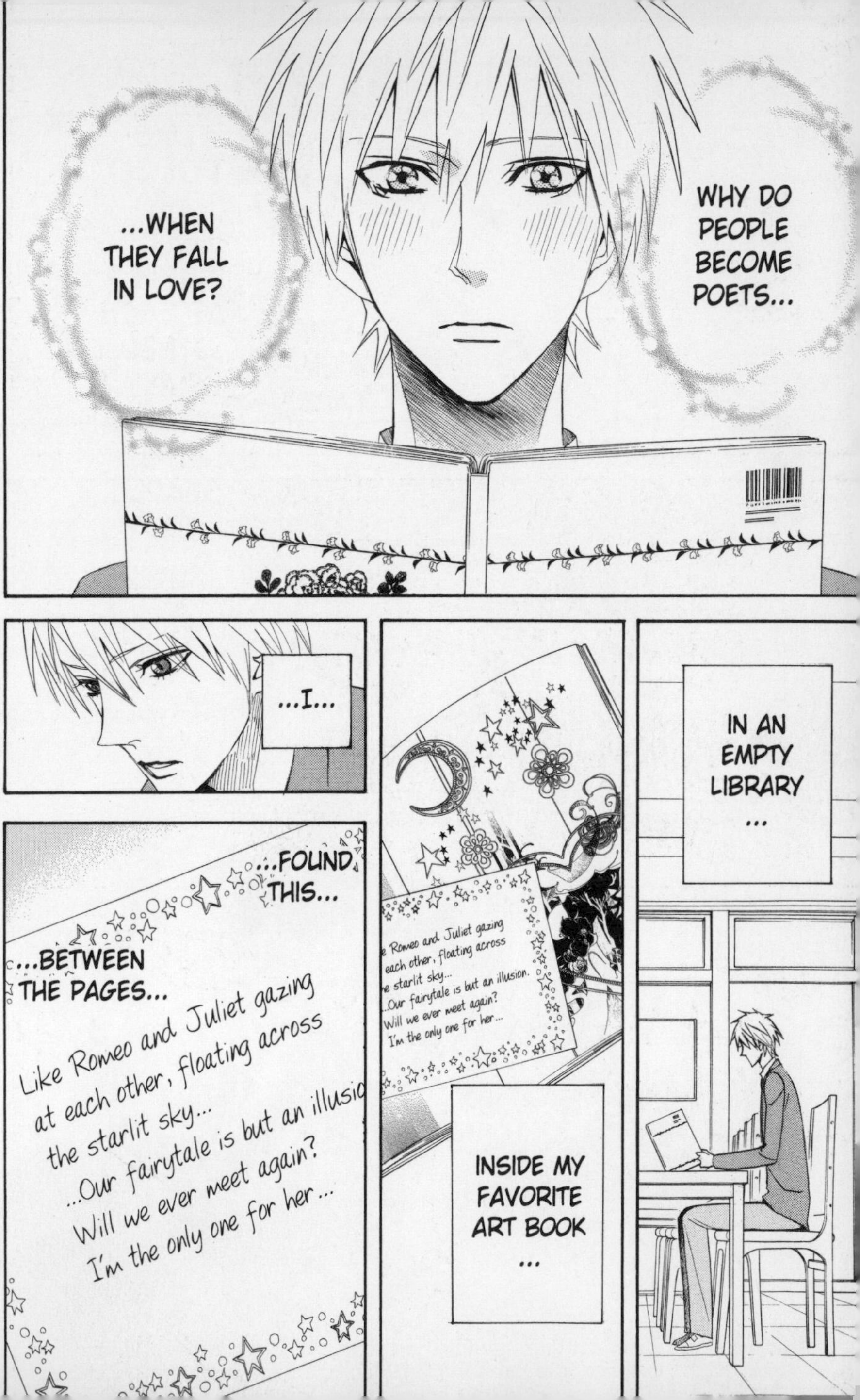
WHY DO PEOPLE BECOME POETS...
...WHEN THEY FALL IN LOVE?
IN AN EMPTY LIBRARY ...
INSIDE MY FAVORITE ART BOOK ...
...I...
...FOUND THIS...
...BETWEEN THE PAGES...
Like Romeo and Juliet gazing at each other, floating across the starlit sky...
...Our fairytale is but an illusio
Will we ever meet again?
I'm the only one for her...

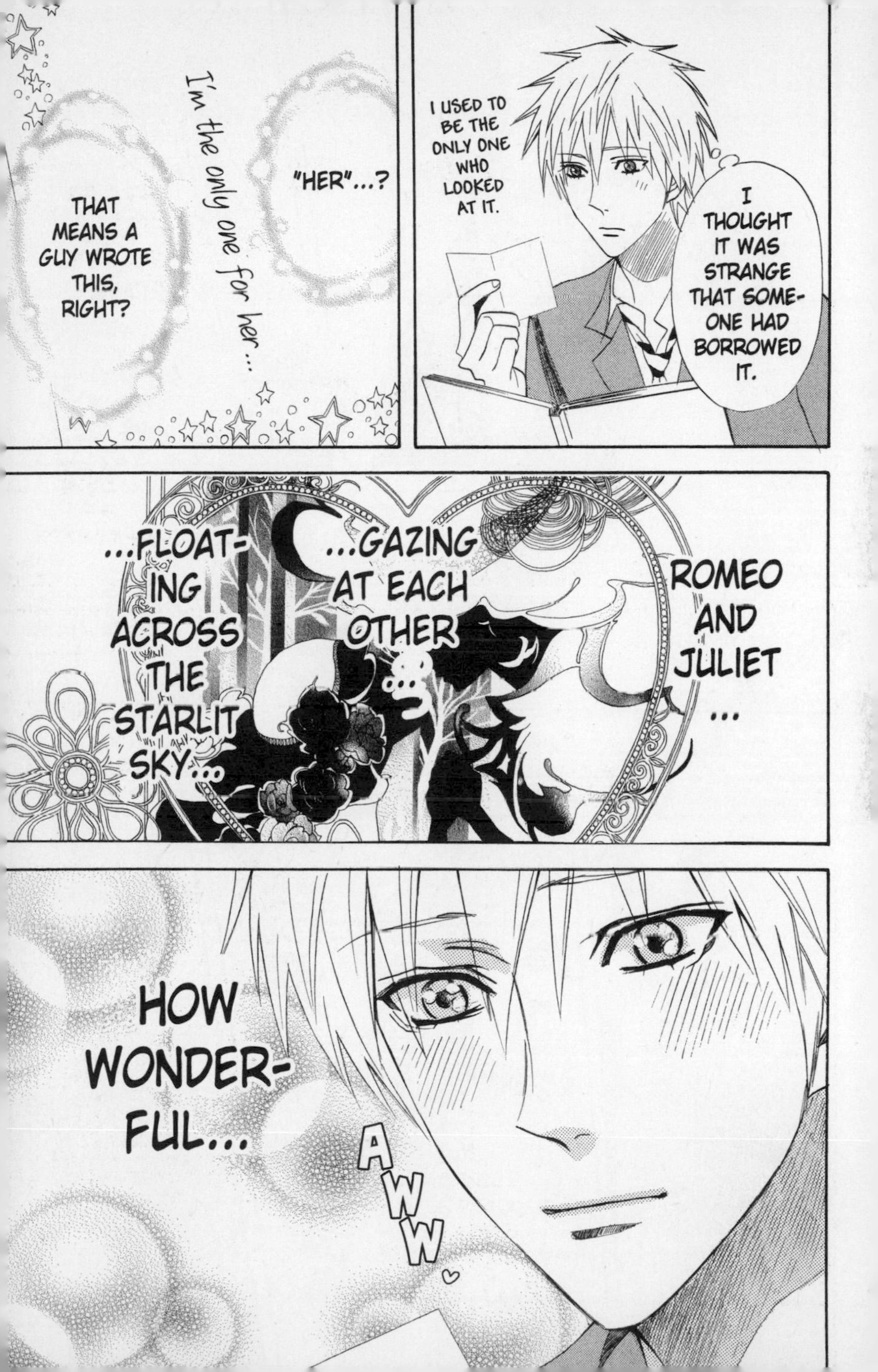
I THOUGHT IT WAS STRANGE THAT SOME-ONE HAD BORROWED IT.
I USED TO BE THE ONLY ONE WHO LOOKED AT IT.
"HER"...?
I'm the only one for her...
THAT MEANS A GUY WROTE THIS, RIGHT?
ROMEO AND JULIET...
...GAZING AT EACH OTHER...
...FLOAT-ING ACROSS THE STARLIT SKY...
HOW WONDER-FUL...
AWW

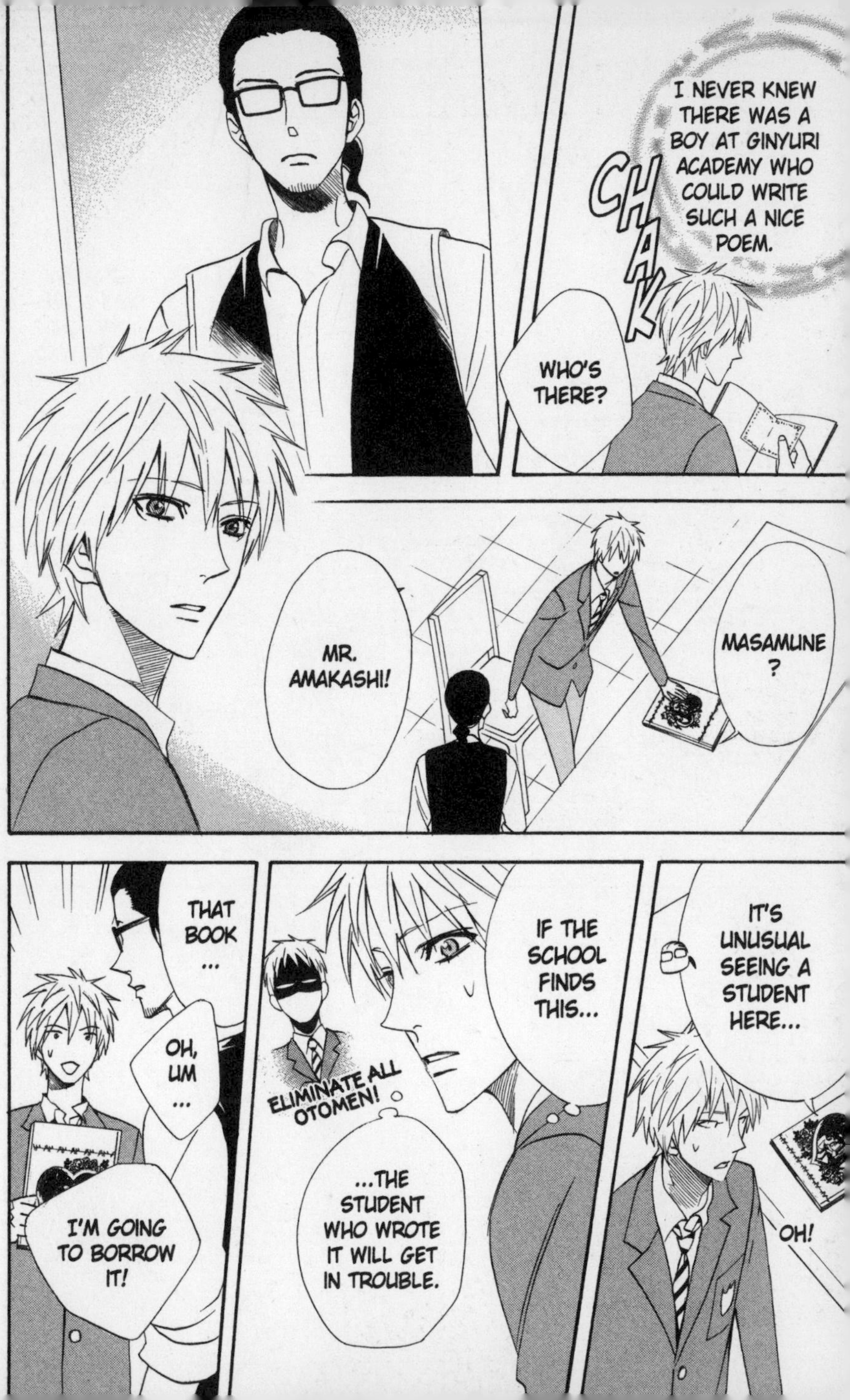
I NEVER KNEW THERE WAS A BOY AT GINYURI ACADEMY WHO COULD WRITE SUCH A NICE POEM.
CHAK
WHO'S THERE?
MASAMUNE?
MR. AMAKASHI!
IT'S UNUSUAL SEEING A STUDENT HERE...
OH!
IF THE SCHOOL FINDS THIS...
...THE STUDENT WHO WROTE IT WILL GET IN TROUBLE.
ELIMINATE ALL OTOMEN!
THAT BOOK ...
OH, UM ...
I'M GOING TO BORROW IT!

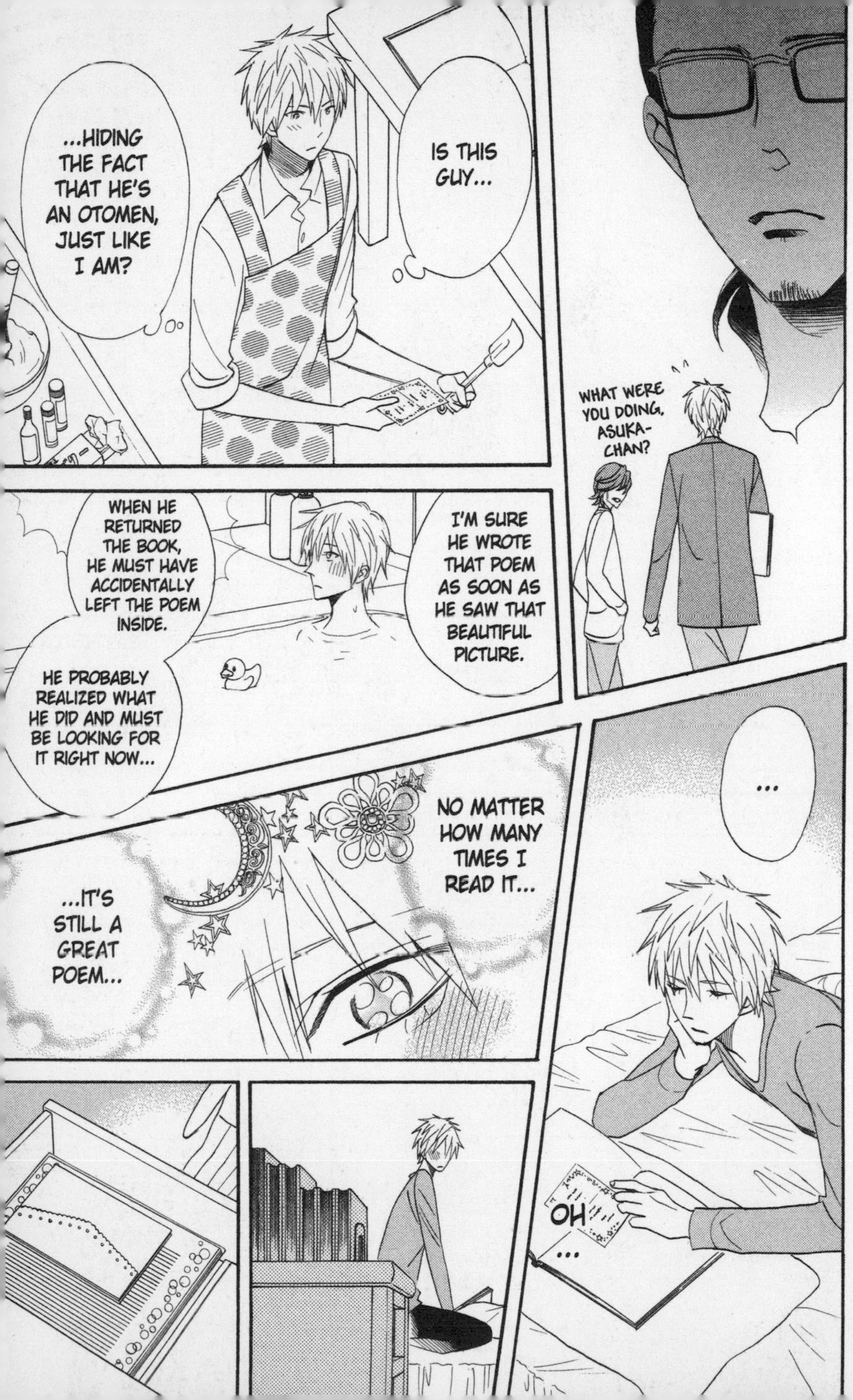
WHAT WERE YOU DOING, ASUKA-CHAN?
IS THIS GUY...
...HIDING THE FACT THAT HE'S AN OTOMEN, JUST LIKE I AM?
I'M SURE HE WROTE THAT POEM AS SOON AS HE SAW THAT BEAUTIFUL PICTURE.
WHEN HE RETURNED THE BOOK, HE MUST HAVE ACCIDENTALLY LEFT THE POEM INSIDE.
HE PROBABLY REALIZED WHAT HE DID AND MUST BE LOOKING FOR IT RIGHT NOW...
...
OH...
NO MATTER HOW MANY TIMES I READ IT...
...IT'S STILL A GREAT POEM...

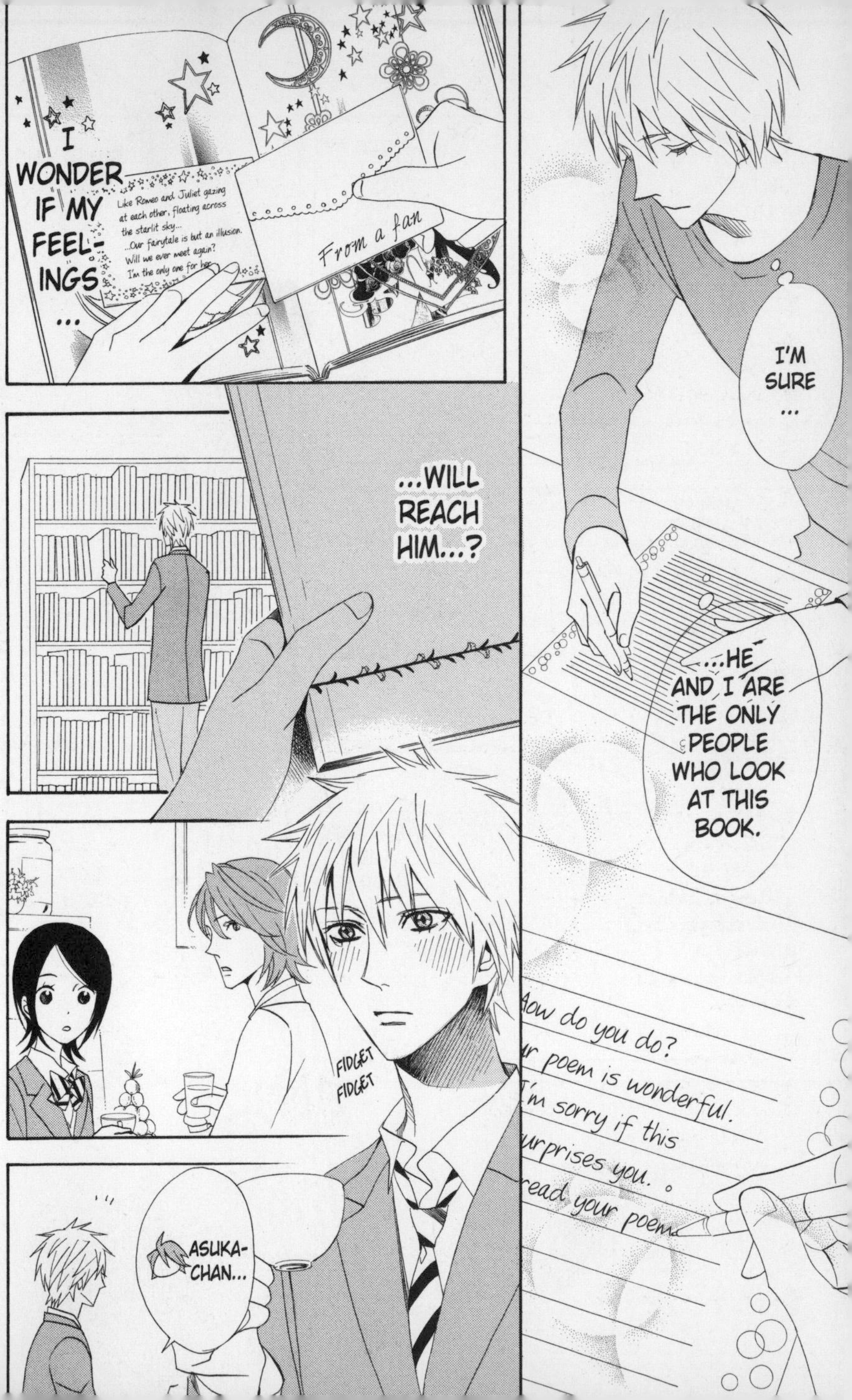

I'M SURE ...
...HE AND I ARE THE ONLY PEOPLE WHO LOOK AT THIS BOOK.
How do you do?
ur poem is wonderful.
I'm sorry if this
urprises you.
read your poem.
Like Romeo and Juliet gazing at each other, floating across the starlit sky... ...Our fairytale is but an illusion. Will we ever meet again? I'm the only one for her
From a fan
I WONDER IF MY FEEL-INGS ...
...WILL REACH HIM...?
FIDGET FIDGET
ASUKA-CHAN...

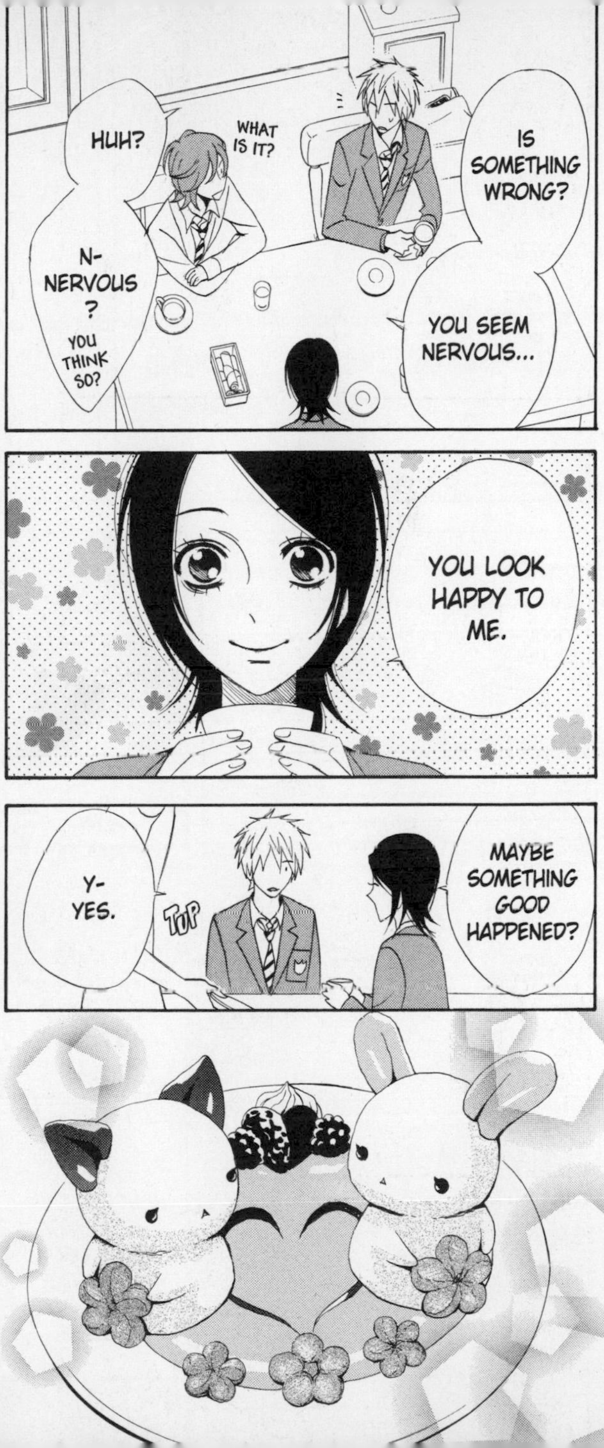
IS SOMETHING WRONG?
WHAT IS IT?
HUH?
YOU SEEM NERVOUS...
N-NERVOUS?
YOU THINK SO?
YOU LOOK HAPPY TO ME.
MAYBE SOMETHING GOOD HAPPENED?
TUP
Y-YES.

By the way, I went to France for an autograph session the other day.
It was my first time in France.
It's a great country. I fell in love with it.
My readers in France were as passionate and as wonderful as my readers in Japan and Taiwan.
The company that publishes my comic there is full of wonderful people too.
I keep saying things were wonderful, but they really were.
The people, the streets...
Even their way of thinking.

Thank you so much to everyone in France.
I'd like to go back again.

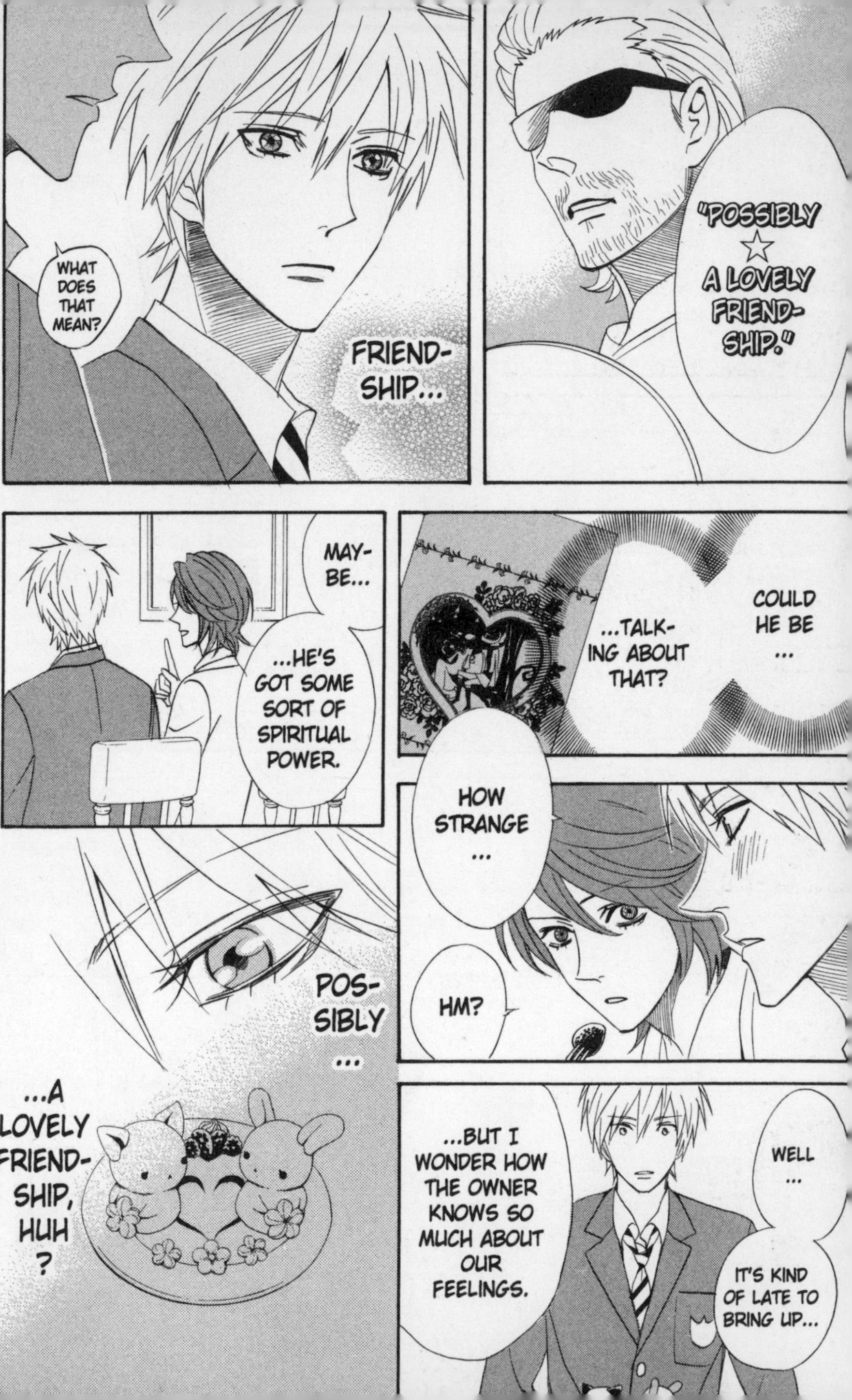
"POSSIBLY ☆ A LOVELY FRIEND-SHIP."
WHAT DOES THAT MEAN?
FRIEND-SHIP...
COULD HE BE ...
...TALK-ING ABOUT THAT?
MAY-BE...
...HE'S GOT SOME SORT OF SPIRITUAL POWER.
HOW STRANGE ...
HM?
WELL ...
IT'S KIND OF LATE TO BRING UP...
...BUT I WONDER HOW THE OWNER KNOWS SO MUCH ABOUT OUR FEELINGS.
POS-SIBLY ...
...A LOVELY FRIEND-SHIP, HUH ?

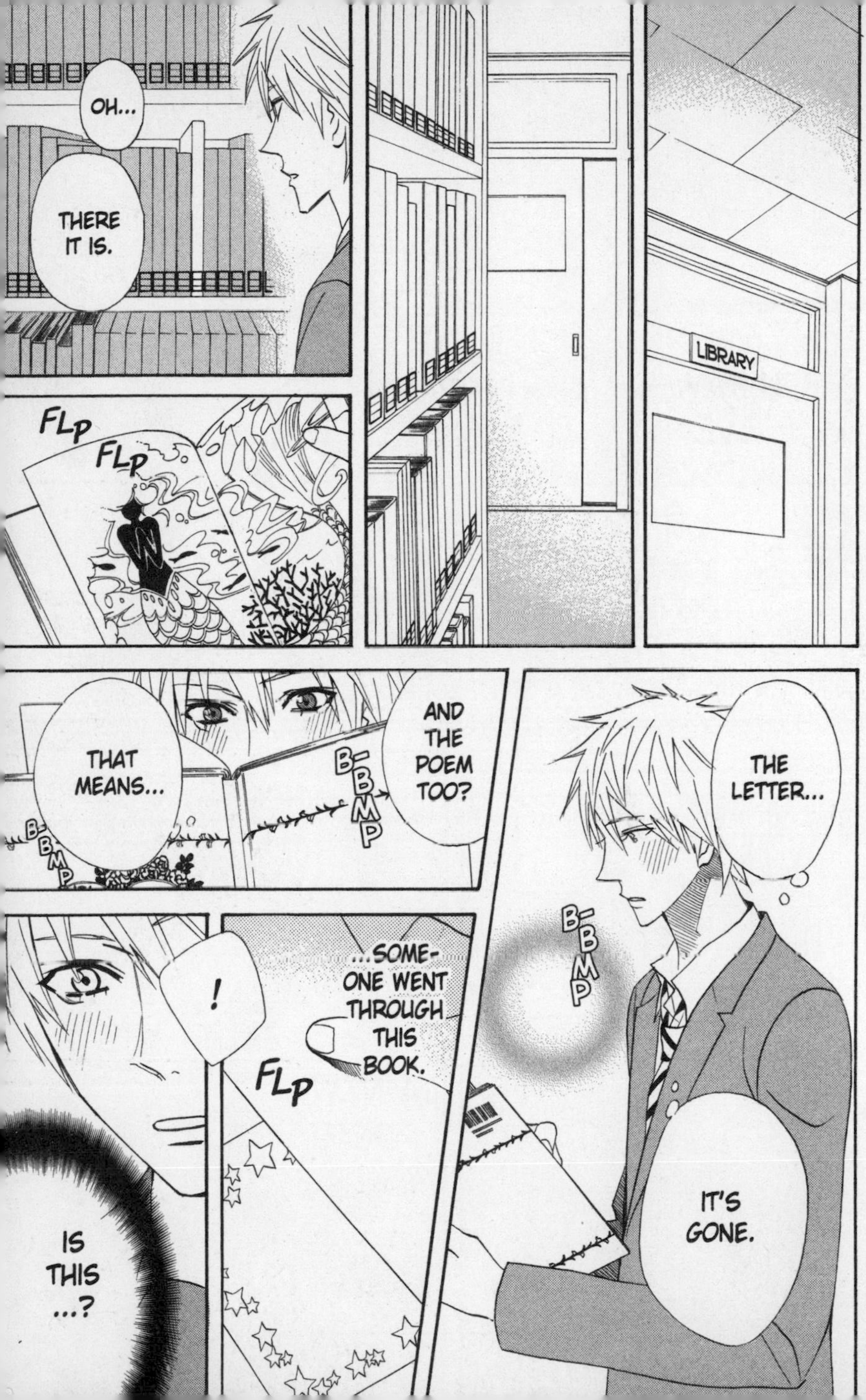
LIBRARY
OH...
THERE IT IS.
FLP
FLP
THE LETTER...
B-BMP
IT'S GONE.
AND THE POEM TOO?
B-BMP
THAT MEANS...
B-BMP
...SOME-ONE WENT THROUGH THIS BOOK.
FLP
!
IS THIS ...?

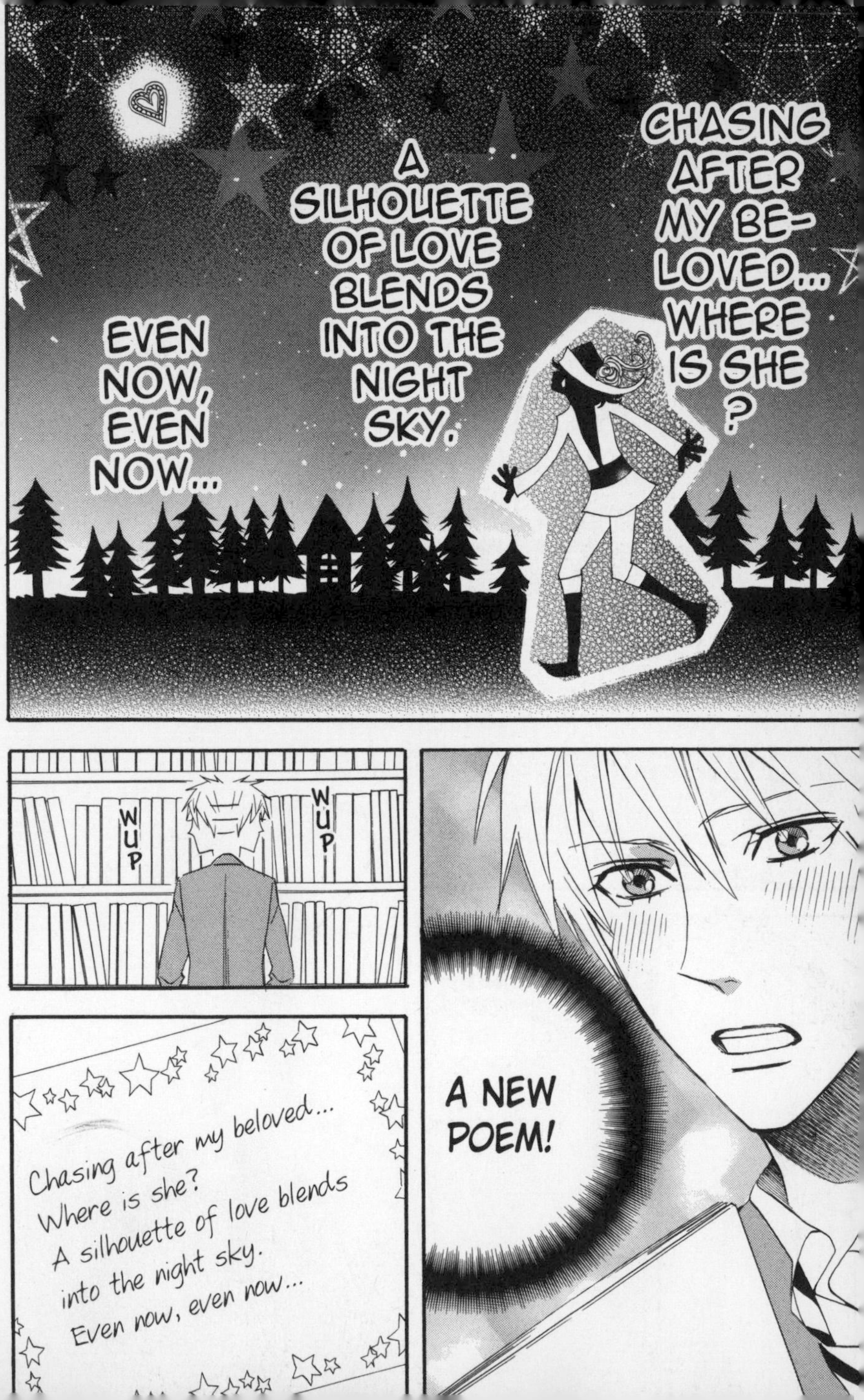
CHASING AFTER MY BE-LOVED... WHERE IS SHE?
A SILHOUETTE OF LOVE BLENDS INTO THE NIGHT SKY.
EVEN NOW, EVEN NOW...
A NEW POEM!
WUP
WUP
Chasing after my beloved...
Where is she?
A silhouette of love blends
into the night sky.
Even now, even now...

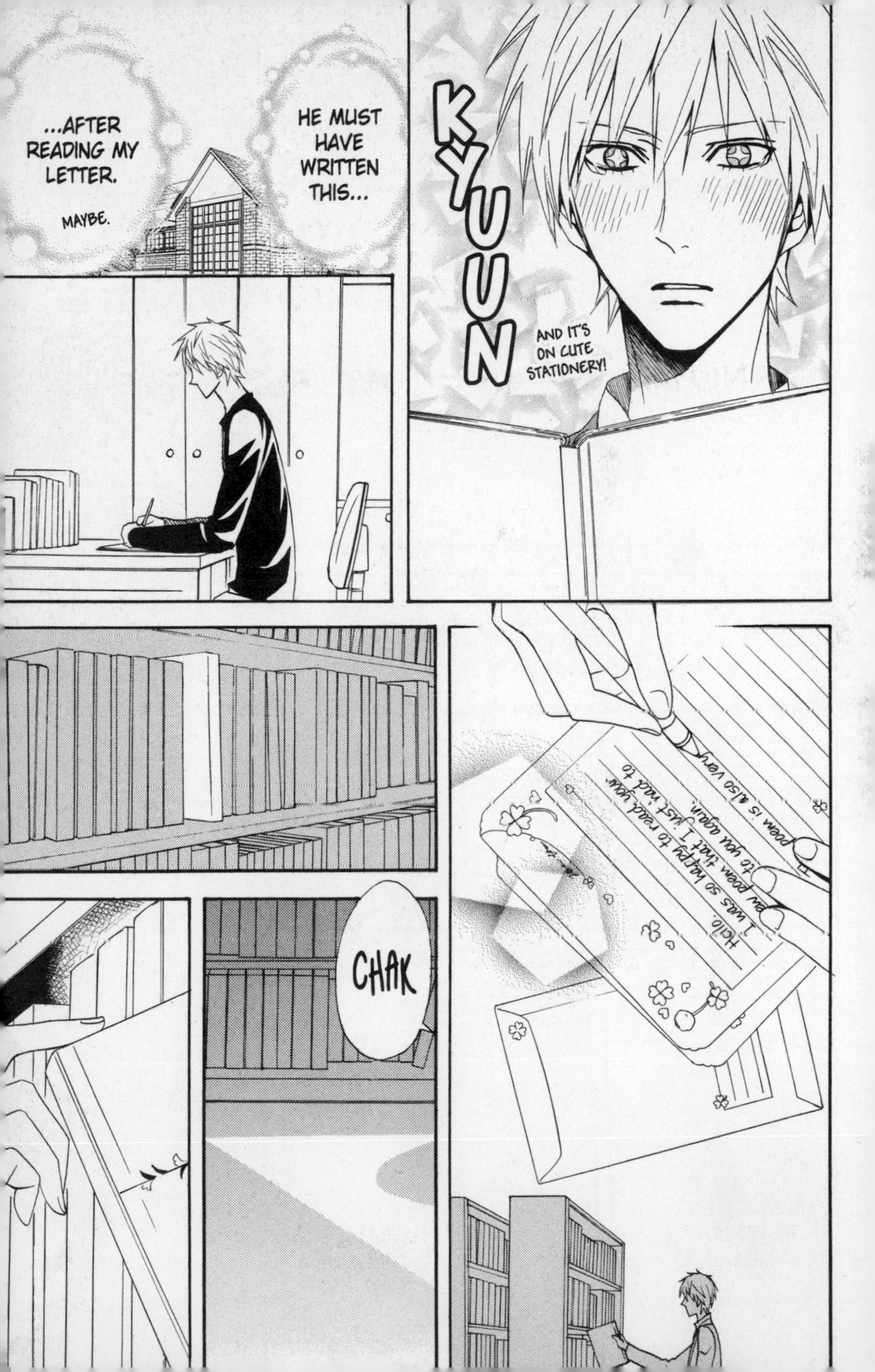
KYUUN
AND IT'S ON CUTE STATIONERY!
HE MUST HAVE WRITTEN THIS...
...AFTER READING MY LETTER.
MAYBE.
Hello.
I was so happy to read your
new poem that I just had to
to you again.
poem is also very
CHAK

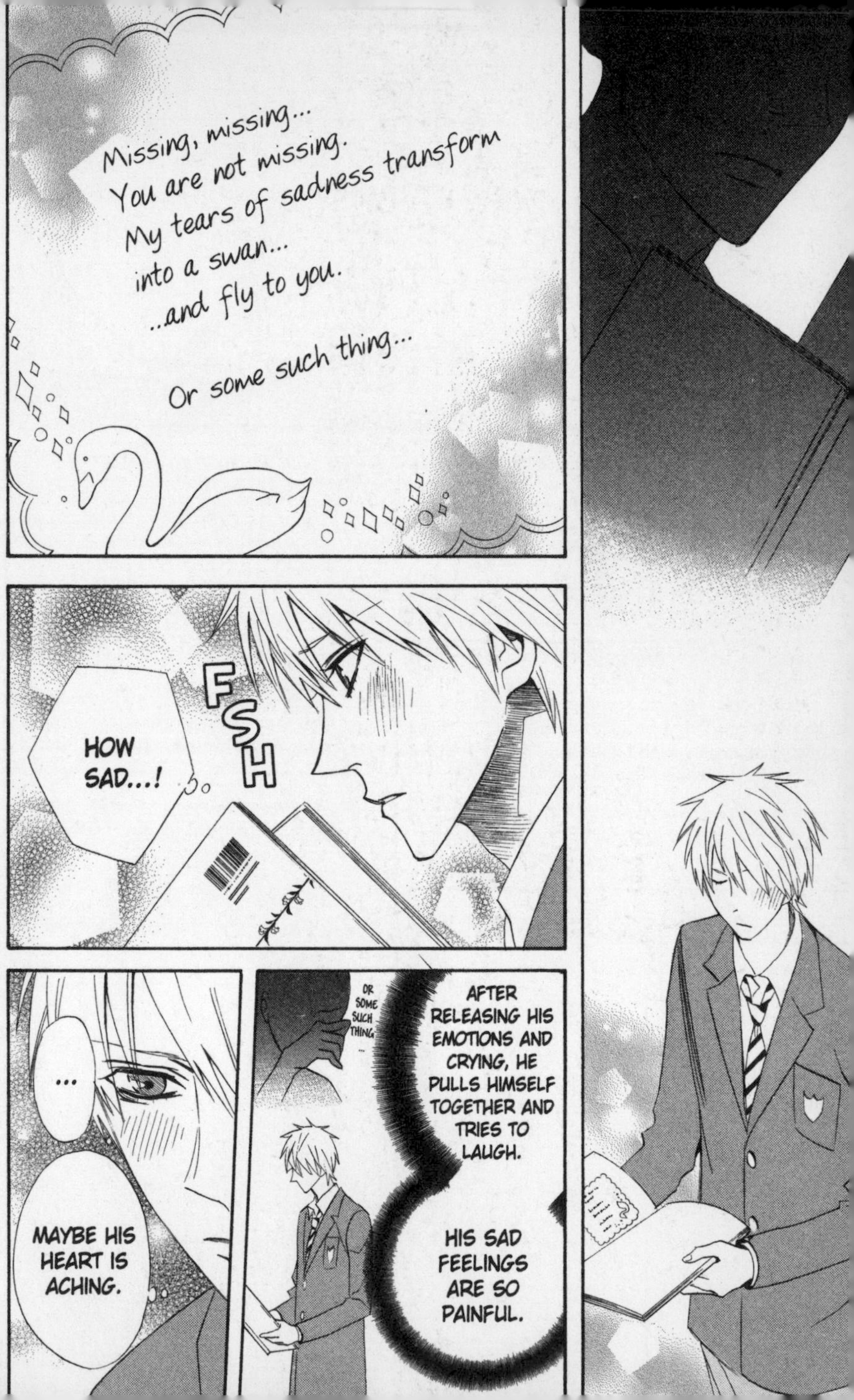
Missing, missing...
You are not missing.
My tears of sadness transform
into a swan...
...and fly to you.
Or some such thing...
FSH
HOW SAD...!
OR SOME SUCH THING...
AFTER RELEASING HIS EMOTIONS AND CRYING, HE PULLS HIMSELF TOGETHER AND TRIES TO LAUGH.
HIS SAD FEELINGS ARE SO PAINFUL.
...
MAYBE HIS HEART IS ACHING.

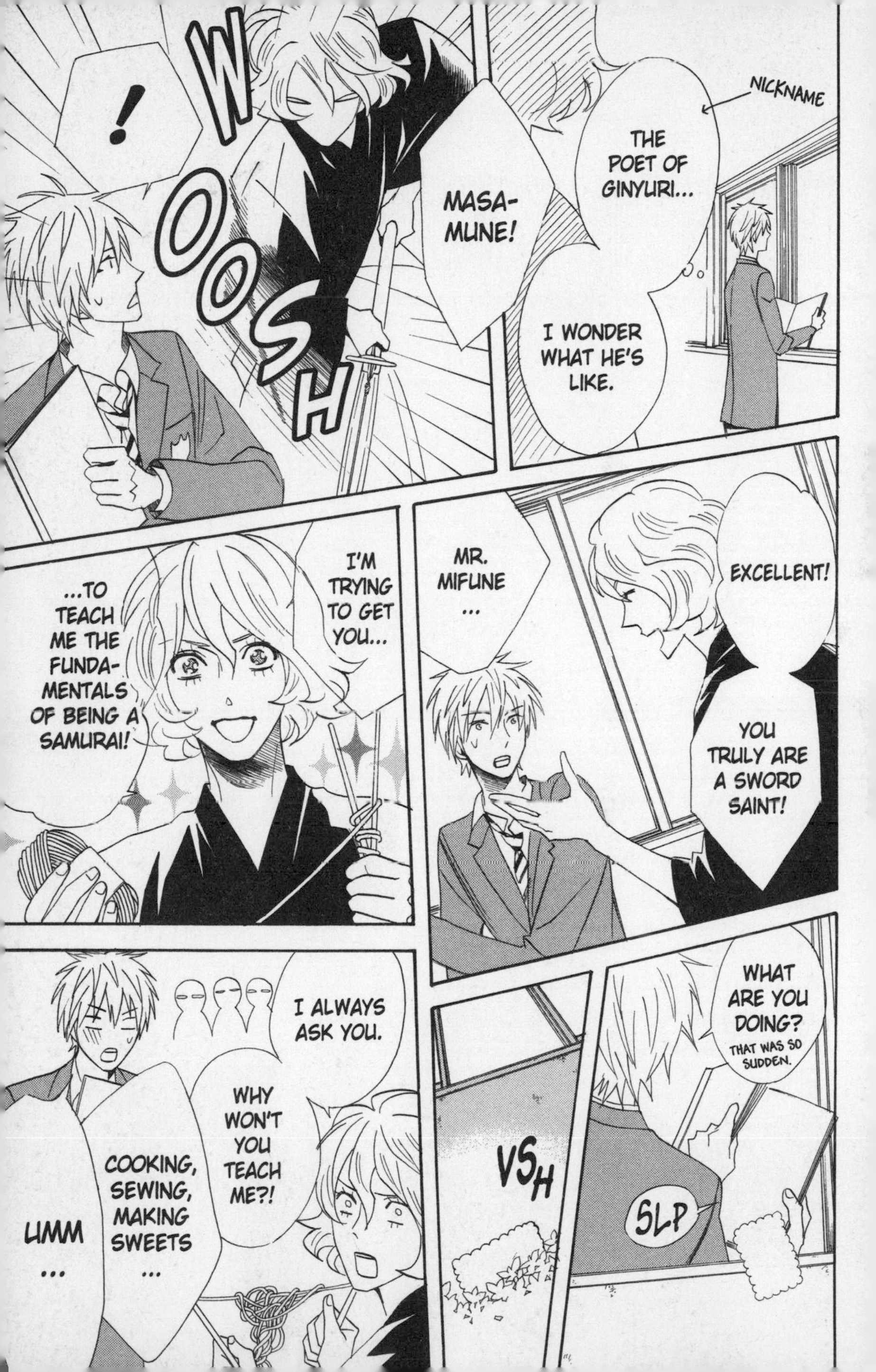
NICKNAME
THE POET OF GINYURI...
I WONDER WHAT HE'S LIKE.
MASA-MUNE!
!
WOOSH
EXCELLENT!
YOU TRULY ARE A SWORD SAINT!
MR. MIFUNE ...
I'M TRYING TO GET YOU...
...TO TEACH ME THE FUNDA-MENTALS OF BEING A SAMURAI!
WHAT ARE YOU DOING? THAT WAS SO SUDDEN.
SLP
VSH
I ALWAYS ASK YOU.
WHY WON'T YOU TEACH ME?!
COOKING, SEWING, MAKING SWEETS ...
UMM ...

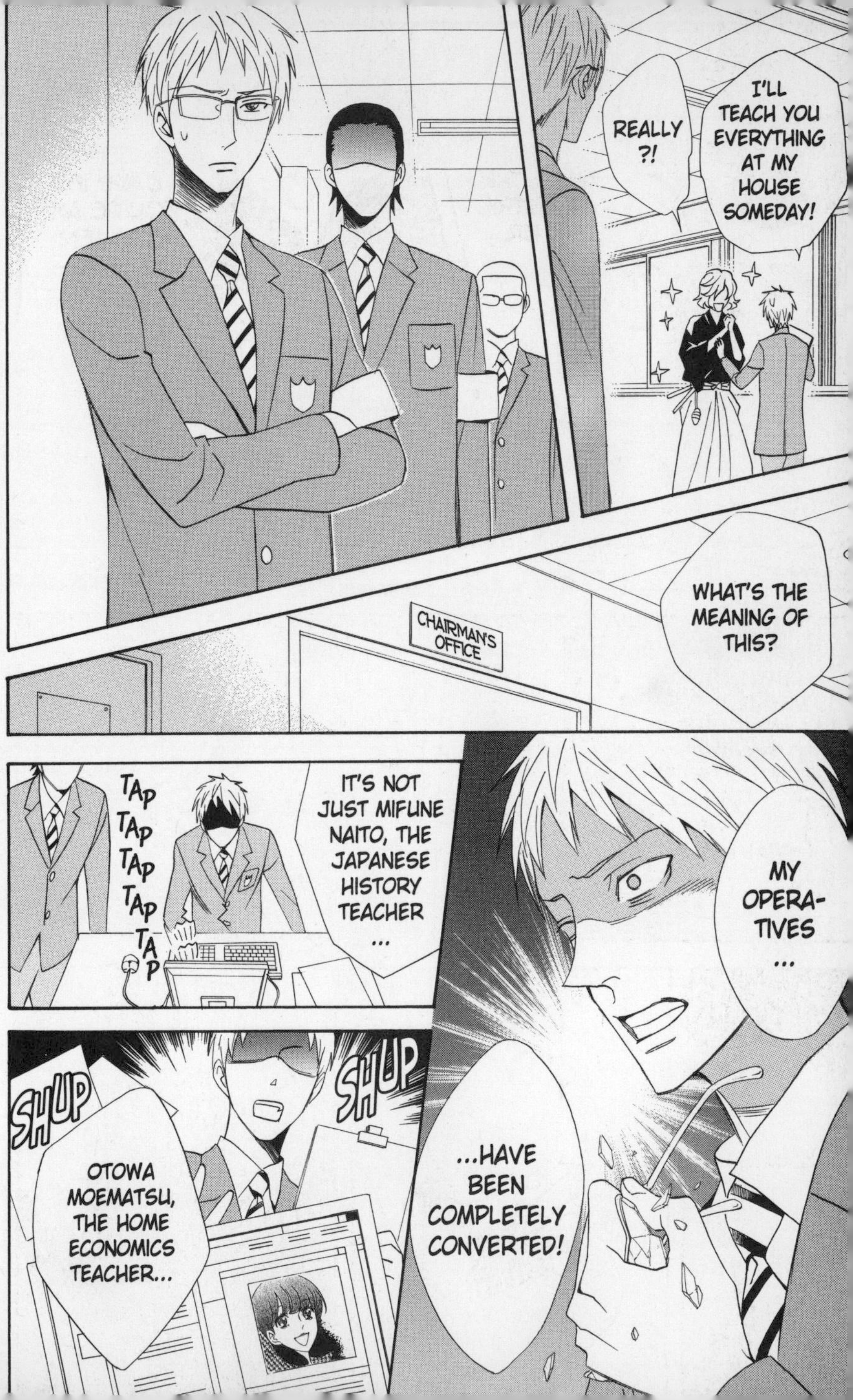
I'LL TEACH YOU EVERYTHING AT MY HOUSE SOMEDAY!
REALLY ?!
WHAT'S THE MEANING OF THIS?
CHAIRMAN'S OFFICE
MY OPERA-TIVES ...
...HAVE BEEN COMPLETELY CONVERTED!
IT'S NOT JUST MIFUNE NAITO, THE JAPANESE HISTORY TEACHER ...
TAP TAP TAP TAP TAP
SHUP
OTOWA MOEMATSU, THE HOME ECONOMICS TEACHER...
SHUP

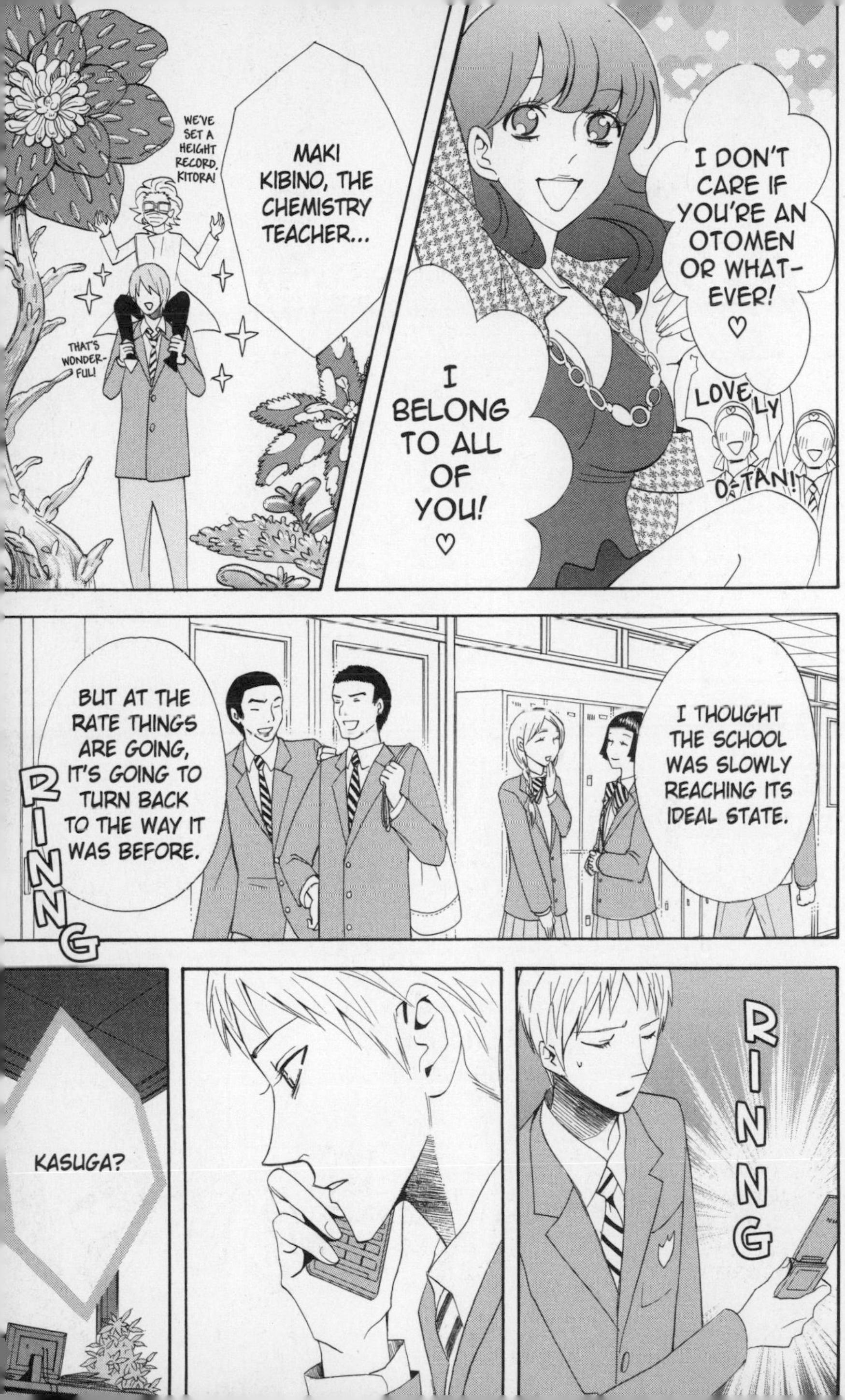
I DON'T CARE IF YOU'RE AN OTOMEN OR WHATEVER! ♡
I BELONG TO ALL OF YOU! ♡
LOVELY O-TAN!
MAKI KIBINO, THE CHEMISTRY TEACHER...
WE'VE SET A HEIGHT RECORD, KITORA!
THAT'S WONDERFUL!
I THOUGHT THE SCHOOL WAS SLOWLY REACHING ITS IDEAL STATE.
BUT AT THE RATE THINGS ARE GOING, IT'S GOING TO TURN BACK TO THE WAY IT WAS BEFORE.
RINNG
RINNG
KASUGA?

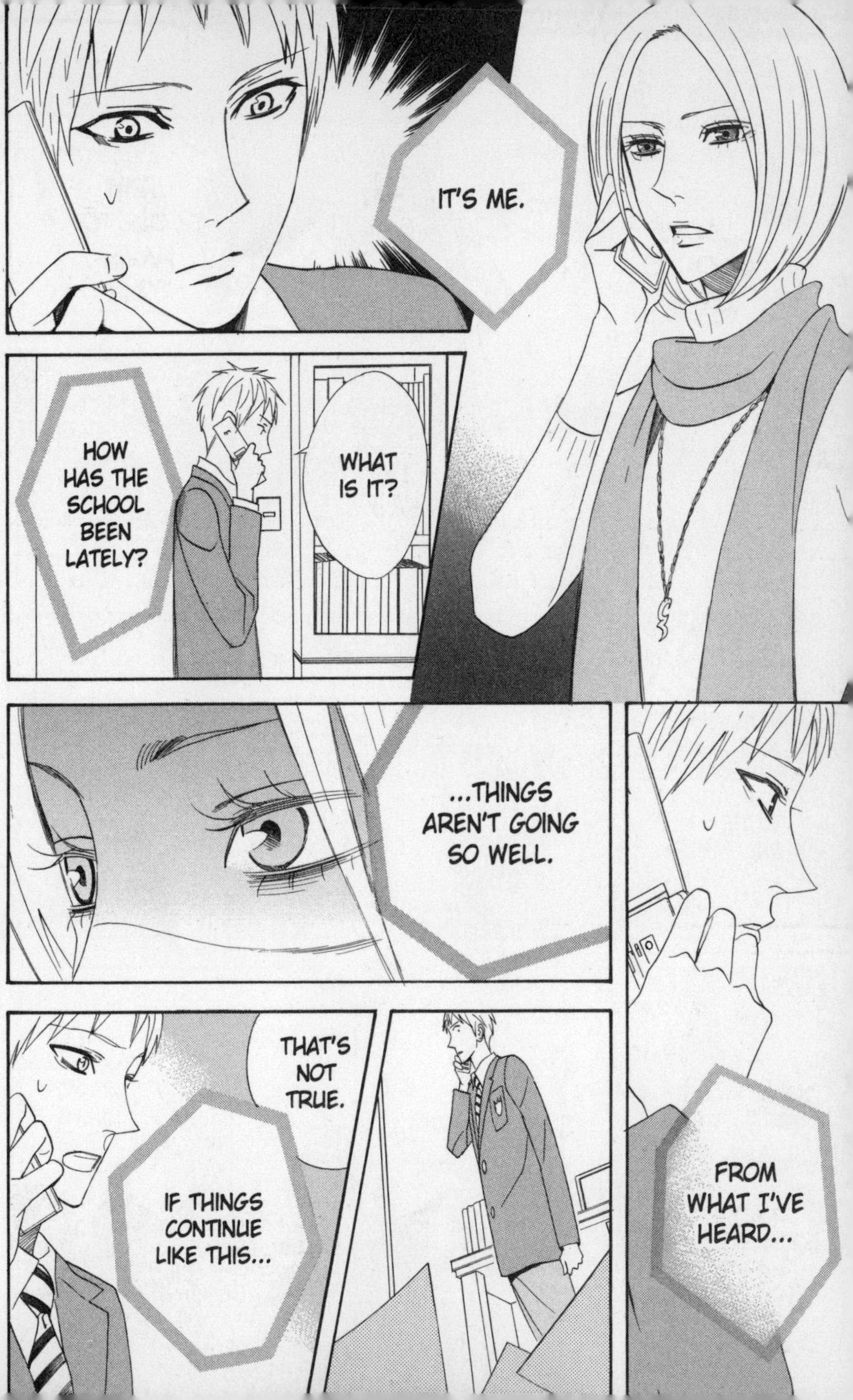
IT'S ME.
WHAT IS IT?
HOW HAS THE SCHOOL BEEN LATELY?
FROM WHAT I'VE HEARD...
...THINGS AREN'T GOING SO WELL.
THAT'S NOT TRUE.
IF THINGS CONTINUE LIKE THIS...

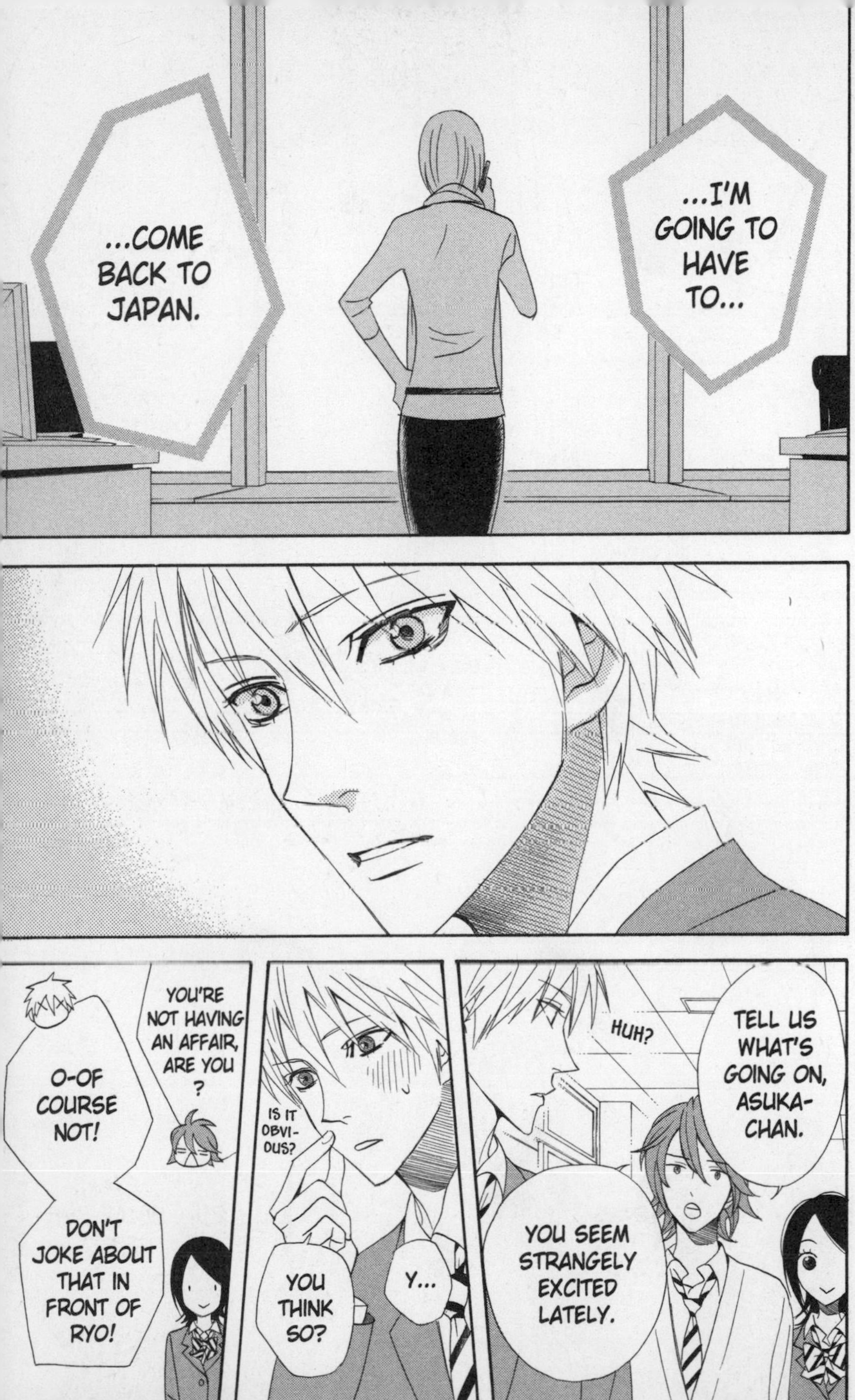
...I'M GOING TO HAVE TO...
...COME BACK TO JAPAN.
TELL US WHAT'S GOING ON, ASUKA-CHAN.
HUH?
YOU SEEM STRANGELY EXCITED LATELY.
Y...
YOU THINK SO?
IS IT OBVI-OUS?
YOU'RE NOT HAVING AN AFFAIR, ARE YOU?
O-OF COURSE NOT!
DON'T JOKE ABOUT THAT IN FRONT OF RYO!

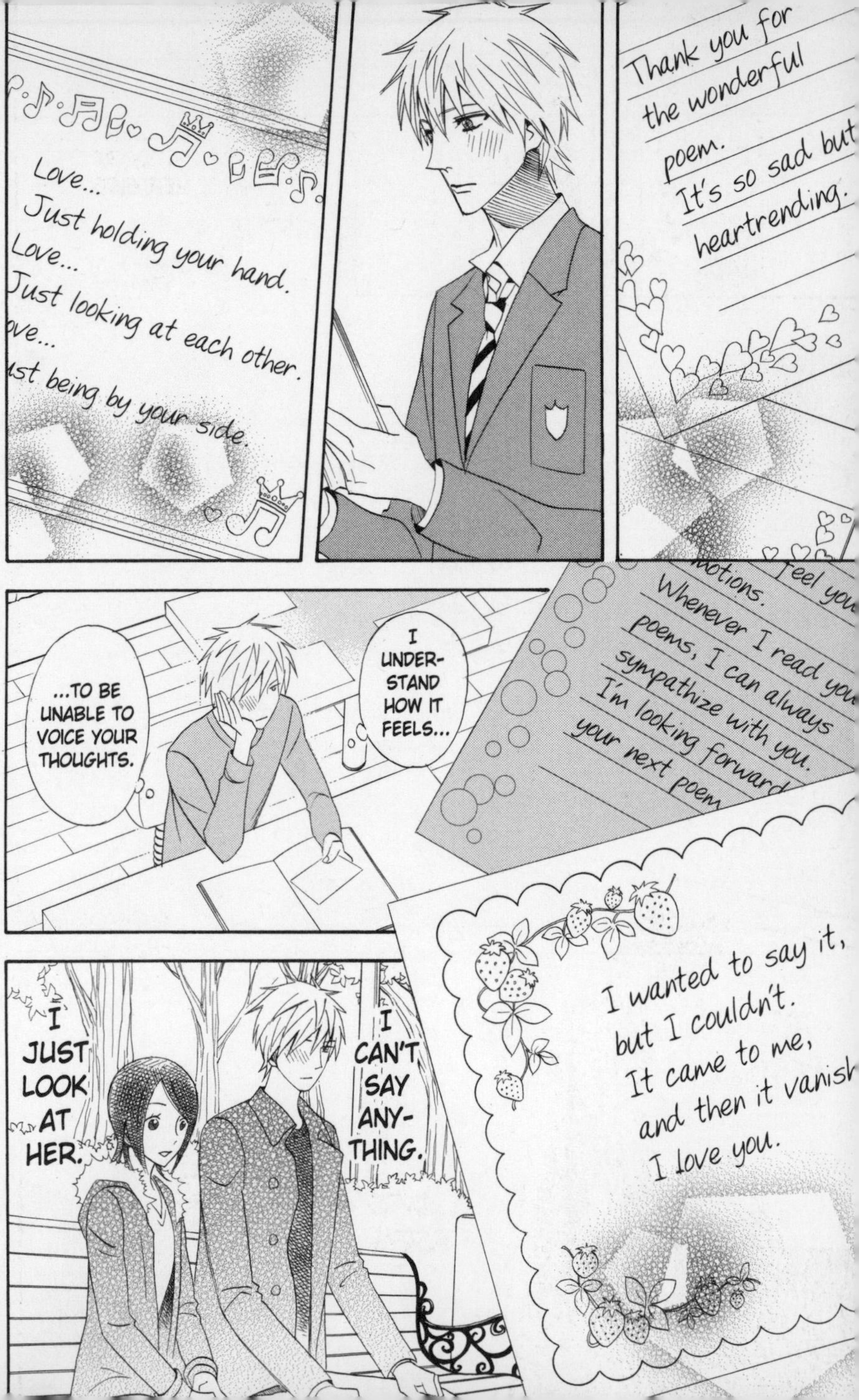

Thank you for the wonderful poem. It's so sad but heartrending.
Love... Just holding your hand. Love... Just looking at each other. ove... ust being by your side.
feel you motions. Whenever I read you poems, I can always sympathize with you. I'm looking forward your next poem
I UNDER-STAND HOW IT FEELS...
...TO BE UNABLE TO VOICE YOUR THOUGHTS.
I wanted to say it, but I couldn't. It came to me, and then it vanish I love you.
I CAN'T SAY ANY-THING.
I JUST LOOK AT HER.

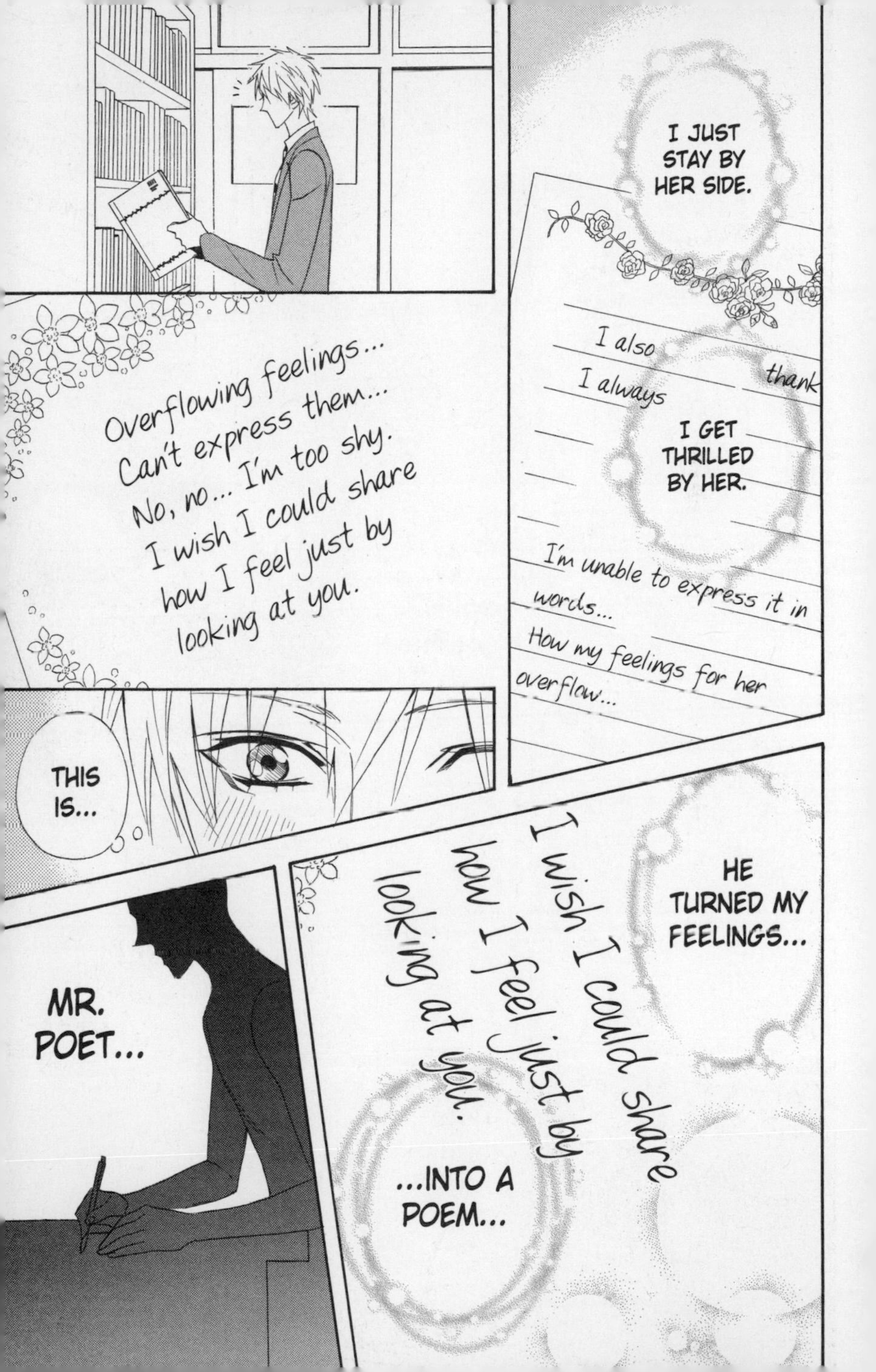

I JUST STAY BY HER SIDE.
I also
thank
I always
I GET THRILLED BY HER.
I'm unable to express it in words...
How my feelings for her overflow...
Overflowing feelings...
Can't express them...
No, no... I'm too shy.
I wish I could share how I feel just by looking at you.
THIS IS...
HE TURNED MY FEELINGS...
I wish I could share how I feel just by looking at you.
...INTO A POEM...
MR. POET...

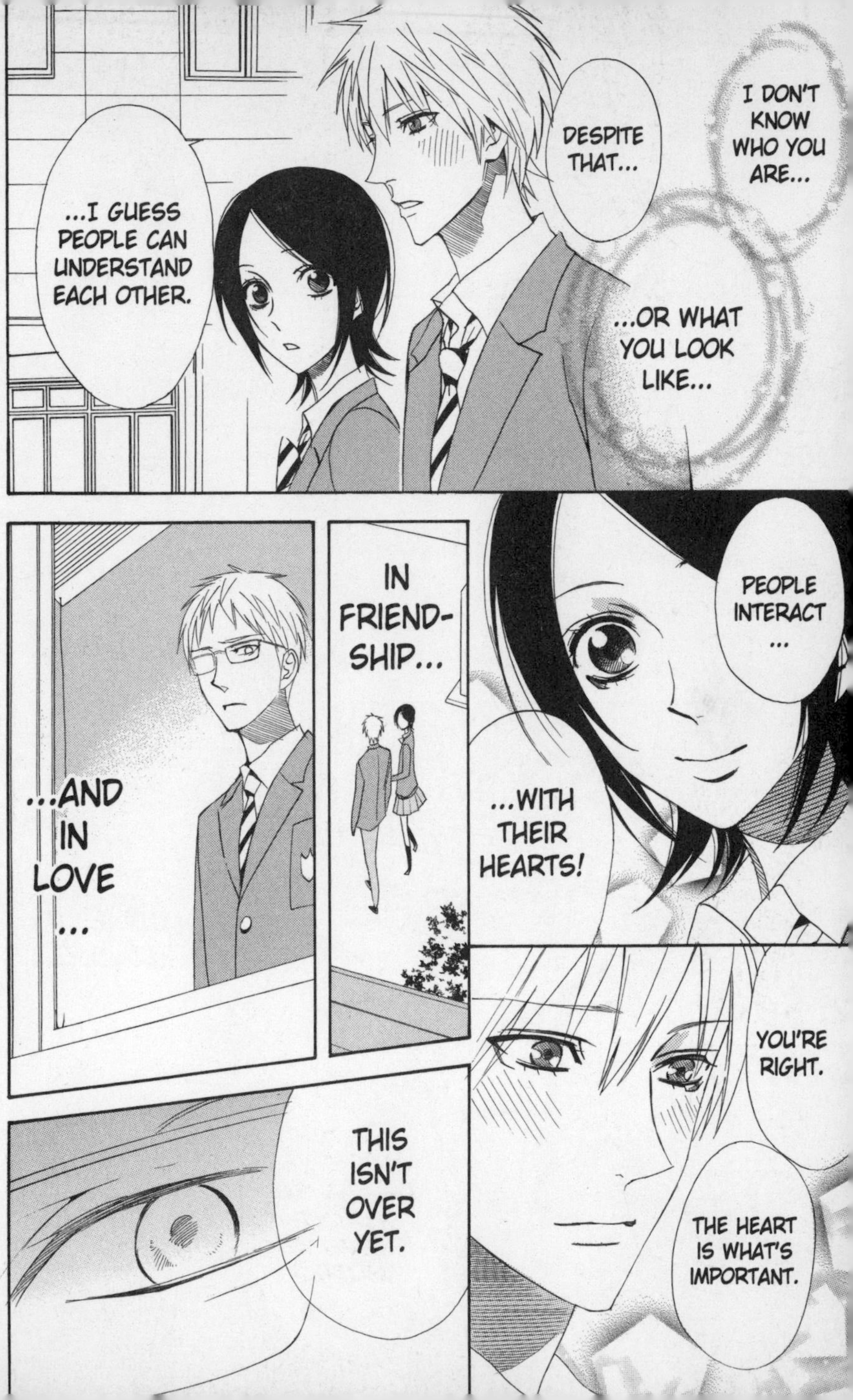
I DON'T KNOW WHO YOU ARE...
...OR WHAT YOU LOOK LIKE...
DESPITE THAT...
...I GUESS PEOPLE CAN UNDERSTAND EACH OTHER.
PEOPLE INTERACT ...
...WITH THEIR HEARTS!
YOU'RE RIGHT.
THE HEART IS WHAT'S IMPORTANT.
IN FRIEND-SHIP...
...AND IN LOVE ...
THIS ISN'T OVER YET.

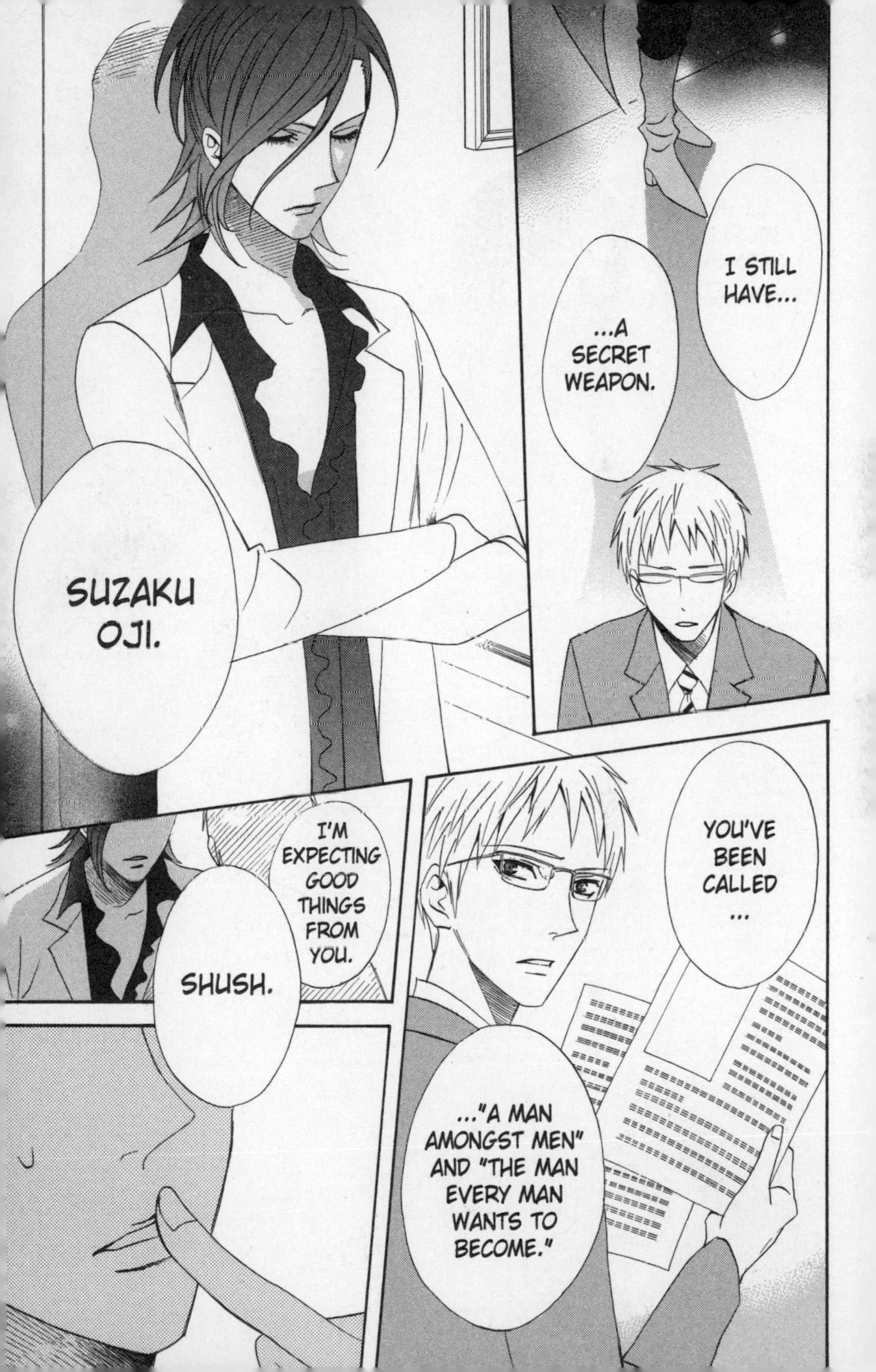
I STILL HAVE...
...A SECRET WEAPON.
SUZAKU OJI.
YOU'VE BEEN CALLED ...
..."A MAN AMONGST MEN" AND "THE MAN EVERY MAN WANTS TO BECOME."
I'M EXPECTING GOOD THINGS FROM YOU.
SHUSH.

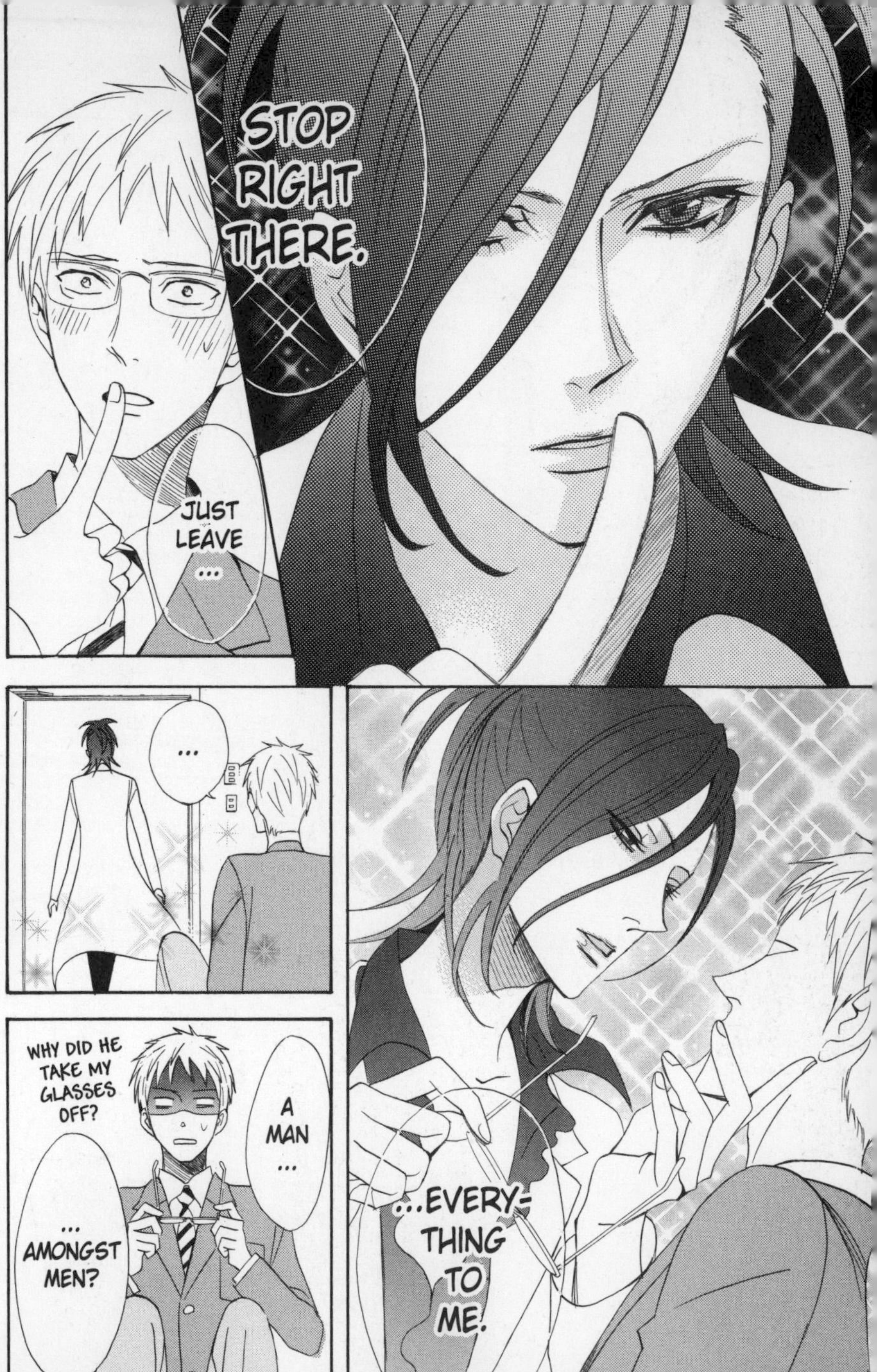

STOP RIGHT THERE.
JUST LEAVE ...
...EVERY-THING TO ME.
...
A MAN ...
... AMONGST MEN?
WHY DID HE TAKE MY GLASSES OFF?

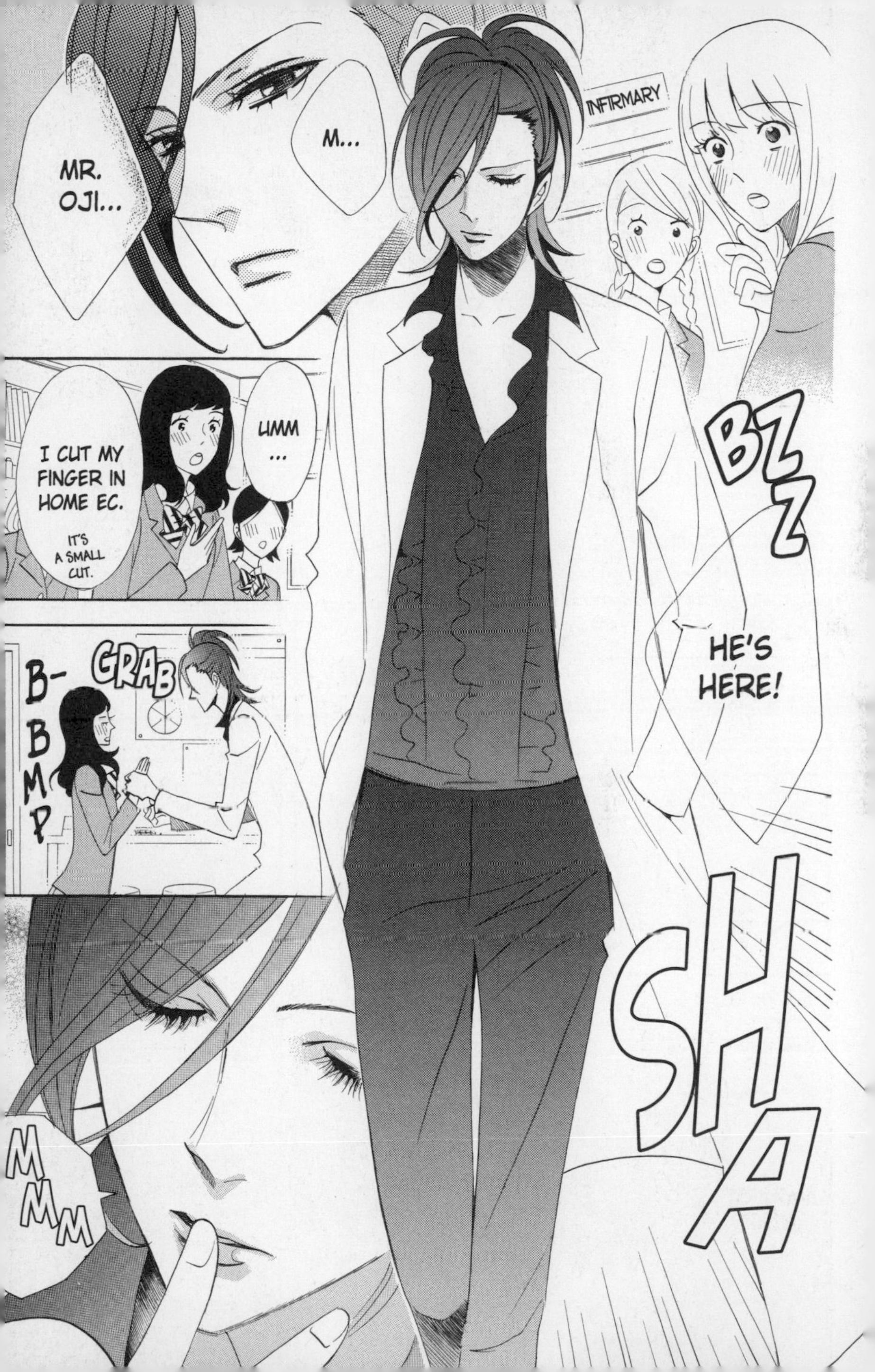
INFIRMARY
BZZZ
HE'S HERE!
SHA
M...
MR. OJI...
UMM ...
I CUT MY FINGER IN HOME EC.
IT'S A SMALL CUT.
GRAB
B-BMP
MMMM

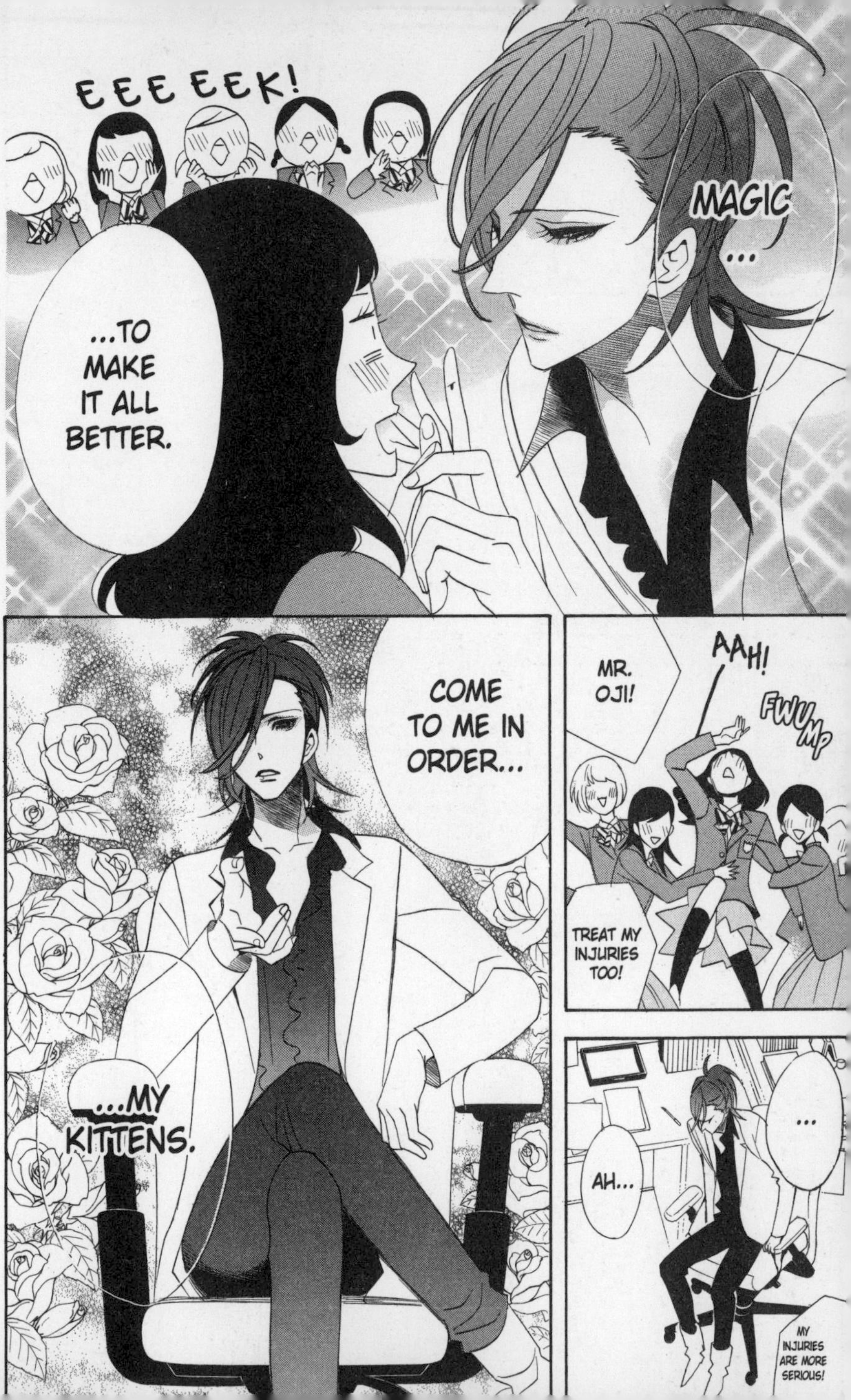
MAGIC...
...TO MAKE IT ALL BETTER.
EEE EEK!
AAH!
MR. OJI!
FWUMP
TREAT MY INJURIES TOO!
...
AH...
MY INJURIES ARE MORE SERIOUS!
COME TO ME IN ORDER...
...MY KITTENS.

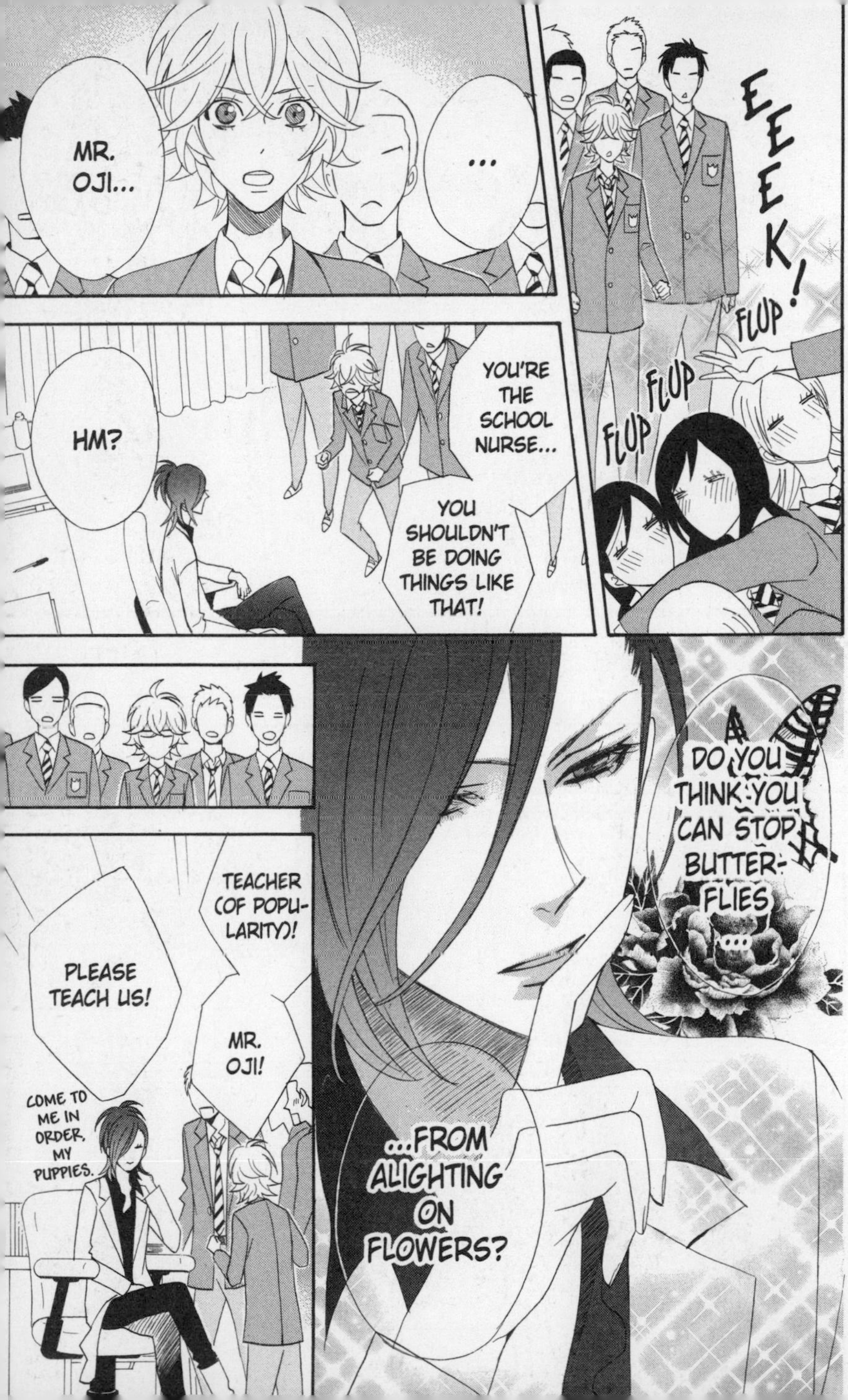
EEEK!
FLUP
FLUP
FLUP
FLUP
...
MR. OJI...
YOU'RE THE SCHOOL NURSE...
YOU SHOULDN'T BE DOING THINGS LIKE THAT!
HM?
DO YOU THINK YOU CAN STOP BUTTER-FLIES...
...FROM ALIGHTING ON FLOWERS?
TEACHER (OF POPULARITY)!
MR. OJI!
PLEASE TEACH US!
COME TO ME IN ORDER, MY PUPPIES.

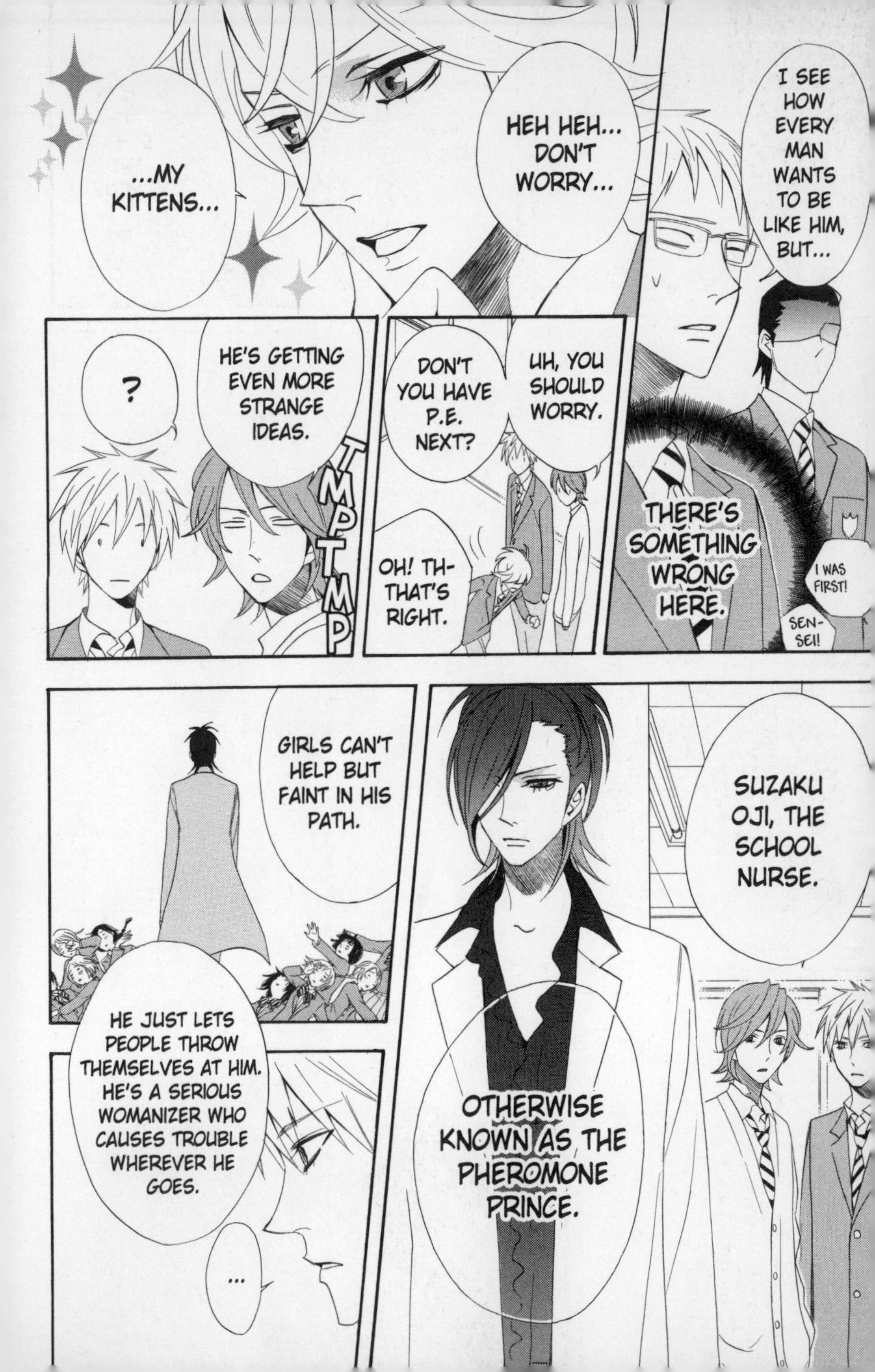
I SEE HOW EVERY MAN WANTS TO BE LIKE HIM, BUT...
THERE'S SOMETHING WRONG HERE.
I WAS FIRST!
SEN-SEI!
HEH HEH... DON'T WORRY...
...MY KITTENS...
UH, YOU SHOULD WORRY.
DON'T YOU HAVE P.E. NEXT?
OH! TH-THAT'S RIGHT.
TMPTMP
HE'S GETTING EVEN MORE STRANGE IDEAS.
?
SUZAKU OJI, THE SCHOOL NURSE.
OTHERWISE KNOWN AS THE PHEROMONE PRINCE.
GIRLS CAN'T HELP BUT FAINT IN HIS PATH.
HE JUST LETS PEOPLE THROW THEMSELVES AT HIM. HE'S A SERIOUS WOMANIZER WHO CAUSES TROUBLE WHEREVER HE GOES.
...

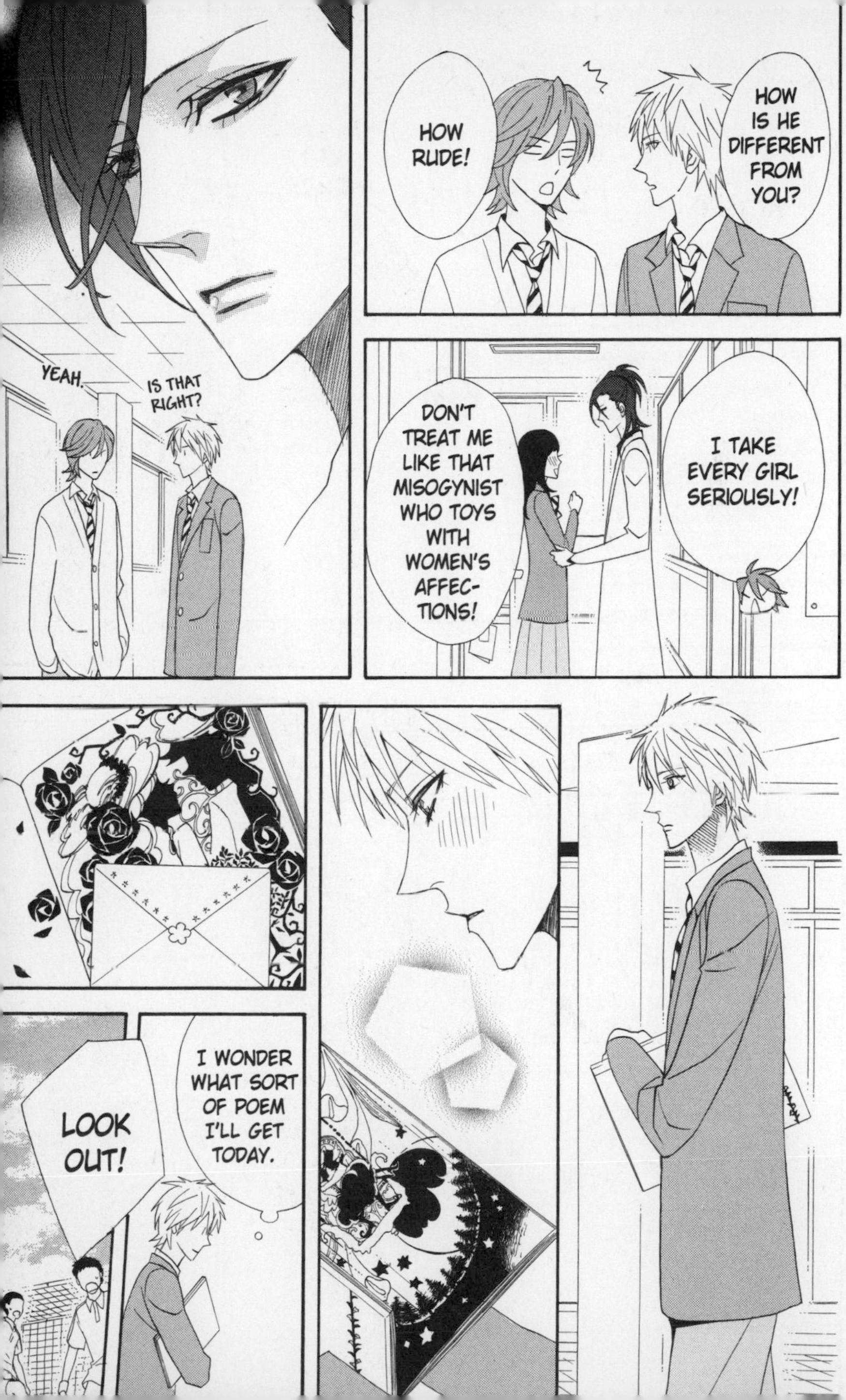
HOW IS HE DIFFERENT FROM YOU?
HOW RUDE!
I TAKE EVERY GIRL SERIOUSLY!
DON'T TREAT ME LIKE THAT MISOGYNIST WHO TOYS WITH WOMEN'S AFFEC-TIONS!
IS THAT RIGHT?
YEAH.
I WONDER WHAT SORT OF POEM I'LL GET TODAY.
LOOK OUT!

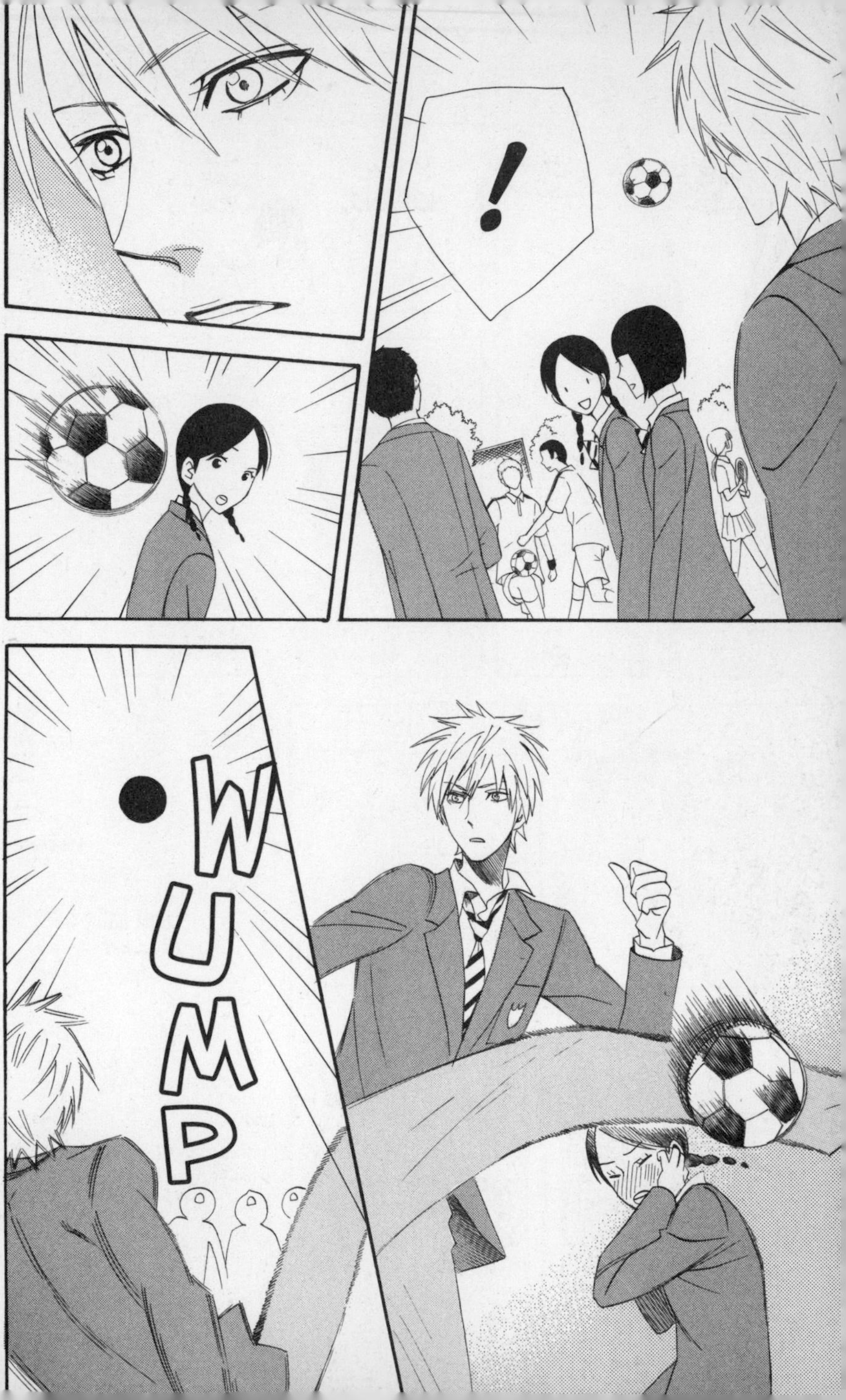
!
WUMP

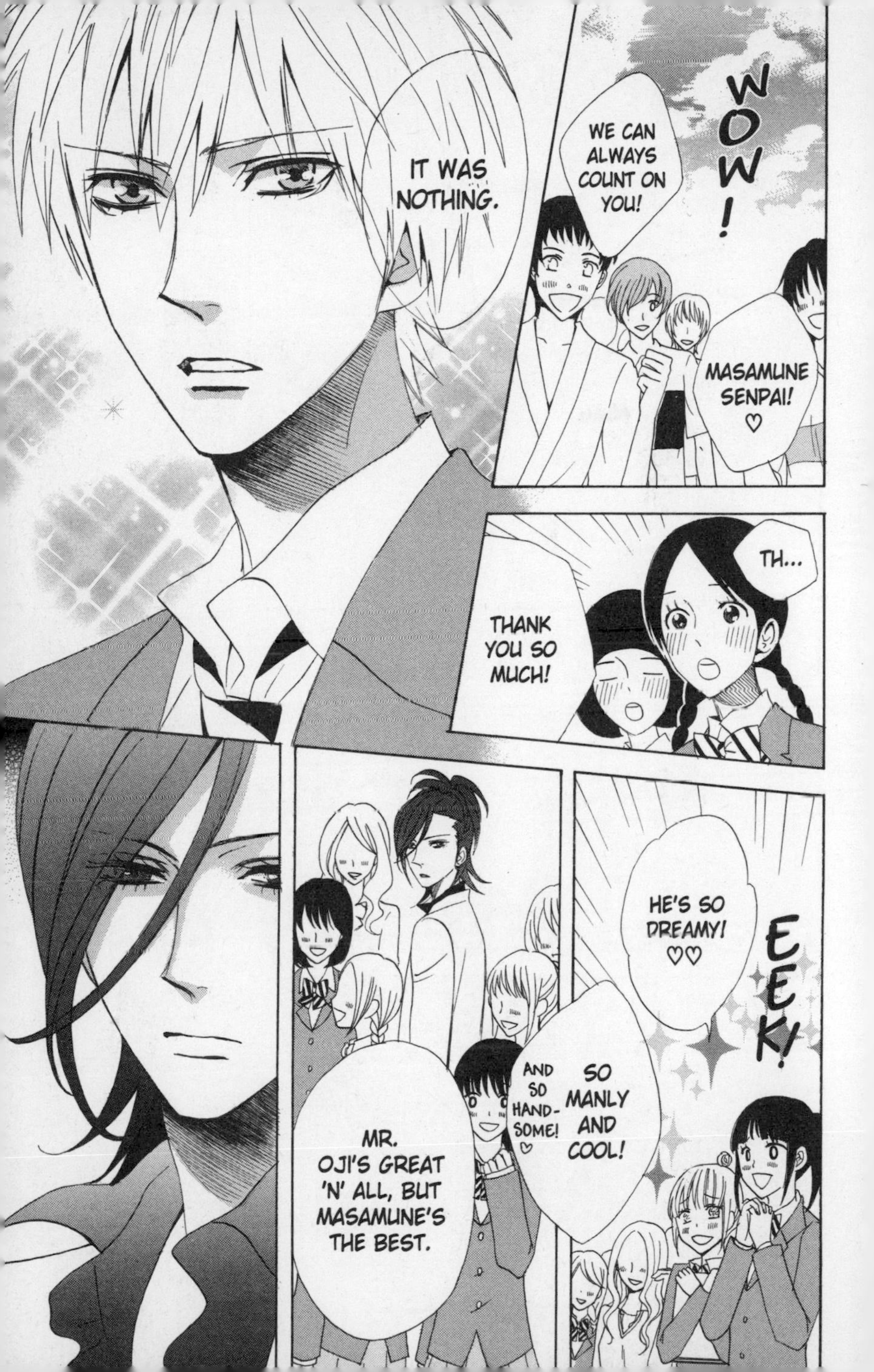
WOW!
WE CAN ALWAYS COUNT ON YOU!
MASAMUNE SENPAI! ♡
TH...
THANK YOU SO MUCH!
IT WAS NOTHING.
EEK!
HE'S SO DREAMY! ♡♡
SO MANLY AND COOL!
AND SO HAND-SOME! ♡
MR. OJI'S GREAT 'N' ALL, BUT MASAMUNE'S THE BEST.

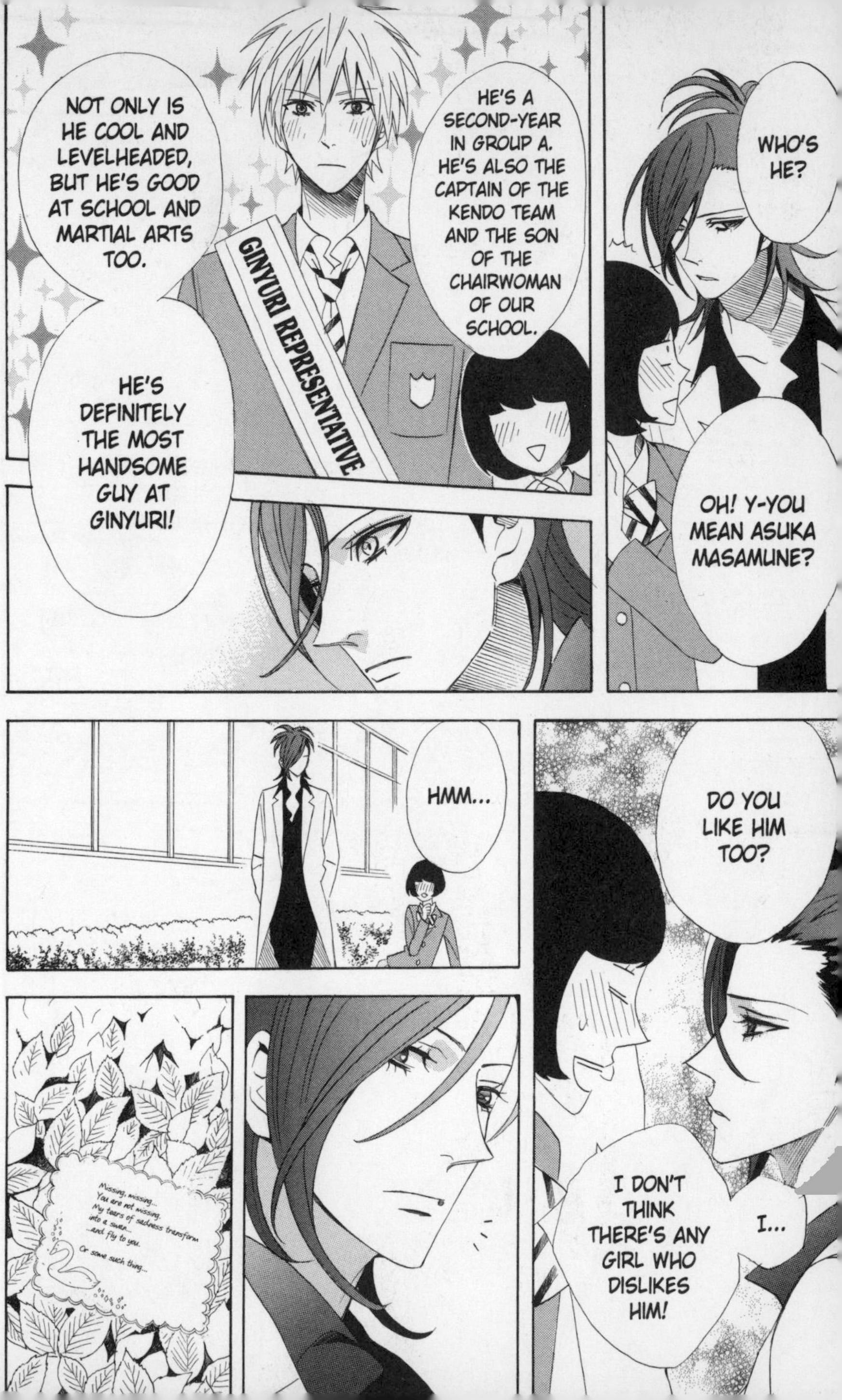
WHO'S HE?
OH! Y-YOU MEAN ASUKA MASAMUNE?
HE'S A SECOND-YEAR IN GROUP A. HE'S ALSO THE CAPTAIN OF THE KENDO TEAM AND THE SON OF THE CHAIRWOMAN OF OUR SCHOOL.
GINYURI REPRESENTATIVE
NOT ONLY IS HE COOL AND LEVELHEADED, BUT HE'S GOOD AT SCHOOL AND MARTIAL ARTS TOO.
HE'S DEFINITELY THE MOST HANDSOME GUY AT GINYURI!
DO YOU LIKE HIM TOO?
HMM...
I...
I DON'T THINK THERE'S ANY GIRL WHO DISLIKES HIM!
Missing, missing... You are not missing. My tears of sadness transform into a swan... ...and fly to you.
Or some such thing...

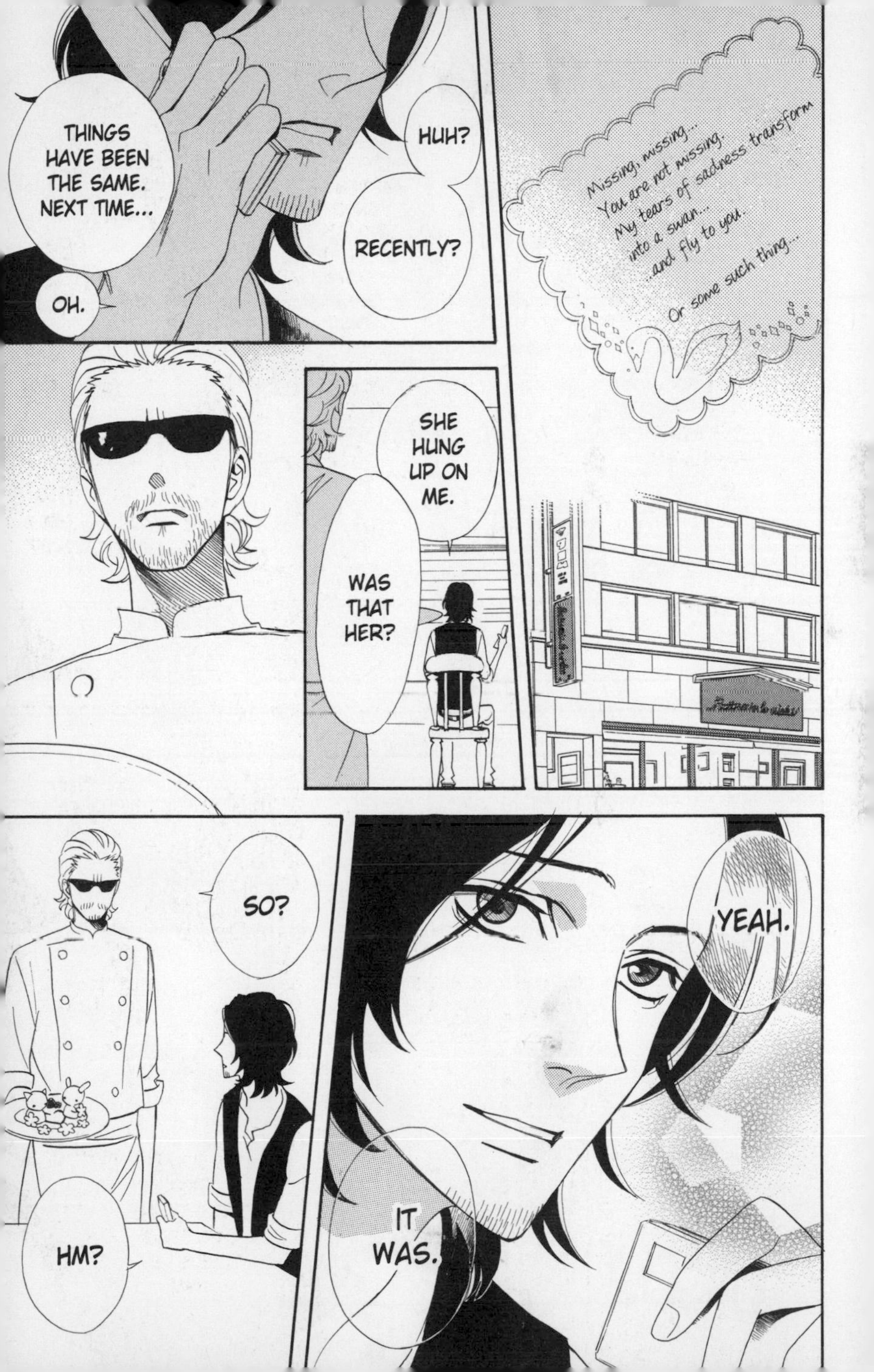
Missing, missing...
You are not missing.
My tears of sadness transform
into a swan...
...and fly to you.
Or some such thing...
HUH?
RECENTLY?
THINGS HAVE BEEN THE SAME. NEXT TIME...
OH.
SHE HUNG UP ON ME.
WAS THAT HER?
YEAH.
IT WAS.
SO?
HM?

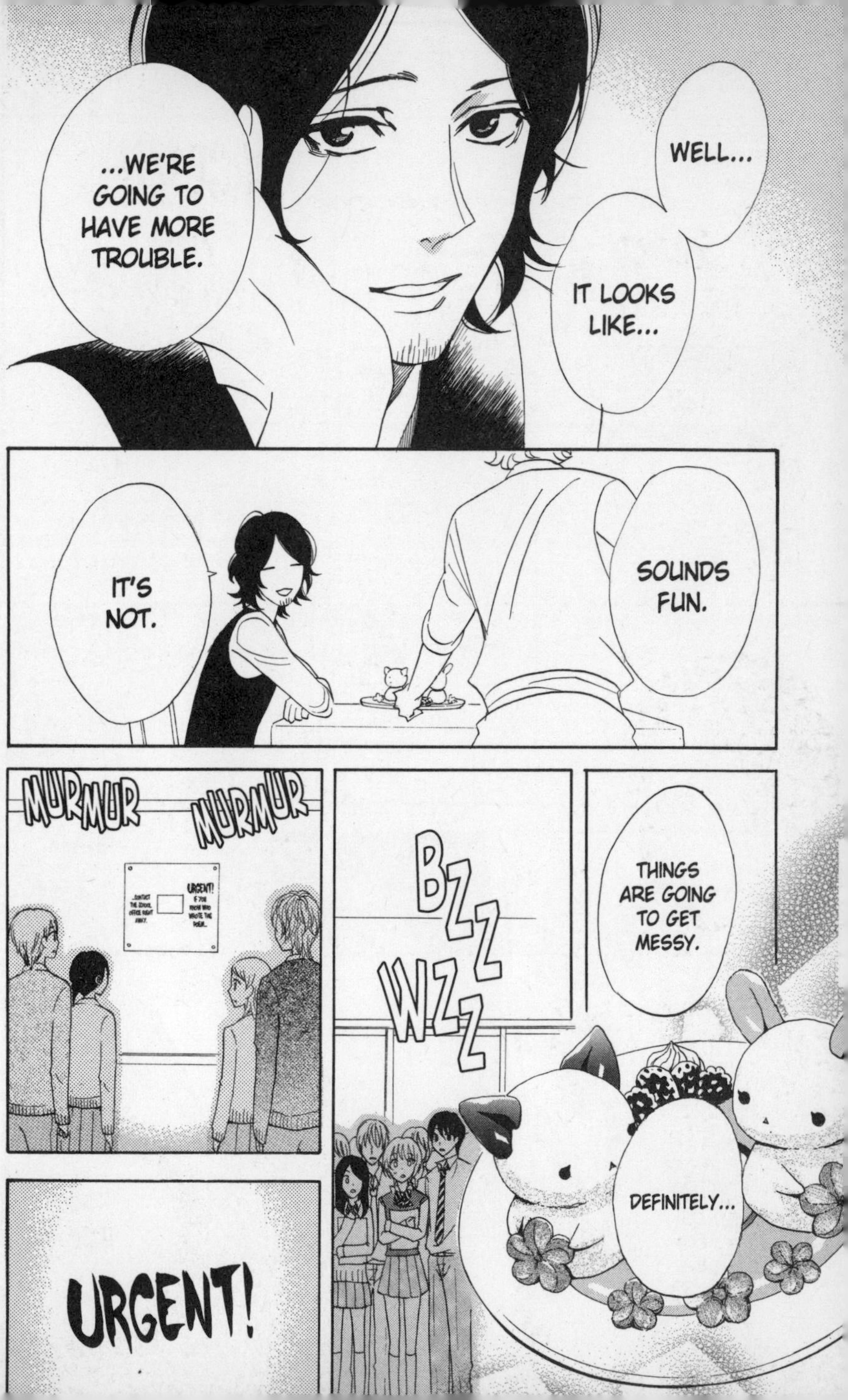
WELL...
IT LOOKS LIKE...
...WE'RE GOING TO HAVE MORE TROUBLE.
SOUNDS FUN.
IT'S NOT.
THINGS ARE GOING TO GET MESSY.
BZZ
WZZ
DEFINITELY...
MURMUR
MURMUR
URGENT!
URGENT!

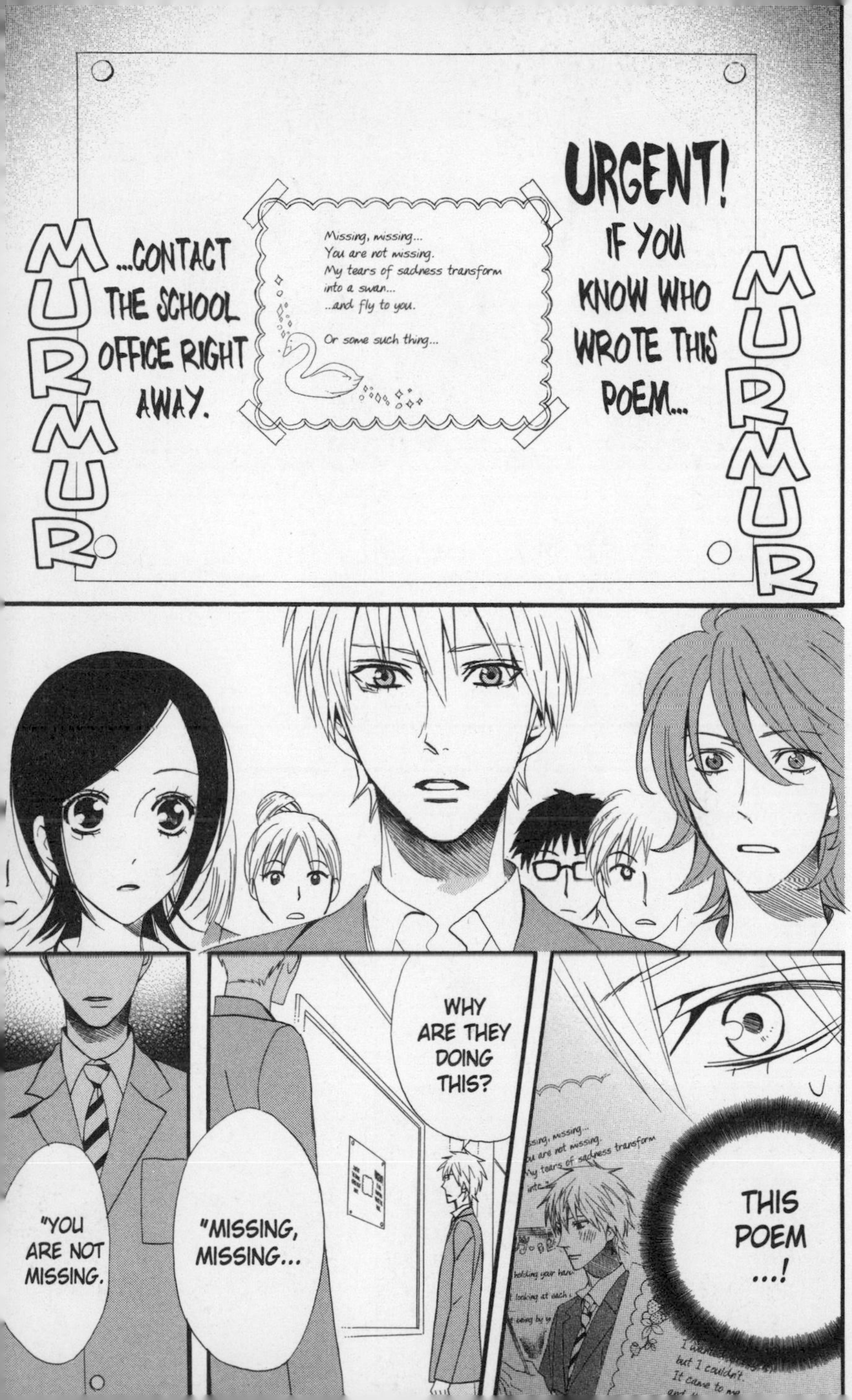
URGENT!
IF YOU KNOW WHO WROTE THIS POEM...
MURMUR
Missing, missing...
You are not missing.
My tears of sadness transform
into a swan...
...and fly to you.
Or some such thing...
...CONTACT THE SCHOOL OFFICE RIGHT AWAY.
MURMUR
THIS POEM ...!
WHY ARE THEY DOING THIS?
"MISSING, MISSING...
"YOU ARE NOT MISSING.

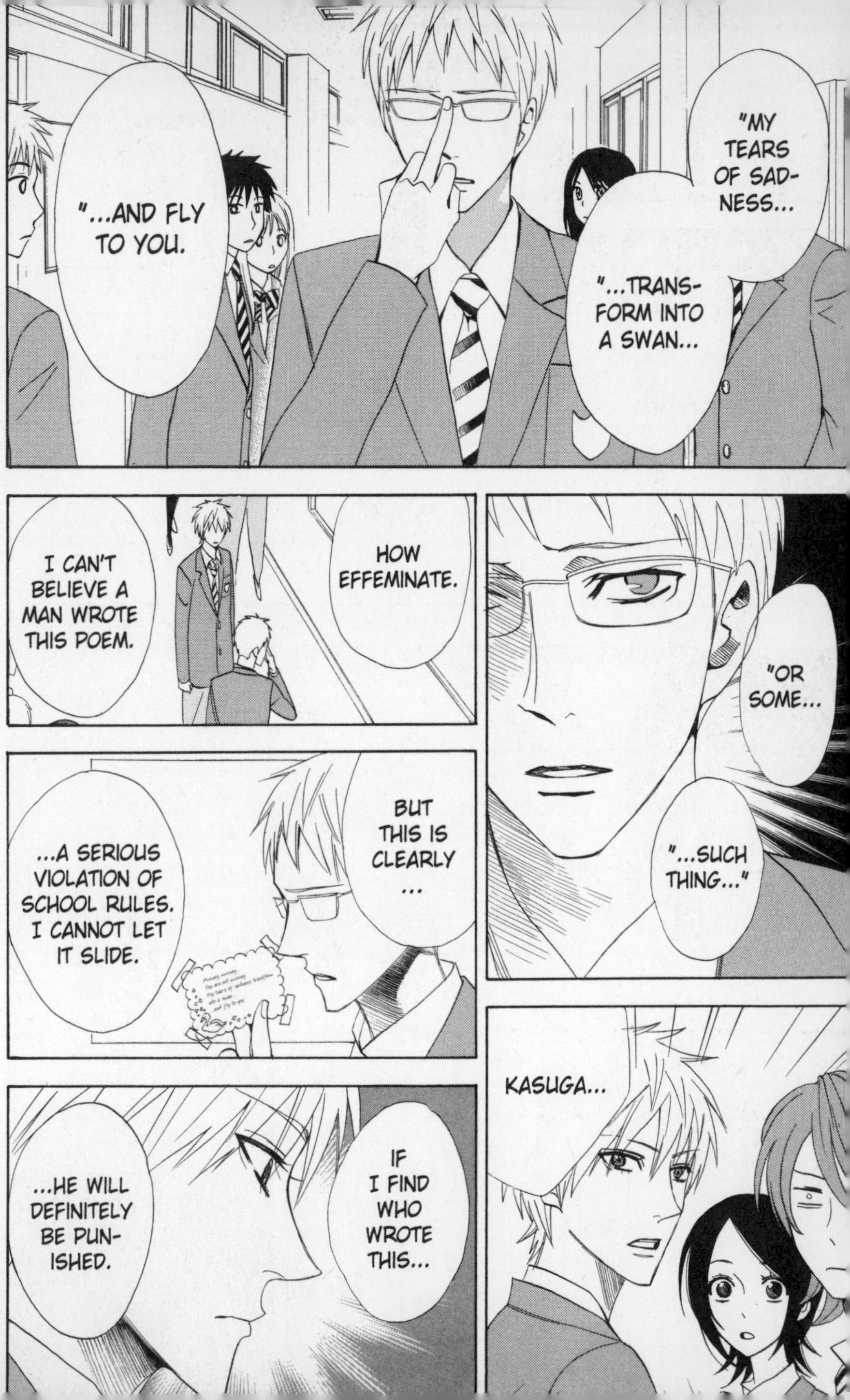
"MY TEARS OF SAD-NESS...
"...TRANS-FORM INTO A SWAN...
"...AND FLY TO YOU.
"OR SOME...
"...SUCH THING..."
HOW EFFEMINATE.
I CAN'T BELIEVE A MAN WROTE THIS POEM.
BUT THIS IS CLEARLY ...
...A SERIOUS VIOLATION OF SCHOOL RULES. I CANNOT LET IT SLIDE.
KASUGA...
IF I FIND WHO WROTE THIS...
...HE WILL DEFINITELY BE PUN-ISHED.

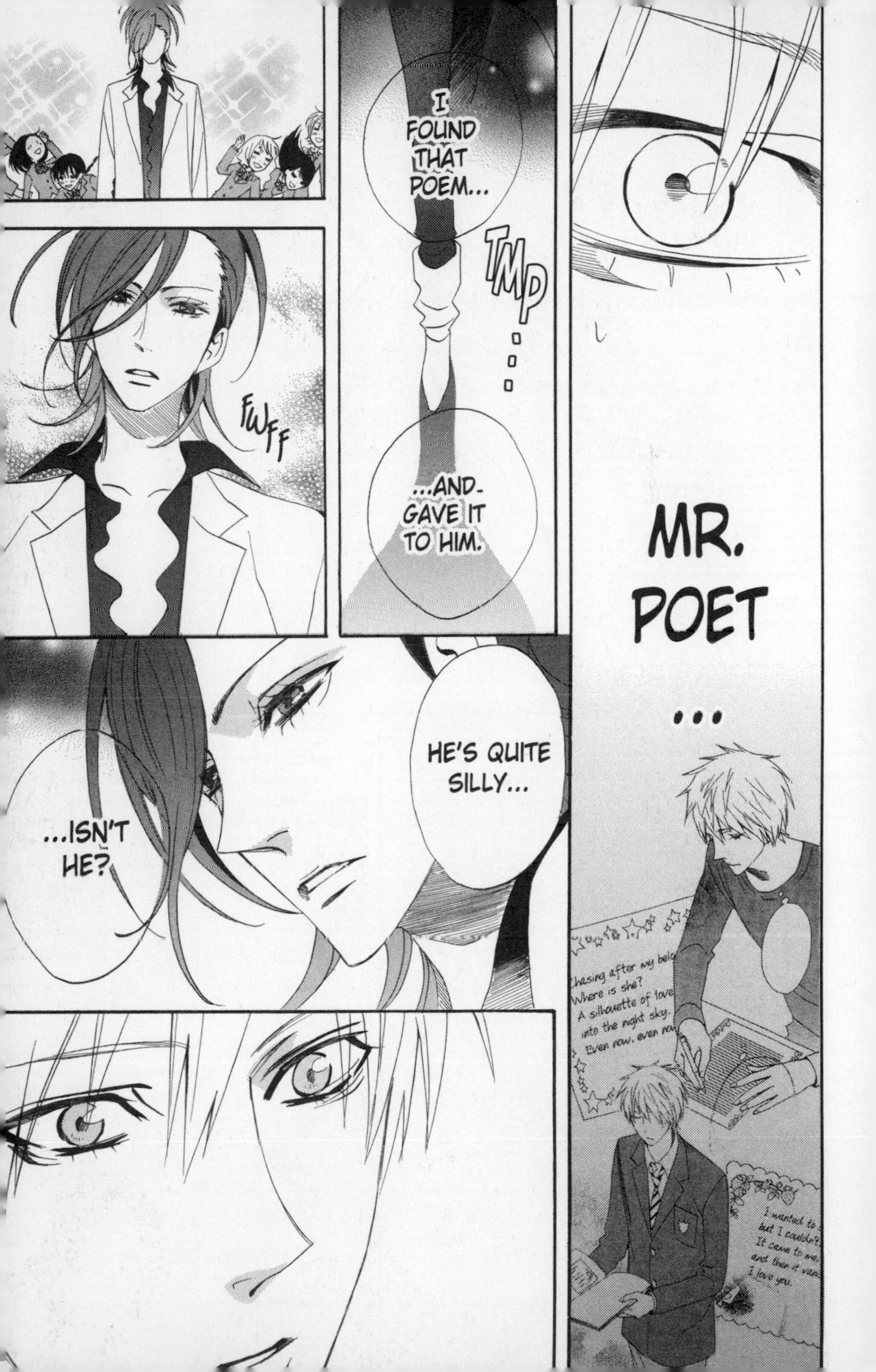
MR. POET...
Chasing after my bel
Where is she?
A silhouette of love
into the night sky.
Even now, even now
I wanted to
but I couldn't
It came to me,
and then it van
I love you.
I FOUND THAT POEM...
TMP...
...AND GAVE IT TO HIM.
FWFF
HE'S QUITE SILLY...
...ISN'T HE?

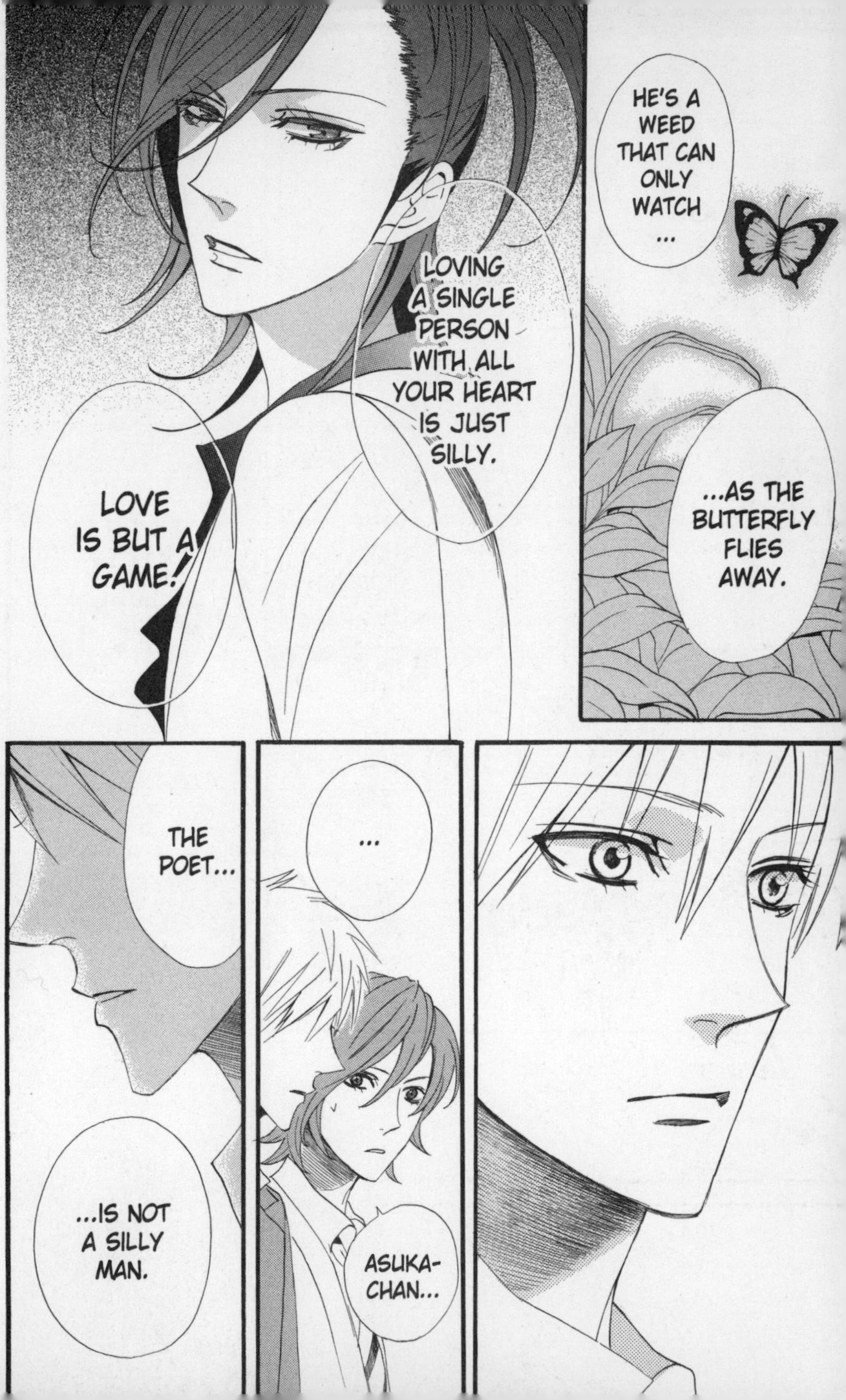
HE'S A WEED THAT CAN ONLY WATCH ...
...AS THE BUTTERFLY FLIES AWAY.
LOVING A SINGLE PERSON WITH ALL YOUR HEART IS JUST SILLY.
LOVE IS BUT A GAME!
...
ASUKA-CHAN...
THE POET...
...IS NOT A SILLY MAN.

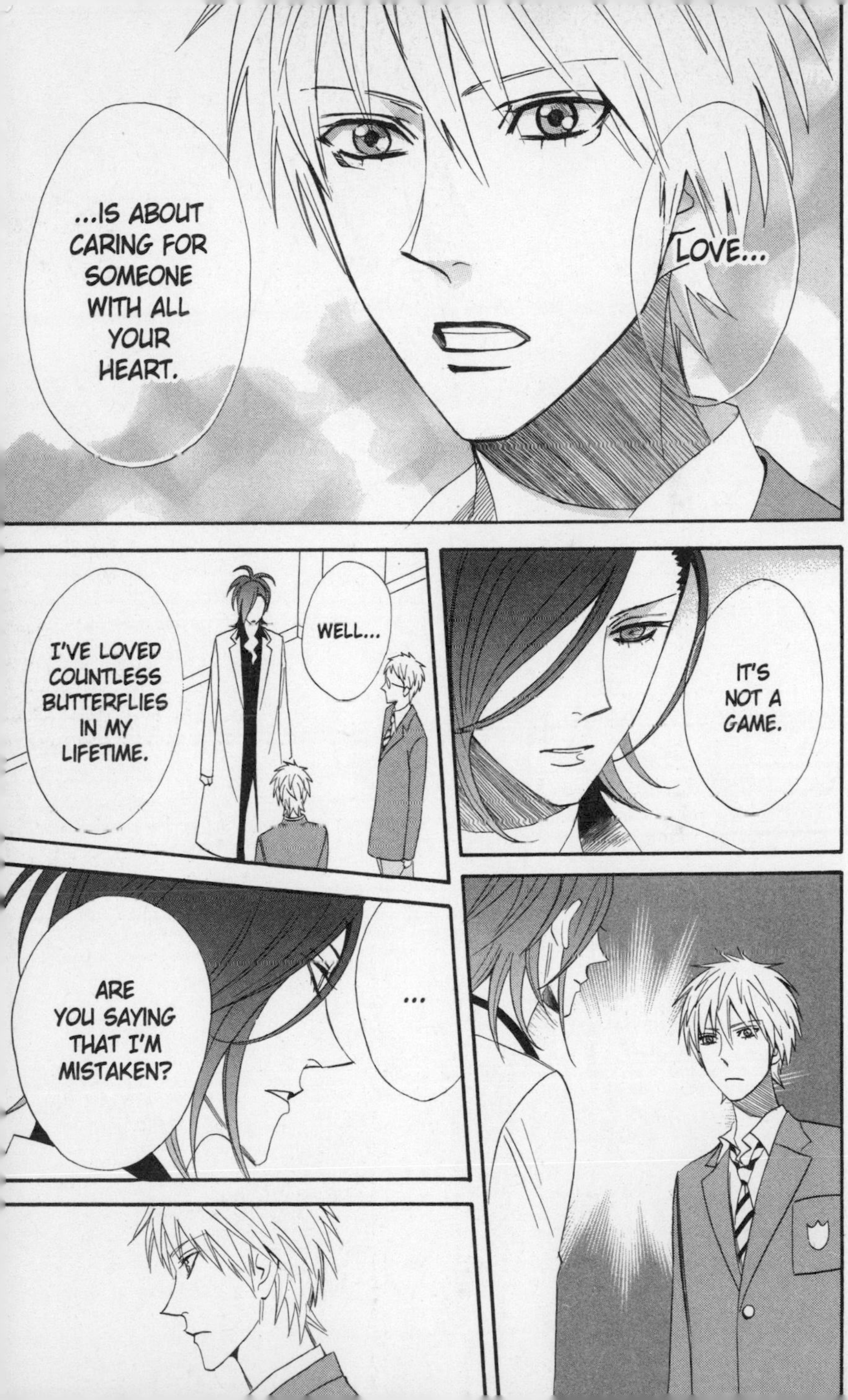
LOVE...
...IS ABOUT CARING FOR SOMEONE WITH ALL YOUR HEART.
IT'S NOT A GAME.
WELL...
I'VE LOVED COUNTLESS BUTTERFLIES IN MY LIFETIME.
...
ARE YOU SAYING THAT I'M MISTAKEN?

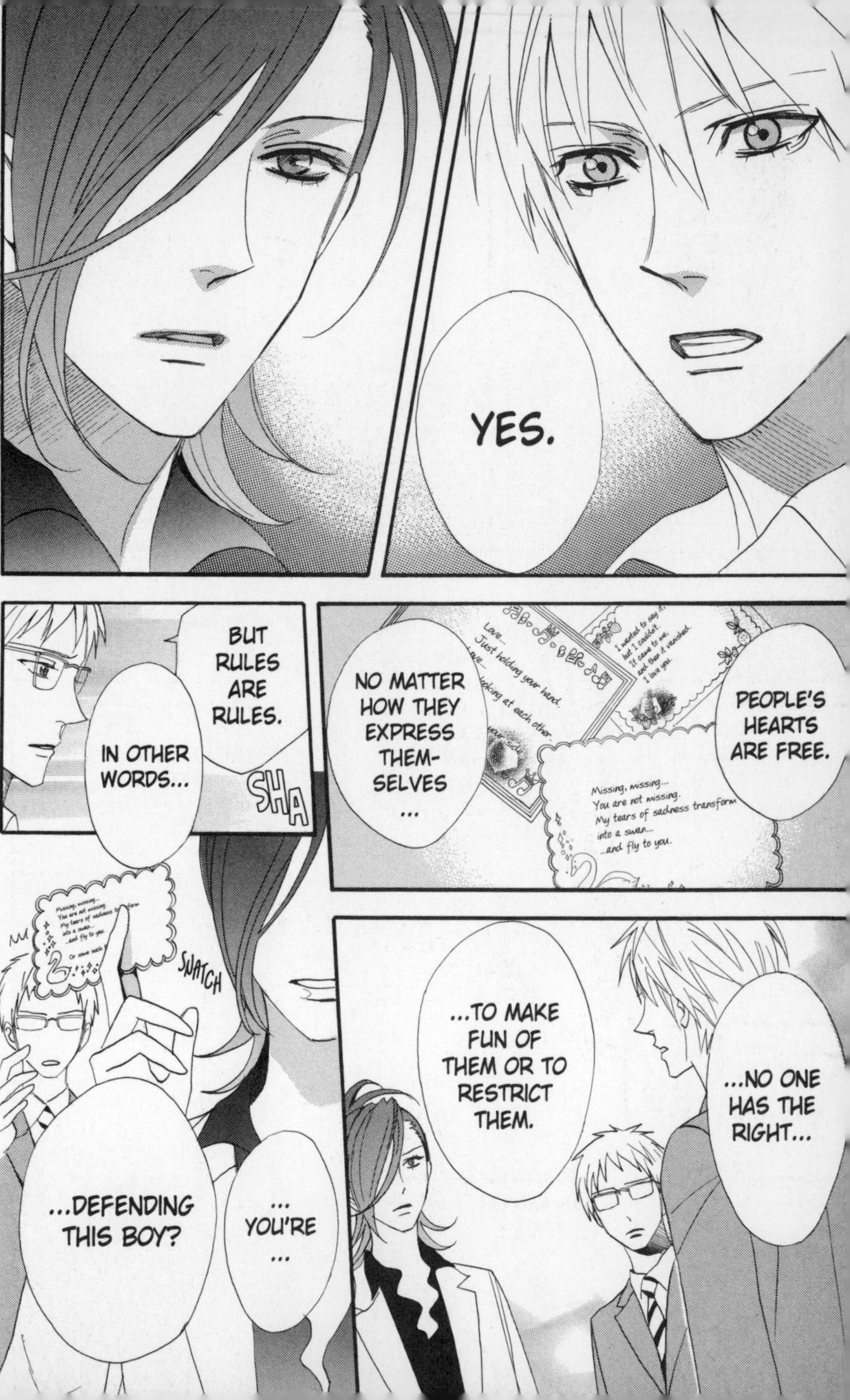
YES.
PEOPLE'S HEARTS ARE FREE.
I wanted to say it, but I couldn't. It came to me, and then it vanished. I love you.
Missing, missing... You are not missing. My tears of sadness transform into a swan... ...and fly to you.
NO MATTER HOW THEY EXPRESS THEM-SELVES...
BUT RULES ARE RULES.
SHA
IN OTHER WORDS...
...NO ONE HAS THE RIGHT...
...TO MAKE FUN OF THEM OR TO RESTRICT THEM.
SNATCH
...YOU'RE...
...DEFENDING THIS BOY?

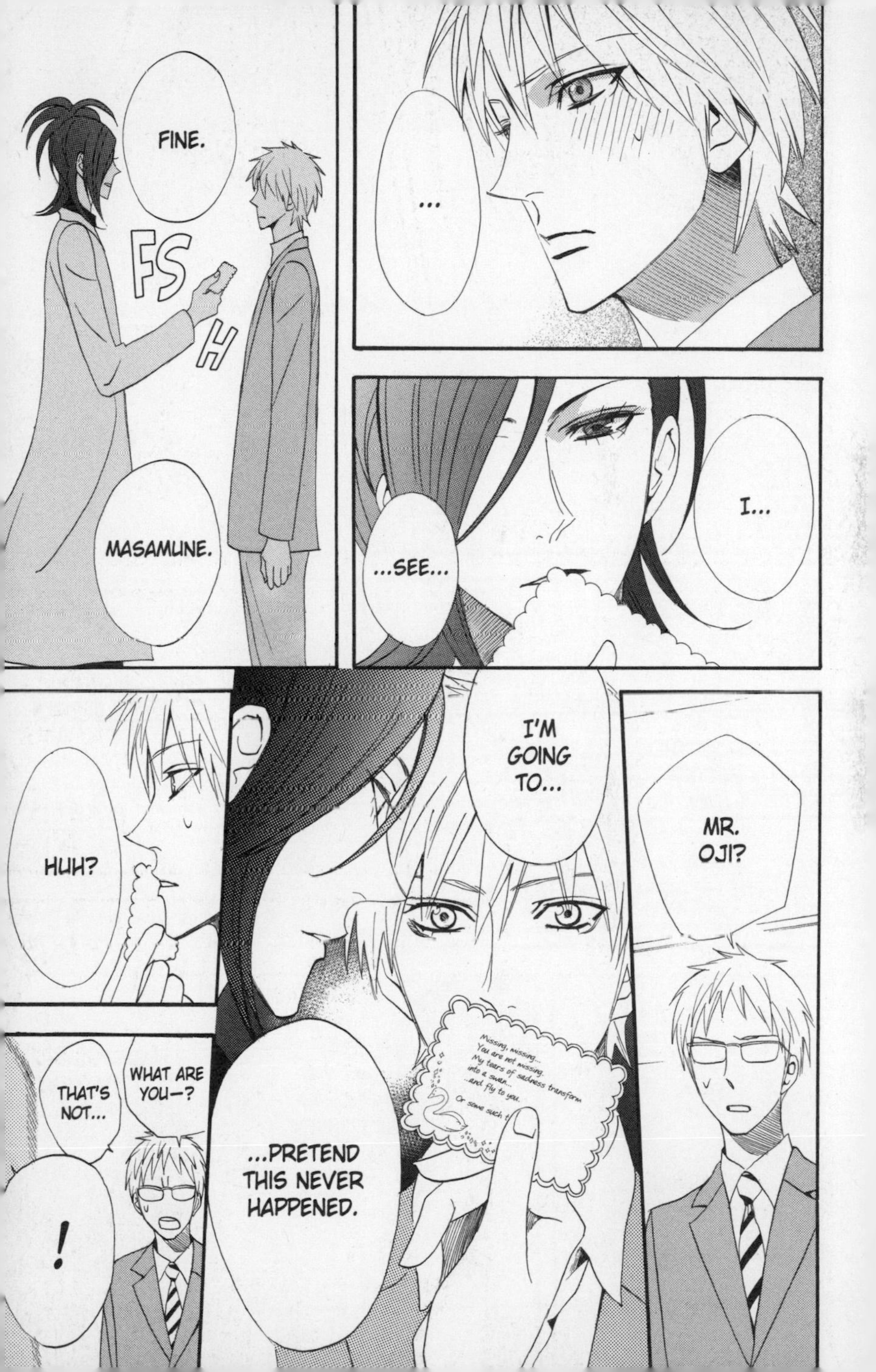
...
I...
...SEE...
FINE.
FSH
MASAMUNE.
MR. OJI?
I'M GOING TO...
...PRETEND THIS NEVER HAPPENED.
Missing, missing...
You are not missing...
My tears of sadness transform
into a swan...
...and fly to you.
HUH?
WHAT ARE YOU—?
THAT'S NOT...
!

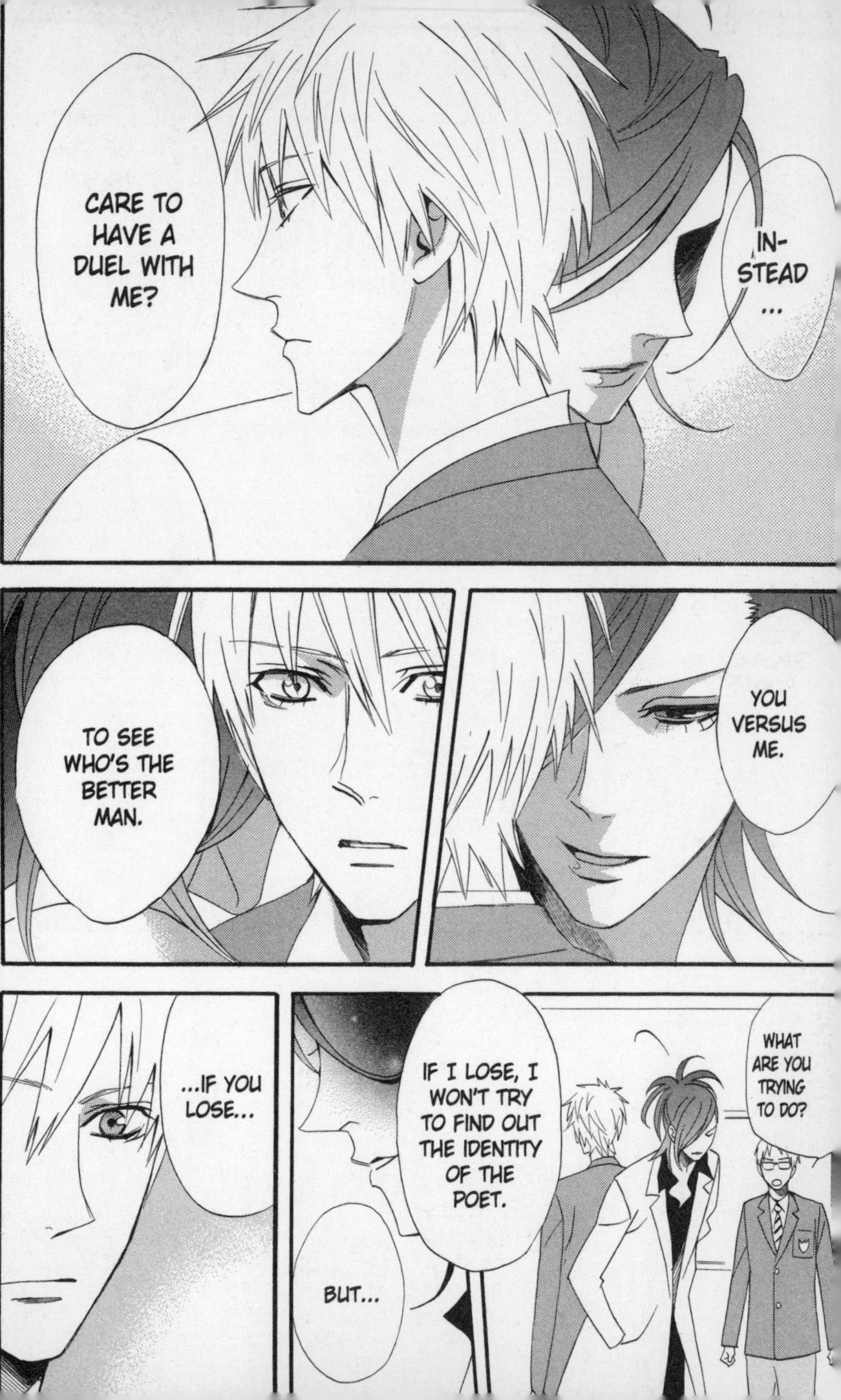
IN-STEAD...
CARE TO HAVE A DUEL WITH ME?
YOU VERSUS ME.
TO SEE WHO'S THE BETTER MAN.
WHAT ARE YOU TRYING TO DO?
IF I LOSE, I WON'T TRY TO FIND OUT THE IDENTITY OF THE POET.
BUT...
...IF YOU LOSE...

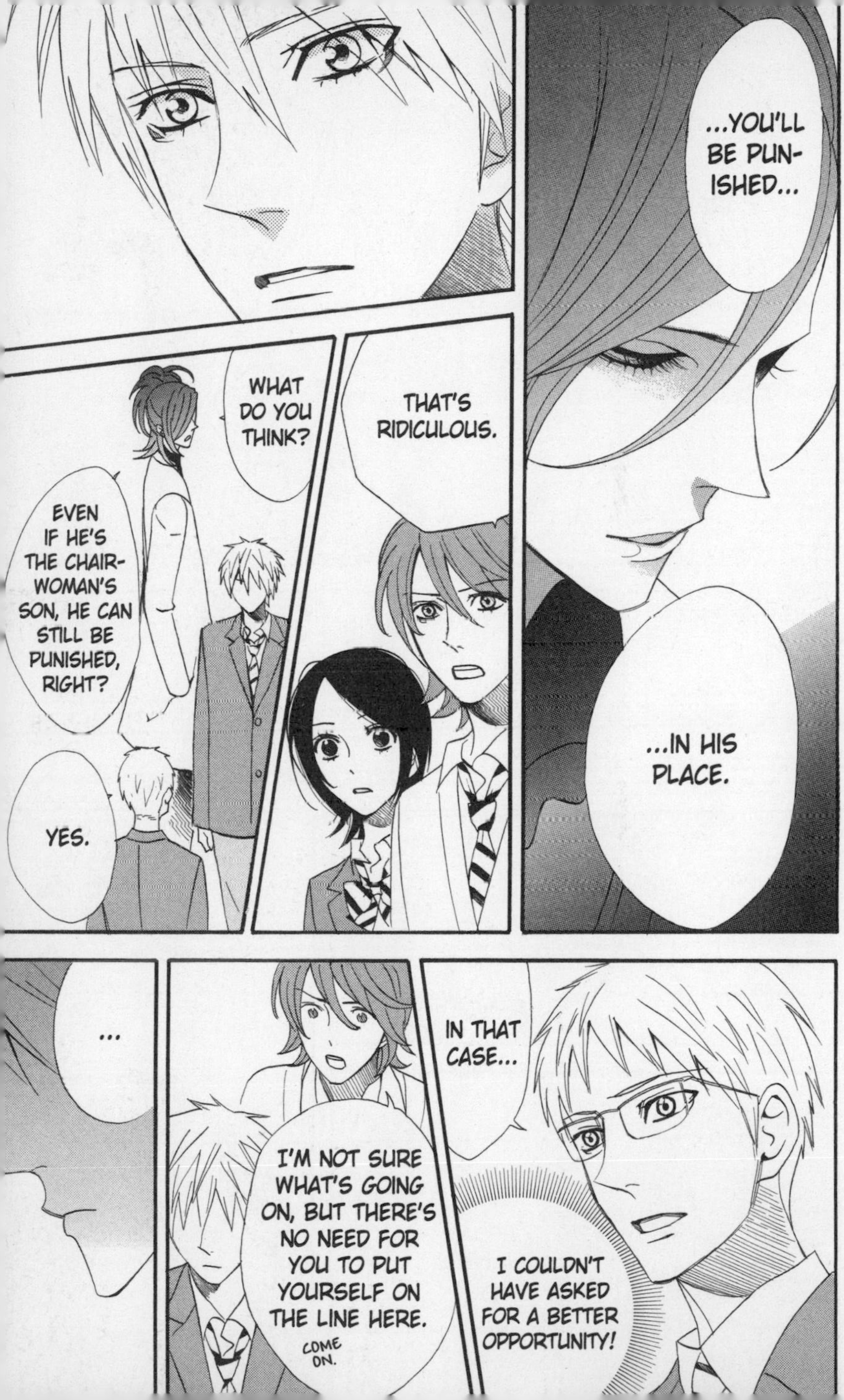
...YOU'LL BE PUN- ISHED...
...IN HIS PLACE.
THAT'S RIDICULOUS.
WHAT DO YOU THINK?
EVEN IF HE'S THE CHAIR- WOMAN'S SON, HE CAN STILL BE PUNISHED, RIGHT?
YES.
IN THAT CASE...
I COULDN'T HAVE ASKED FOR A BETTER OPPORTUNITY!
I'M NOT SURE WHAT'S GOING ON, BUT THERE'S NO NEED FOR YOU TO PUT YOURSELF ON THE LINE HERE.
COME ON.
...

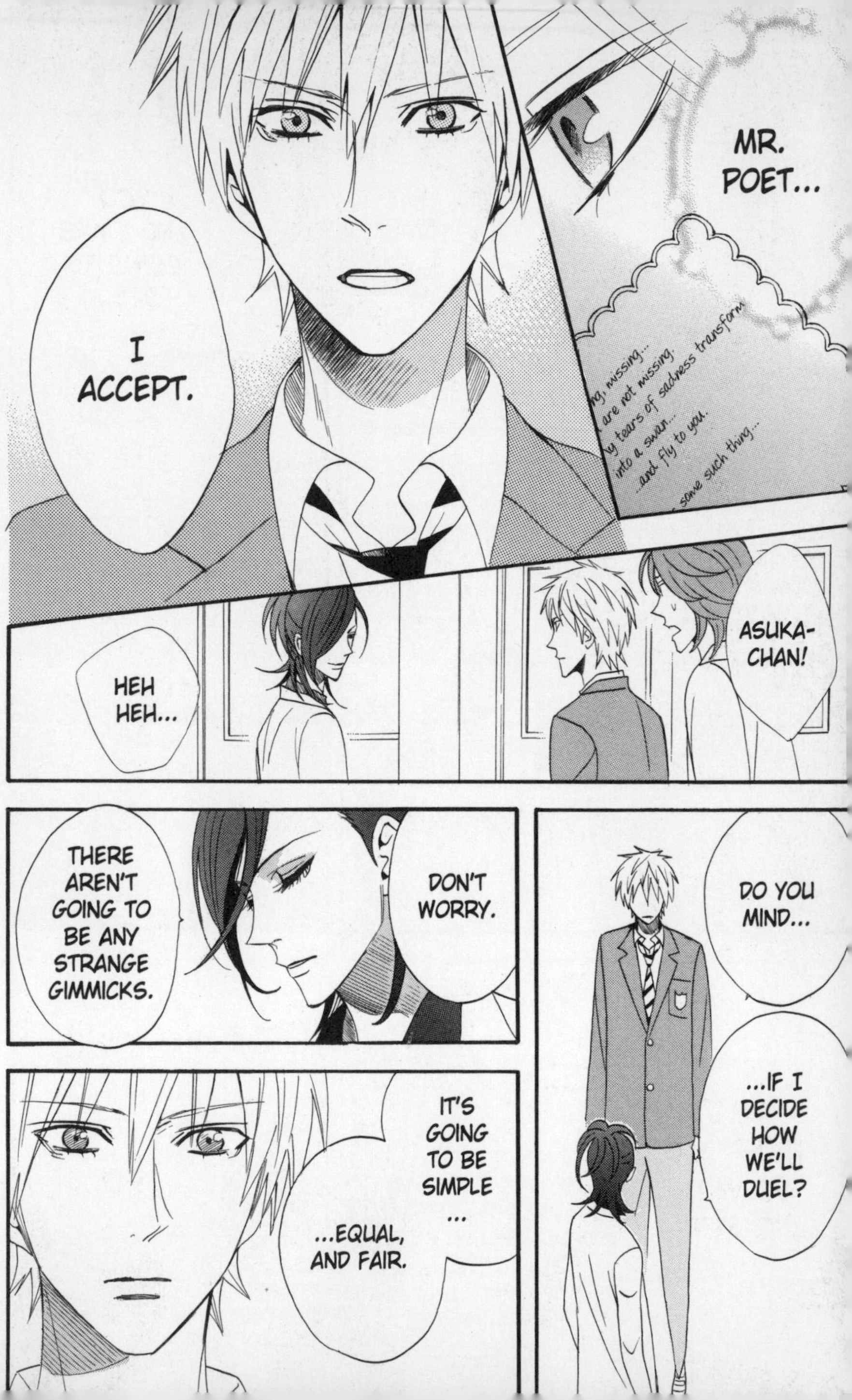
MR. POET...
ng, missing...
are not missing.
y tears of sadness transform
into a swan...
...and fly to you.
...some such thing...
I ACCEPT.
ASUKA-CHAN!
HEH HEH...
DO YOU MIND...
...IF I DECIDE HOW WE'LL DUEL?
DON'T WORRY.
THERE AREN'T GOING TO BE ANY STRANGE GIMMICKS.
IT'S GOING TO BE SIMPLE...
...EQUAL, AND FAIR.

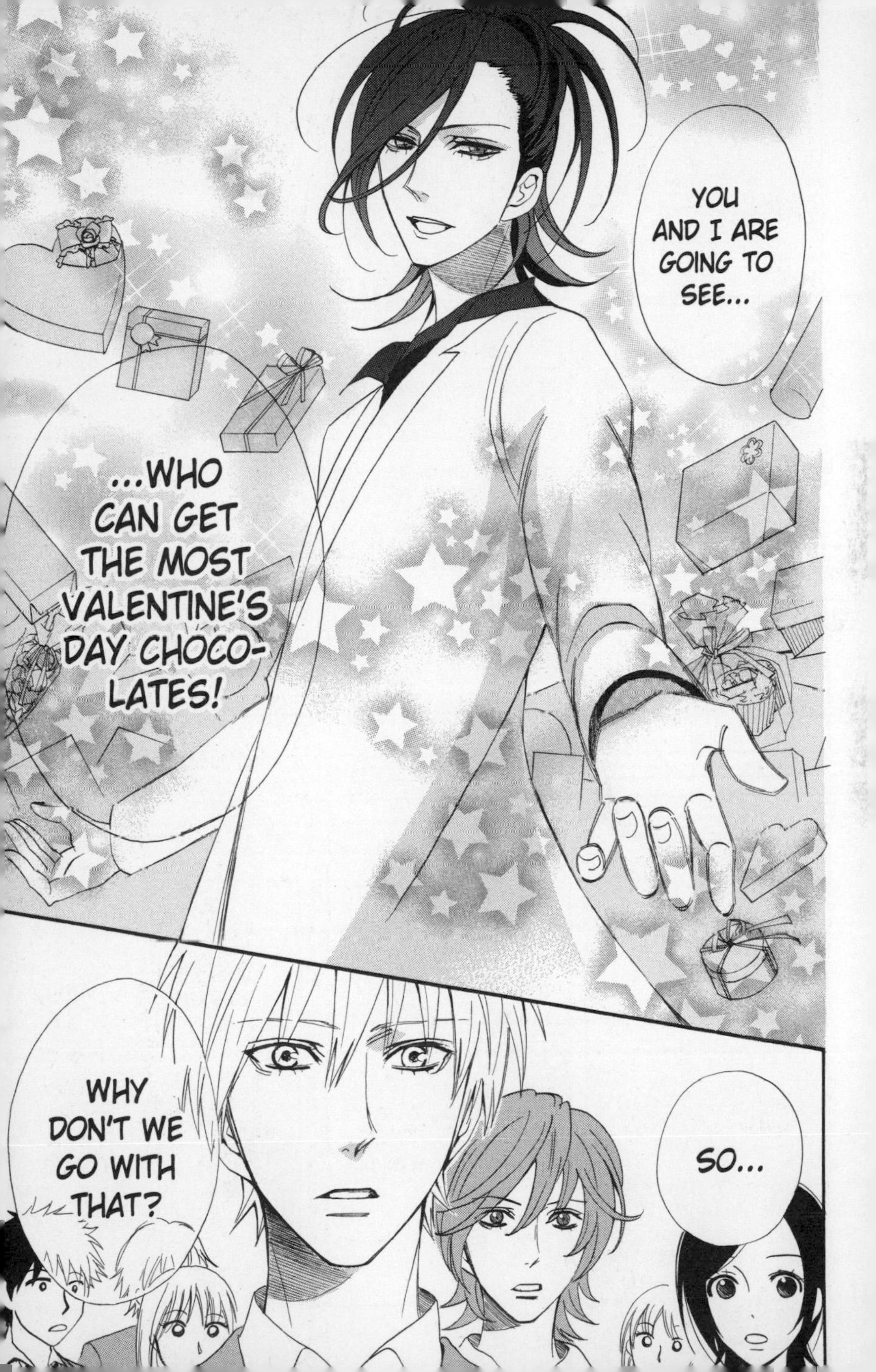
YOU AND I ARE GOING TO SEE...
...WHO CAN GET THE MOST VALENTINE'S DAY CHOCO-LATES!
SO...
WHY DON'T WE GO WITH THAT?

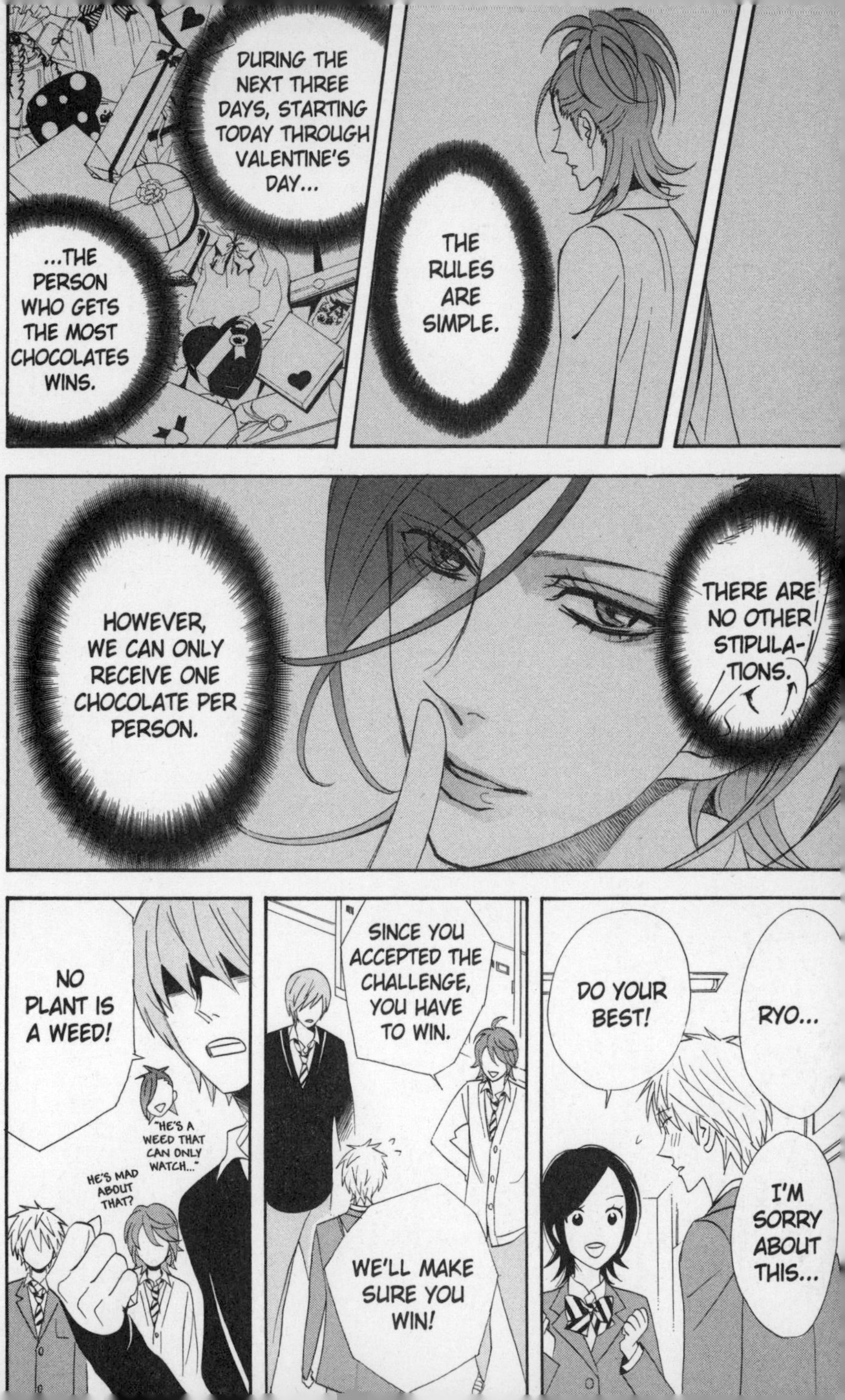
THE RULES ARE SIMPLE.
DURING THE NEXT THREE DAYS, STARTING TODAY THROUGH VALENTINE'S DAY...
...THE PERSON WHO GETS THE MOST CHOCOLATES WINS.
HOWEVER, WE CAN ONLY RECEIVE ONE CHOCOLATE PER PERSON.
THERE ARE NO OTHER STIPULA-TIONS.
RYO...
DO YOUR BEST!
I'M SORRY ABOUT THIS...
SINCE YOU ACCEPTED THE CHALLENGE, YOU HAVE TO WIN.
WE'LL MAKE SURE YOU WIN!
NO PLANT IS A WEED!
"HE'S A WEED THAT CAN ONLY WATCH..."
HE'S MAD ABOUT THAT?

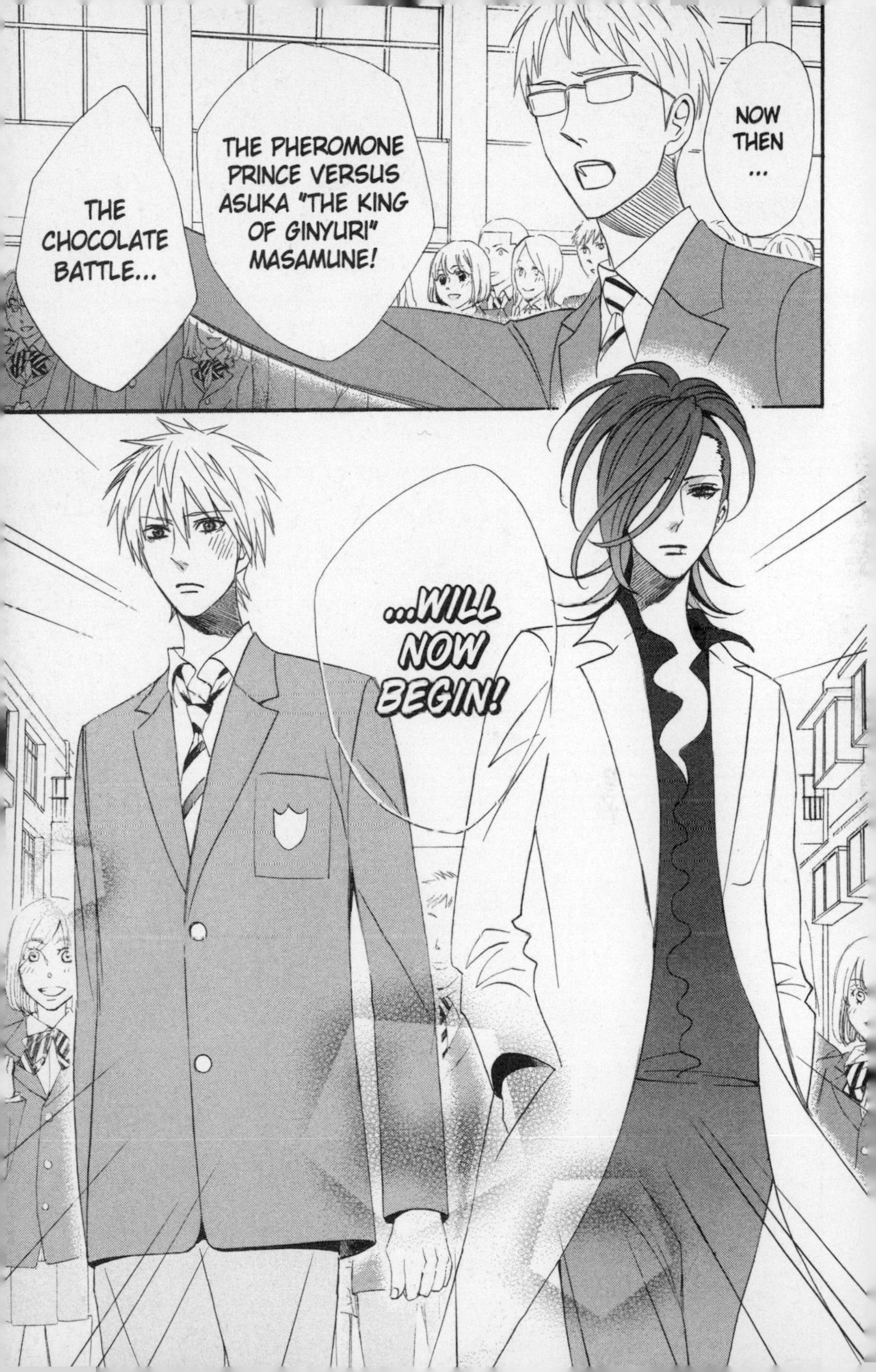
NOW THEN ...
THE PHEROMONE PRINCE VERSUS ASUKA "THE KING OF GINYURI" MASAMUNE!
THE CHOCOLATE BATTLE...
...WILL NOW BEGIN!

OTOMEN

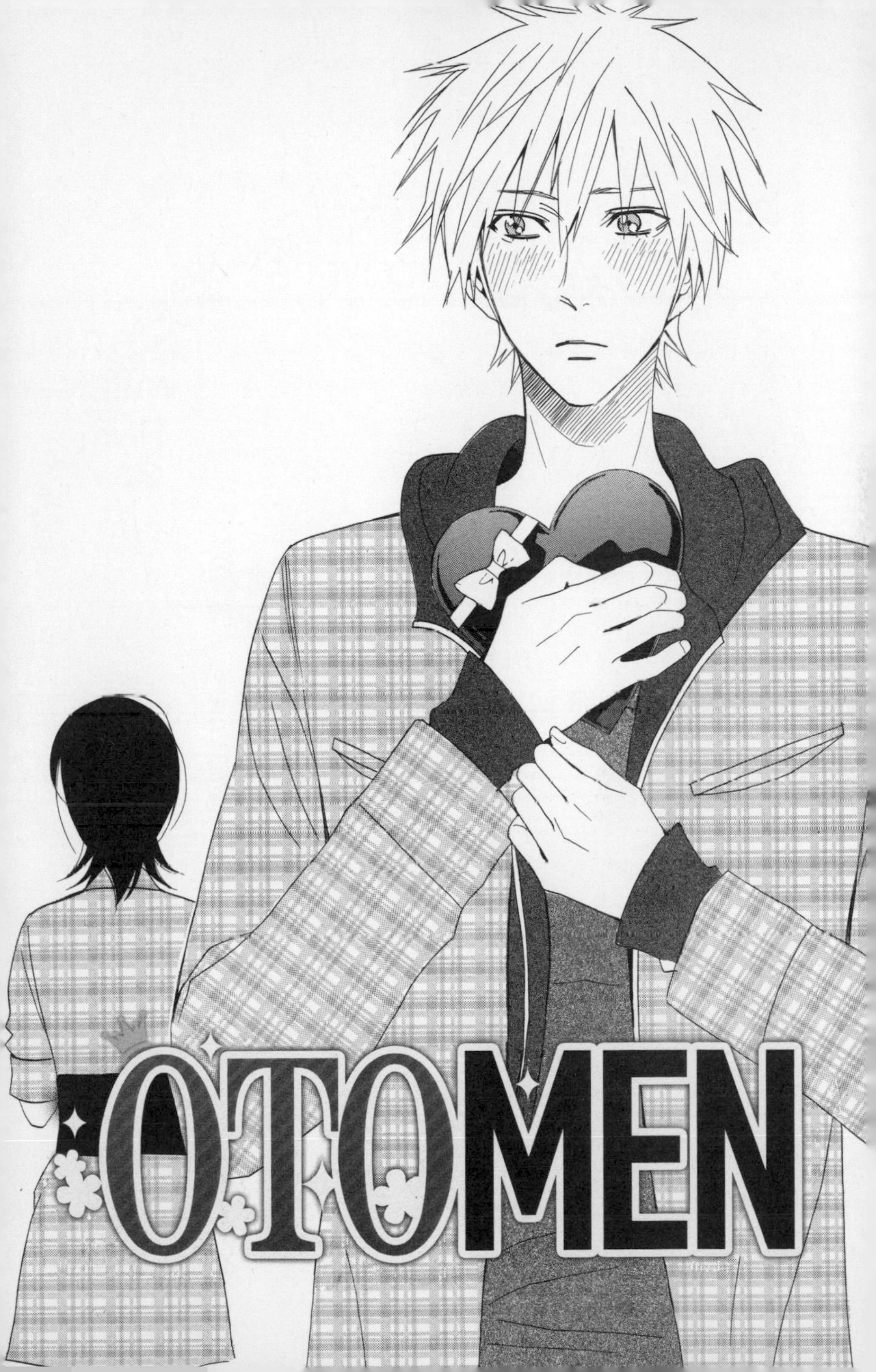
OTOMEN

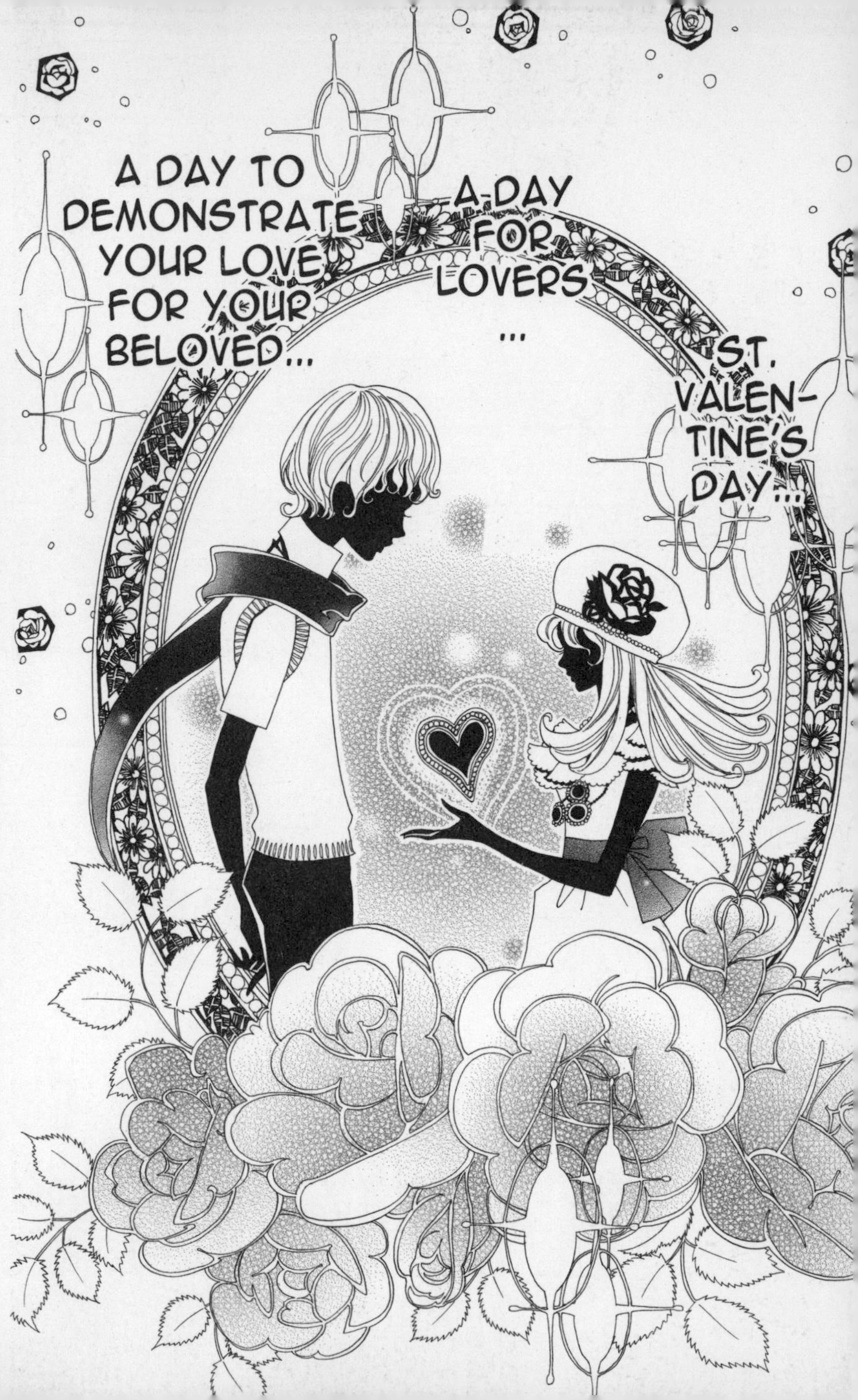
ST. VALENTINE'S DAY...
A DAY FOR LOVERS...
A DAY TO DEMONSTRATE YOUR LOVE FOR YOUR BELOVED...

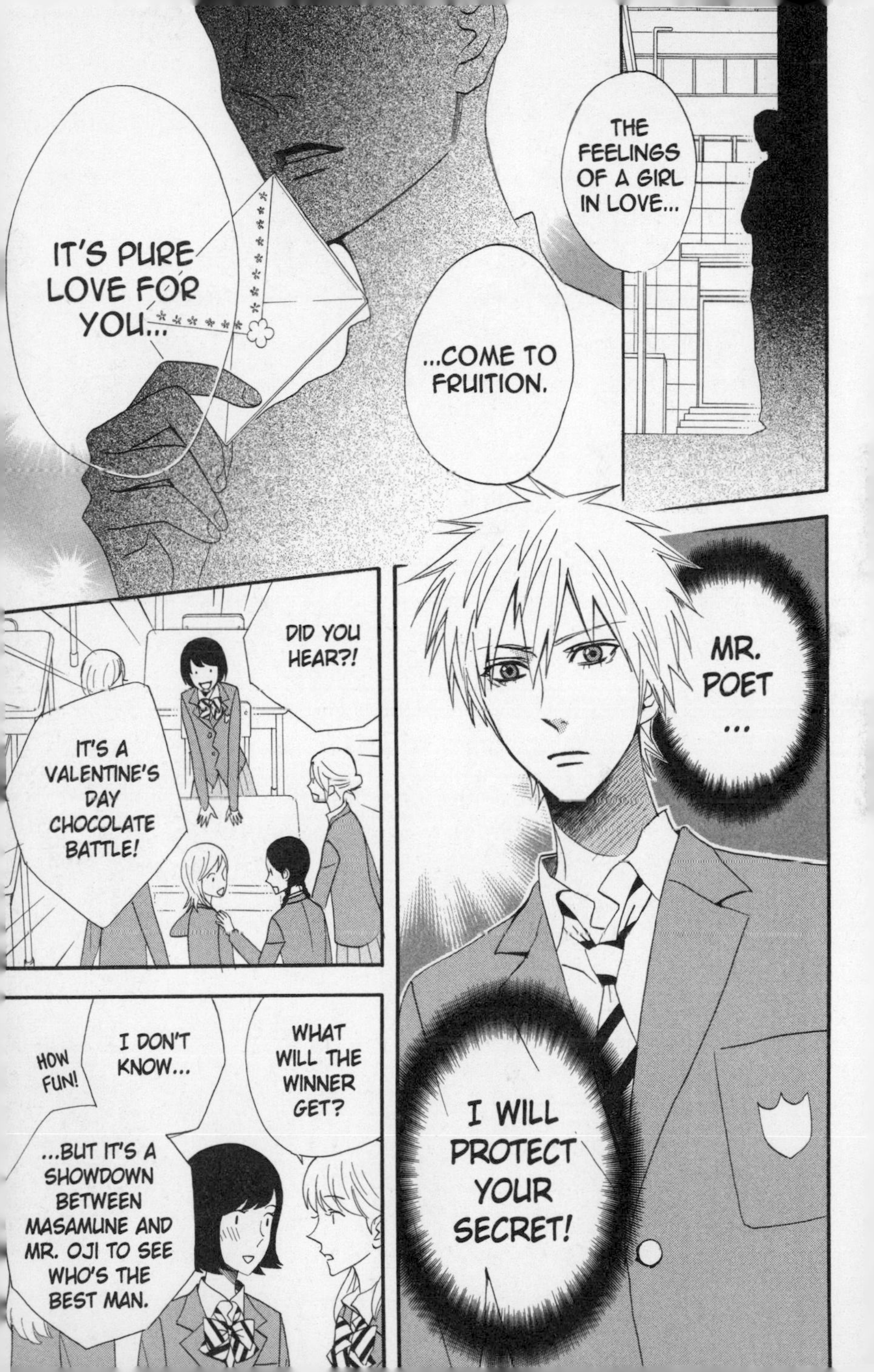
THE FEELINGS OF A GIRL IN LOVE...
...COME TO FRUITION.
IT'S PURE LOVE FOR YOU...
MR. POET...
I WILL PROTECT YOUR SECRET!
DID YOU HEAR?!
IT'S A VALENTINE'S DAY CHOCOLATE BATTLE!
WHAT WILL THE WINNER GET?
I DON'T KNOW...
HOW FUN!
...BUT IT'S A SHOWDOWN BETWEEN MASAMUNE AND MR. OJI TO SEE WHO'S THE BEST MAN.

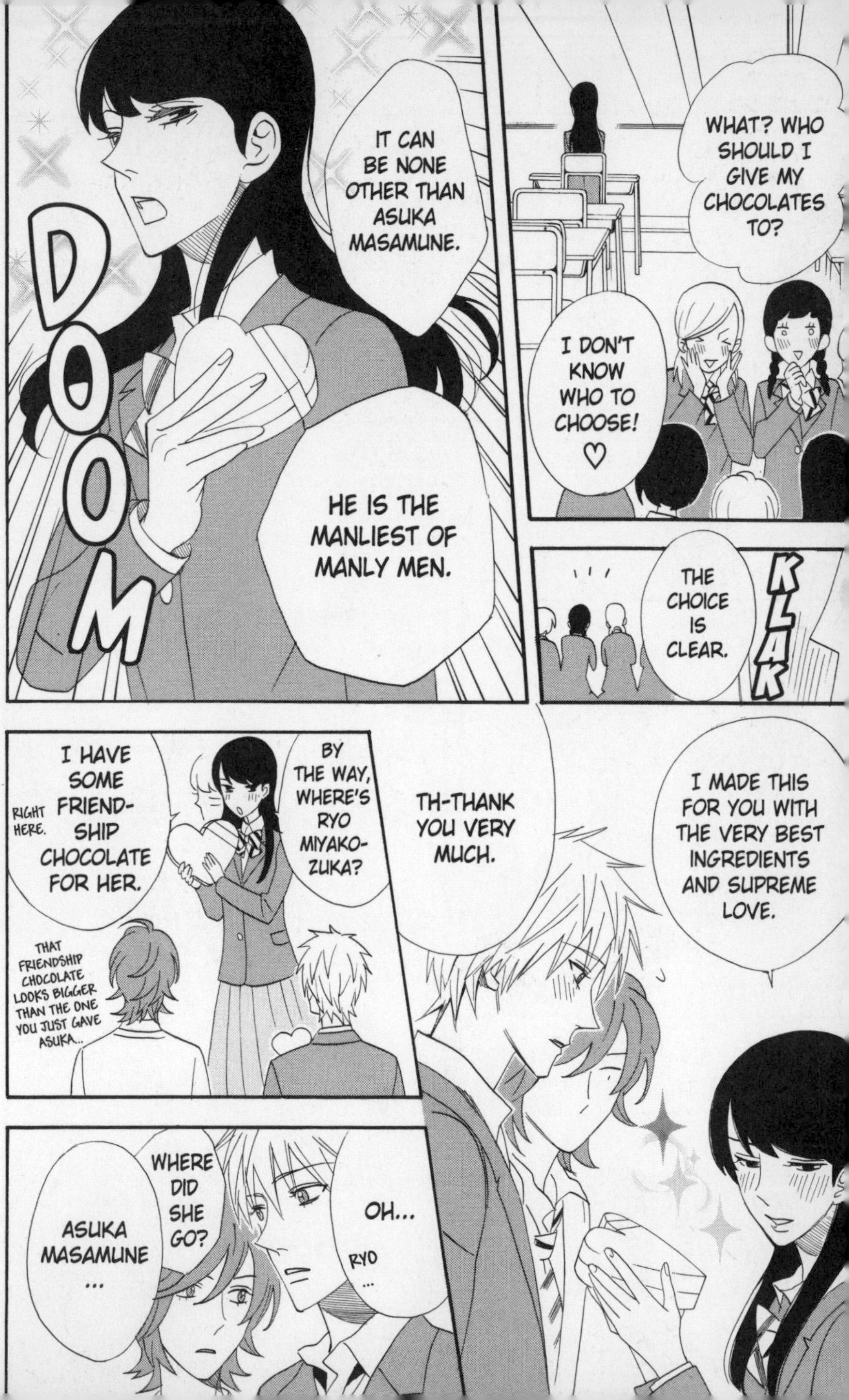
WHAT? WHO SHOULD I GIVE MY CHOCOLATES TO?
I DON'T KNOW WHO TO CHOOSE! ♡
KLAK
THE CHOICE IS CLEAR.
IT CAN BE NONE OTHER THAN ASUKA MASAMUNE.
DOOOM
HE IS THE MANLIEST OF MANLY MEN.
I MADE THIS FOR YOU WITH THE VERY BEST INGREDIENTS AND SUPREME LOVE.
TH-THANK YOU VERY MUCH.
BY THE WAY, WHERE'S RYO MIYAKO-ZUKA?
I HAVE SOME FRIENDSHIP CHOCOLATE FOR HER.
RIGHT HERE.
THAT FRIENDSHIP CHOCOLATE LOOKS BIGGER THAN THE ONE YOU JUST GAVE ASUKA...
WHERE DID SHE GO?
OH...
RYO ...
ASUKA MASAMUNE ...

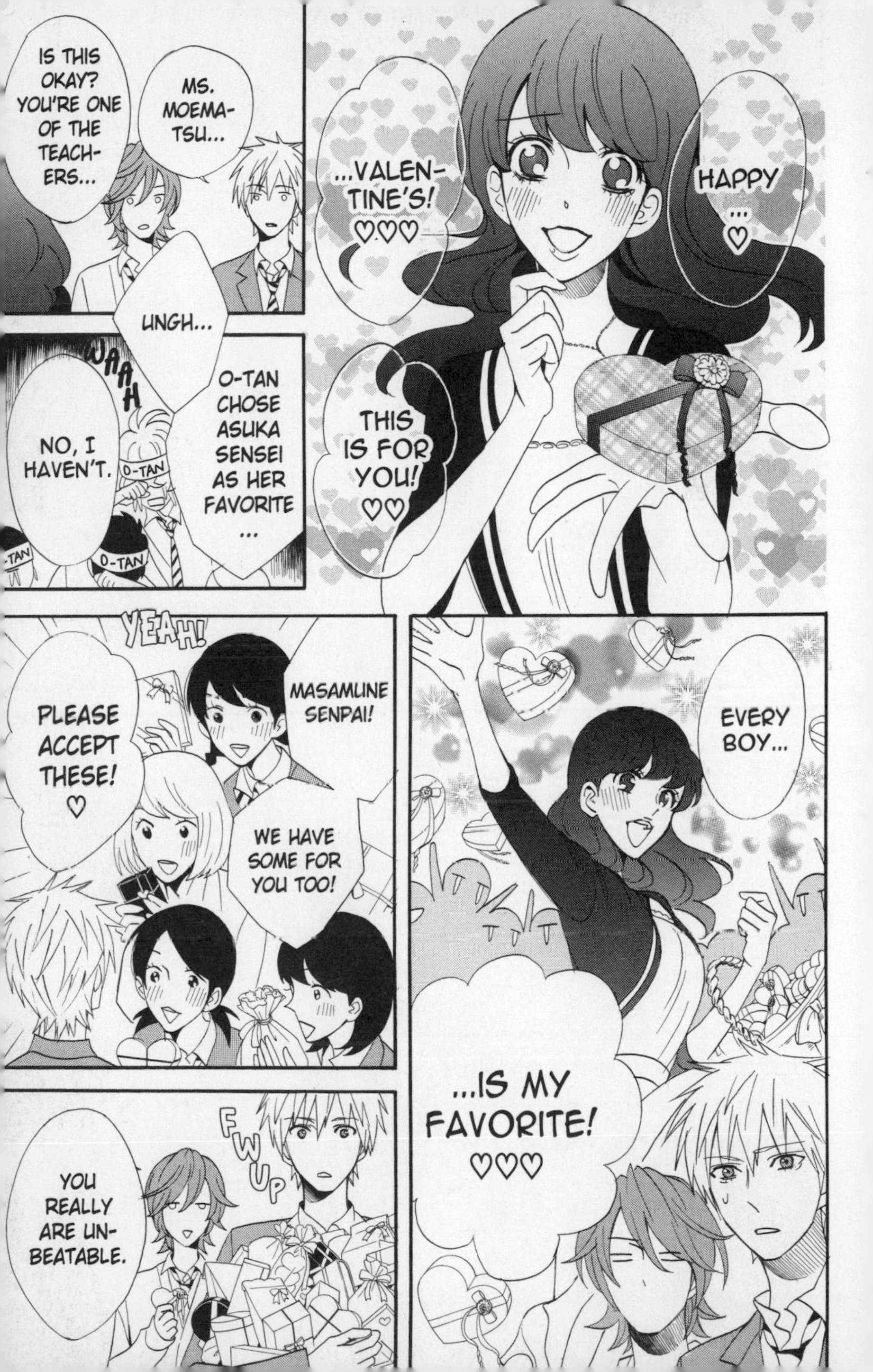
HAPPY ... ♡
...VALENTINE'S! ♡♡♡
THIS IS FOR YOU! ♡♡
MS. MOEMATSU...
IS THIS OKAY? YOU'RE ONE OF THE TEACHERS...
UNGH...
O-TAN CHOSE ASUKA SENSEI AS HER FAVORITE...
WAAH
NO, I HAVEN'T.
O-TAN
O-TAN
O-TAN
EVERY BOY...
...IS MY FAVORITE! ♡♡♡
YEAH!
MASAMUNE SENPAI!
PLEASE ACCEPT THESE! ♡
WE HAVE SOME FOR YOU TOO!
FWUP
YOU REALLY ARE UNBEATABLE.

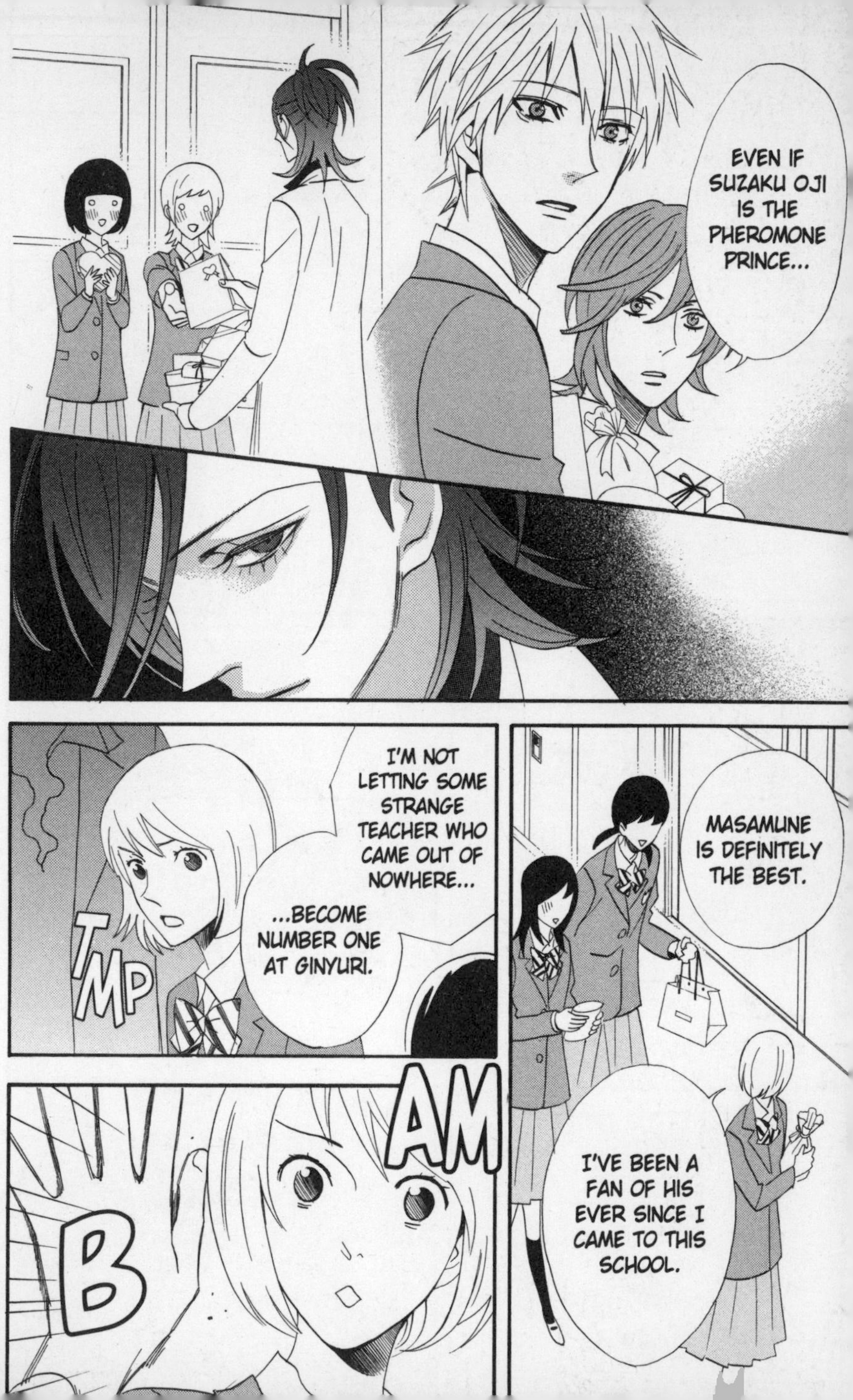
EVEN IF SUZAKU OJI IS THE PHEROMONE PRINCE...
MASAMUNE IS DEFINITELY THE BEST.
I'VE BEEN A FAN OF HIS EVER SINCE I CAME TO THIS SCHOOL.
I'M NOT LETTING SOME STRANGE TEACHER WHO CAME OUT OF NOWHERE...
...BECOME NUMBER ONE AT GINYURI.
TMP
B
AM

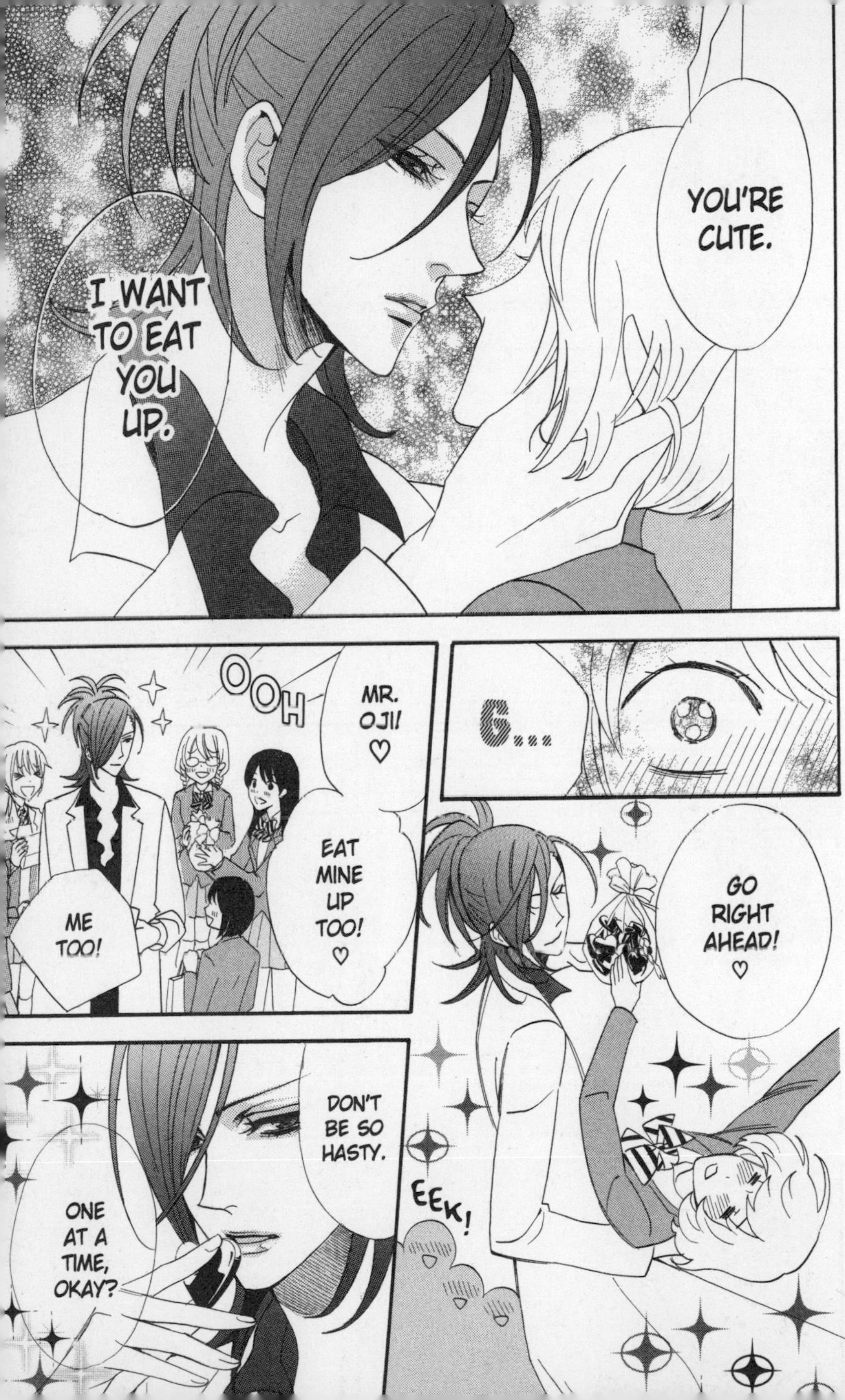
YOU'RE CUTE.
I WANT TO EAT YOU UP.
G...
OOH
MR. OJI! ♡
EAT MINE UP TOO! ♡
ME TOO!
GO RIGHT AHEAD! ♡
EEK!
DON'T BE SO HASTY.
ONE AT A TIME, OKAY?

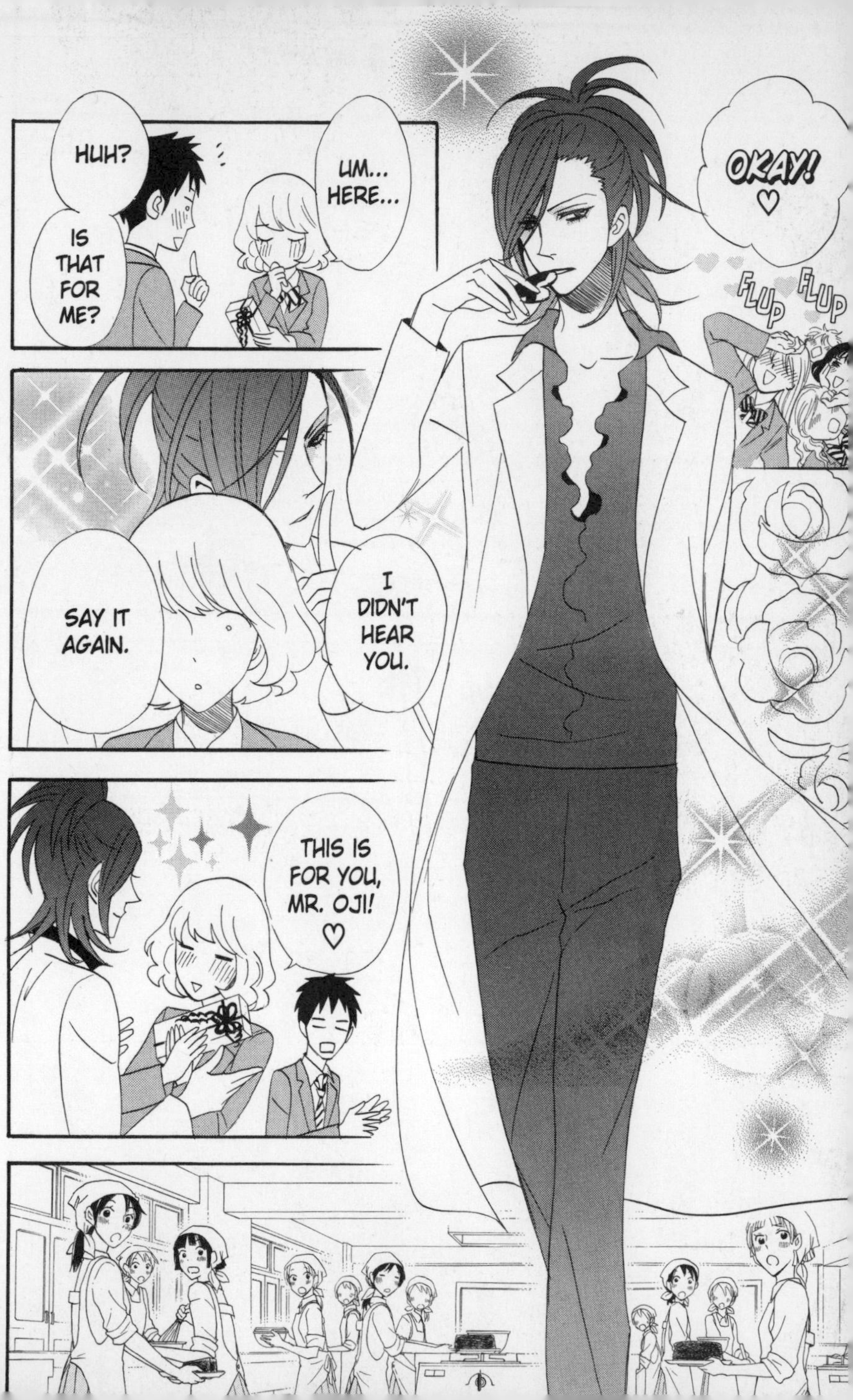
OKAY! ♥
FLUP FLUP
UM... HERE...
HUH?
IS THAT FOR ME?
I DIDN'T HEAR YOU.
SAY IT AGAIN.
THIS IS FOR YOU, MR. OJI! ♥

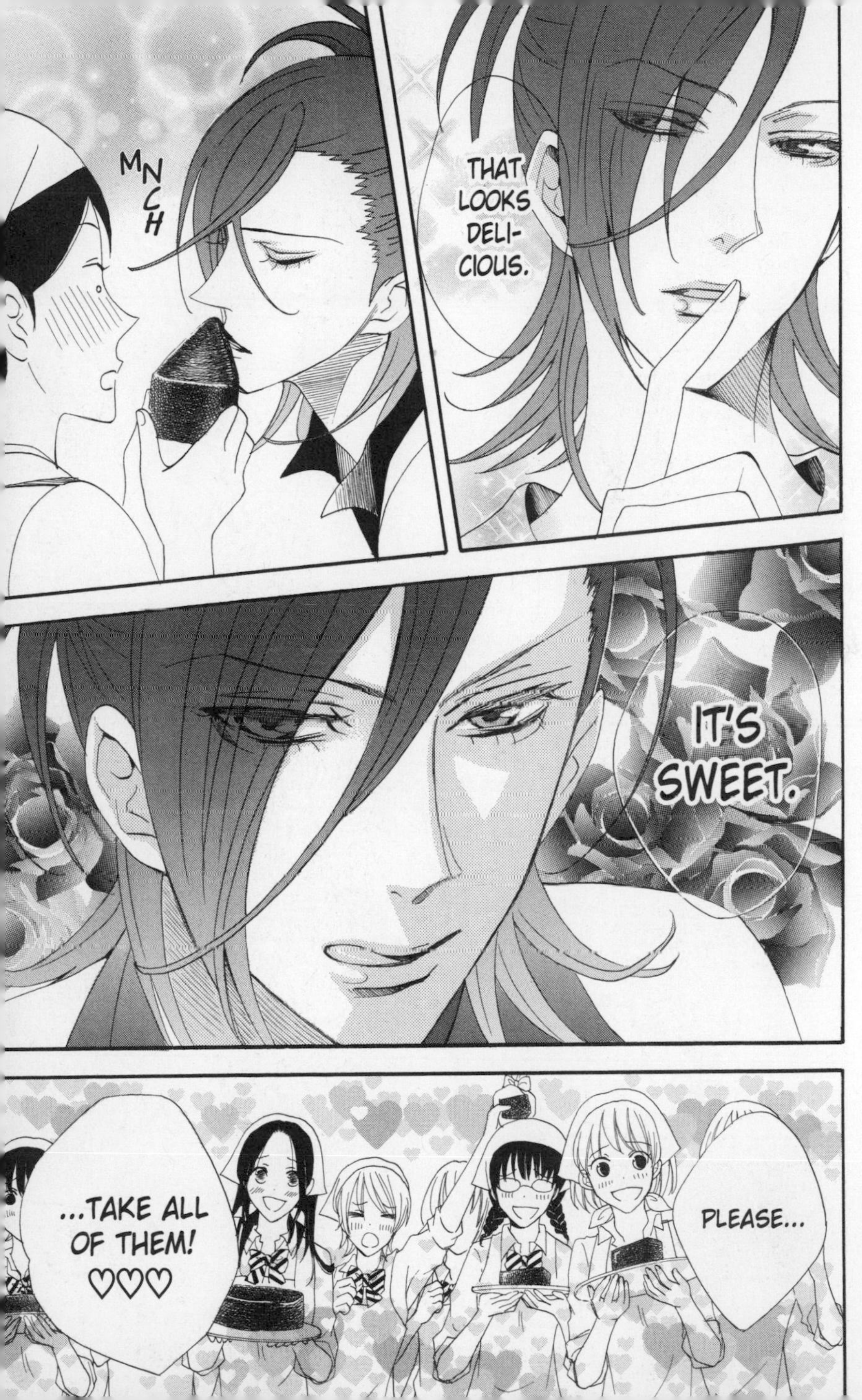
THAT LOOKS DELI-CIOUS.
MNCH
IT'S SWEET.
PLEASE...
...TAKE ALL OF THEM! ♡♡♡

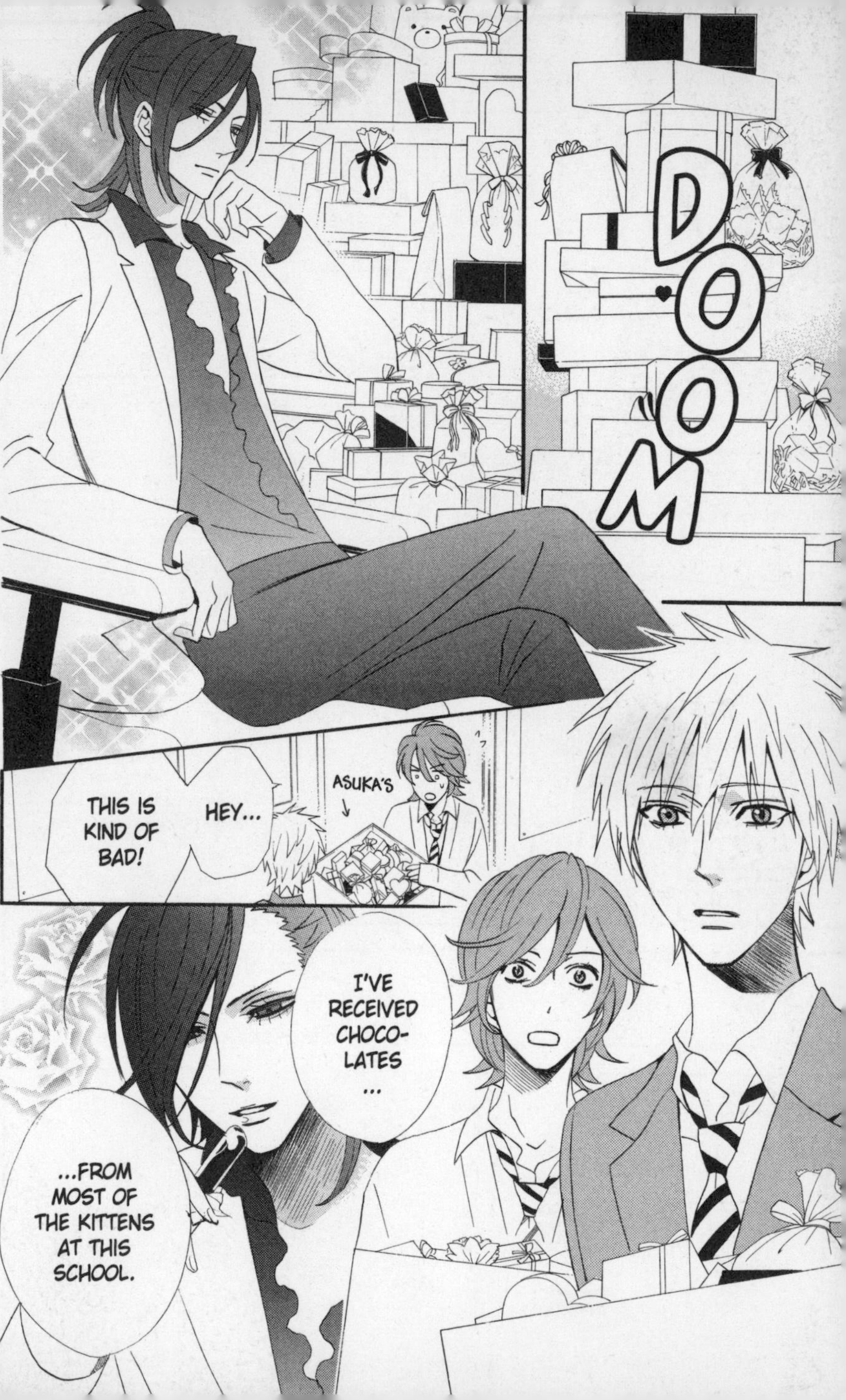
DOOM
ASUKA'S
HEY...
THIS IS KIND OF BAD!
I'VE RECEIVED CHOCO-LATES ...
...FROM MOST OF THE KITTENS AT THIS SCHOOL.

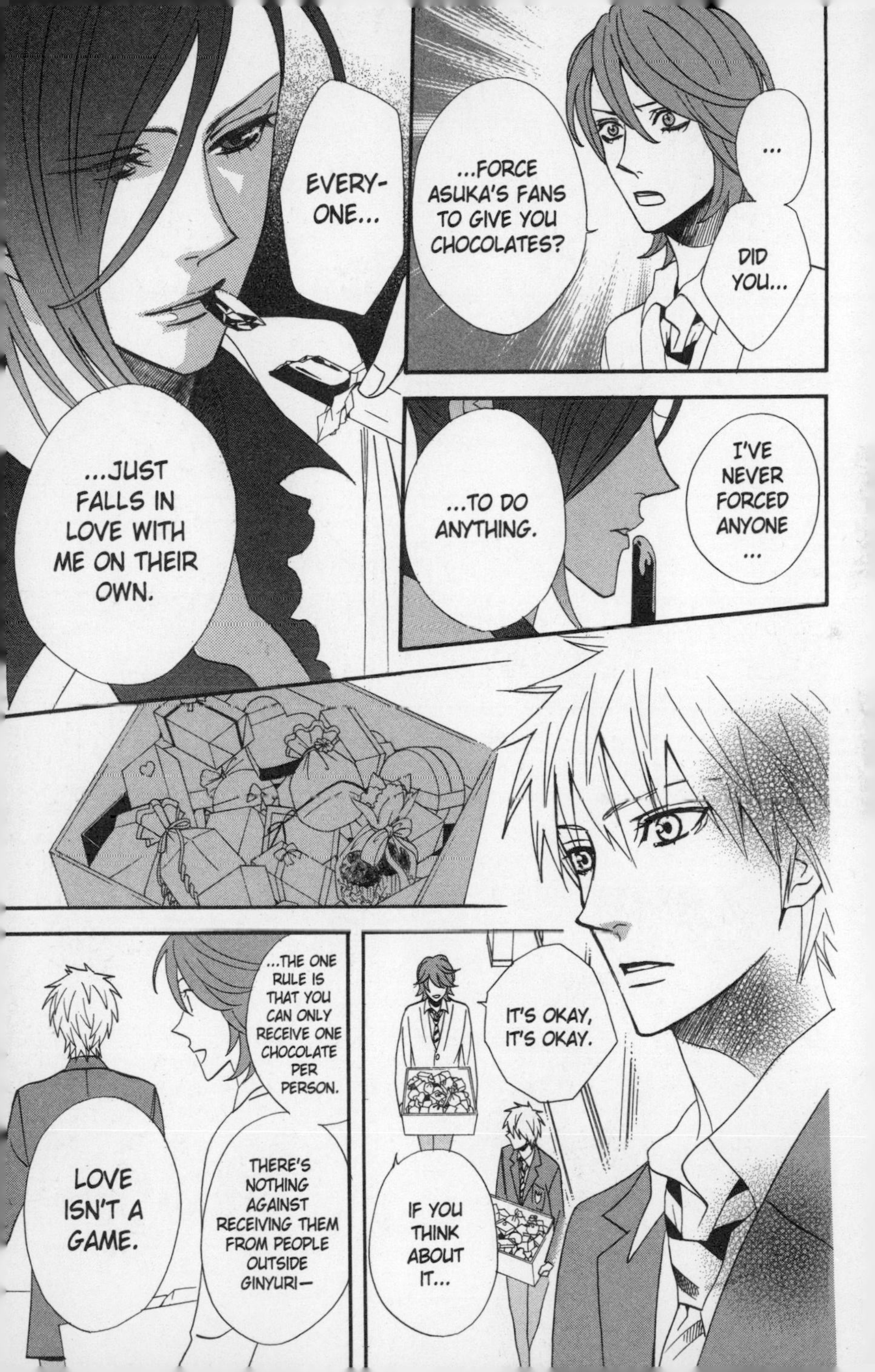
...
DID YOU...
...FORCE ASUKA'S FANS TO GIVE YOU CHOCOLATES?
I'VE NEVER FORCED ANYONE...
...TO DO ANYTHING.
EVERY-ONE...
...JUST FALLS IN LOVE WITH ME ON THEIR OWN.
IT'S OKAY, IT'S OKAY.
IF YOU THINK ABOUT IT...
...THE ONE RULE IS THAT YOU CAN ONLY RECEIVE ONE CHOCOLATE PER PERSON.
THERE'S NOTHING AGAINST RECEIVING THEM FROM PEOPLE OUTSIDE GINYURI—
LOVE ISN'T A GAME.

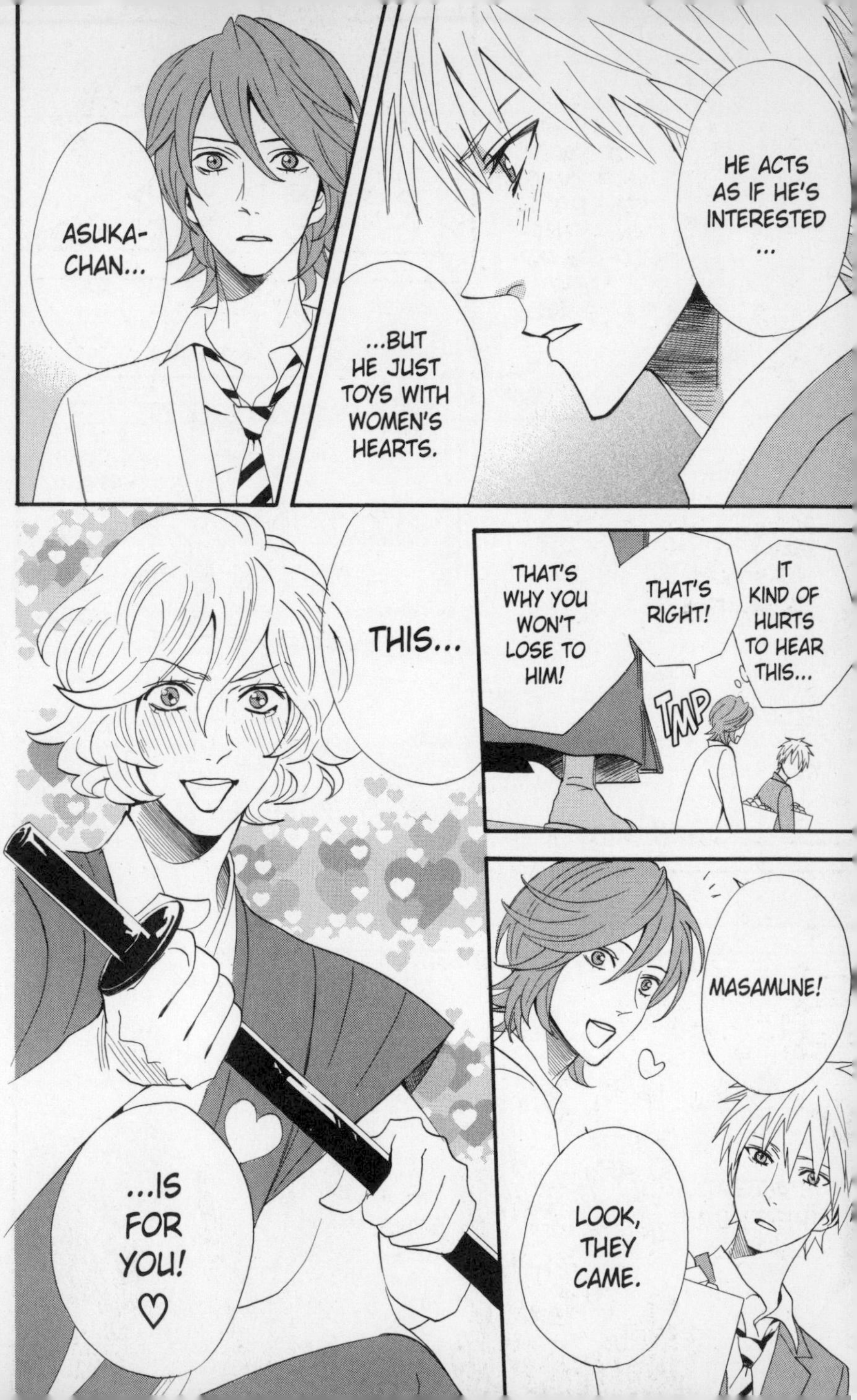
HE ACTS AS IF HE'S INTERESTED ...
...BUT HE JUST TOYS WITH WOMEN'S HEARTS.
ASUKA-CHAN...
IT KIND OF HURTS TO HEAR THIS...
THAT'S RIGHT!
THAT'S WHY YOU WON'T LOSE TO HIM!
TMP
MASAMUNE!
LOOK, THEY CAME.
THIS...
...IS FOR YOU! ♡

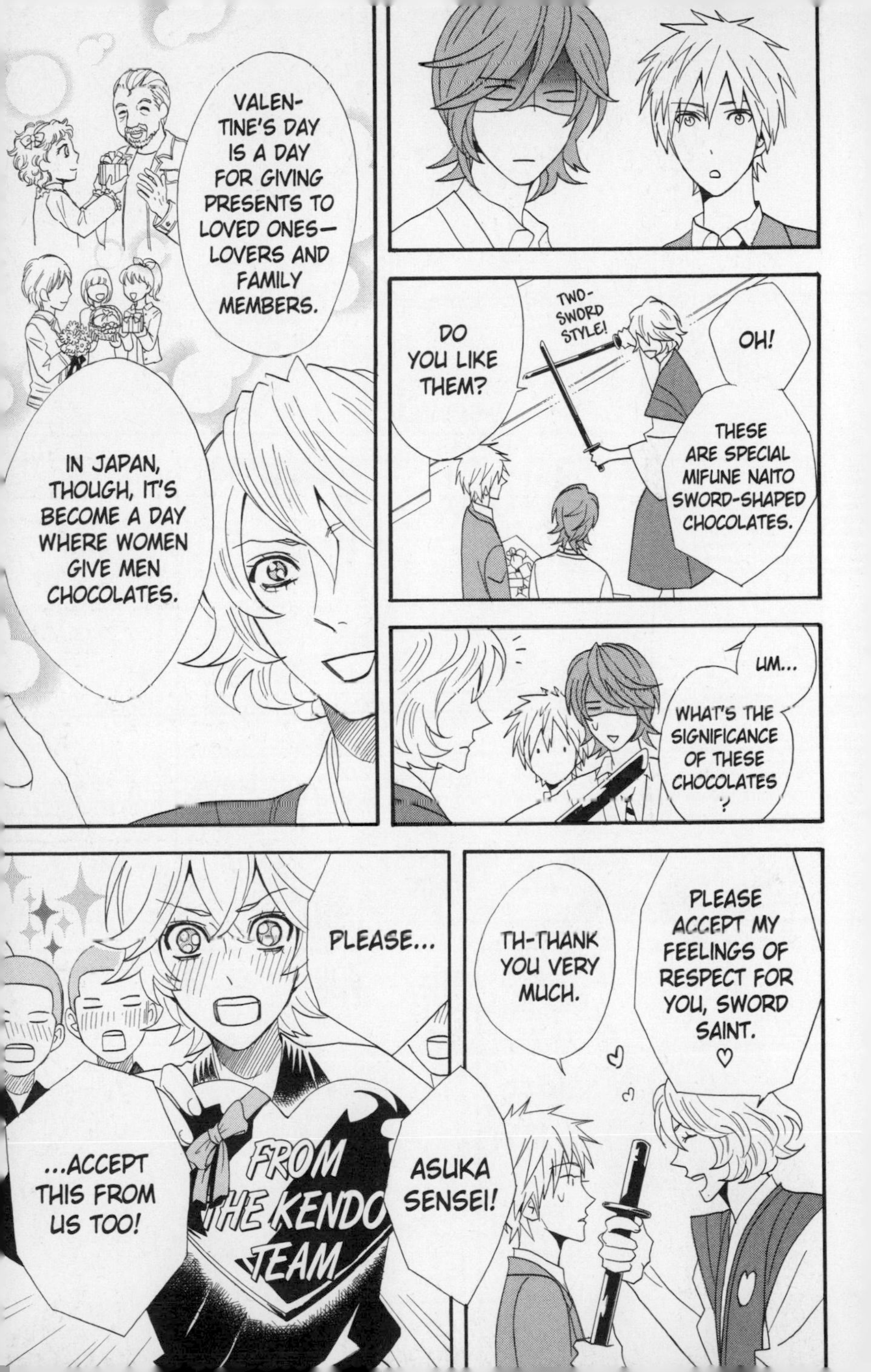
OH!
THESE ARE SPECIAL MIFUNE NAITO SWORD-SHAPED CHOCOLATES.
TWO-SWORD STYLE!
DO YOU LIKE THEM?
UM...
WHAT'S THE SIGNIFICANCE OF THESE CHOCOLATES?
VALEN-TINE'S DAY IS A DAY FOR GIVING PRESENTS TO LOVED ONES—LOVERS AND FAMILY MEMBERS.
IN JAPAN, THOUGH, IT'S BECOME A DAY WHERE WOMEN GIVE MEN CHOCOLATES.
PLEASE ACCEPT MY FEELINGS OF RESPECT FOR YOU, SWORD SAINT. ♡
TH-THANK YOU VERY MUCH.
ASUKA SENSEI!
PLEASE...
...ACCEPT THIS FROM US TOO!
FROM THE KENDO TEAM

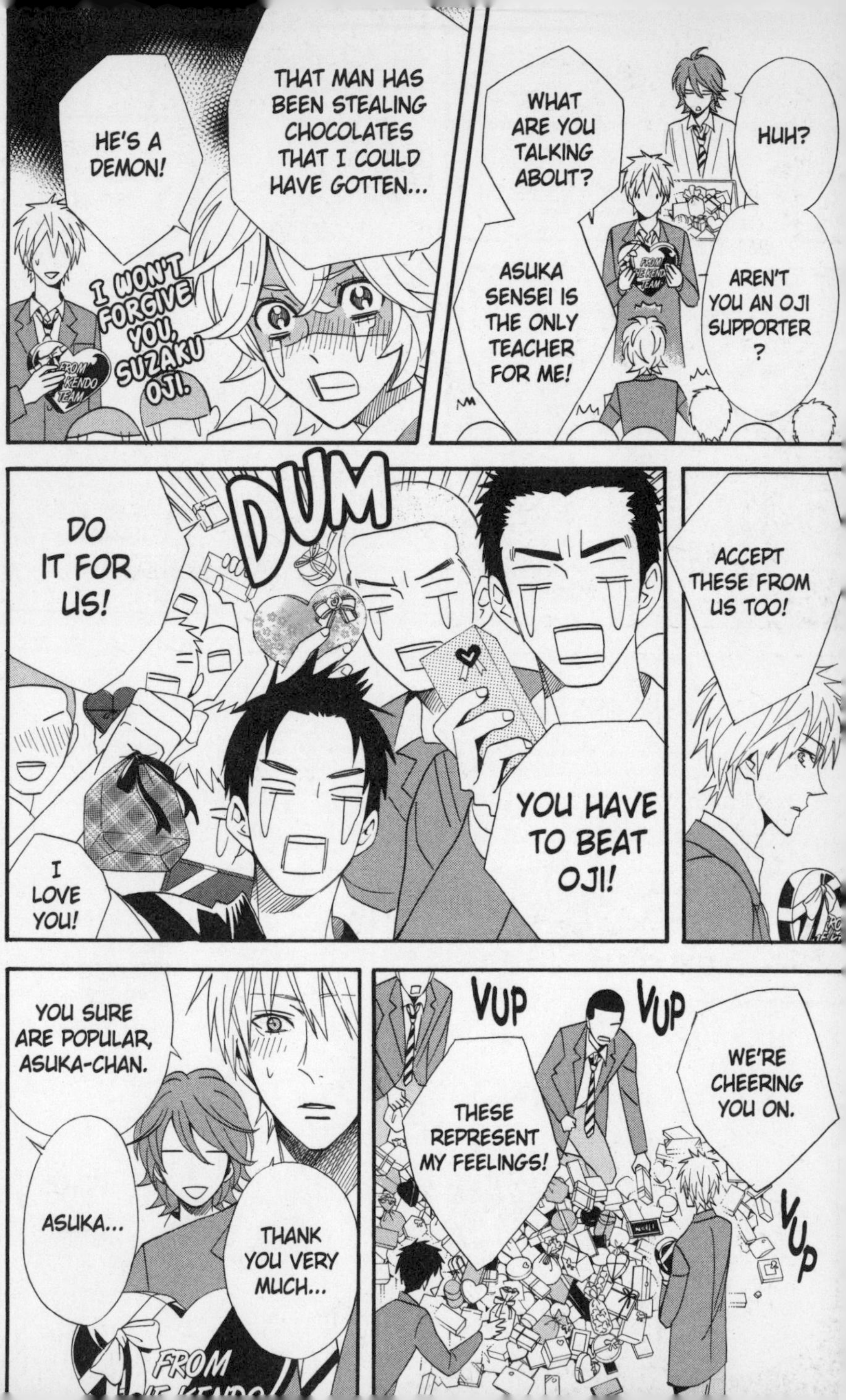
HUH?
AREN'T YOU AN OJI SUPPORTER ?
WHAT ARE YOU TALKING ABOUT?
FROM THE KENDO TEAM
ASUKA SENSEI IS THE ONLY TEACHER FOR ME!
THAT MAN HAS BEEN STEALING CHOCOLATES THAT I COULD HAVE GOTTEN...
HE'S A DEMON!
I WON'T FORGIVE YOU, SUZAKU OJI.
FROM KENDO TEAM
ACCEPT THESE FROM US TOO!
DUM
DO IT FOR US!
YOU HAVE TO BEAT OJI!
I LOVE YOU!
VUP
VUP
WE'RE CHEERING YOU ON.
THESE REPRESENT MY FEELINGS!
VUP
YOU SURE ARE POPULAR, ASUKA-CHAN.
THANK YOU VERY MUCH...
ASUKA...
FROM

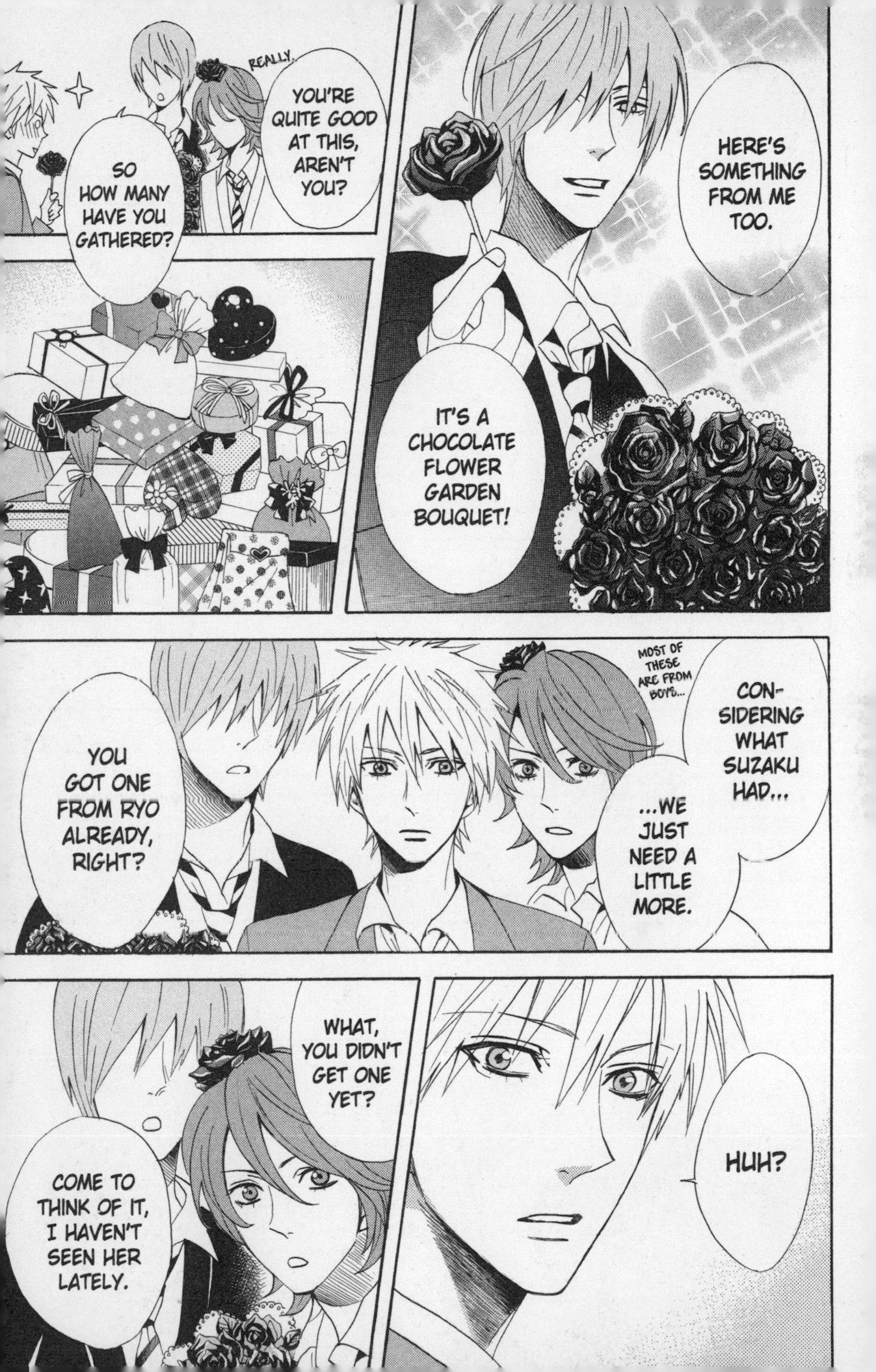
HERE'S SOMETHING FROM ME TOO.
IT'S A CHOCOLATE FLOWER GARDEN BOUQUET!
REALLY.
YOU'RE QUITE GOOD AT THIS, AREN'T YOU?
SO HOW MANY HAVE YOU GATHERED?
CON-SIDERING WHAT SUZAKU HAD...
MOST OF THESE ARE FROM BOYS...
...WE JUST NEED A LITTLE MORE.
YOU GOT ONE FROM RYO ALREADY, RIGHT?
HUH?
WHAT, YOU DIDN'T GET ONE YET?
COME TO THINK OF IT, I HAVEN'T SEEN HER LATELY.

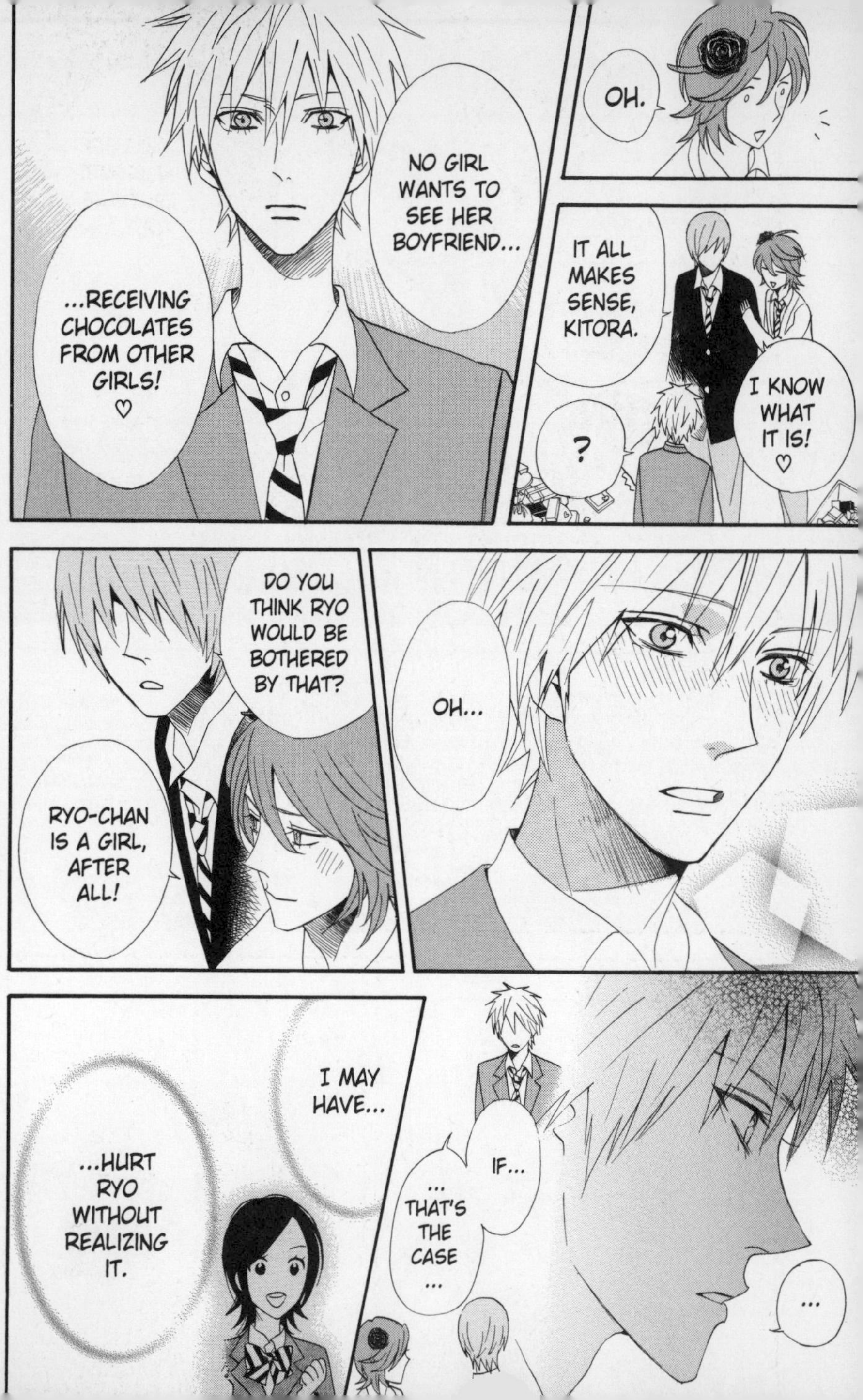
OH.
IT ALL MAKES SENSE, KITORA.
I KNOW WHAT IT IS! ♡
?
NO GIRL WANTS TO SEE HER BOYFRIEND...
...RECEIVING CHOCOLATES FROM OTHER GIRLS! ♡
OH...
DO YOU THINK RYO WOULD BE BOTHERED BY THAT?
RYO-CHAN IS A GIRL, AFTER ALL!
...
IF...
...THAT'S THE CASE...
I MAY HAVE...
...HURT RYO WITHOUT REALIZING IT.

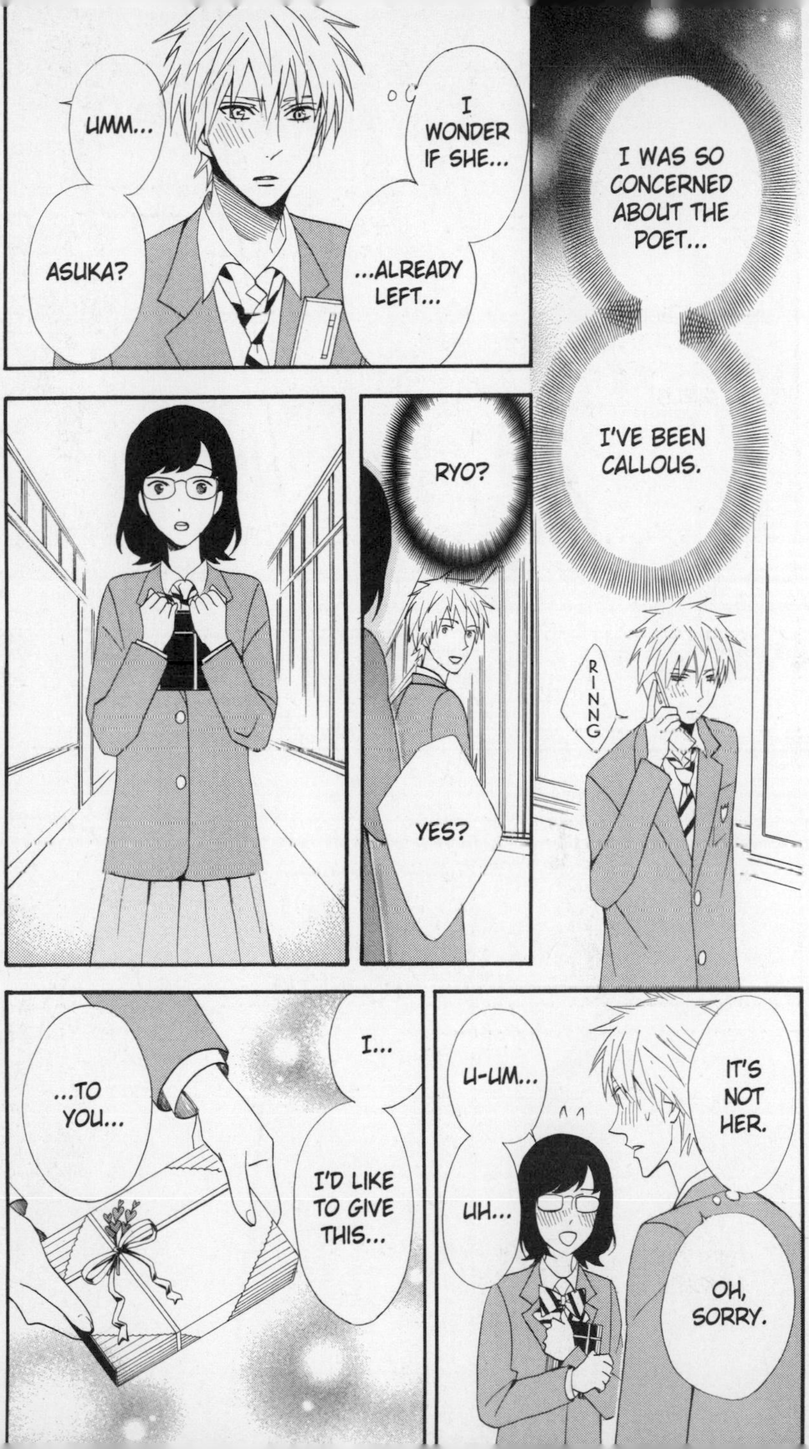
I WAS SO CONCERNED ABOUT THE POET...
I'VE BEEN CALLOUS.
RINNG
I WONDER IF SHE...
...ALREADY LEFT...
UMM...
ASUKA?
RYO?
YES?
IT'S NOT HER.
OH, SORRY.
U-UM...
UH...
I...
I'D LIKE TO GIVE THIS...
...TO YOU...

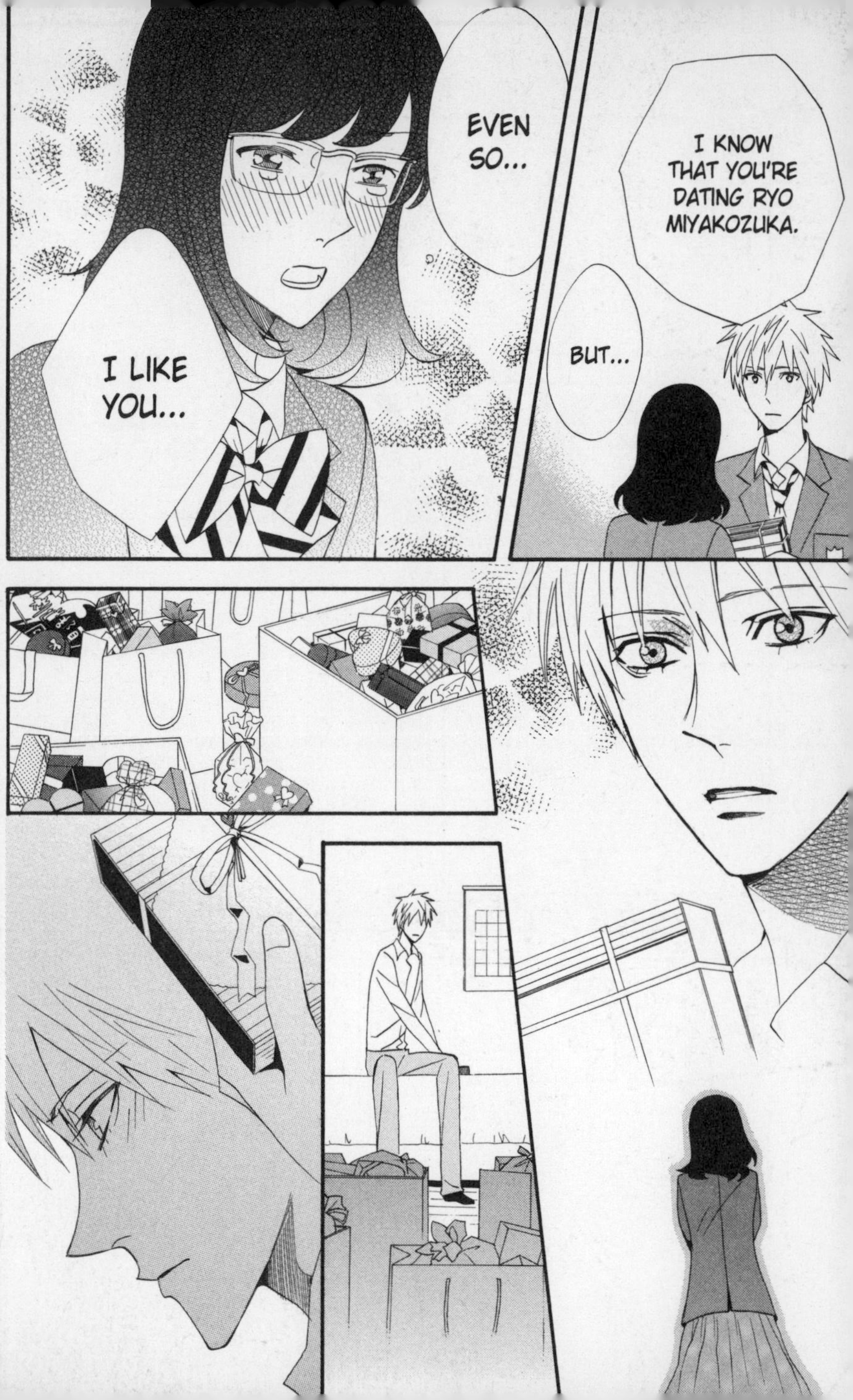
I KNOW THAT YOU'RE DATING RYO MIYAKOZUKA.
BUT...
EVEN SO...
I LIKE YOU...

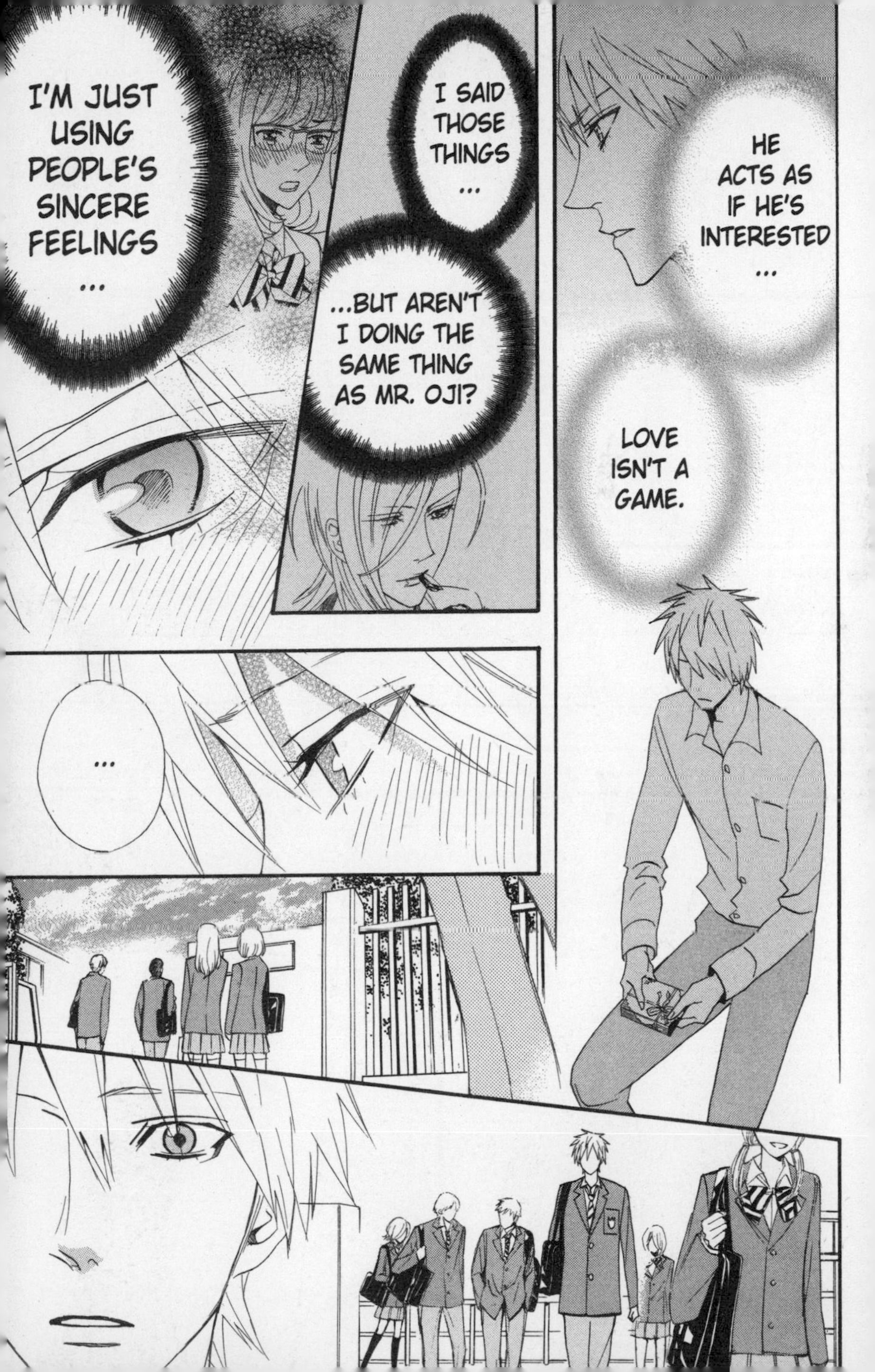
HE ACTS AS IF HE'S INTERESTED...
LOVE ISN'T A GAME.
I SAID THOSE THINGS...
...BUT AREN'T I DOING THE SAME THING AS MR. OJI?
I'M JUST USING PEOPLE'S SINCERE FEELINGS...
...

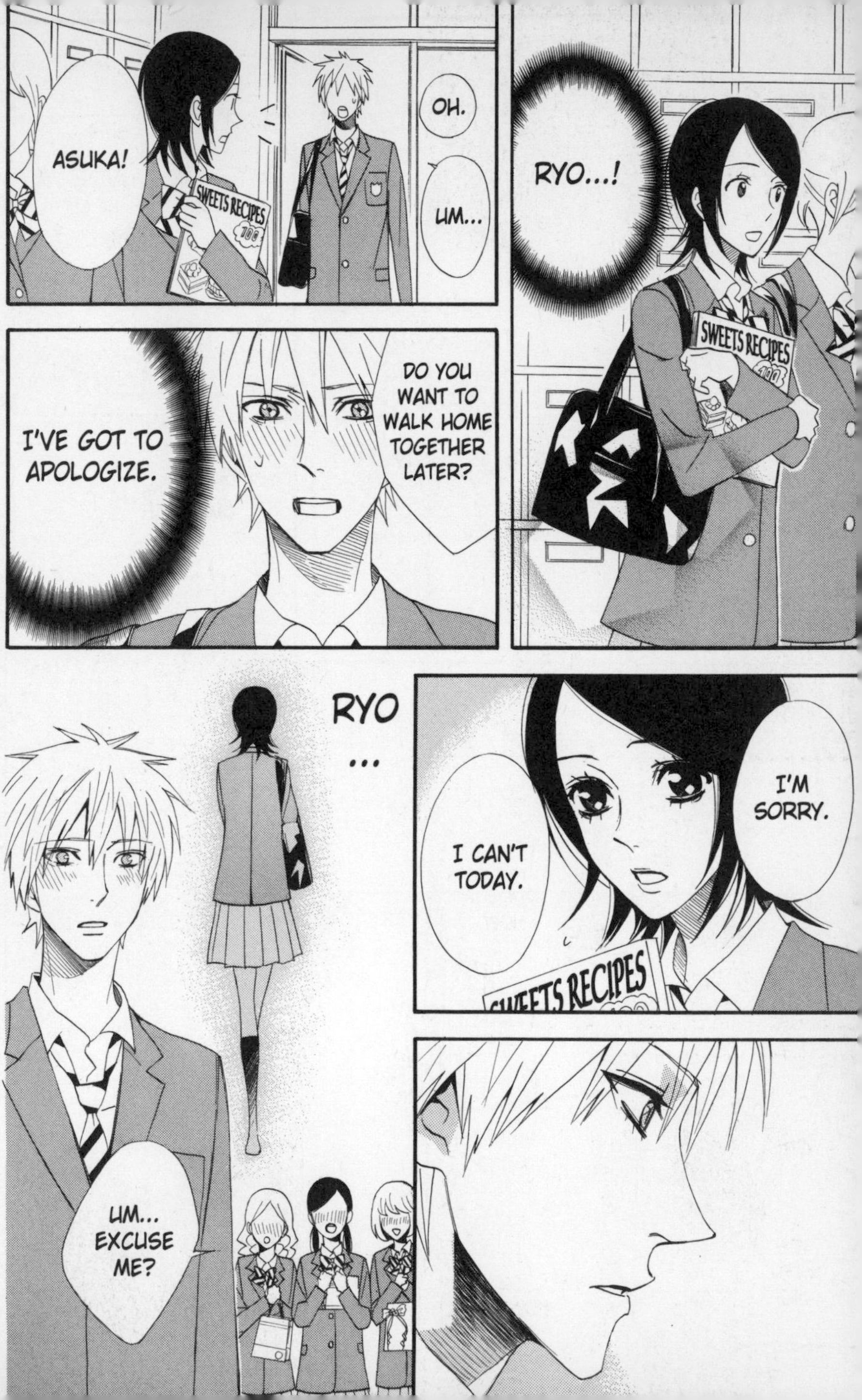
RYO...!
OH.
UM...
ASUKA!
DO YOU WANT TO WALK HOME TOGETHER LATER?
I'VE GOT TO APOLOGIZE.
SWEETS RECIPES
I'M SORRY.
I CAN'T TODAY.
RYO ...
UM... EXCUSE ME?

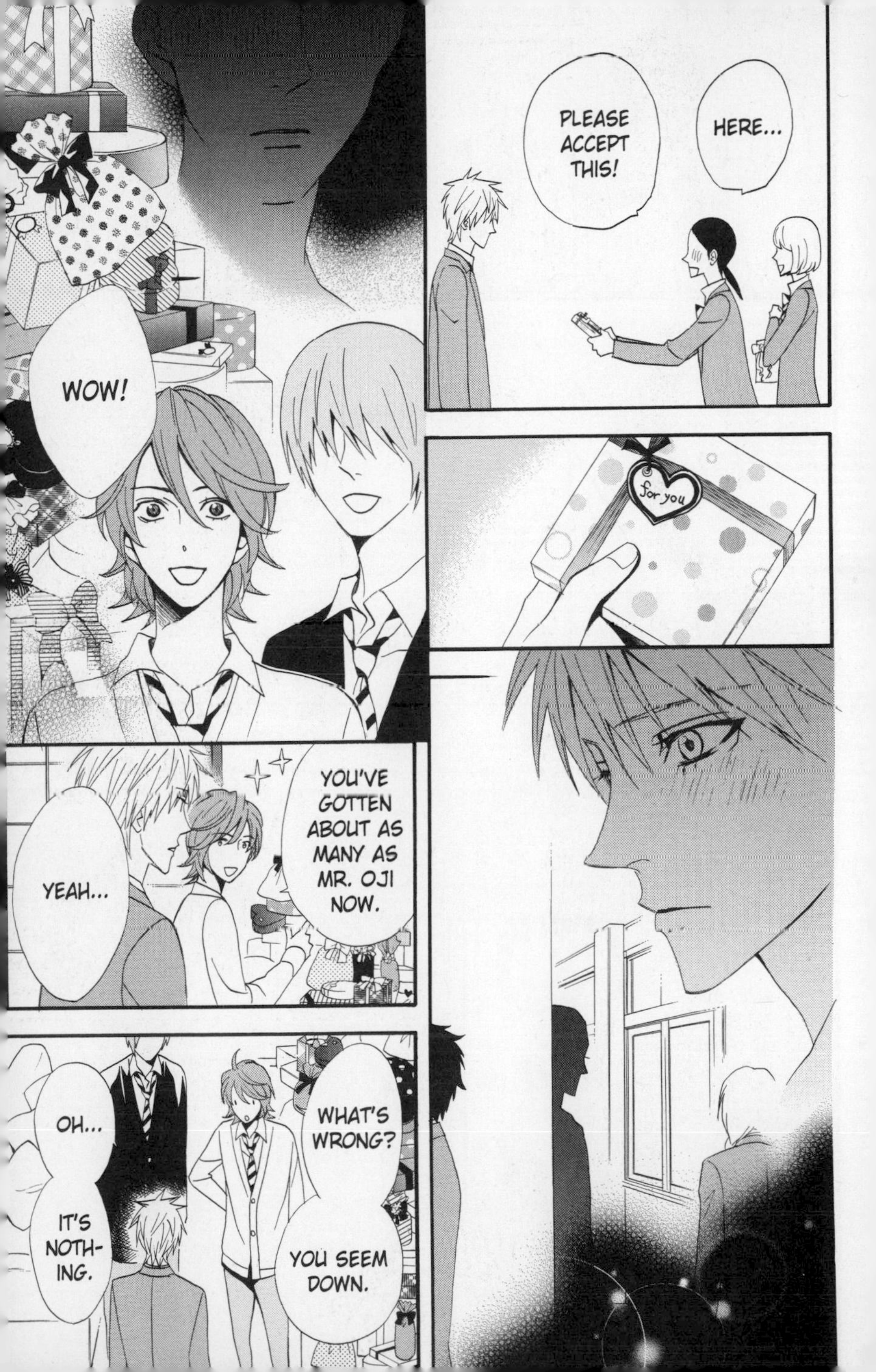
HERE...
PLEASE ACCEPT THIS!
for you
WOW!
YOU'VE GOTTEN ABOUT AS MANY AS MR. OJI NOW.
YEAH...
WHAT'S WRONG?
YOU SEEM DOWN.
OH...
IT'S NOTHING.

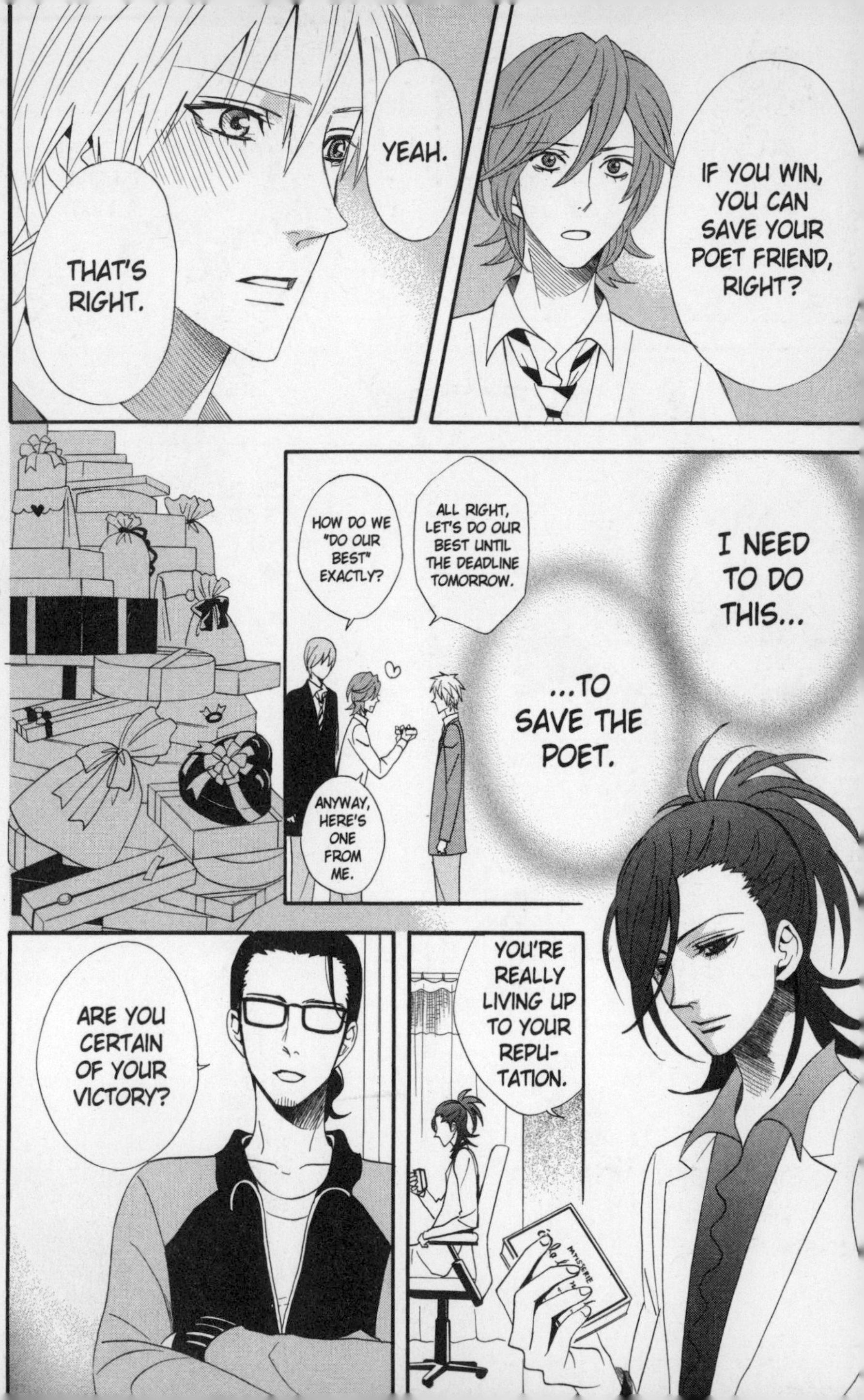
IF YOU WIN, YOU CAN SAVE YOUR POET FRIEND, RIGHT?
YEAH.
THAT'S RIGHT.
I NEED TO DO THIS...
...TO SAVE THE POET.
ALL RIGHT, LET'S DO OUR BEST UNTIL THE DEADLINE TOMORROW.
HOW DO WE "DO OUR BEST" EXACTLY?
ANYWAY, HERE'S ONE FROM ME.
YOU'RE REALLY LIVING UP TO YOUR REPU-TATION.
ARE YOU CERTAIN OF YOUR VICTORY?

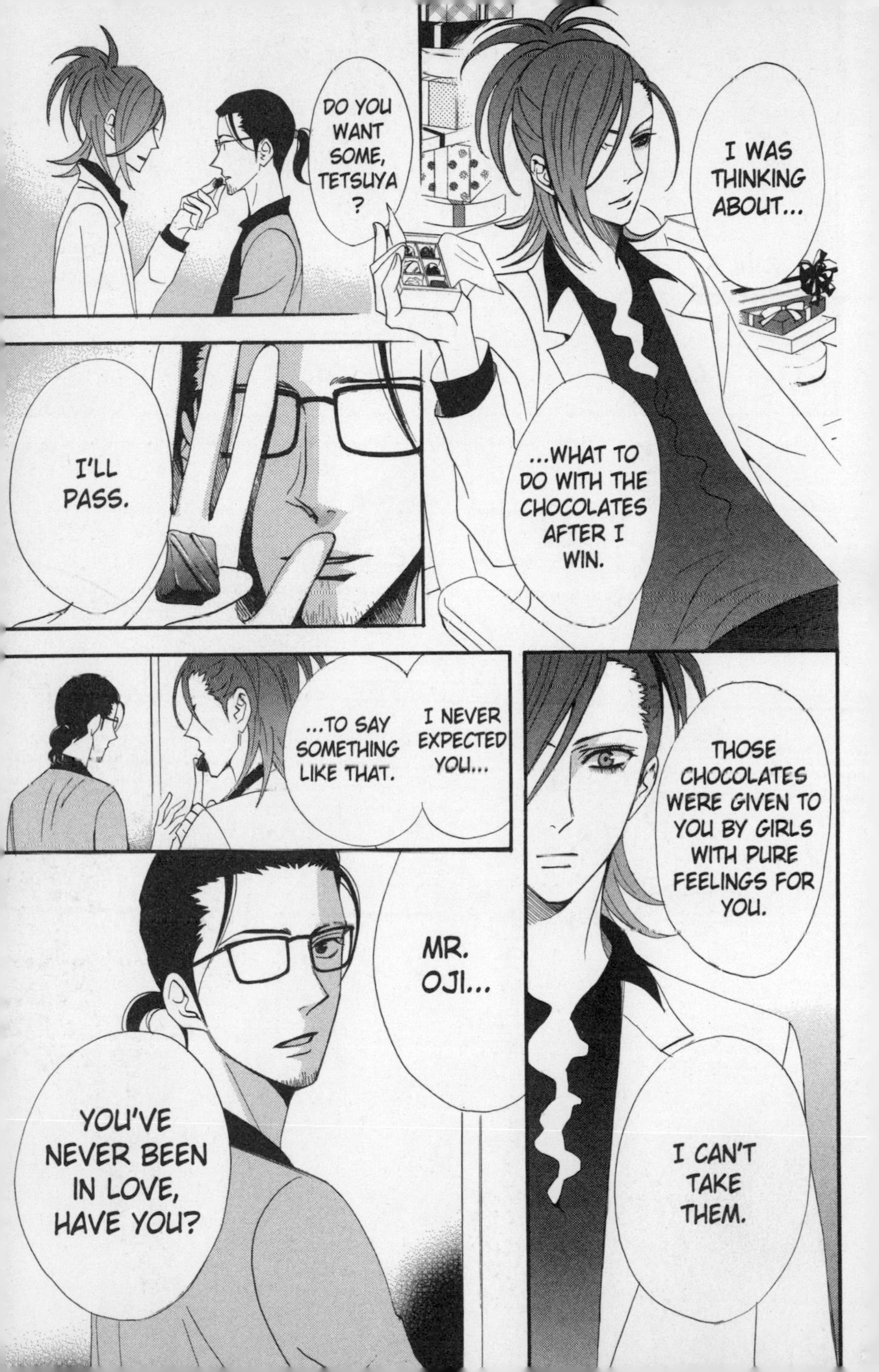
I WAS THINKING ABOUT...
...WHAT TO DO WITH THE CHOCOLATES AFTER I WIN.
DO YOU WANT SOME, TETSUYA?
I'LL PASS.
THOSE CHOCOLATES WERE GIVEN TO YOU BY GIRLS WITH PURE FEELINGS FOR YOU.
I CAN'T TAKE THEM.
I NEVER EXPECTED YOU...
...TO SAY SOMETHING LIKE THAT.
MR. OJI...
YOU'VE NEVER BEEN IN LOVE, HAVE YOU?

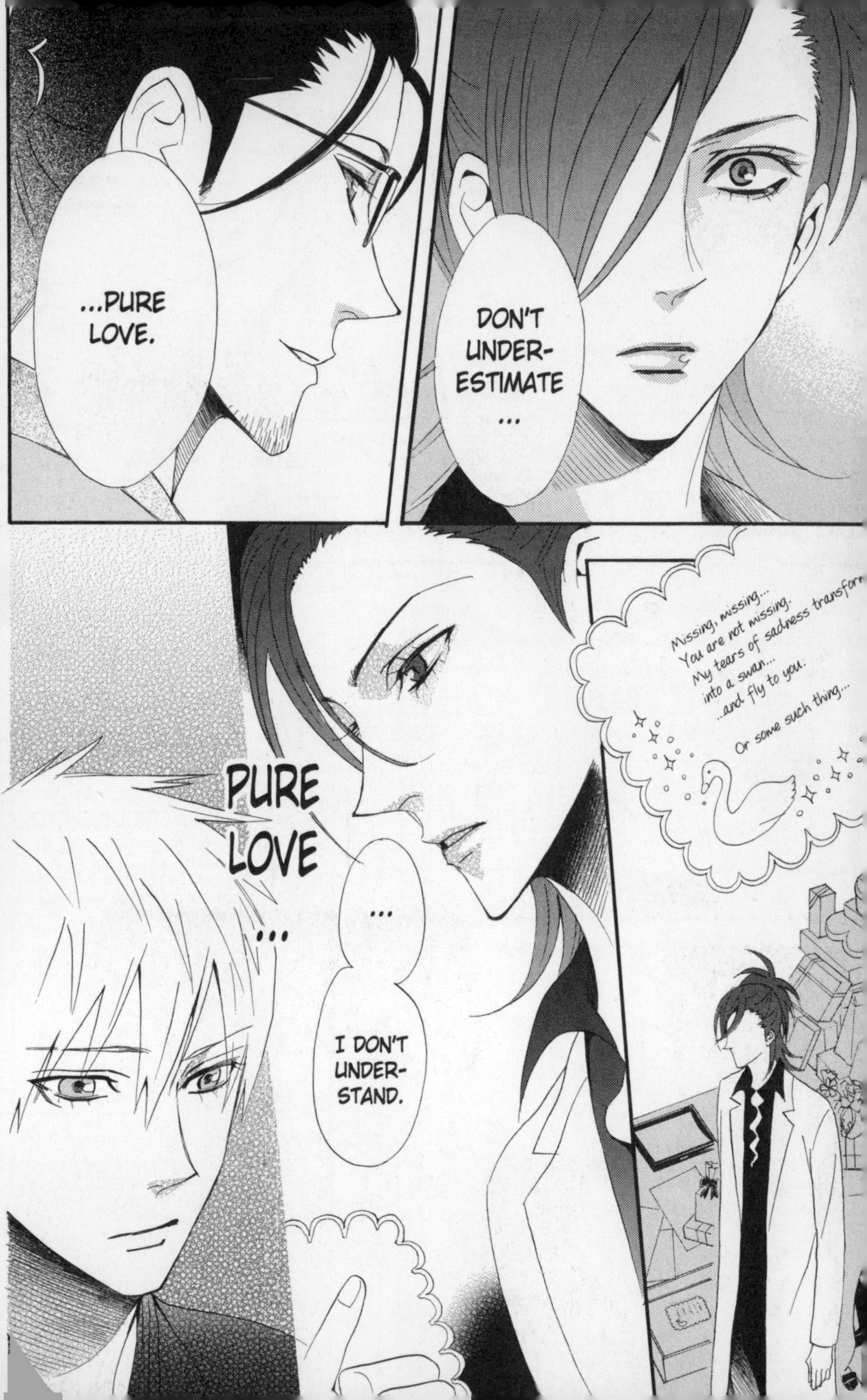
DON'T UNDER-ESTIMATE ...
...PURE LOVE.
Missing, missing... You are not missing. My tears of sadness transform into a swan... ...and fly to you.
Or some such thing...
PURE LOVE
...
...
I DON'T UNDER-STAND.

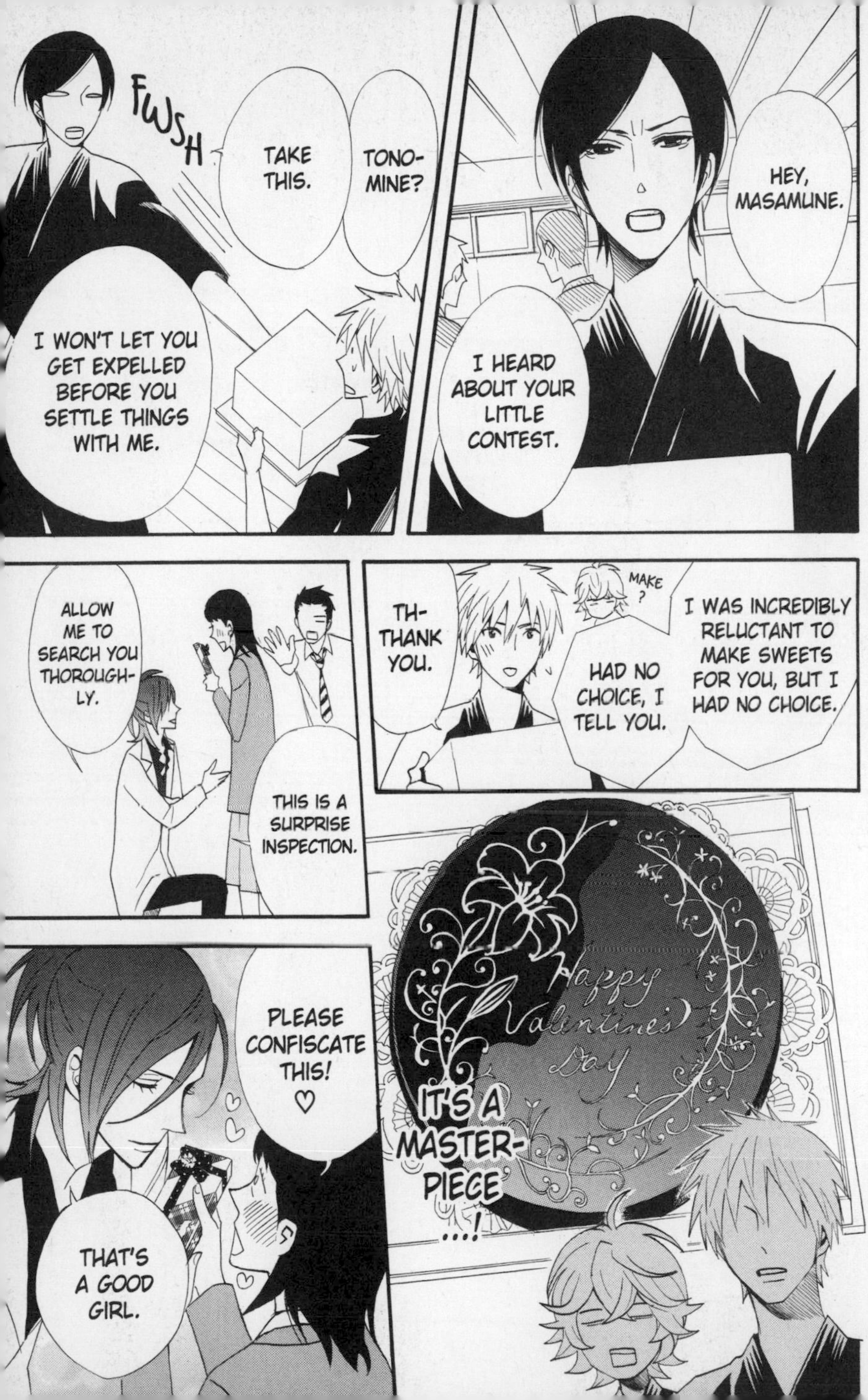
HEY, MASAMUNE.
I HEARD ABOUT YOUR LITTLE CONTEST.
TONO-MINE?
TAKE THIS.
FWSH
I WON'T LET YOU GET EXPELLED BEFORE YOU SETTLE THINGS WITH ME.
I WAS INCREDIBLY RELUCTANT TO MAKE SWEETS FOR YOU, BUT I HAD NO CHOICE.
MAKE ?
HAD NO CHOICE, I TELL YOU.
TH-THANK YOU.
ALLOW ME TO SEARCH YOU THOROUGH-LY.
THIS IS A SURPRISE INSPECTION.
Happy Valentine's Day
IT'S A MASTER-PIECE ...!
PLEASE CONFISCATE THIS! ♡
THAT'S A GOOD GIRL.

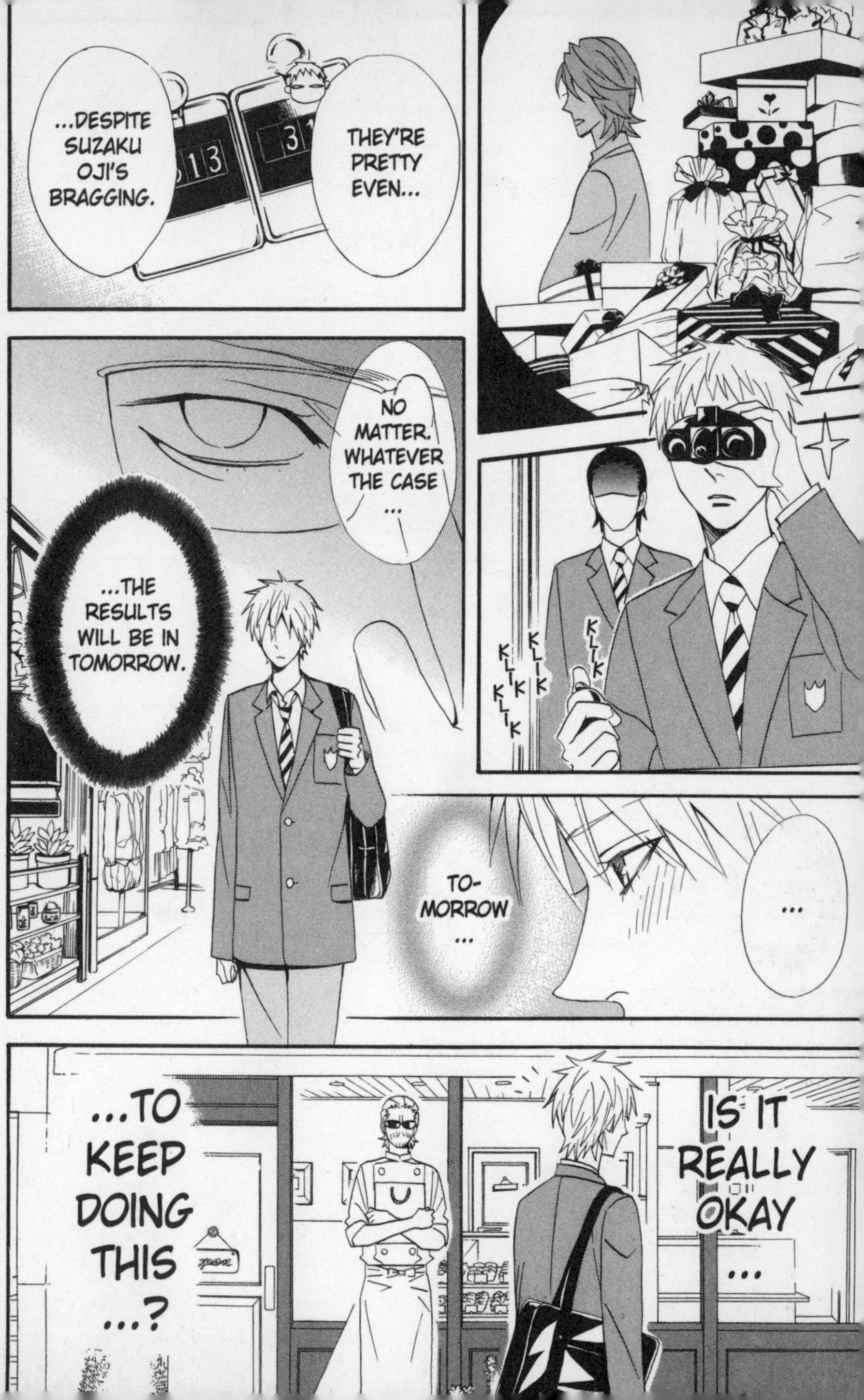
THEY'RE PRETTY EVEN...
...DESPITE SUZAKU OJI'S BRAGGING.
KLIK KLIK KLIK KLIK
...
TO-MORROW...
NO MATTER. WHATEVER THE CASE...
...THE RESULTS WILL BE IN TOMORROW.
IS IT REALLY OKAY...
...TO KEEP DOING THIS...?

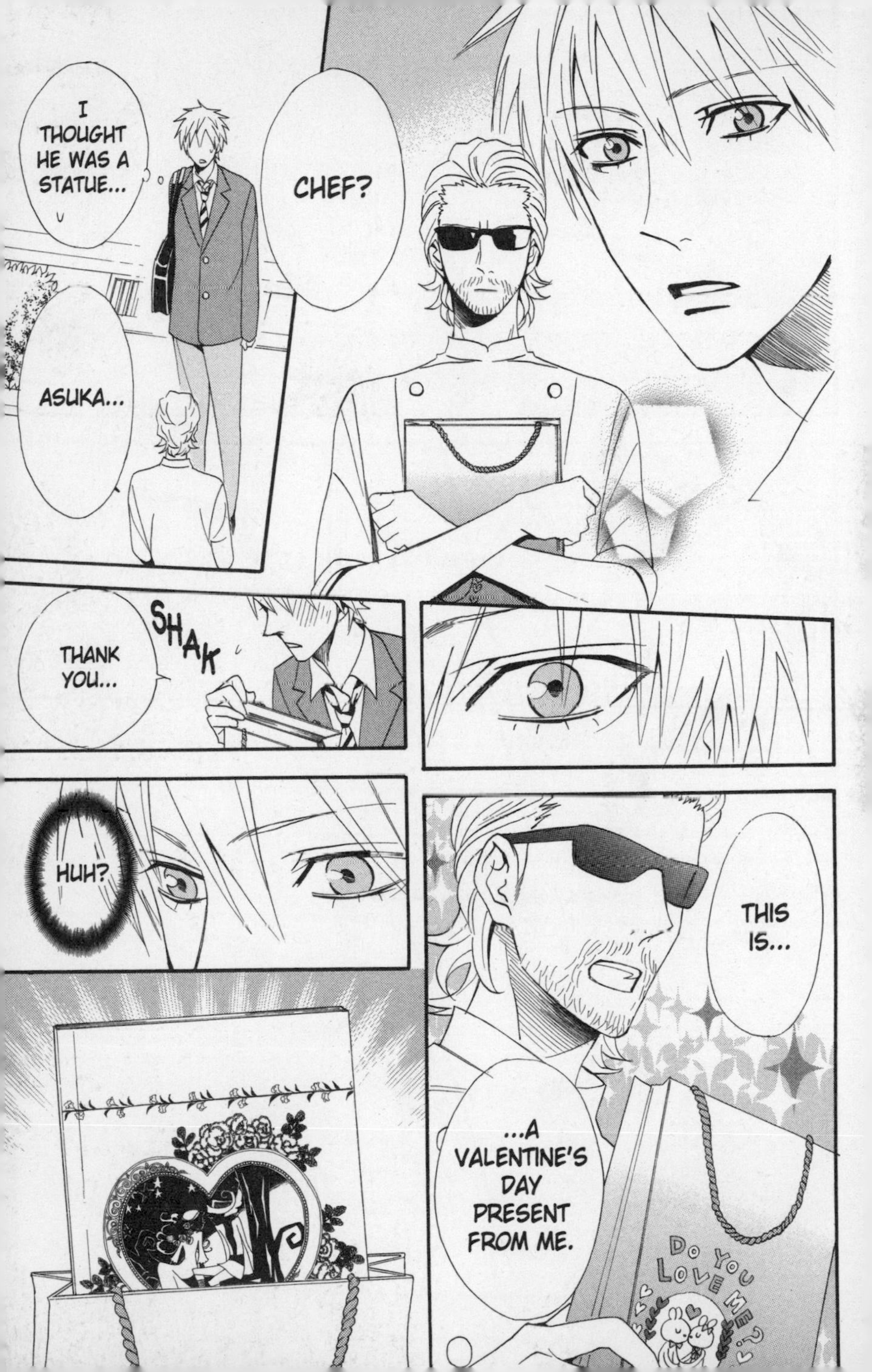
CHEF?
I THOUGHT HE WAS A STATUE...
ASUKA...
SHAK
THANK YOU...
THIS IS...
...A VALENTINE'S DAY PRESENT FROM ME.
DO YOU LOVE ME?
HUH?

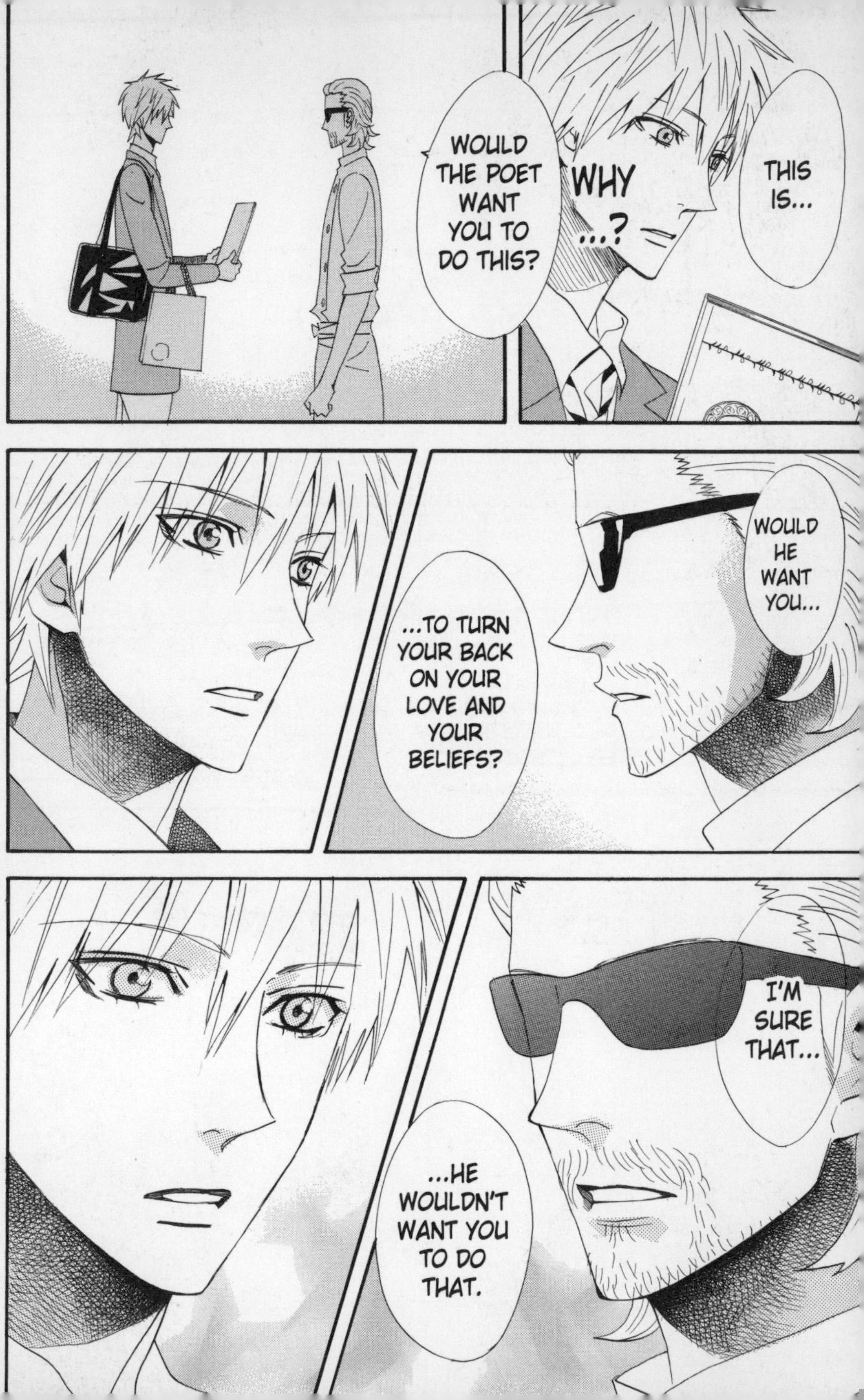
THIS IS...
WHY ...?
WOULD THE POET WANT YOU TO DO THIS?
WOULD HE WANT YOU...
...TO TURN YOUR BACK ON YOUR LOVE AND YOUR BELIEFS?
I'M SURE THAT...
...HE WOULDN'T WANT YOU TO DO THAT.

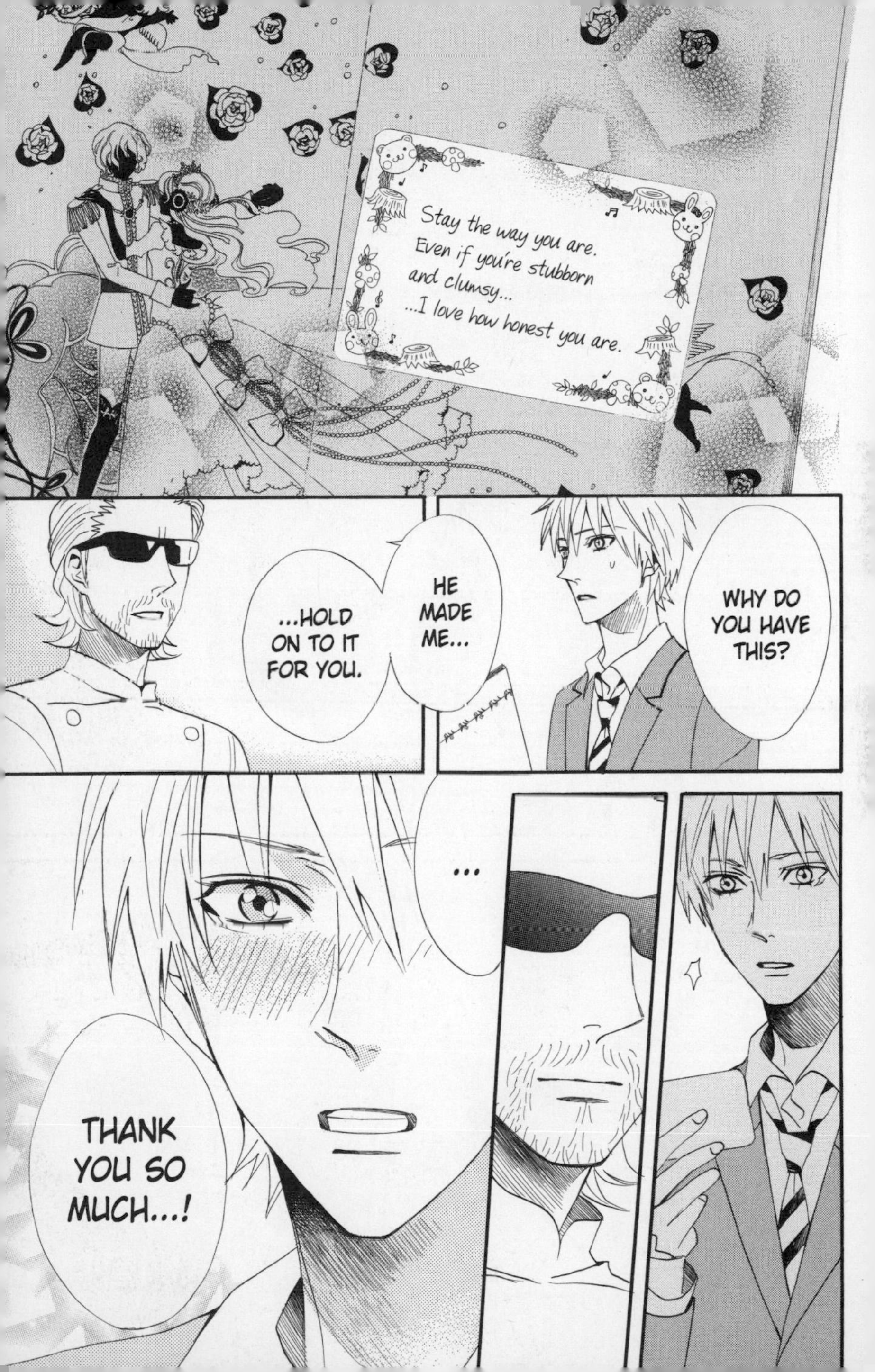
Stay the way you are. Even if you're stubborn and clumsy... ...I love how honest you are.
WHY DO YOU HAVE THIS?
HE MADE ME...
...HOLD ON TO IT FOR YOU.
...
THANK YOU SO MUCH...!

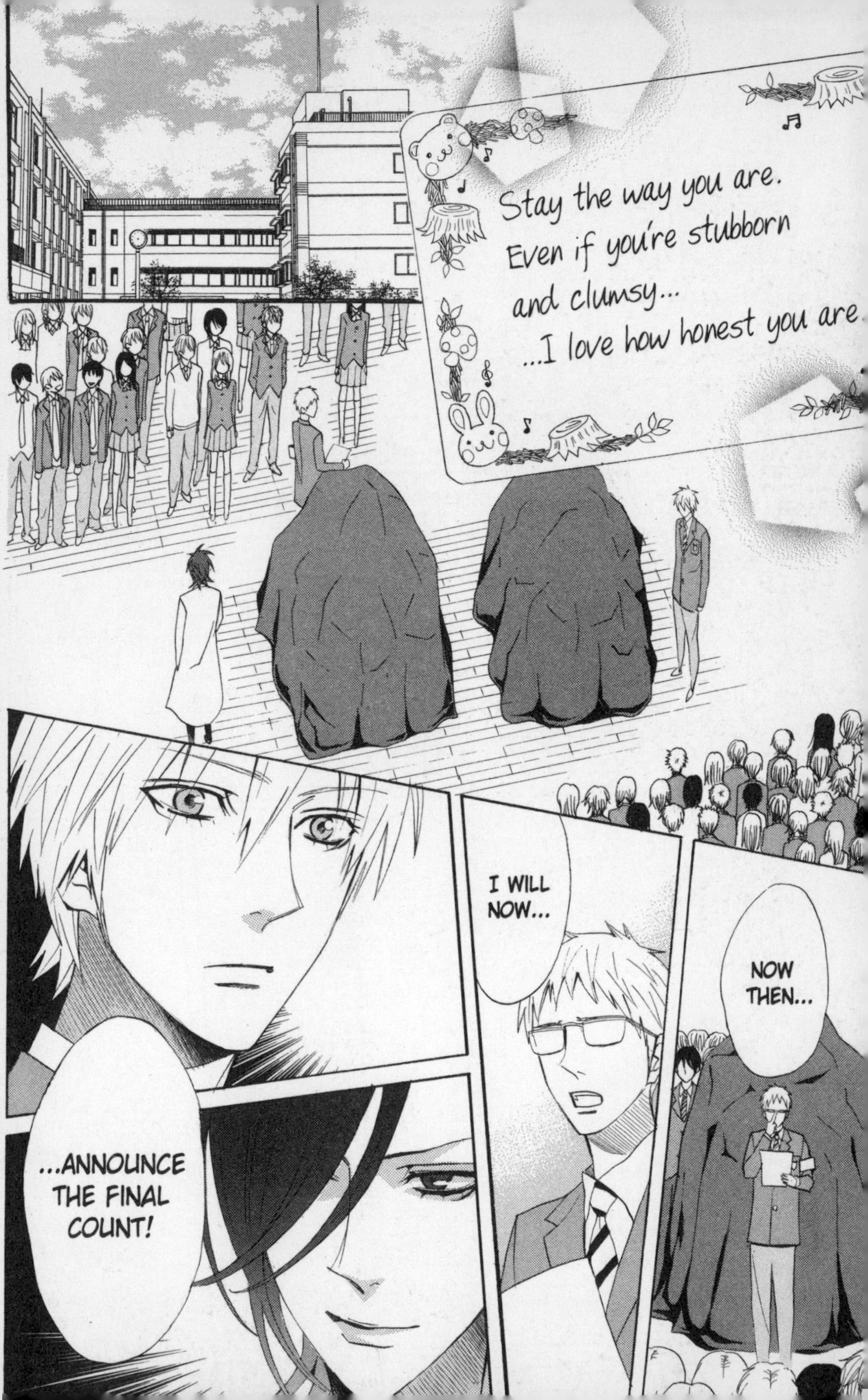
Stay the way you are.
Even if you're stubborn and clumsy...
...I love how honest you are.
NOW THEN...
I WILL NOW...
...ANNOUNCE THE FINAL COUNT!

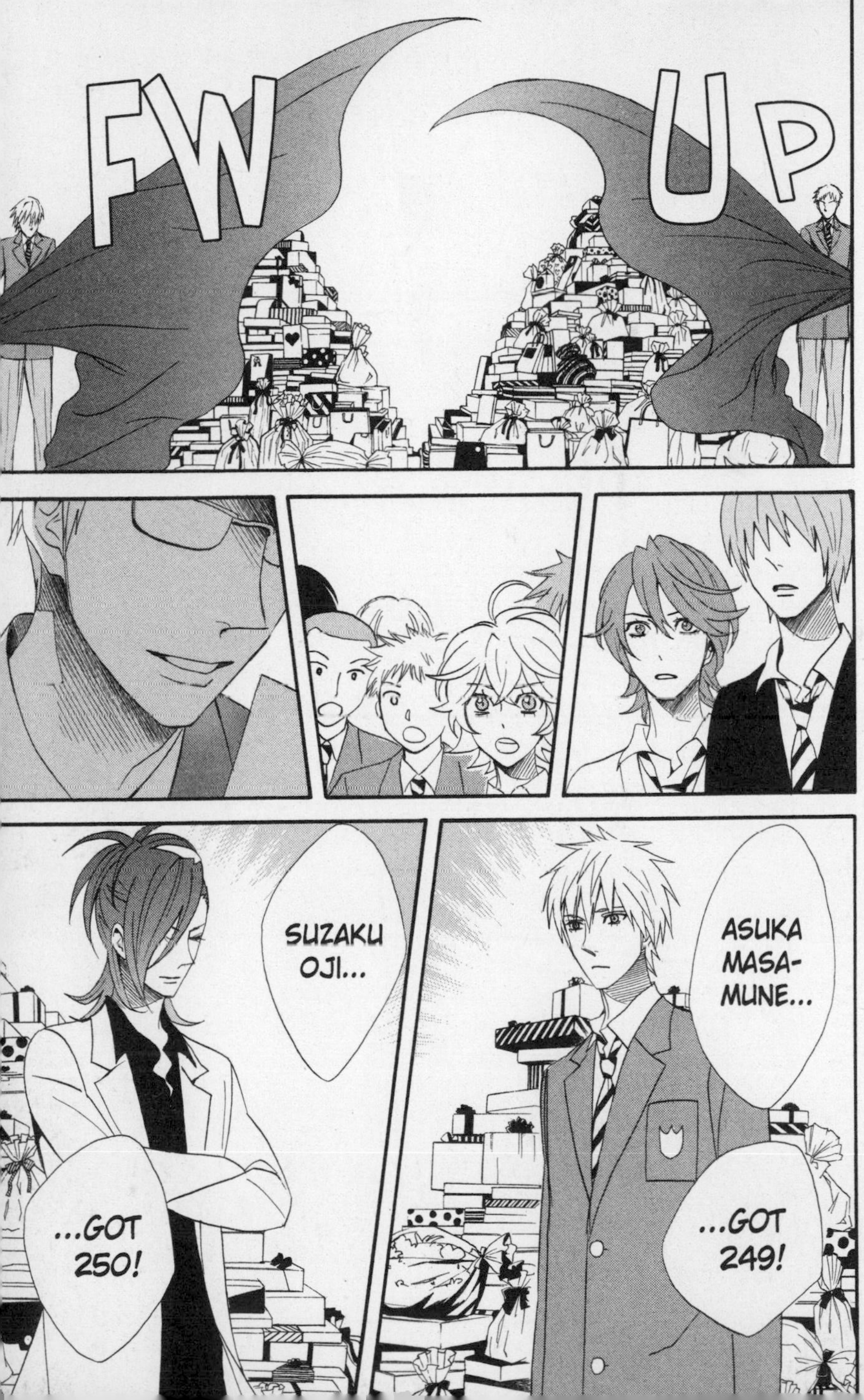
FW UP
ASUKA MASA-MUNE...
...GOT 249!
SUZAKU OJI...
...GOT 250!

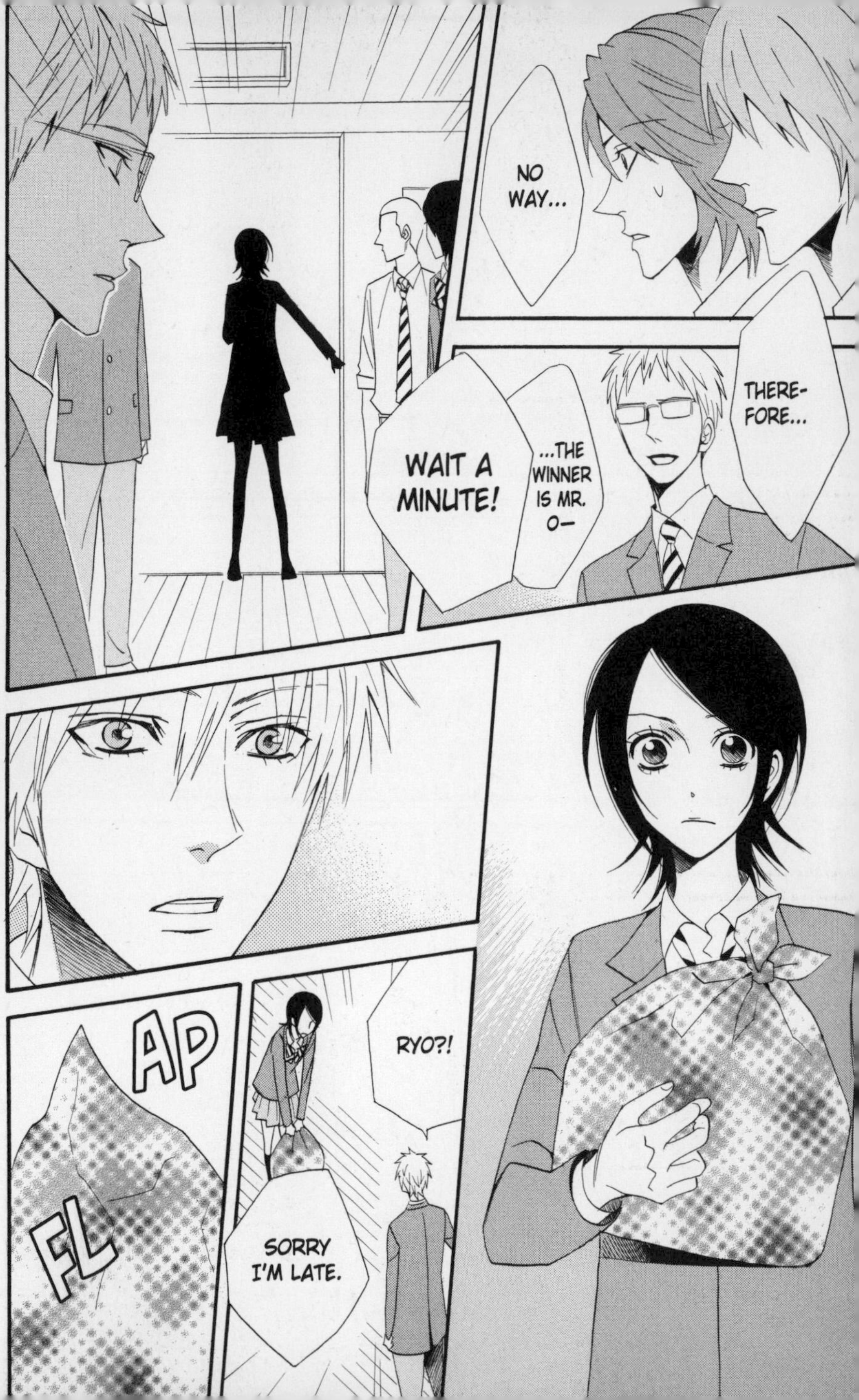

NO WAY...
THERE-FORE...
...THE WINNER IS MR. O—
WAIT A MINUTE!
RYO?!
SORRY I'M LATE.
AP
FL

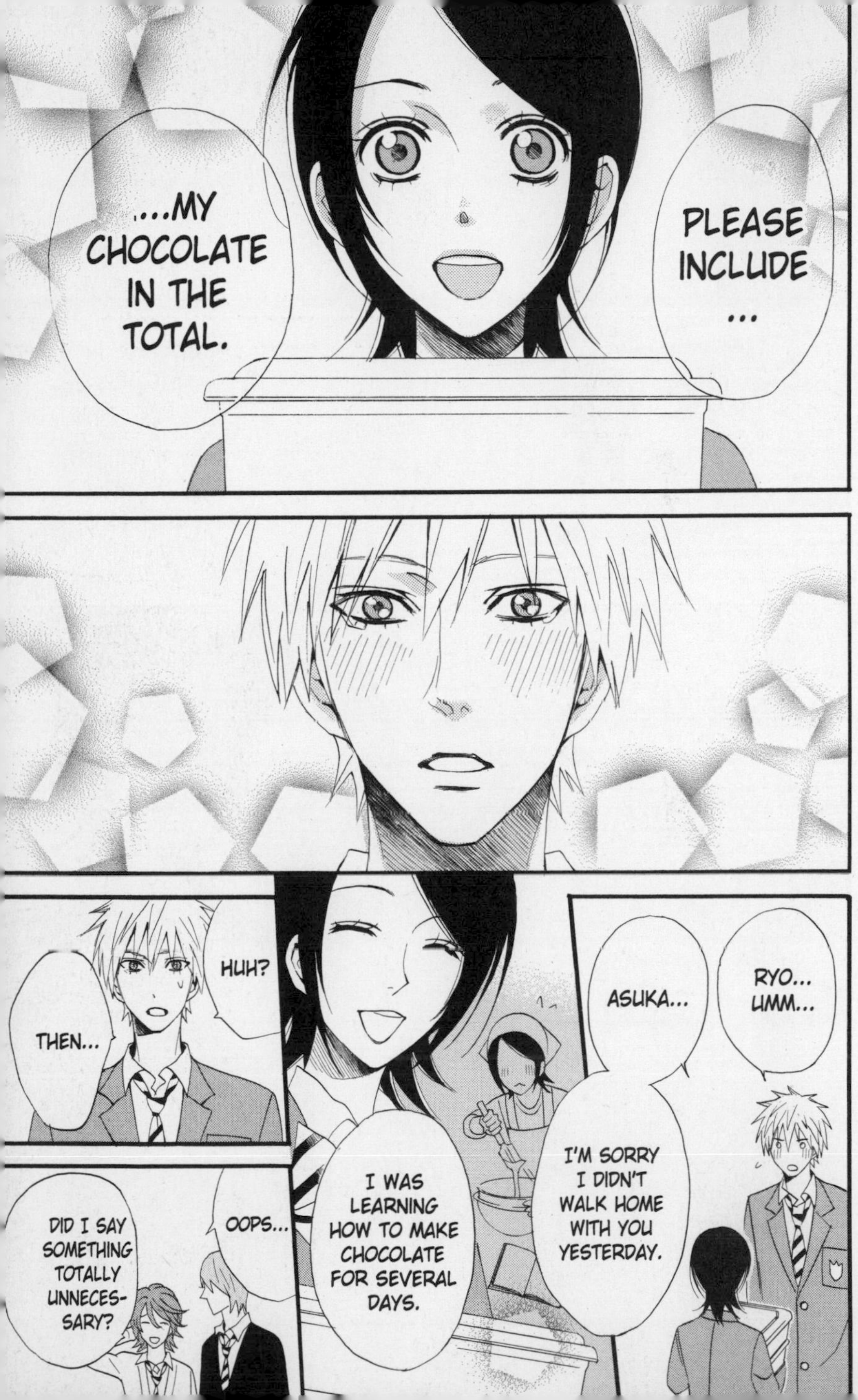
PLEASE INCLUDE ...
....MY CHOCOLATE IN THE TOTAL.
RYO... UMM...
ASUKA...
I'M SORRY I DIDN'T WALK HOME WITH YOU YESTERDAY.
I WAS LEARNING HOW TO MAKE CHOCOLATE FOR SEVERAL DAYS.
HUH?
THEN...
OOPS...
DID I SAY SOMETHING TOTALLY UNNECES-SARY?

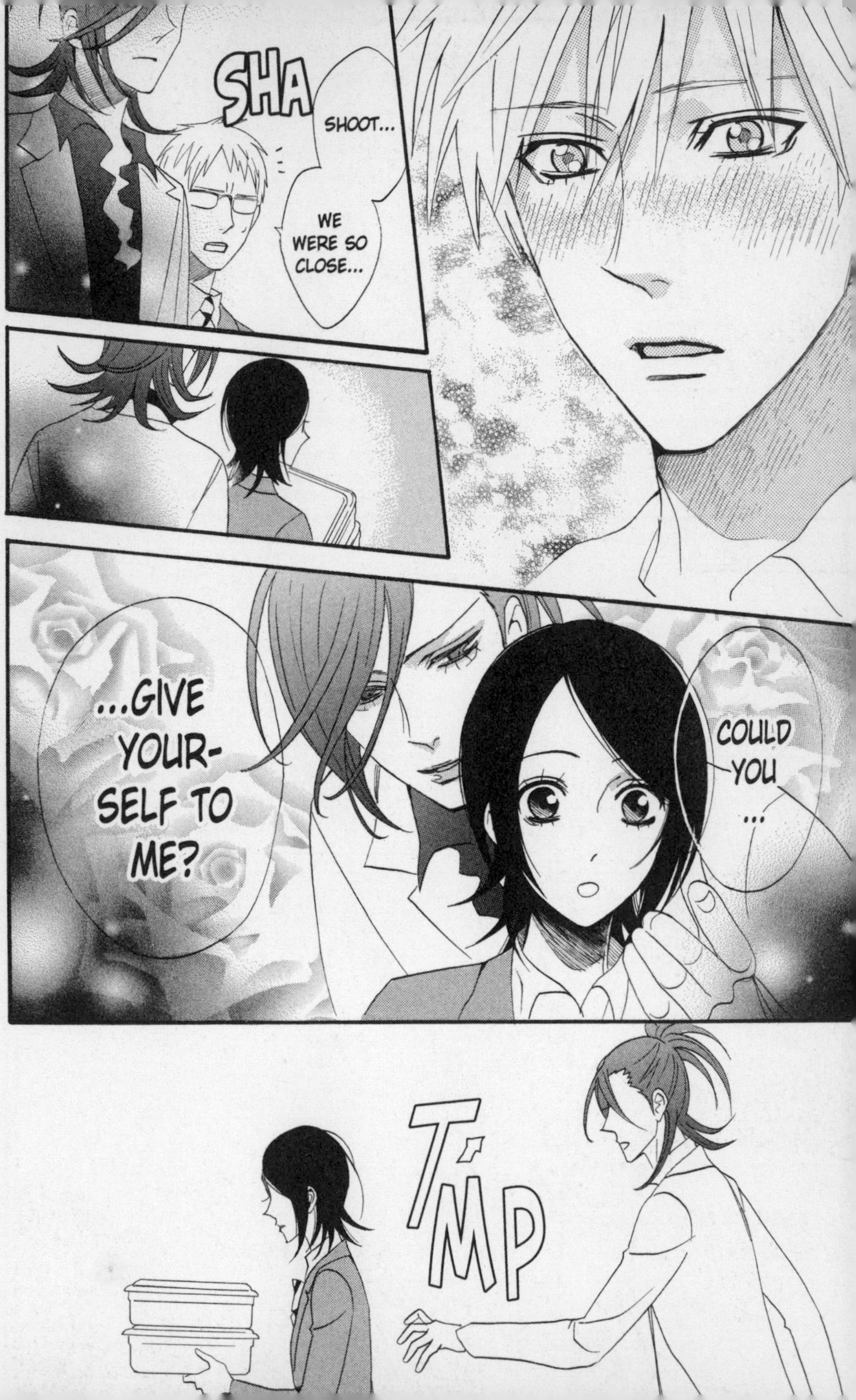
SHA
SHOOT...
WE WERE SO CLOSE...
COULD YOU ...
...GIVE YOUR-SELF TO ME?
TMP

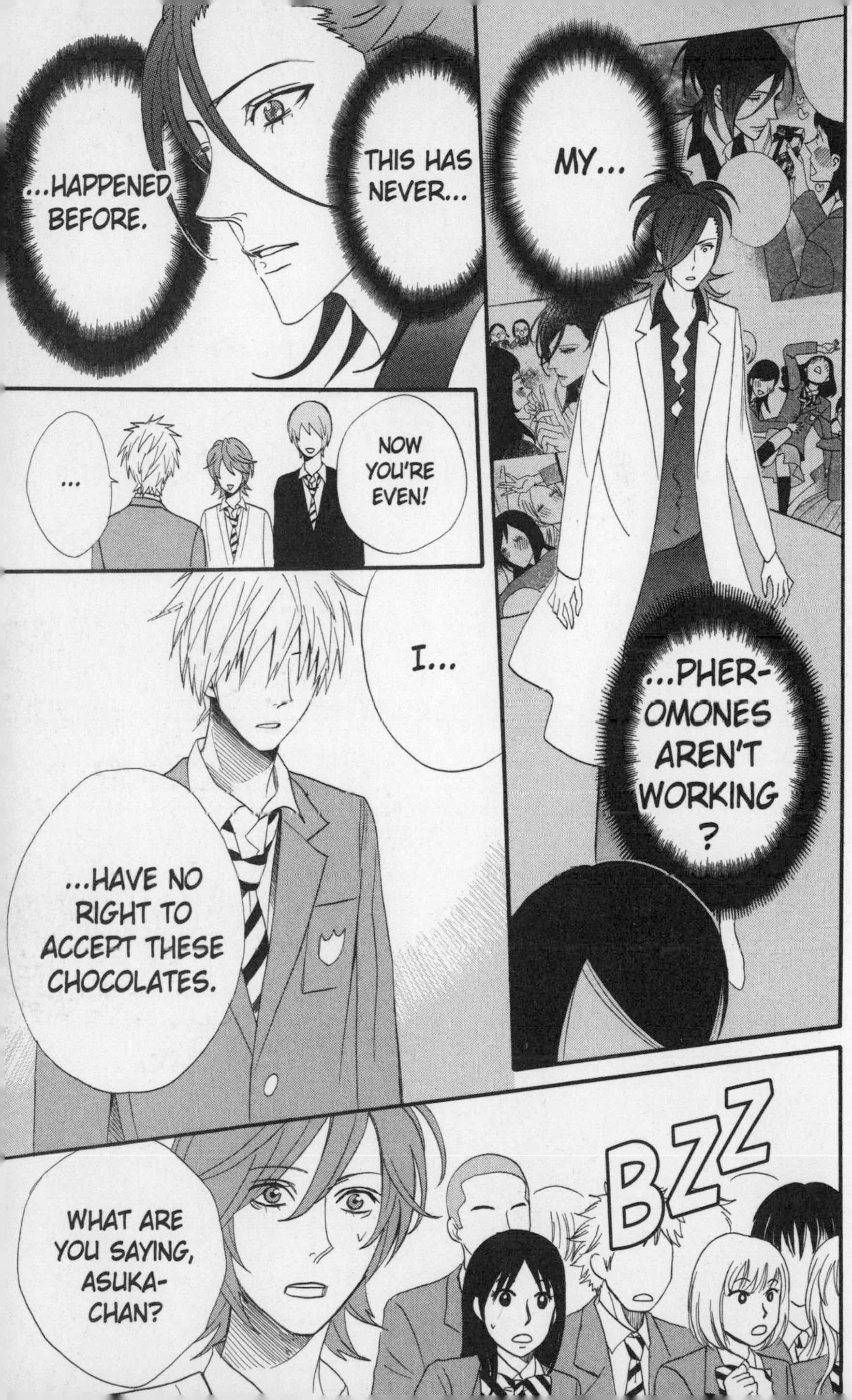
MY...
...PHEROMONES AREN'T WORKING?
THIS HAS NEVER...
...HAPPENED BEFORE.
NOW YOU'RE EVEN!
...
I...
...HAVE NO RIGHT TO ACCEPT THESE CHOCOLATES.
BZZ
WHAT ARE YOU SAYING, ASUKA-CHAN?

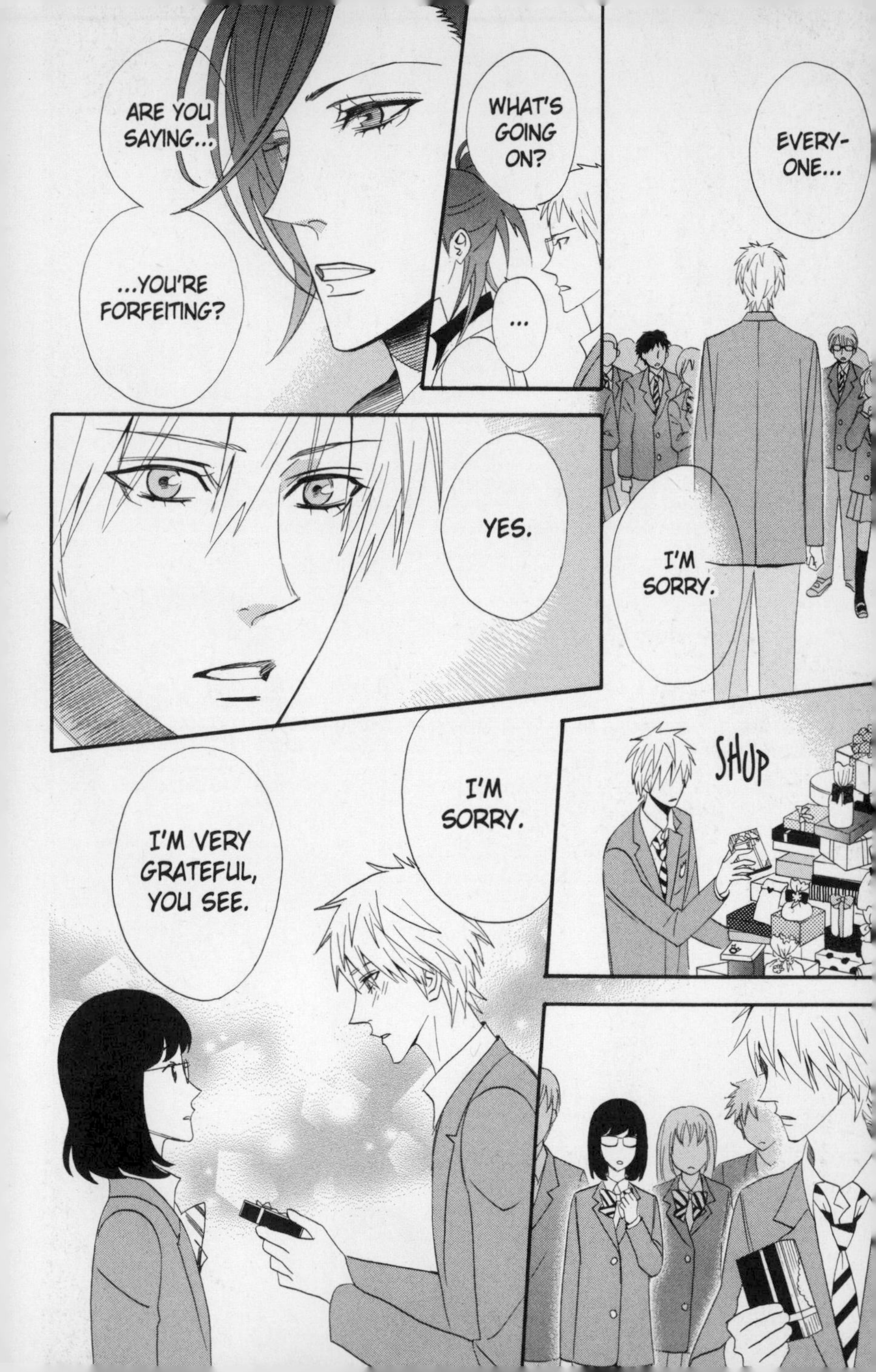
EVERY-ONE...
I'M SORRY.
WHAT'S GOING ON?
...
ARE YOU SAYING...
...YOU'RE FORFEITING?
YES.
SHUP
I'M SORRY.
I'M VERY GRATEFUL, YOU SEE.

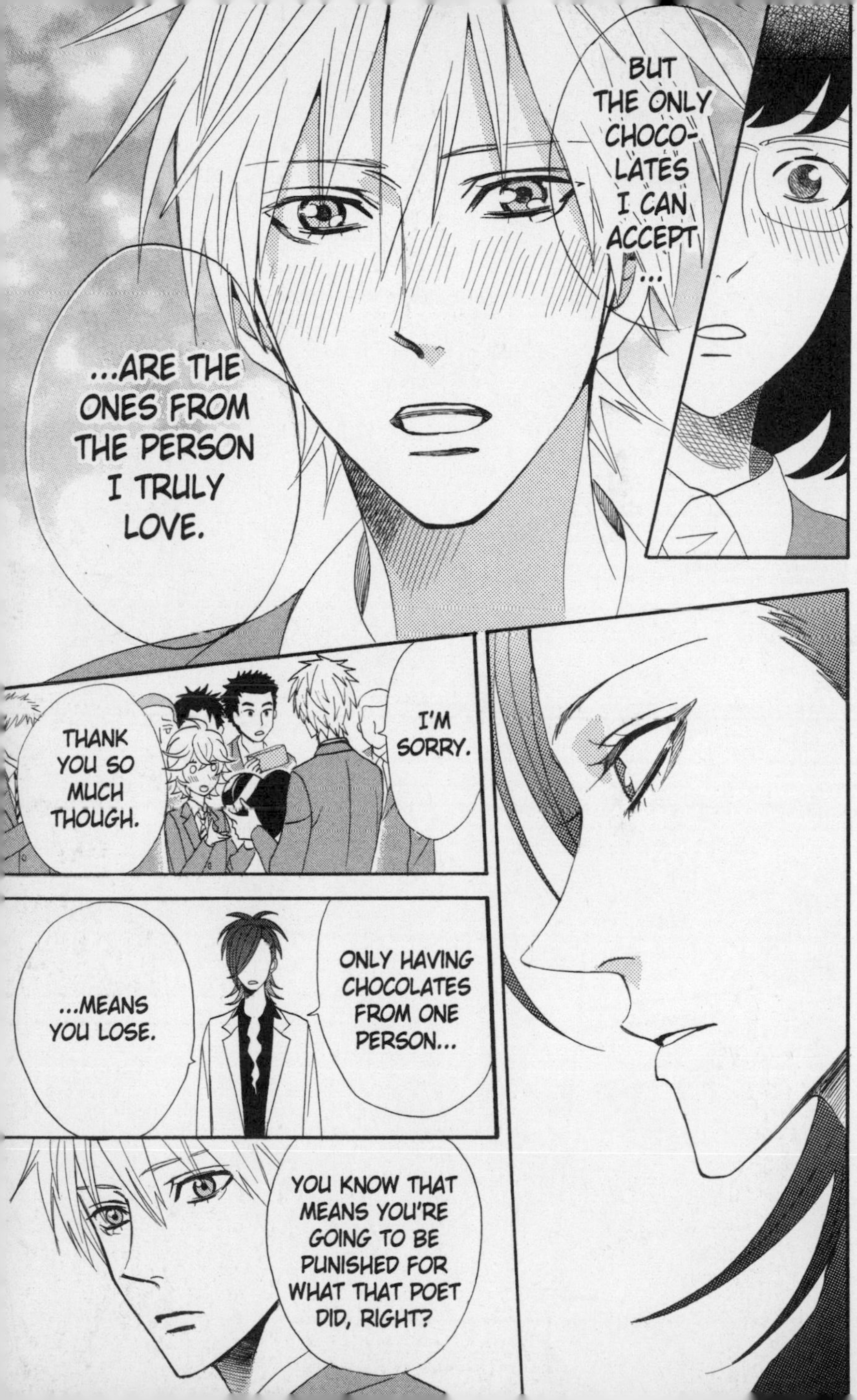
BUT THE ONLY CHOCO-LATES I CAN ACCEPT...
...ARE THE ONES FROM THE PERSON I TRULY LOVE.
I'M SORRY.
THANK YOU SO MUCH THOUGH.
ONLY HAVING CHOCOLATES FROM ONE PERSON...
...MEANS YOU LOSE.
YOU KNOW THAT MEANS YOU'RE GOING TO BE PUNISHED FOR WHAT THAT POET DID, RIGHT?

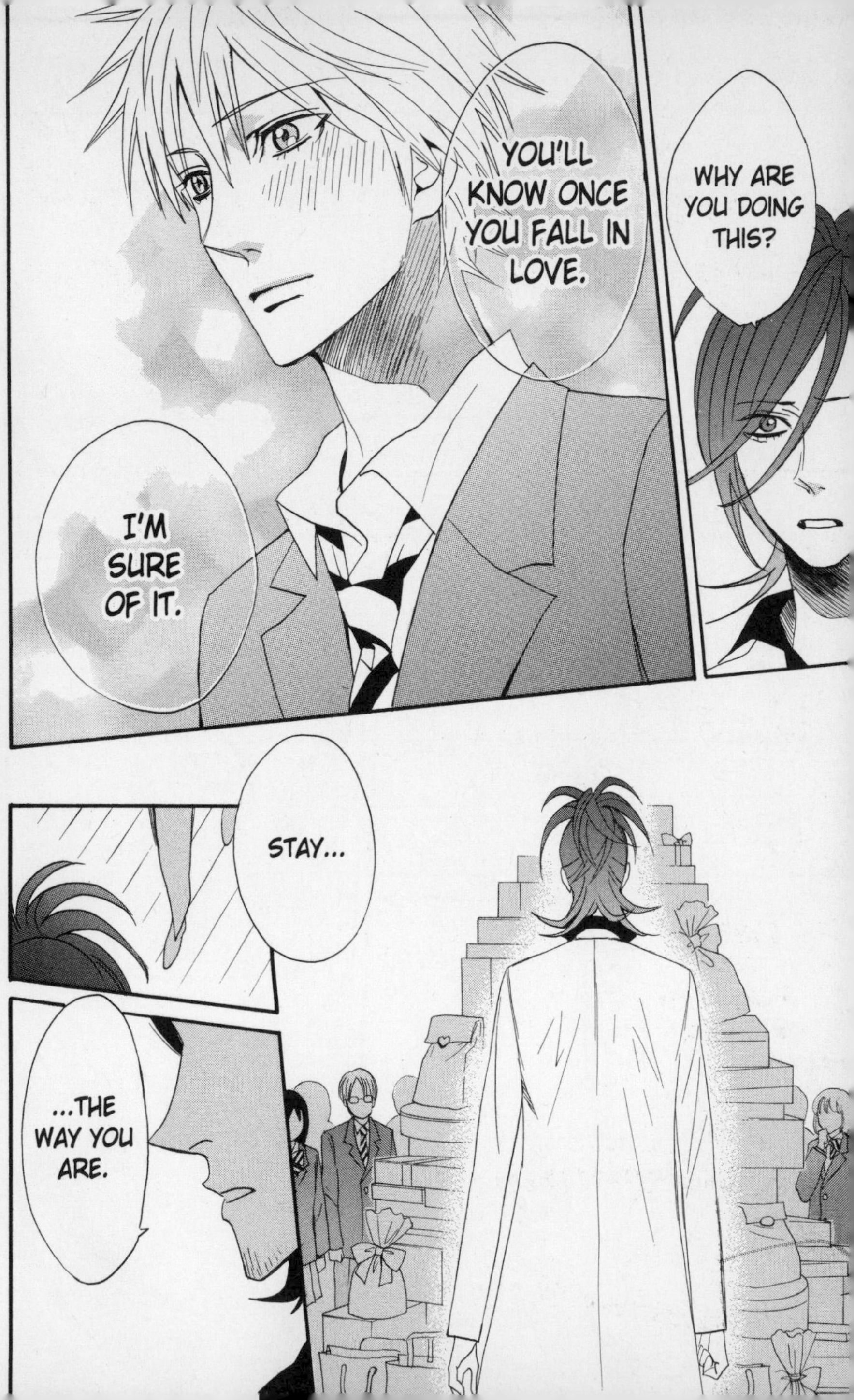
WHY ARE YOU DOING THIS?
YOU'LL KNOW ONCE YOU FALL IN LOVE.
I'M SURE OF IT.
STAY...
...THE WAY YOU ARE.

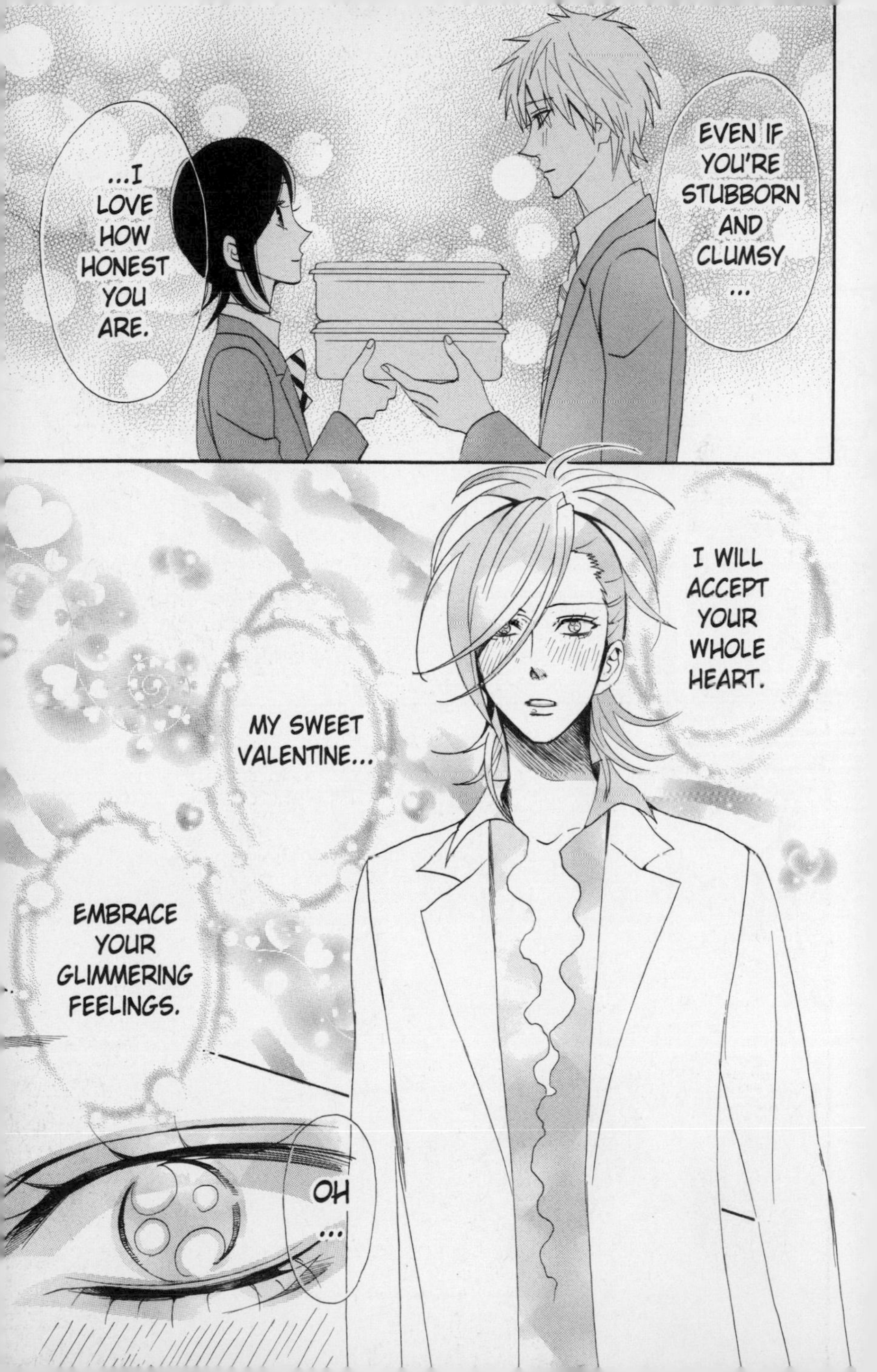
EVEN IF YOU'RE STUBBORN AND CLUMSY...
...I LOVE HOW HONEST YOU ARE.
I WILL ACCEPT YOUR WHOLE HEART.
MY SWEET VALENTINE...
EMBRACE YOUR GLIMMERING FEELINGS.
OH...

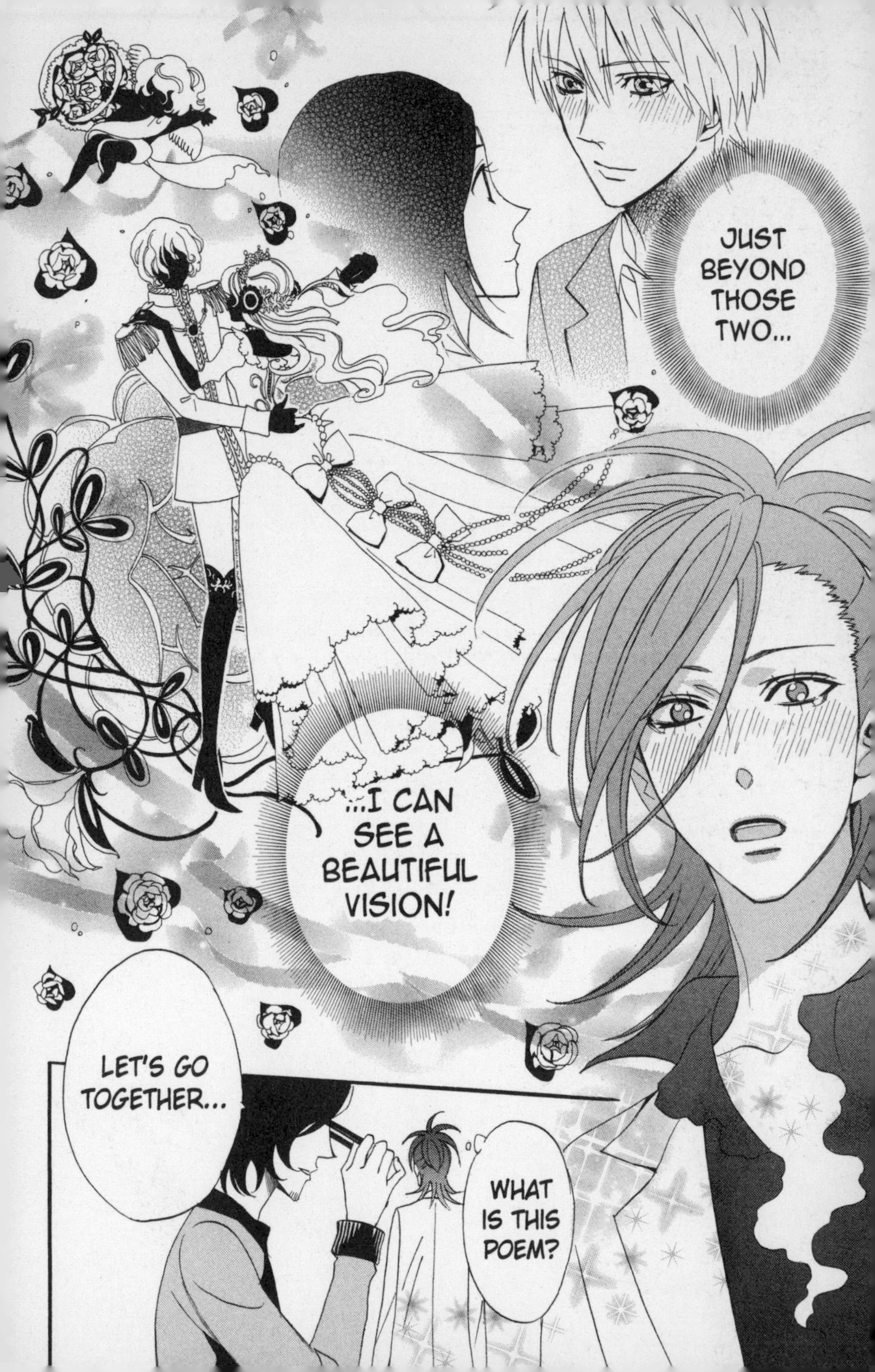
JUST BEYOND THOSE TWO...
...I CAN SEE A BEAUTIFUL VISION!
LET'S GO TOGETHER...
WHAT IS THIS POEM?

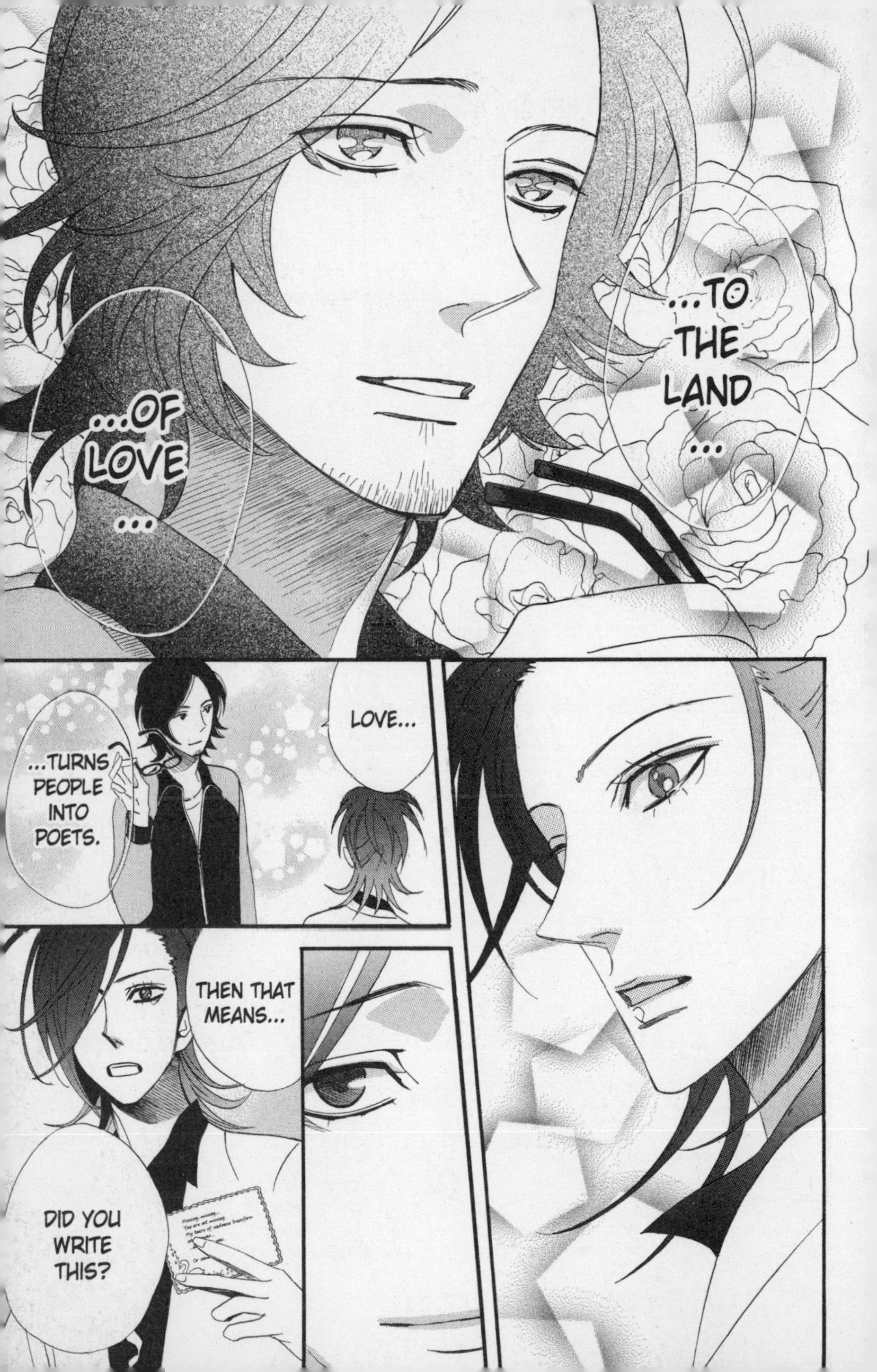
...TO THE LAND...
...OF LOVE...
LOVE...
...TURNS PEOPLE INTO POETS.
THEN THAT MEANS...
DID YOU WRITE THIS?

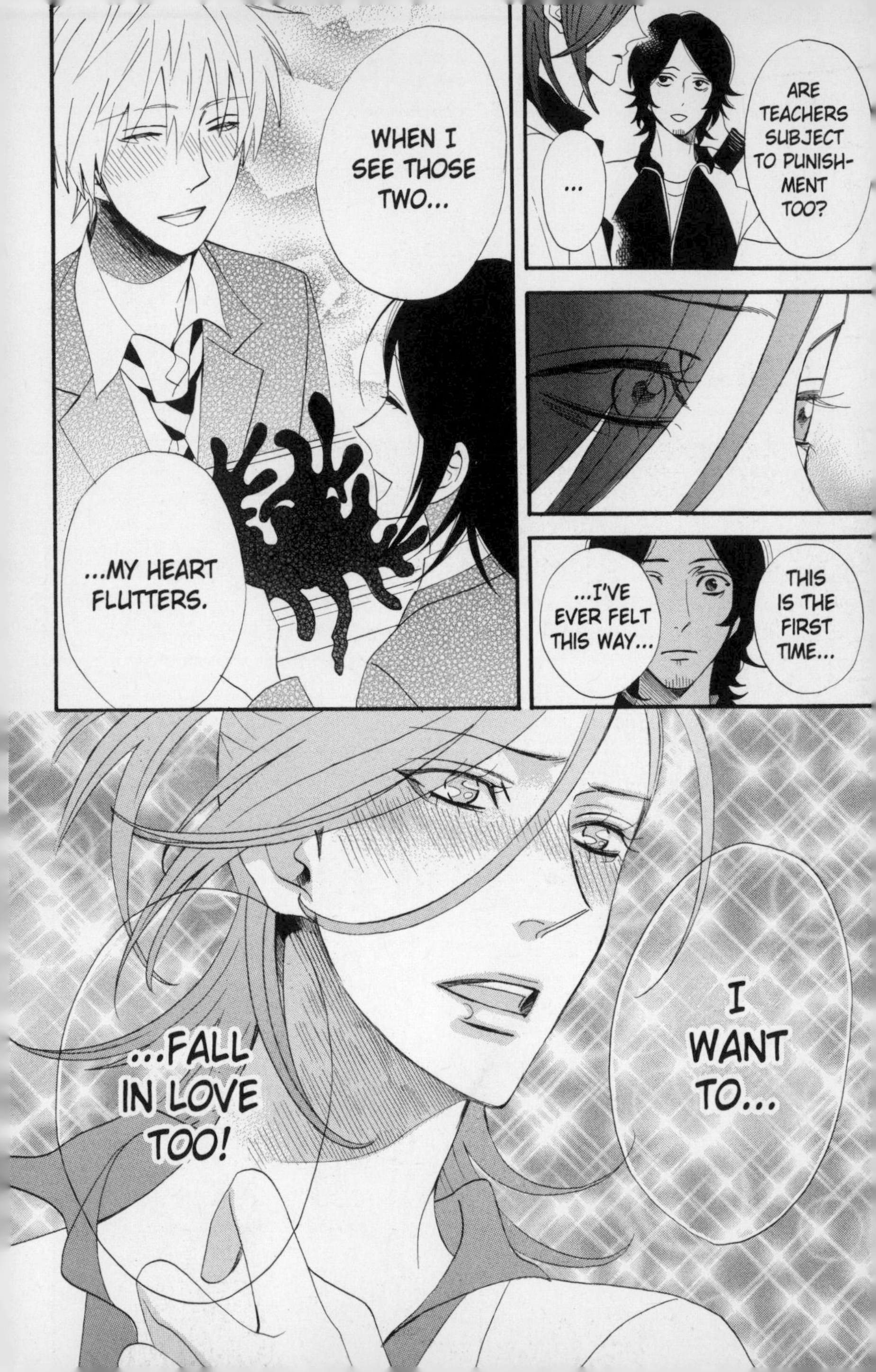
ARE TEACHERS SUBJECT TO PUNISHMENT TOO?
...
THIS IS THE FIRST TIME...
...I'VE EVER FELT THIS WAY...
WHEN I SEE THOSE TWO...
...MY HEART FLUTTERS.
I WANT TO...
...FALL IN LOVE TOO!

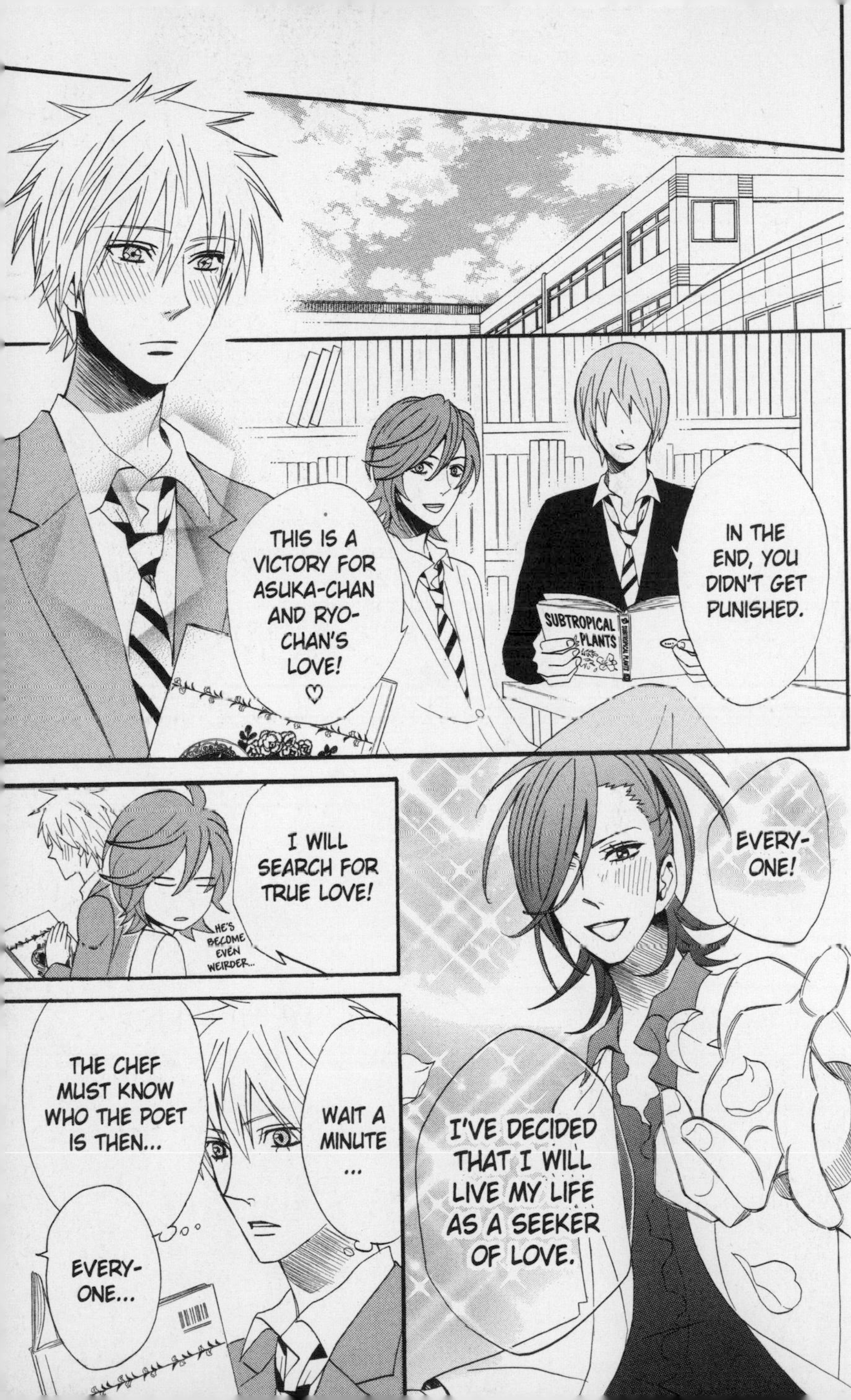
IN THE END, YOU DIDN'T GET PUNISHED.
SUBTROPICAL PLANTS
THIS IS A VICTORY FOR ASUKA-CHAN AND RYO-CHAN'S LOVE! ♡
EVERY-ONE!
I'VE DECIDED THAT I WILL LIVE MY LIFE AS A SEEKER OF LOVE.
I WILL SEARCH FOR TRUE LOVE!
HE'S BECOME EVEN WEIRDER...
WAIT A MINUTE ...
THE CHEF MUST KNOW WHO THE POET IS THEN...
EVERY-ONE...

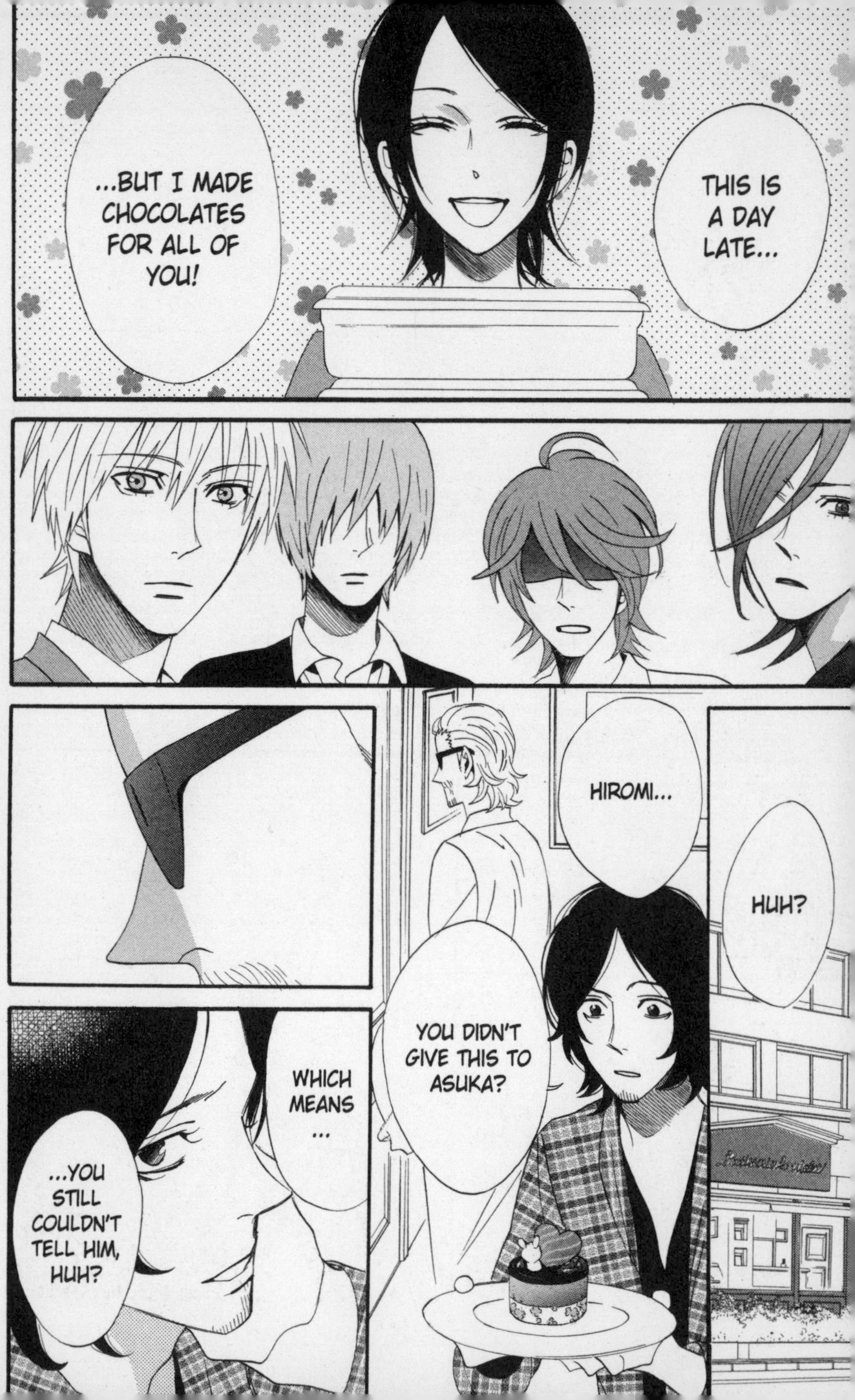
THIS IS A DAY LATE...
...BUT I MADE CHOCOLATES FOR ALL OF YOU!
HIROMI...
HUH?
YOU DIDN'T GIVE THIS TO ASUKA?
WHICH MEANS ...
...YOU STILL COULDN'T TELL HIM, HUH?

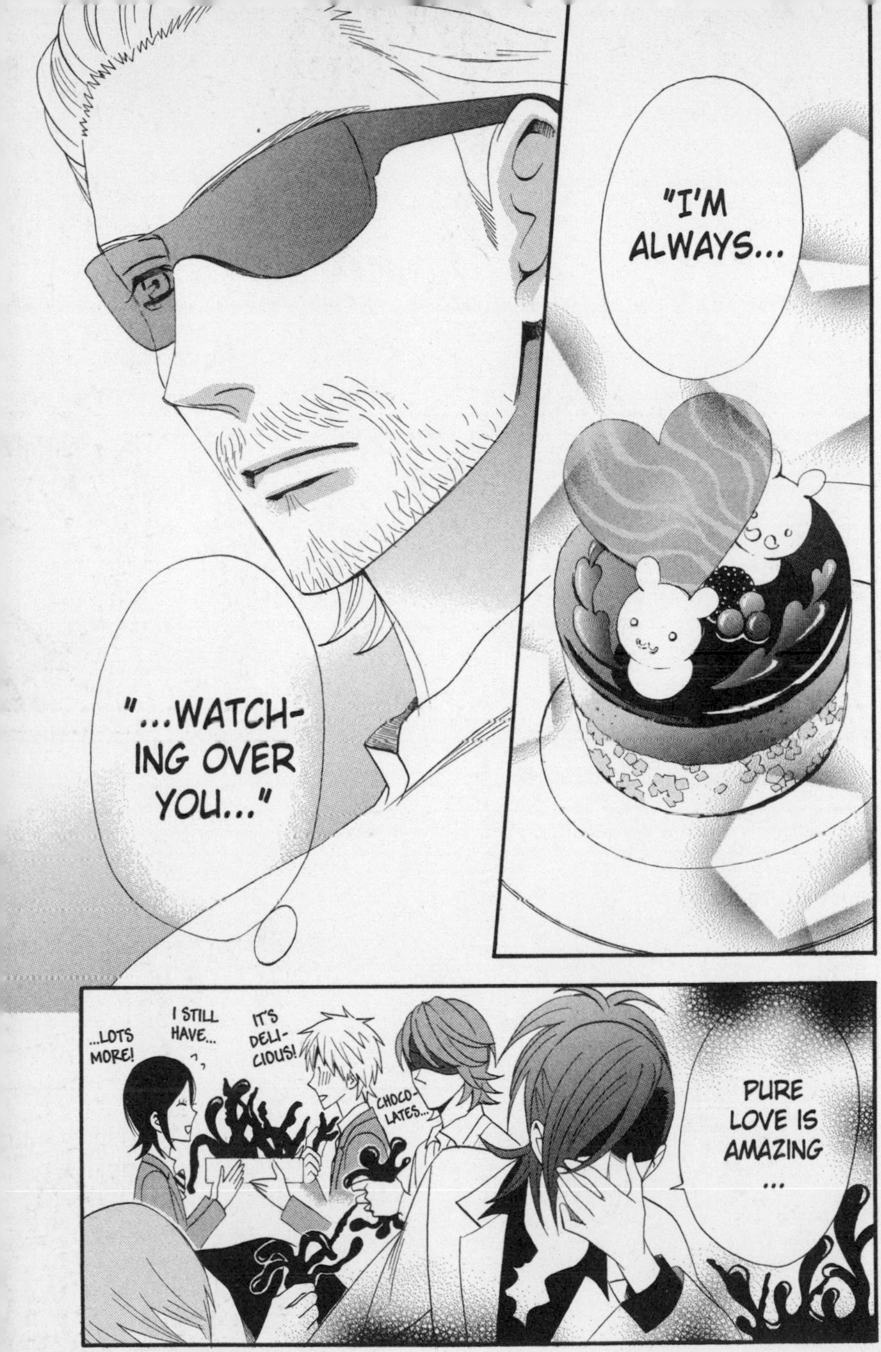
"I'M ALWAYS...
"...WATCHING OVER YOU..."
PURE LOVE IS AMAZING...
CHOCOLATES...
IT'S DELICIOUS!
I STILL HAVE...
...LOTS MORE!

OTOMEN

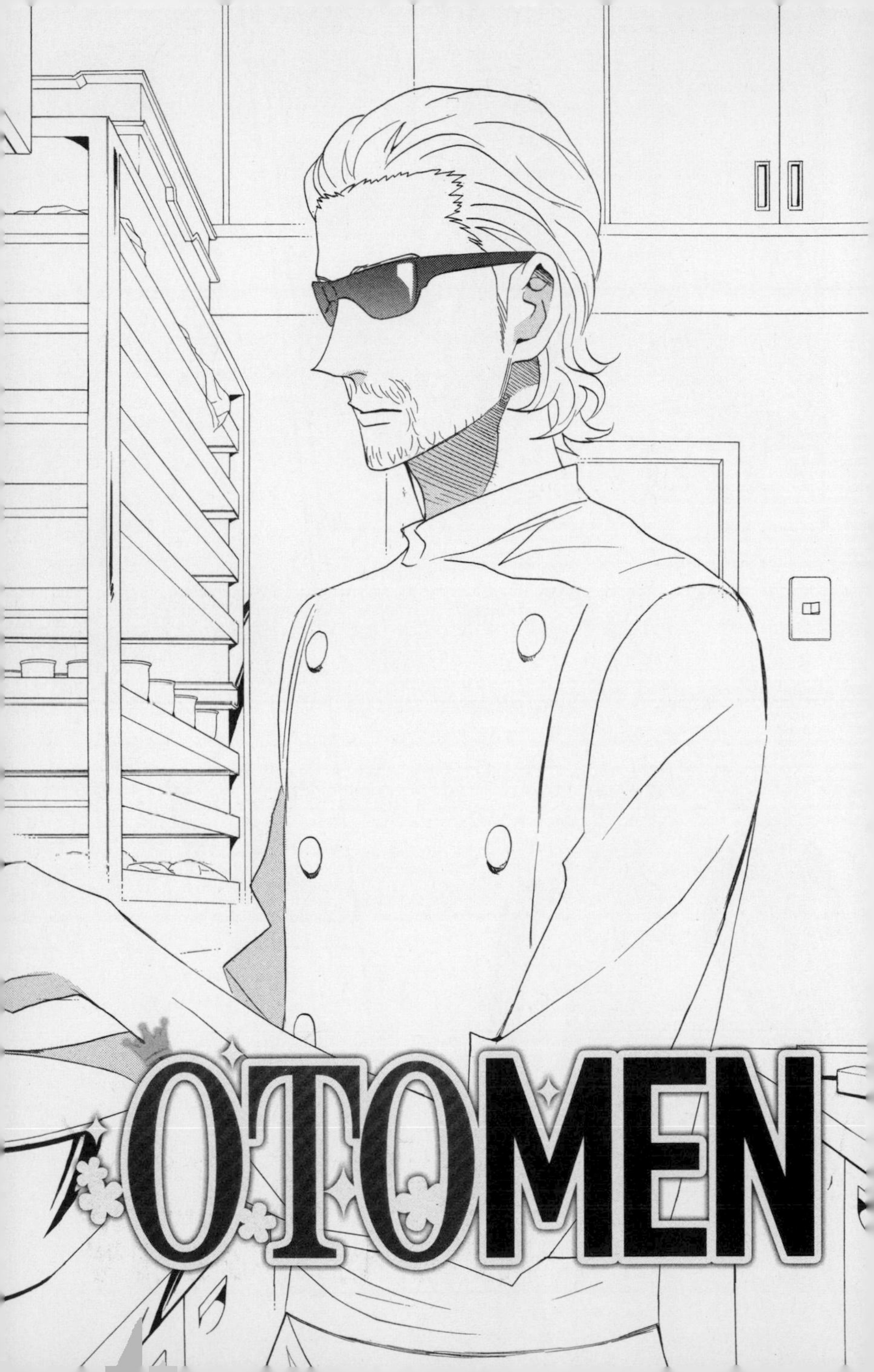
OTOMEN

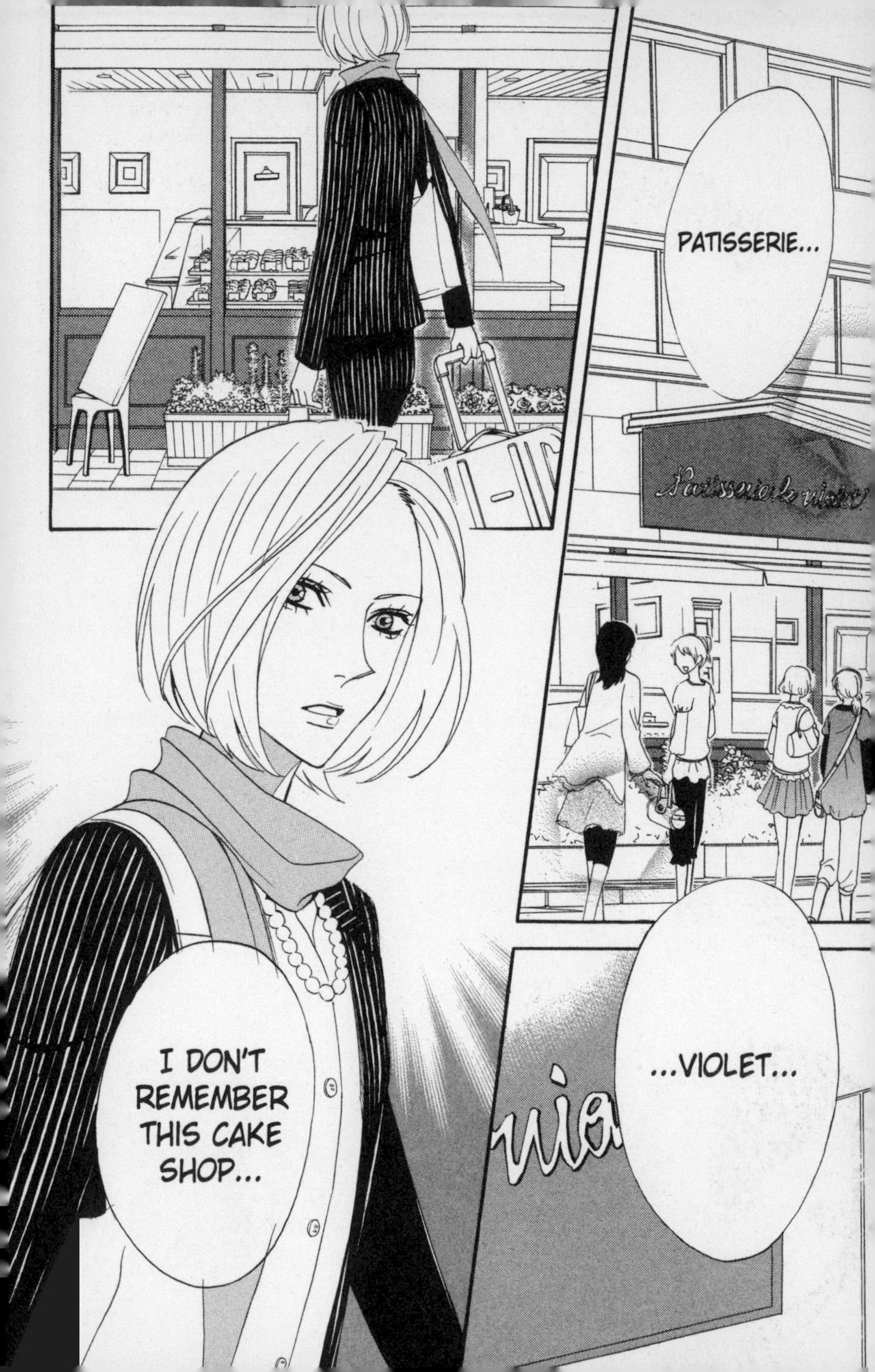
PATISSERIE...
...VIOLET...
I DON'T REMEMBER THIS CAKE SHOP...

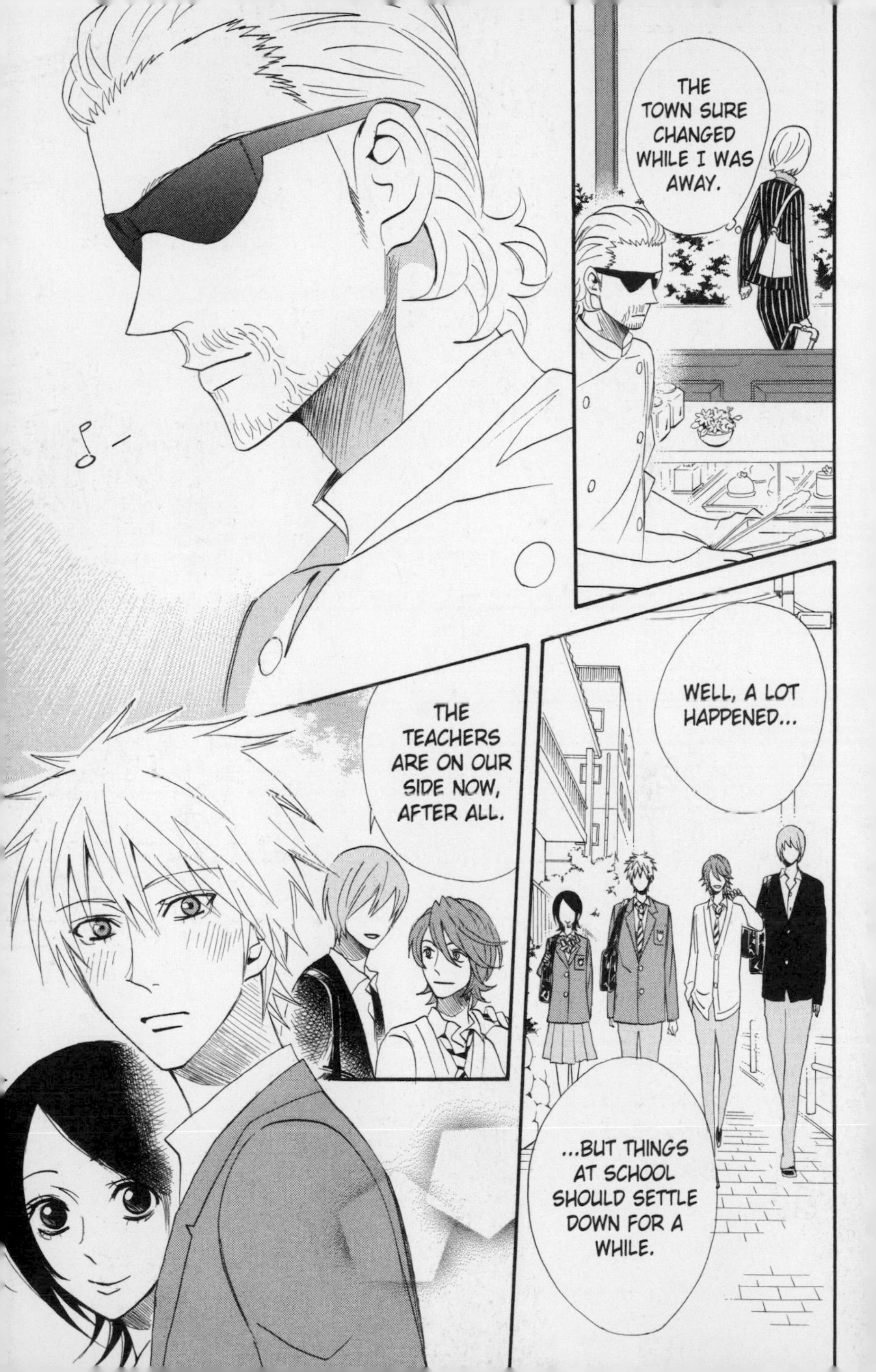
THE TOWN SURE CHANGED WHILE I WAS AWAY.
WELL, A LOT HAPPENED...
...BUT THINGS AT SCHOOL SHOULD SETTLE DOWN FOR A WHILE.
THE TEACHERS ARE ON OUR SIDE NOW, AFTER ALL.

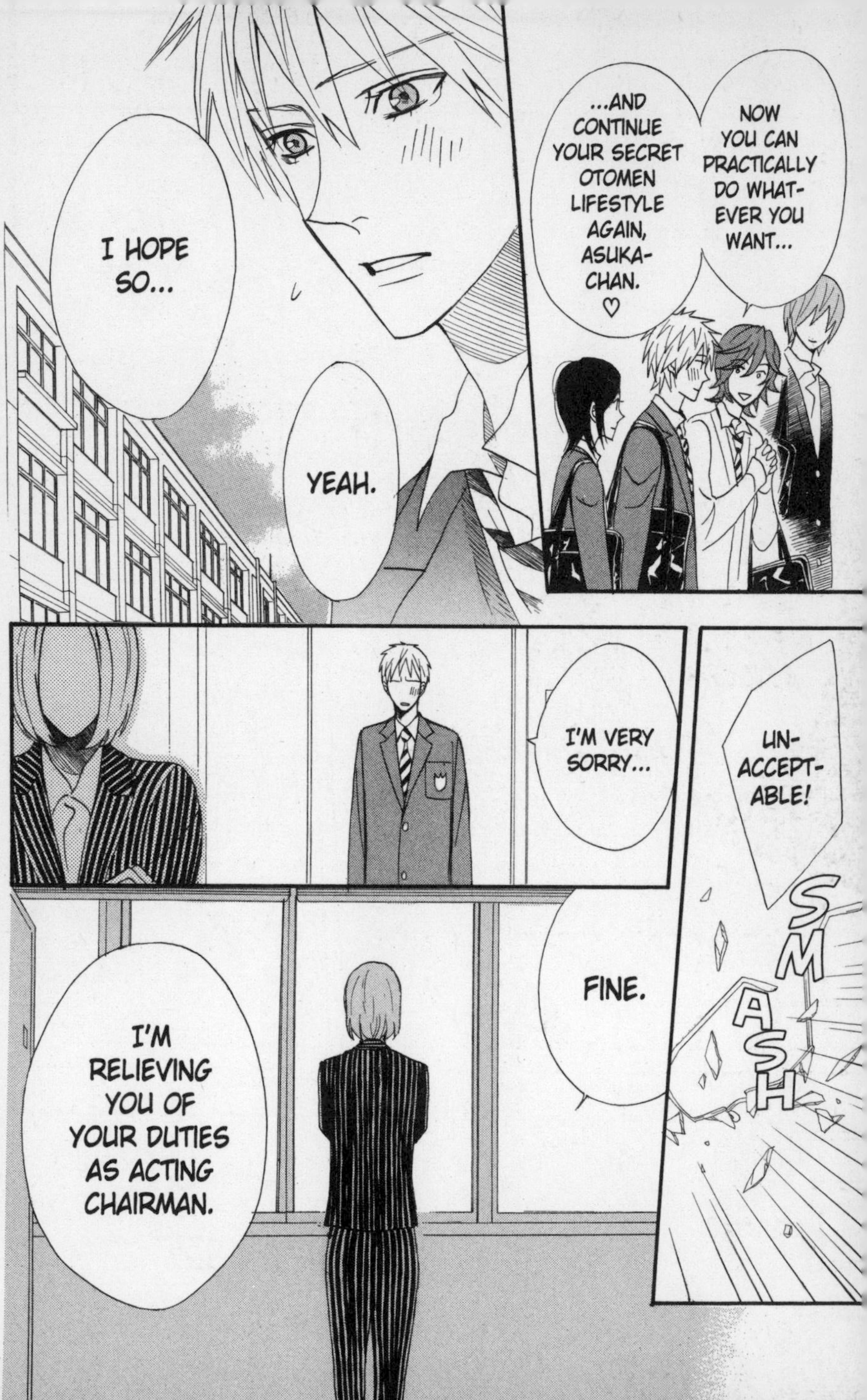
NOW YOU CAN PRACTICALLY DO WHAT-EVER YOU WANT...
...AND CONTINUE YOUR SECRET OTOMEN LIFESTYLE AGAIN, ASUKA-CHAN. ♡
YEAH.
I HOPE SO...
UN-ACCEPT-ABLE!
SMASH
I'M VERY SORRY...
FINE.
I'M RELIEVING YOU OF YOUR DUTIES AS ACTING CHAIRMAN.

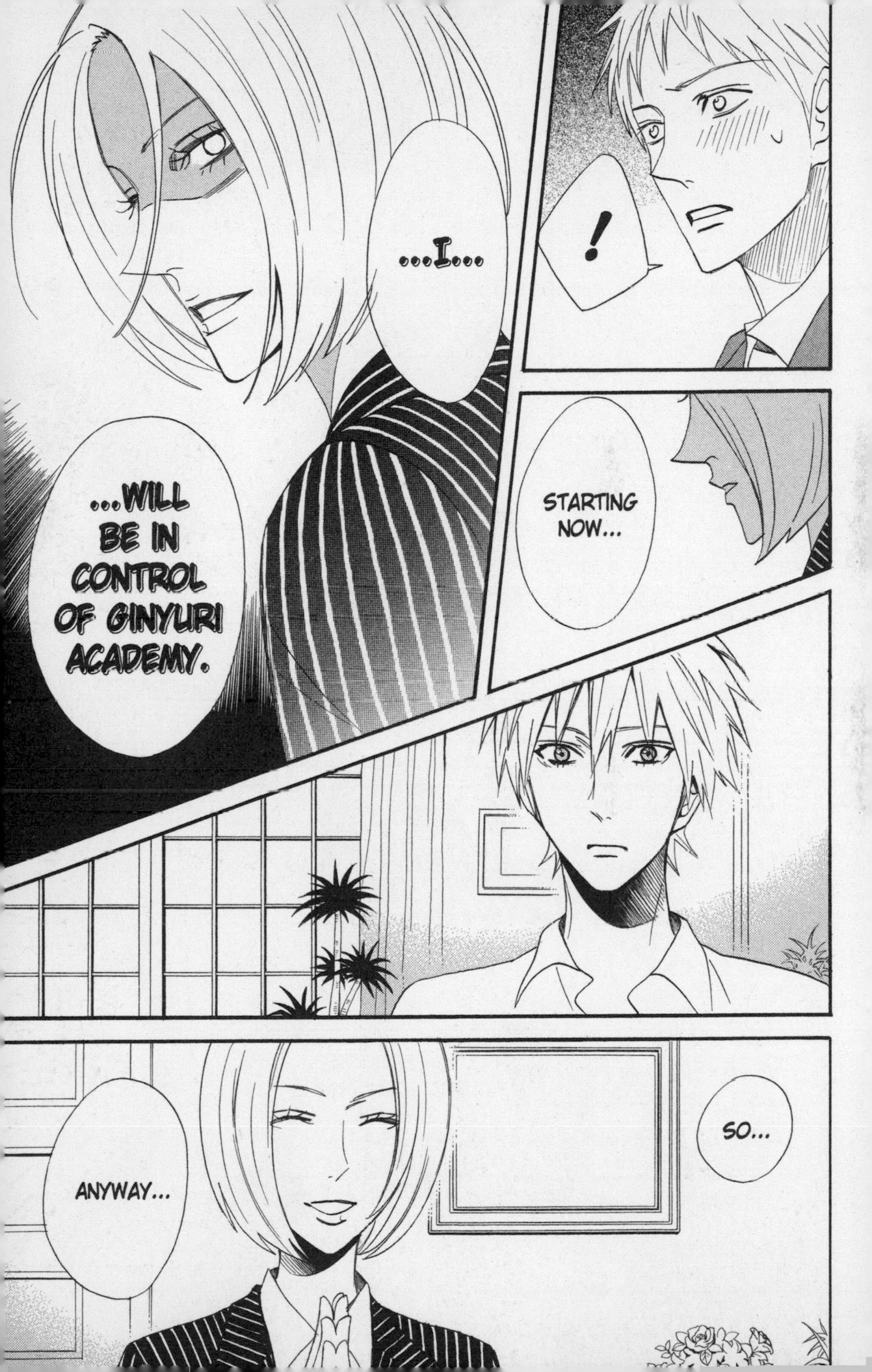
!
STARTING NOW...
...I...
...WILL BE IN CONTROL OF GINYURI ACADEMY.
SO...
ANYWAY...

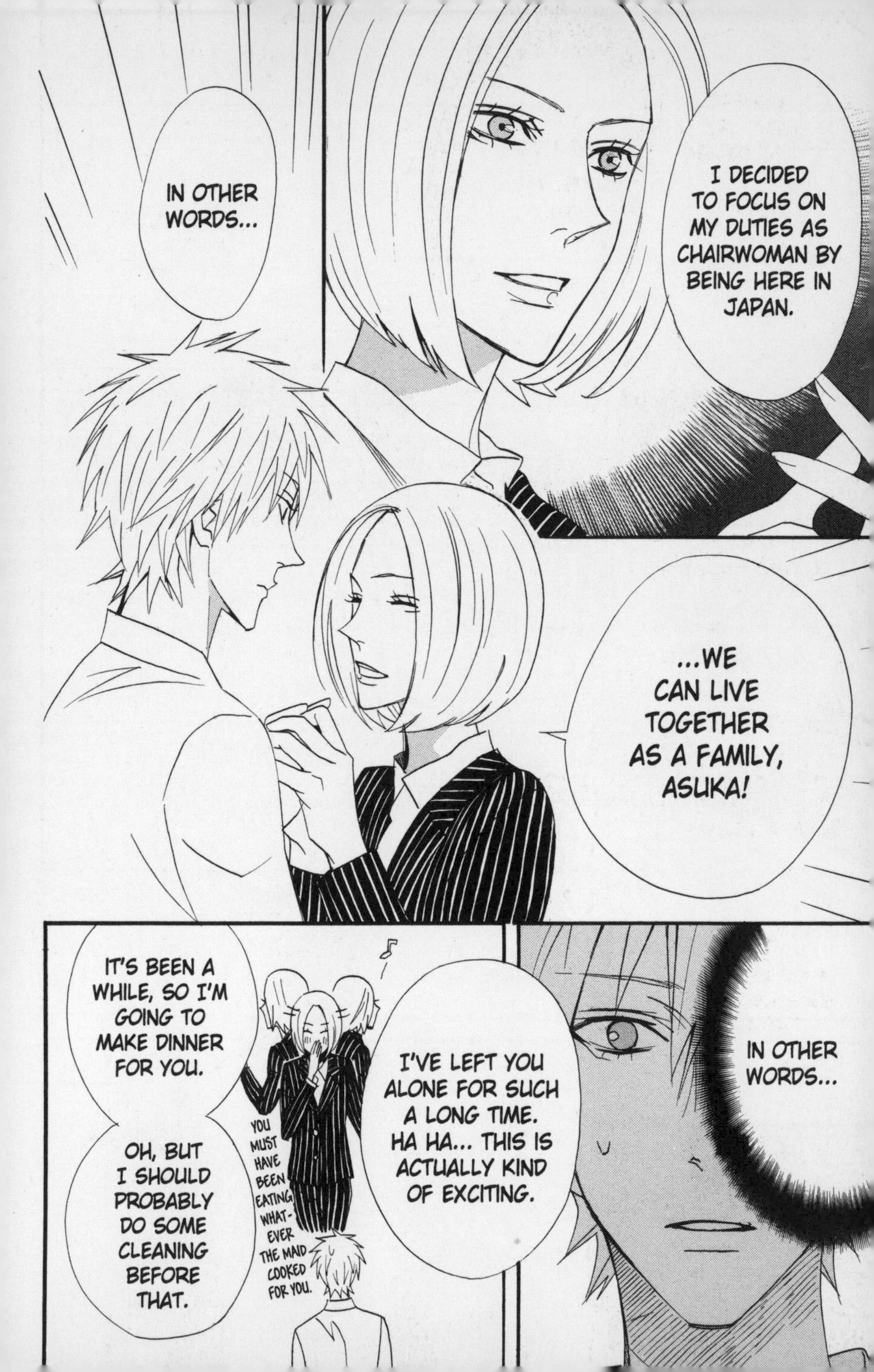
I DECIDED TO FOCUS ON MY DUTIES AS CHAIRWOMAN BY BEING HERE IN JAPAN.
IN OTHER WORDS...
...WE CAN LIVE TOGETHER AS A FAMILY, ASUKA!
IN OTHER WORDS...
I'VE LEFT YOU ALONE FOR SUCH A LONG TIME. HA HA... THIS IS ACTUALLY KIND OF EXCITING.
YOU MUST HAVE BEEN EATING WHATEVER THE MAID COOKED FOR YOU.
IT'S BEEN A WHILE, SO I'M GOING TO MAKE DINNER FOR YOU.
OH, BUT I SHOULD PROBABLY DO SOME CLEANING BEFORE THAT.

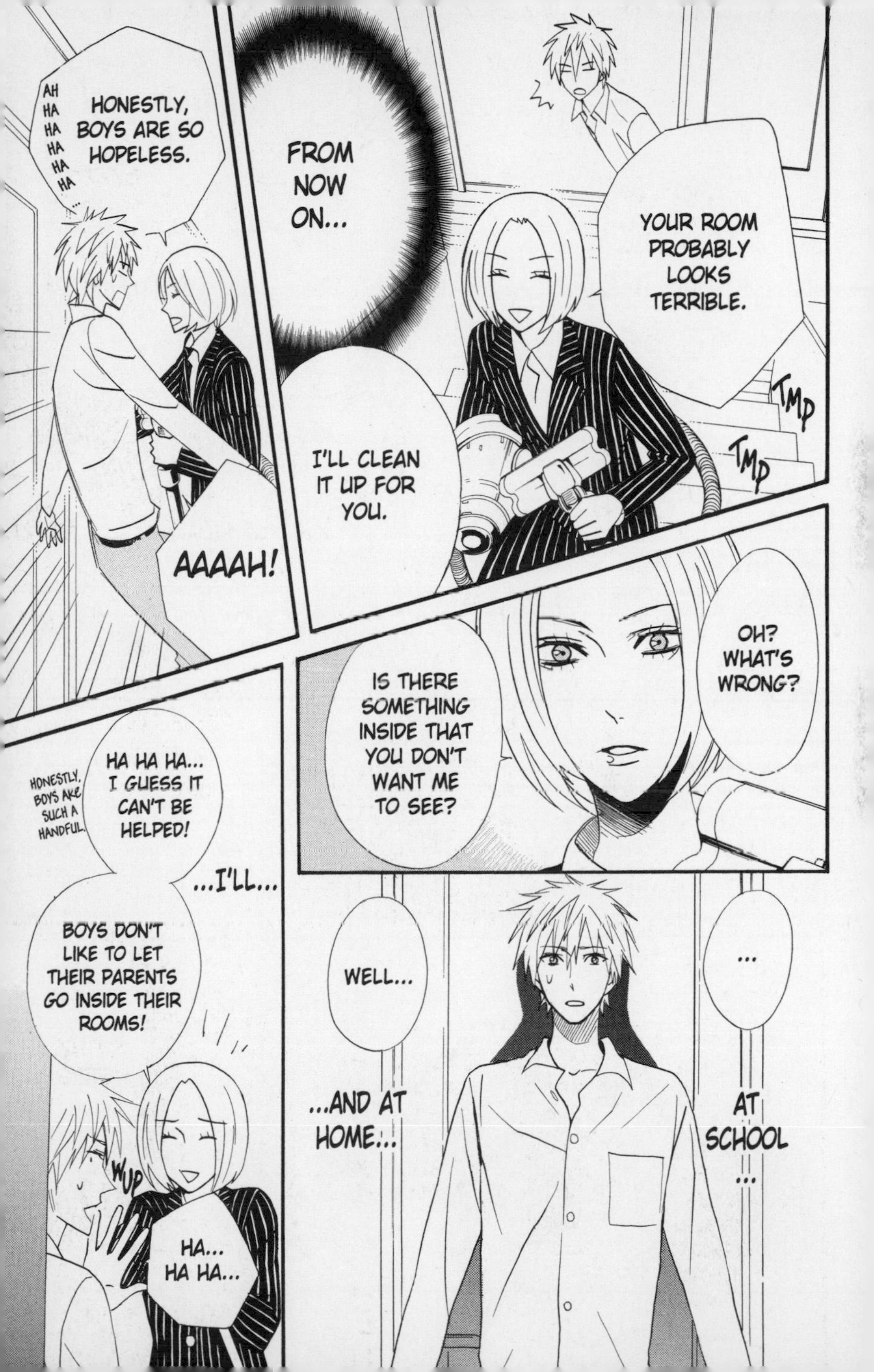
YOUR ROOM PROBABLY LOOKS TERRIBLE.
TMP
TMP
I'LL CLEAN IT UP FOR YOU.
FROM NOW ON...
HONESTLY, BOYS ARE SO HOPELESS.
AH HA HA HA HA HA...
AAAAH!
OH? WHAT'S WRONG?
IS THERE SOMETHING INSIDE THAT YOU DON'T WANT ME TO SEE?
...
AT SCHOOL...
WELL...
...AND AT HOME...
HA HA HA... I GUESS IT CAN'T BE HELPED!
HONESTLY, BOYS ARE SUCH A HANDFUL.
...I'LL...
BOYS DON'T LIKE TO LET THEIR PARENTS GO INSIDE THEIR ROOMS!
WUP
HA... HA HA...

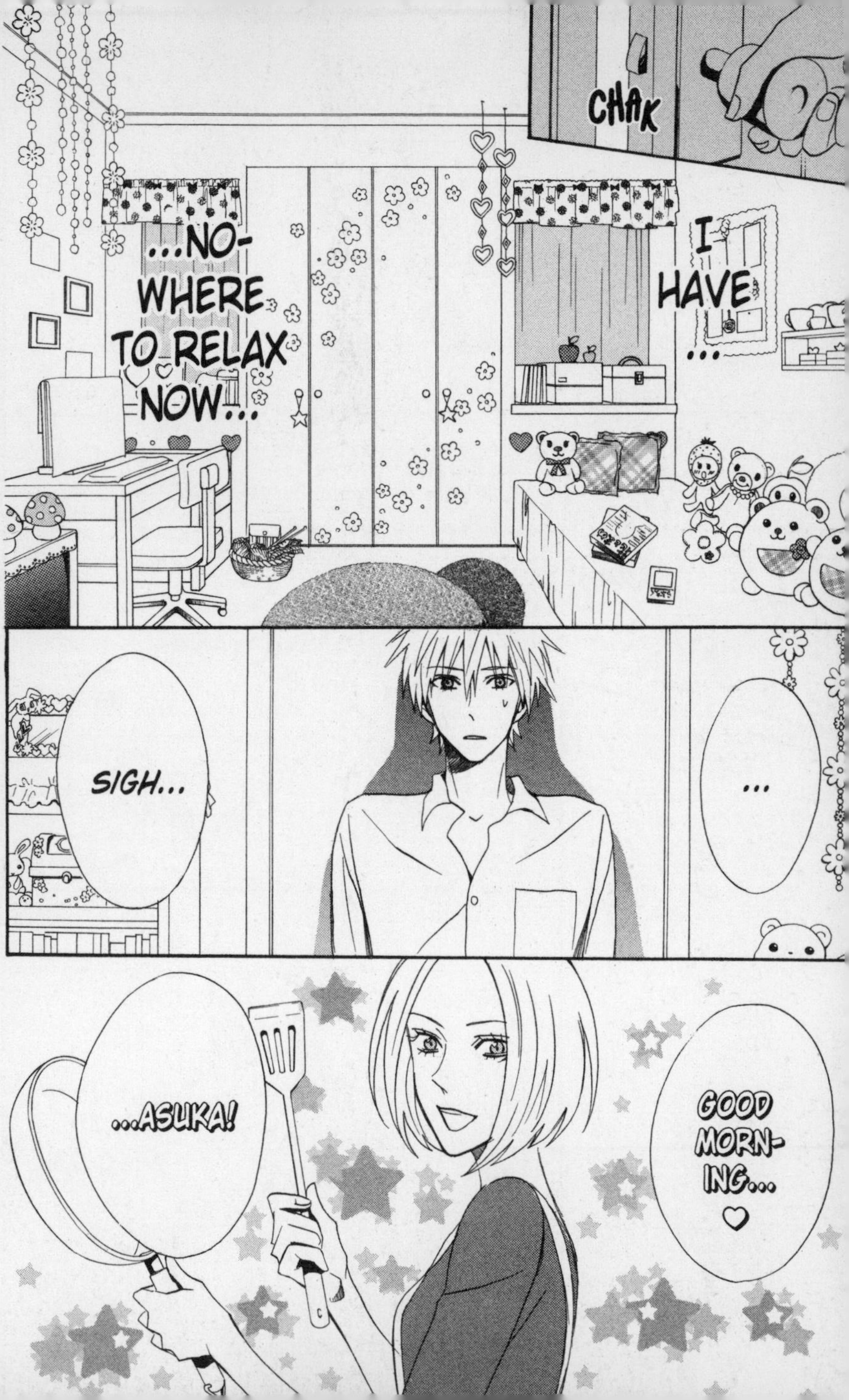
CHAK
I HAVE...
...NO-WHERE TO RELAX NOW...
...
SIGH...
GOOD MORNING... ♡
...ASUKA!

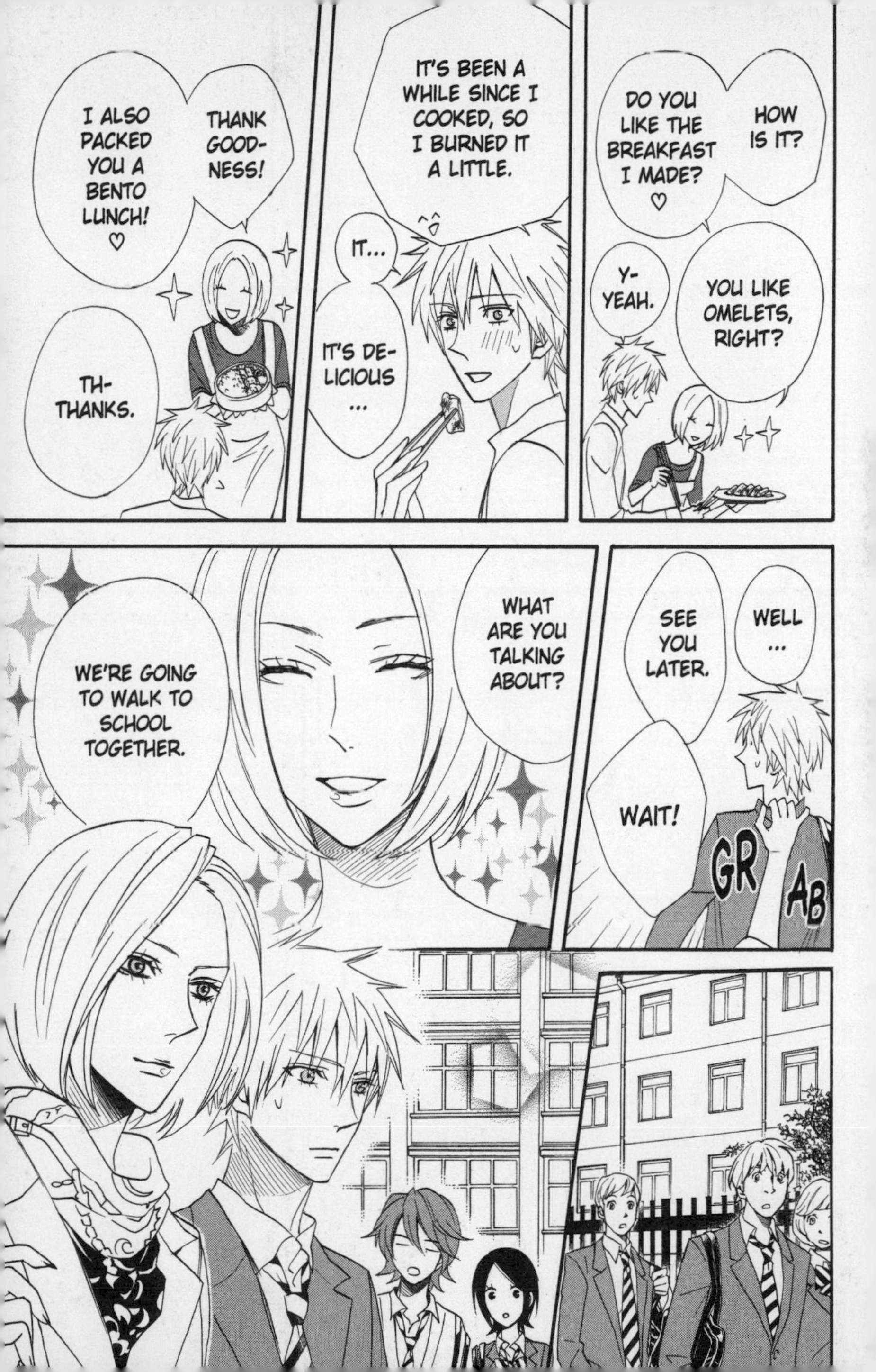
HOW IS IT?
DO YOU LIKE THE BREAKFAST I MADE? ♡
YOU LIKE OMELETS, RIGHT?
Y-YEAH.
IT'S BEEN A WHILE SINCE I COOKED, SO I BURNED IT A LITTLE.
IT...
IT'S DE-LICIOUS ...
THANK GOOD-NESS!
I ALSO PACKED YOU A BENTO LUNCH! ♡
TH-THANKS.
WELL ...
SEE YOU LATER.
WAIT!
GR
AB
WHAT ARE YOU TALKING ABOUT?
WE'RE GOING TO WALK TO SCHOOL TOGETHER.

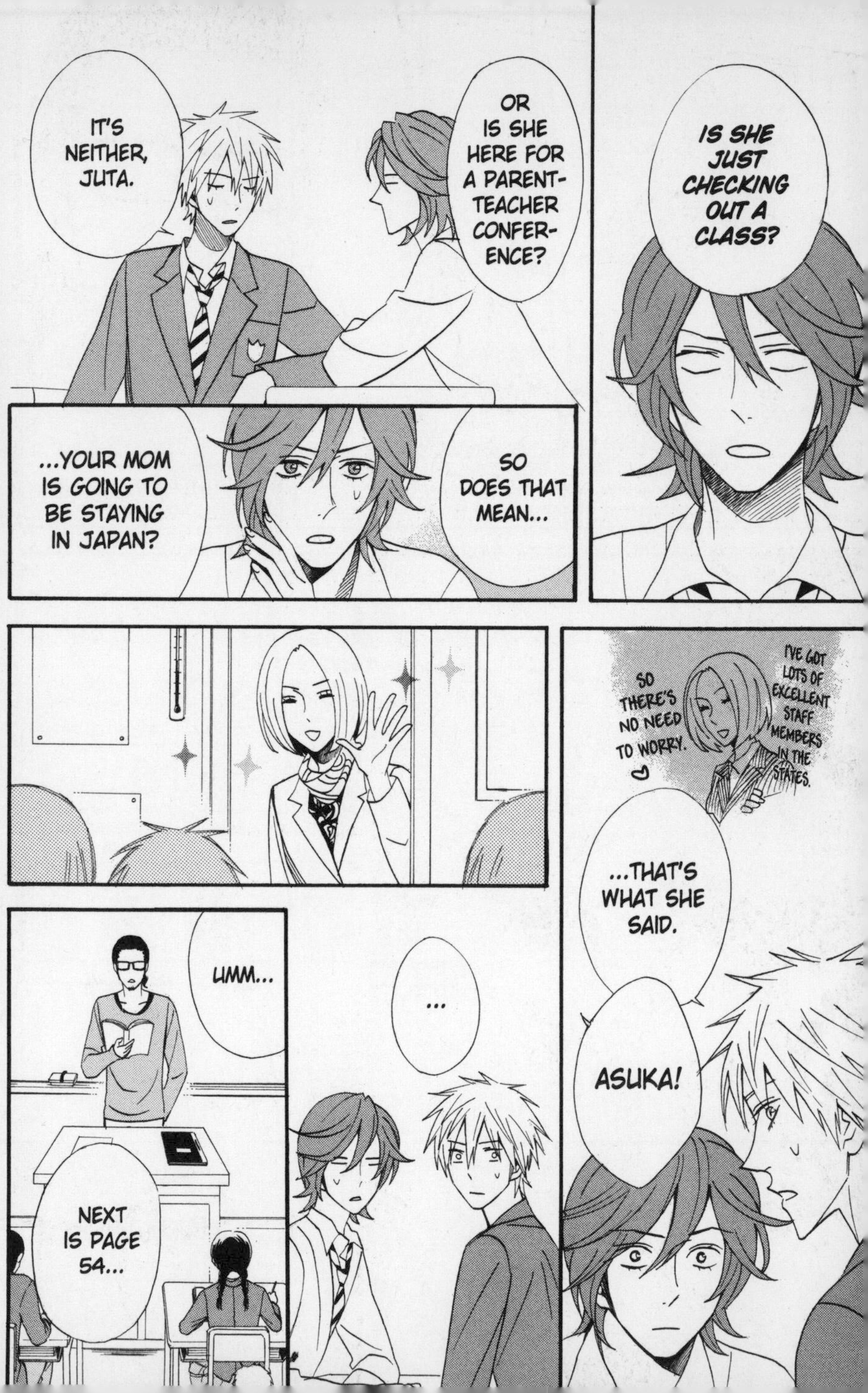
IS SHE JUST CHECKING OUT A CLASS?
OR IS SHE HERE FOR A PARENT-TEACHER CONFERENCE?
IT'S NEITHER, JUTA.
SO DOES THAT MEAN...
...YOUR MOM IS GOING TO BE STAYING IN JAPAN?
I'VE GOT LOTS OF EXCELLENT STAFF MEMBERS IN THE STATES.
SO THERE'S NO NEED TO WORRY. ♥
...THAT'S WHAT SHE SAID.
ASUKA!
...
UMM...
NEXT IS PAGE 54...

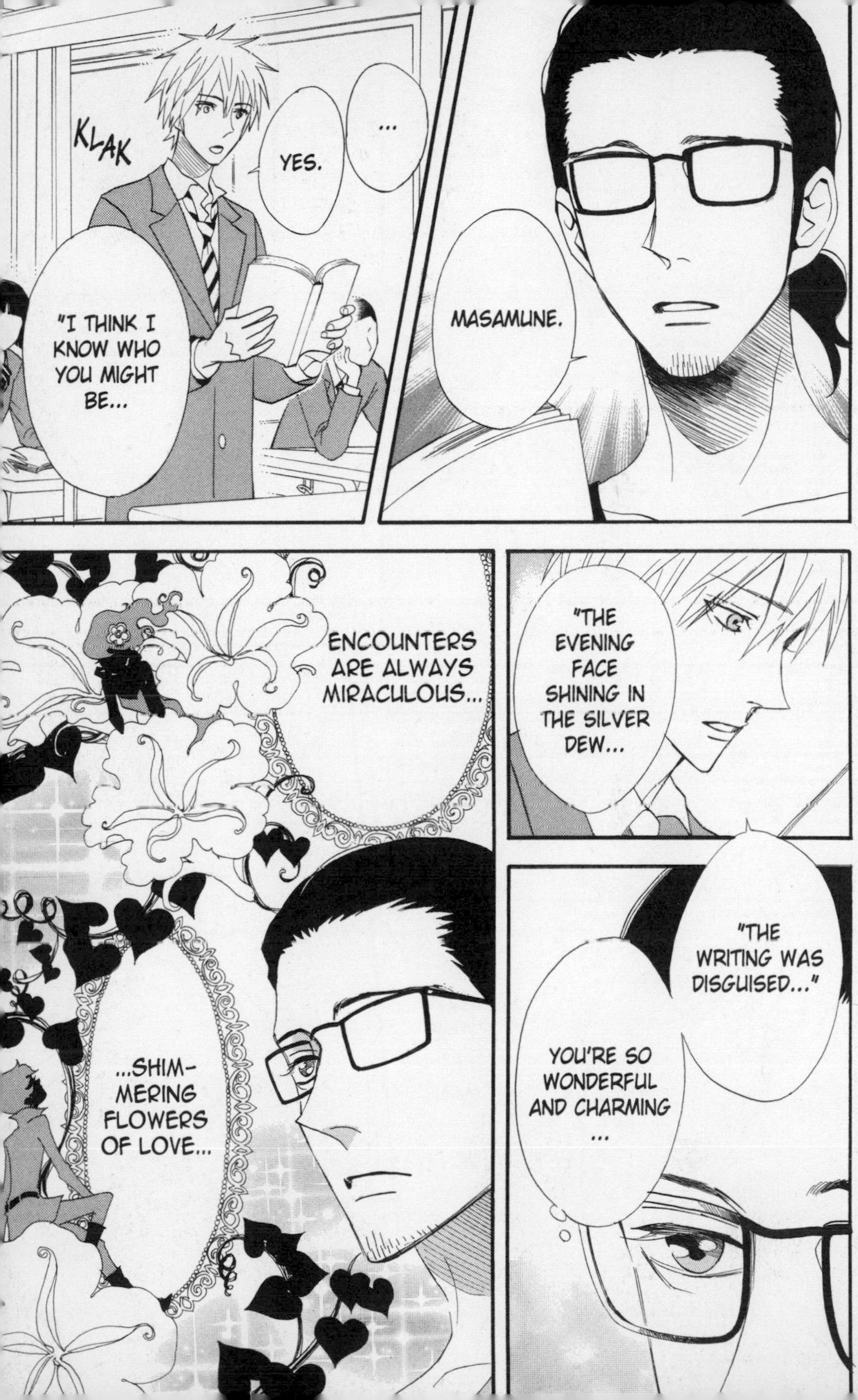
MASAMUNE.
...
YES.
KLAK
"I THINK I KNOW WHO YOU MIGHT BE...
"THE EVENING FACE SHINING IN THE SILVER DEW...
"THE WRITING WAS DISGUISED..."
YOU'RE SO WONDERFUL AND CHARMING ...
ENCOUNTERS ARE ALWAYS MIRACULOUS...
...SHIM-MERING FLOWERS OF LOVE...

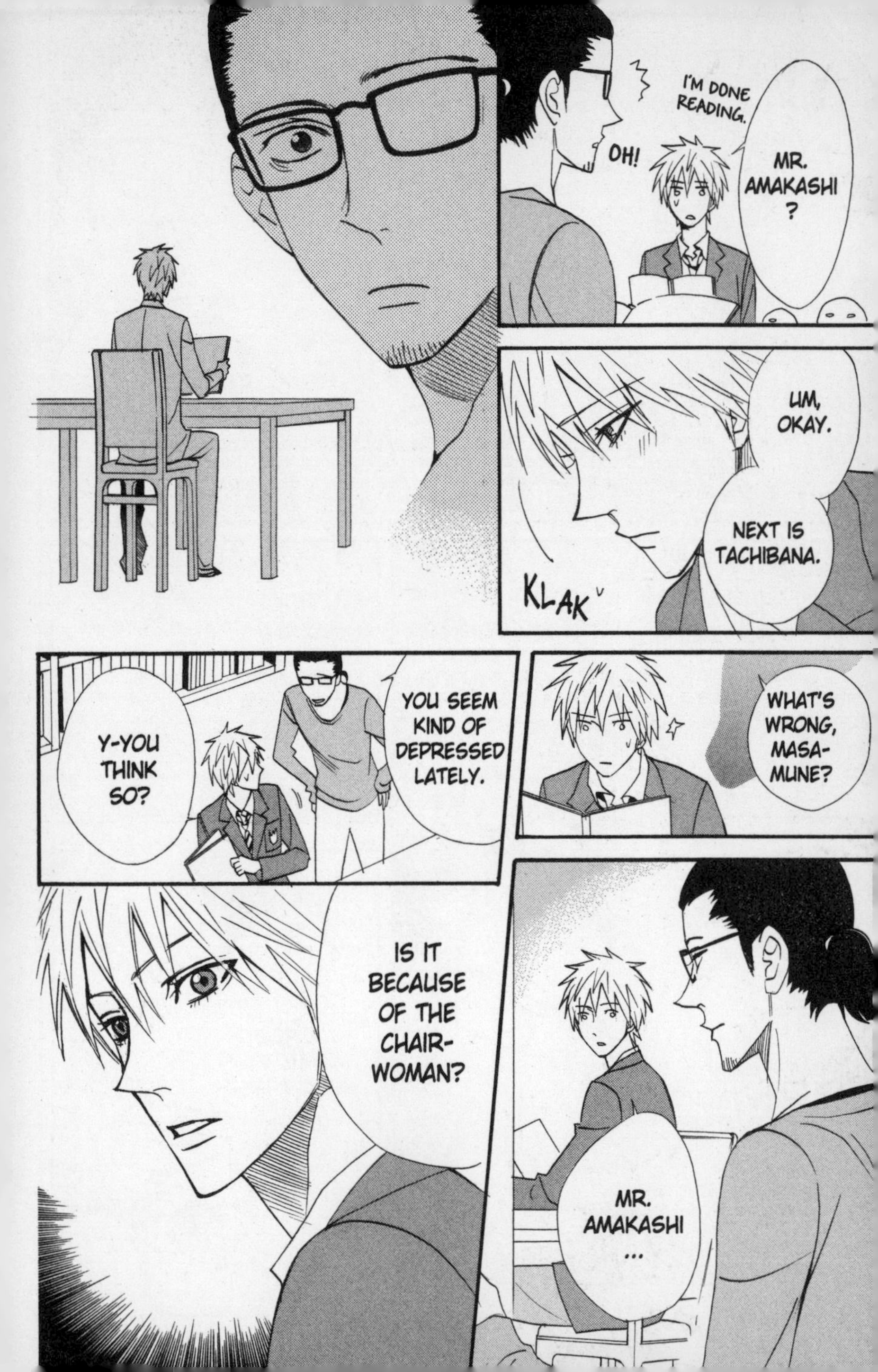
MR. AMAKASHI?
I'M DONE READING.
OH!
UM, OKAY.
NEXT IS TACHIBANA.
KLAK
WHAT'S WRONG, MASAMUNE?
YOU SEEM KIND OF DEPRESSED LATELY.
Y-YOU THINK SO?
MR. AMAKASHI...
IS IT BECAUSE OF THE CHAIR-WOMAN?

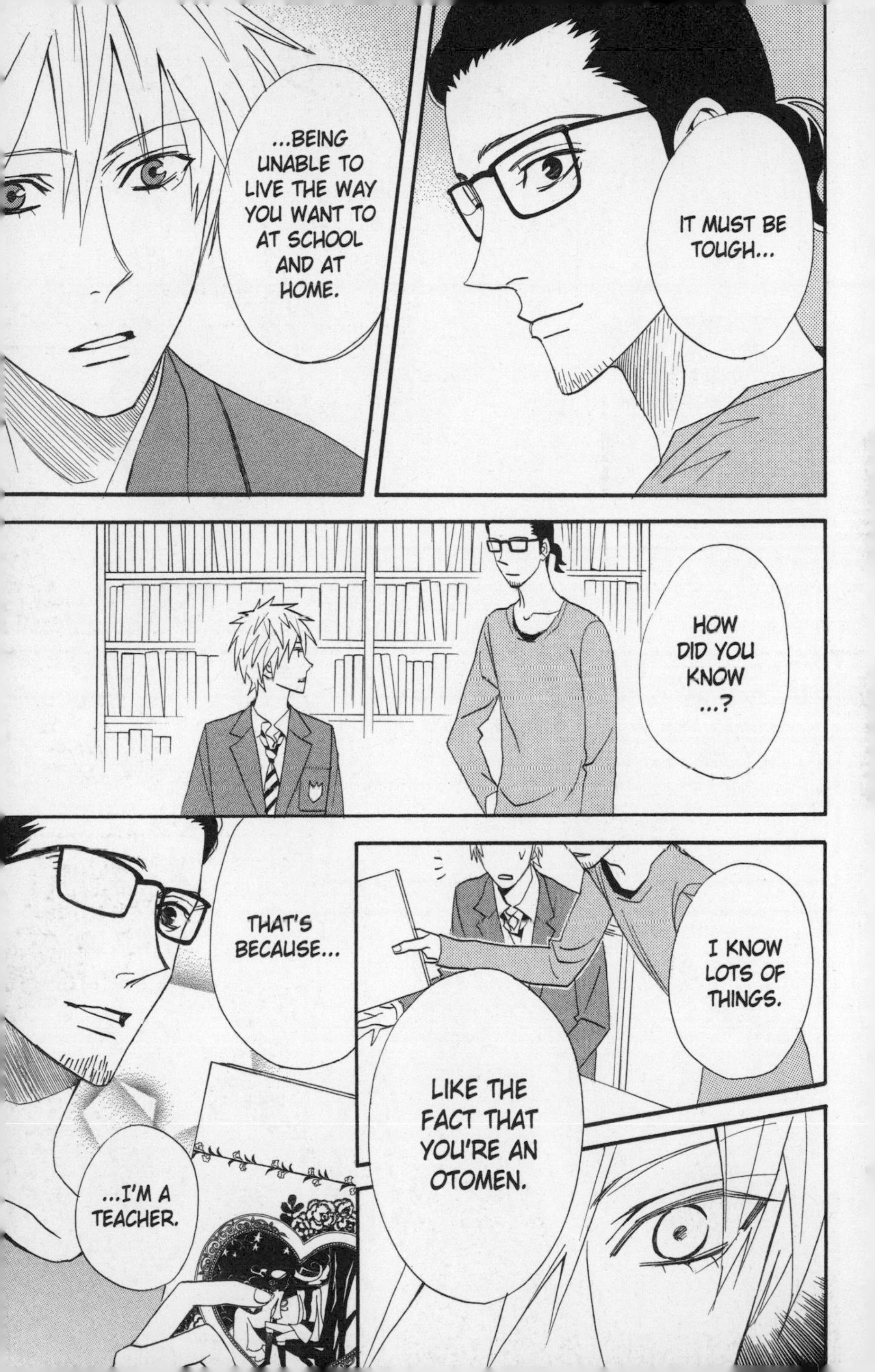
IT MUST BE TOUGH...
...BEING UNABLE TO LIVE THE WAY YOU WANT TO AT SCHOOL AND AT HOME.
HOW DID YOU KNOW ...?
I KNOW LOTS OF THINGS.
LIKE THE FACT THAT YOU'RE AN OTOMEN.
THAT'S BECAUSE...
...I'M A TEACHER.

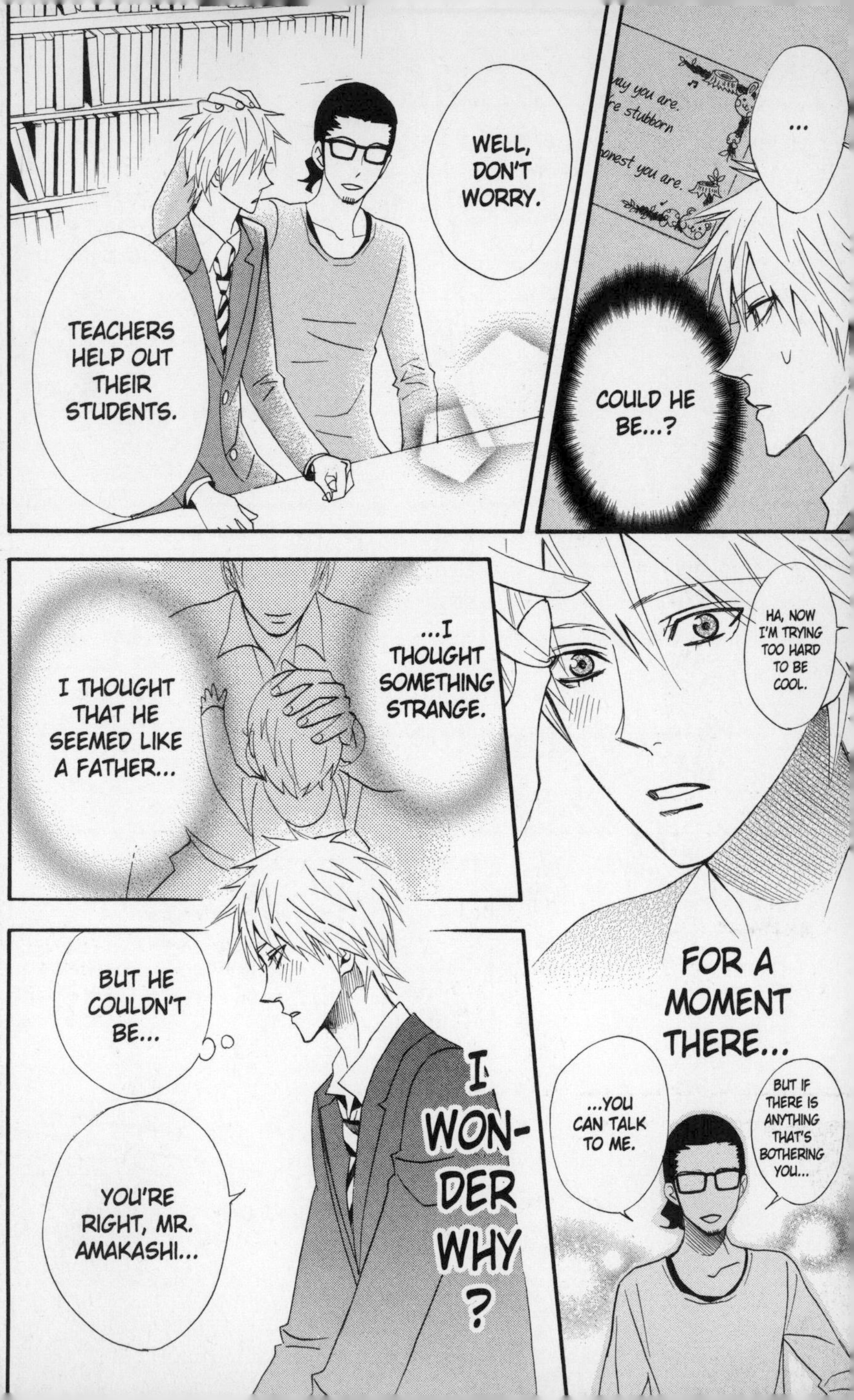
...
COULD HE BE...?
WELL, DON'T WORRY.
TEACHERS HELP OUT THEIR STUDENTS.
HA, NOW I'M TRYING TOO HARD TO BE COOL.
FOR A MOMENT THERE...
BUT IF THERE IS ANYTHING THAT'S BOTHERING YOU...
...YOU CAN TALK TO ME.
...I THOUGHT SOMETHING STRANGE.
I THOUGHT THAT HE SEEMED LIKE A FATHER...
I WONDER WHY?
BUT HE COULDN'T BE...
YOU'RE RIGHT, MR. AMAKASHI...

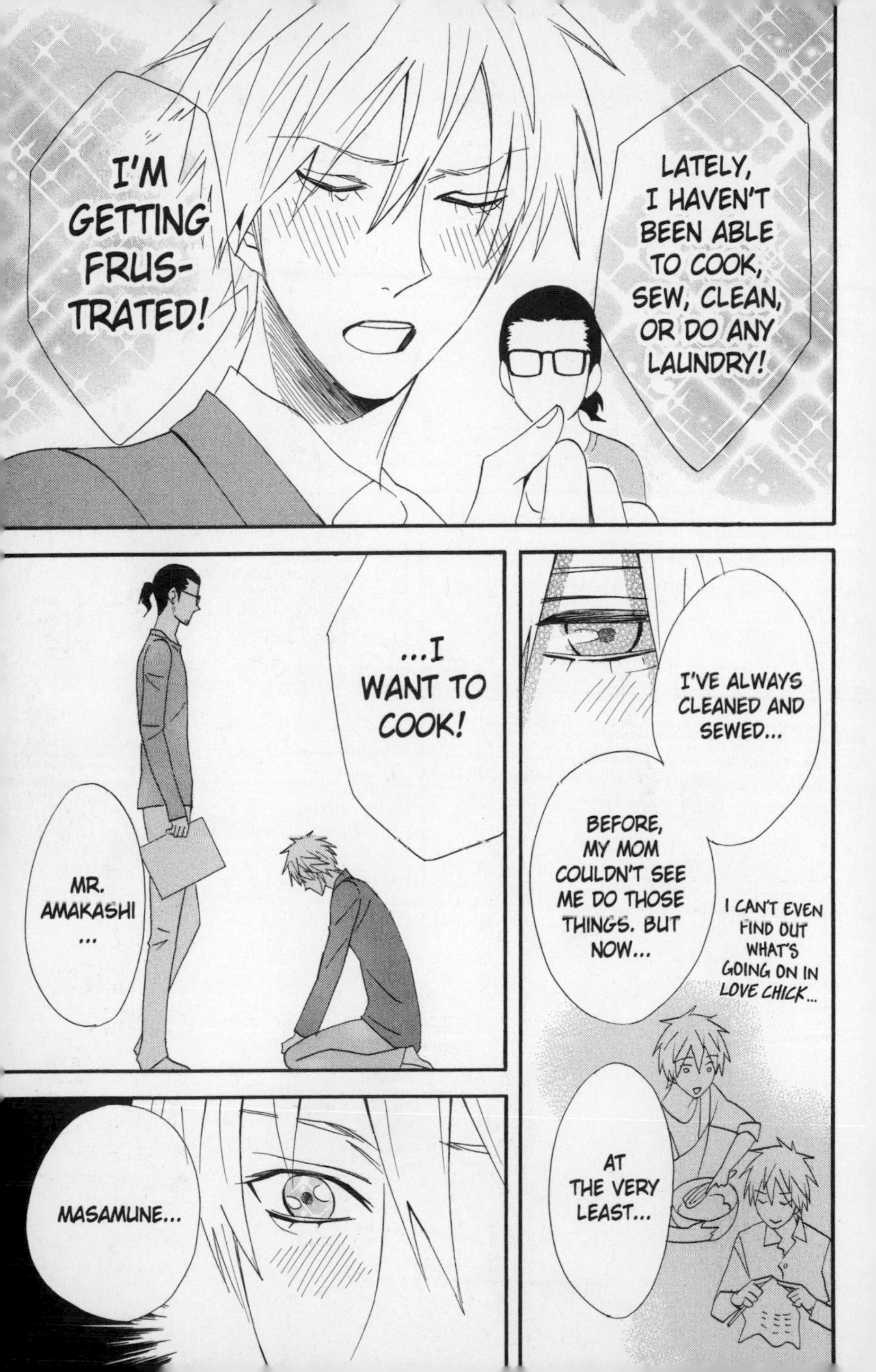
LATELY, I HAVEN'T BEEN ABLE TO COOK, SEW, CLEAN, OR DO ANY LAUNDRY!
I'M GETTING FRUS-TRATED!
I'VE ALWAYS CLEANED AND SEWED...
BEFORE, MY MOM COULDN'T SEE ME DO THOSE THINGS. BUT NOW...
I CAN'T EVEN FIND OUT WHAT'S GOING ON IN LOVE CHICK...
AT THE VERY LEAST...
...I WANT TO COOK!
MR. AMAKASHI ...
MASAMUNE...

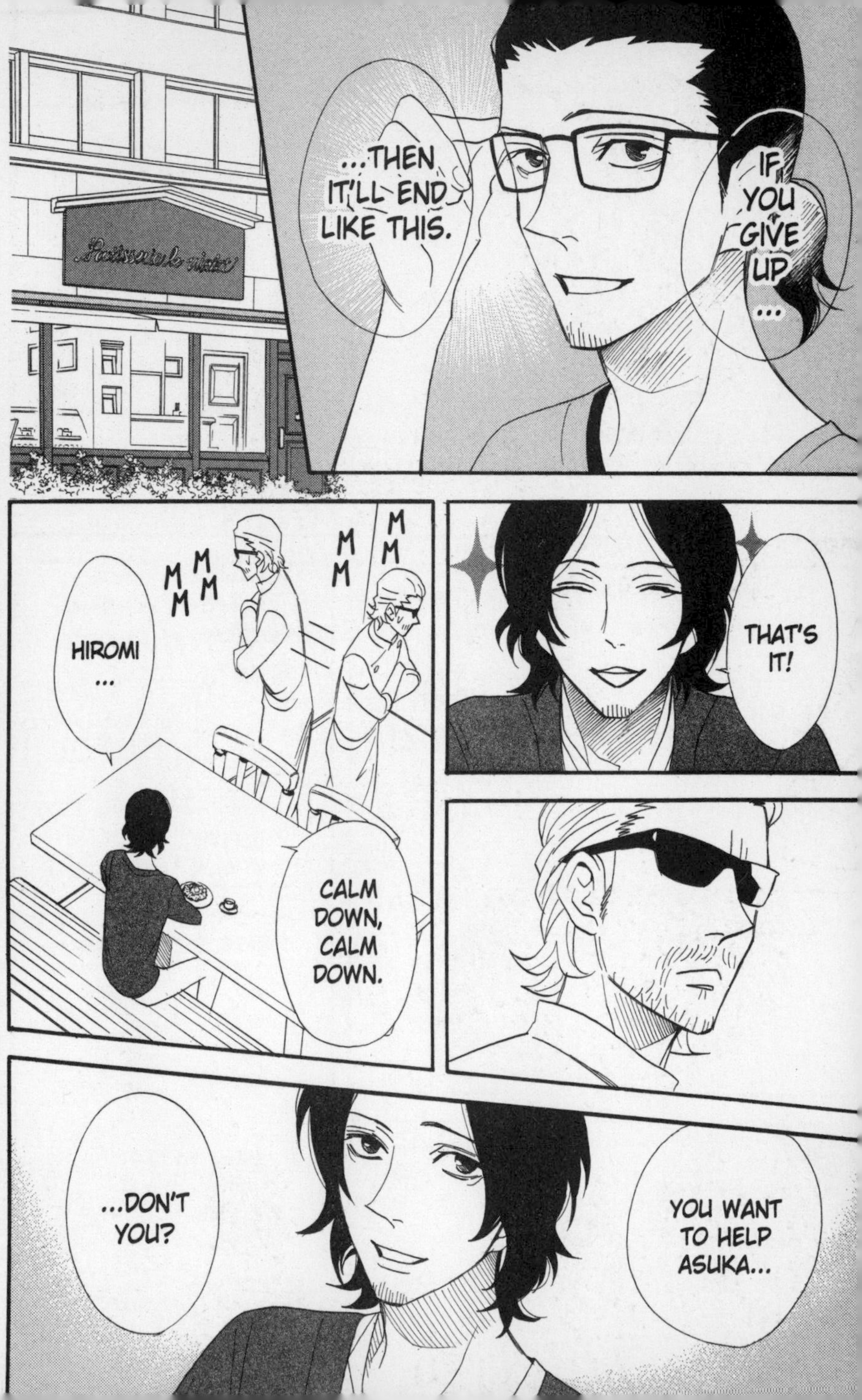
IF YOU GIVE UP...
...THEN IT'LL END LIKE THIS.
THAT'S IT!
MMMM
MMMMM
HIROMI...
CALM DOWN, CALM DOWN.
YOU WANT TO HELP ASUKA...
...DON'T YOU?

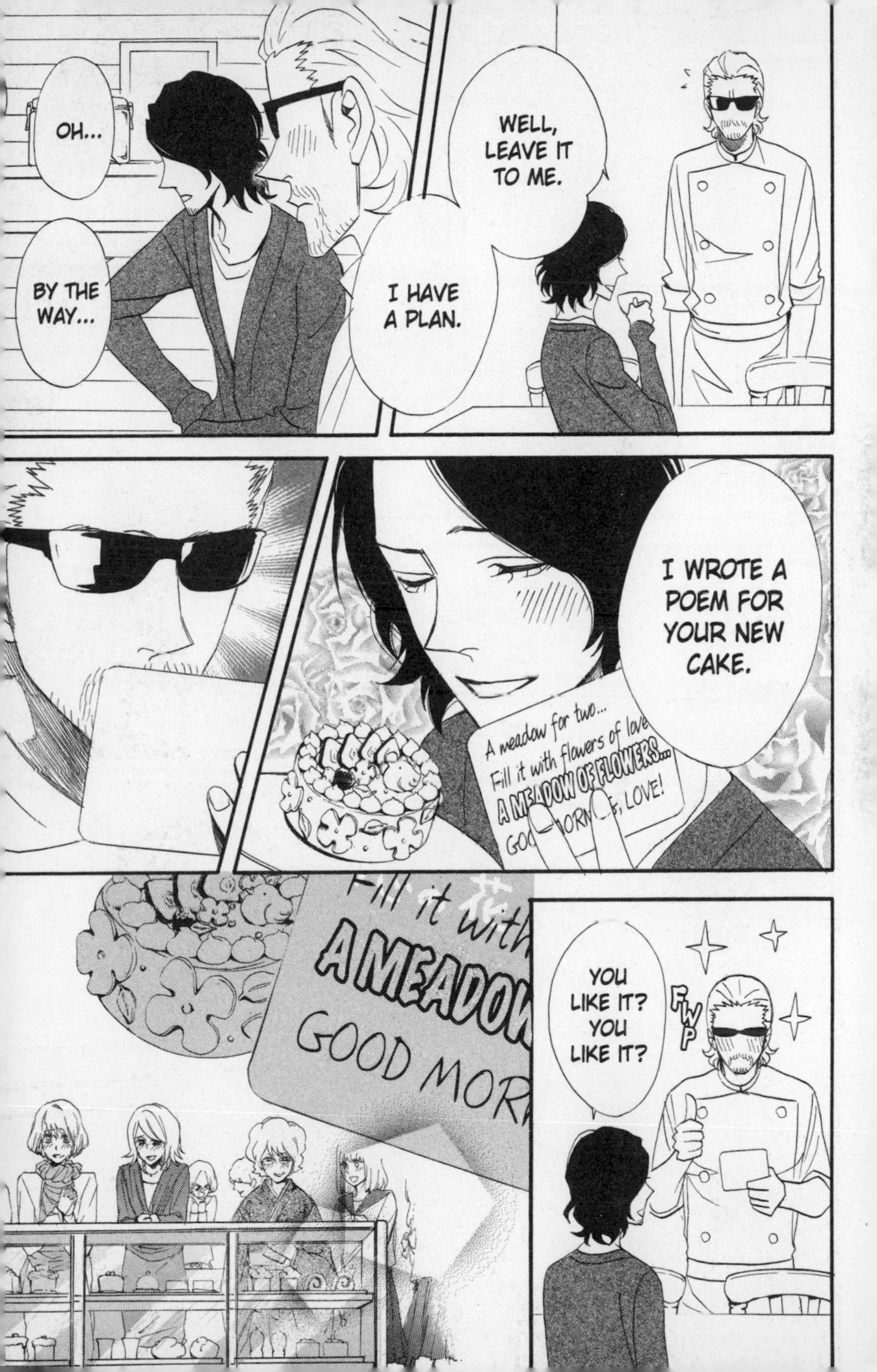
WELL, LEAVE IT TO ME.
I HAVE A PLAN.
OH...
BY THE WAY...
I WROTE A POEM FOR YOUR NEW CAKE.
A meadow for two...
Fill it with flowers of love
A MEADOW OF FLOWERS...
YOU LIKE IT? YOU LIKE IT?
FWP

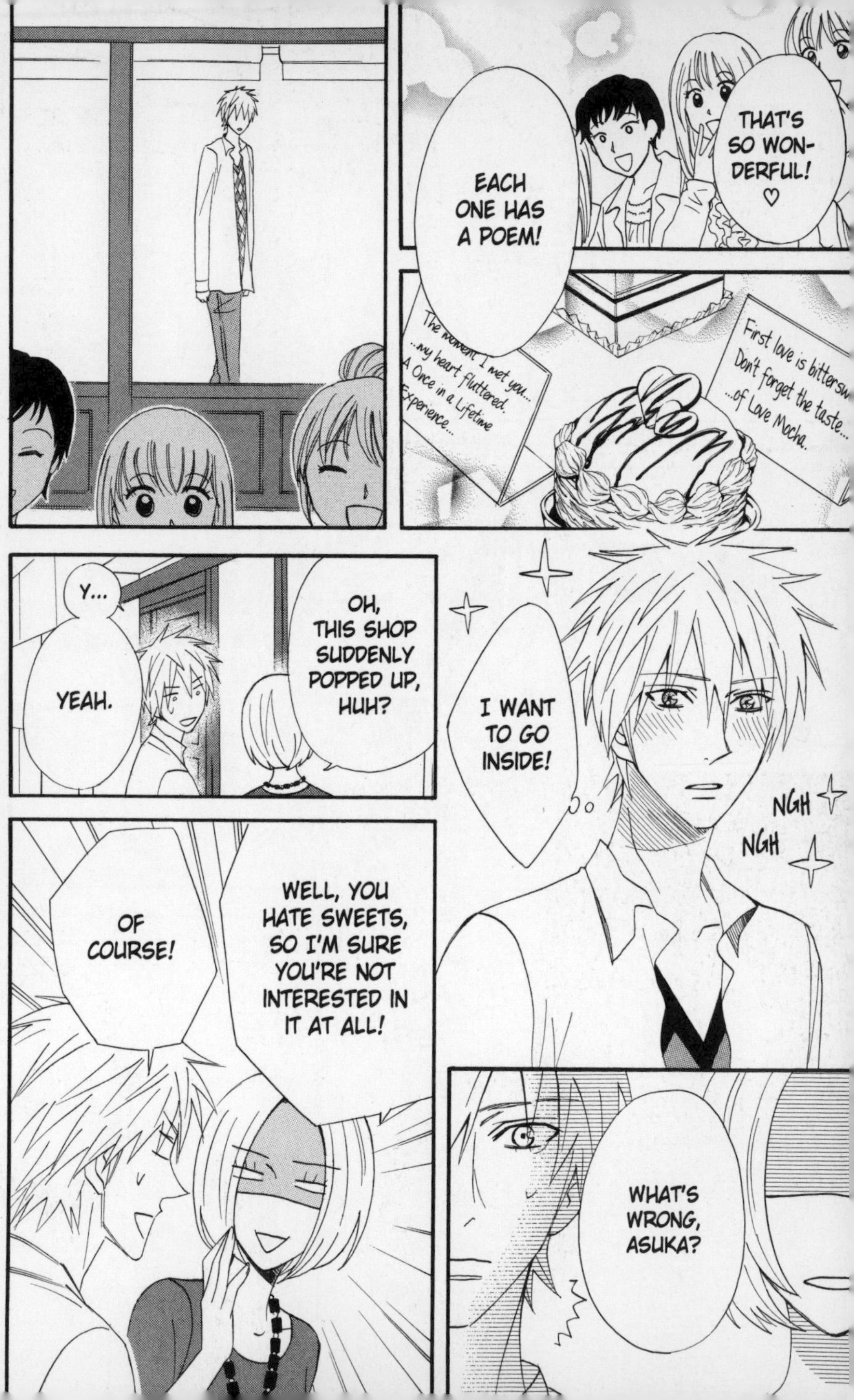
EACH ONE HAS A POEM!
THAT'S SO WON-DERFUL! ♡
First love is bittersw
Don't forget the taste...
...of Love Mocha.
The moment I met you...
...my heart fluttered.
A Once in a Lifetime Experience...
I WANT TO GO INSIDE!
NGH
NGH
OH, THIS SHOP SUDDENLY POPPED UP, HUH?
Y...
YEAH.
WHAT'S WRONG, ASUKA?
WELL, YOU HATE SWEETS, SO I'M SURE YOU'RE NOT INTERESTED IN IT AT ALL!
OF COURSE!

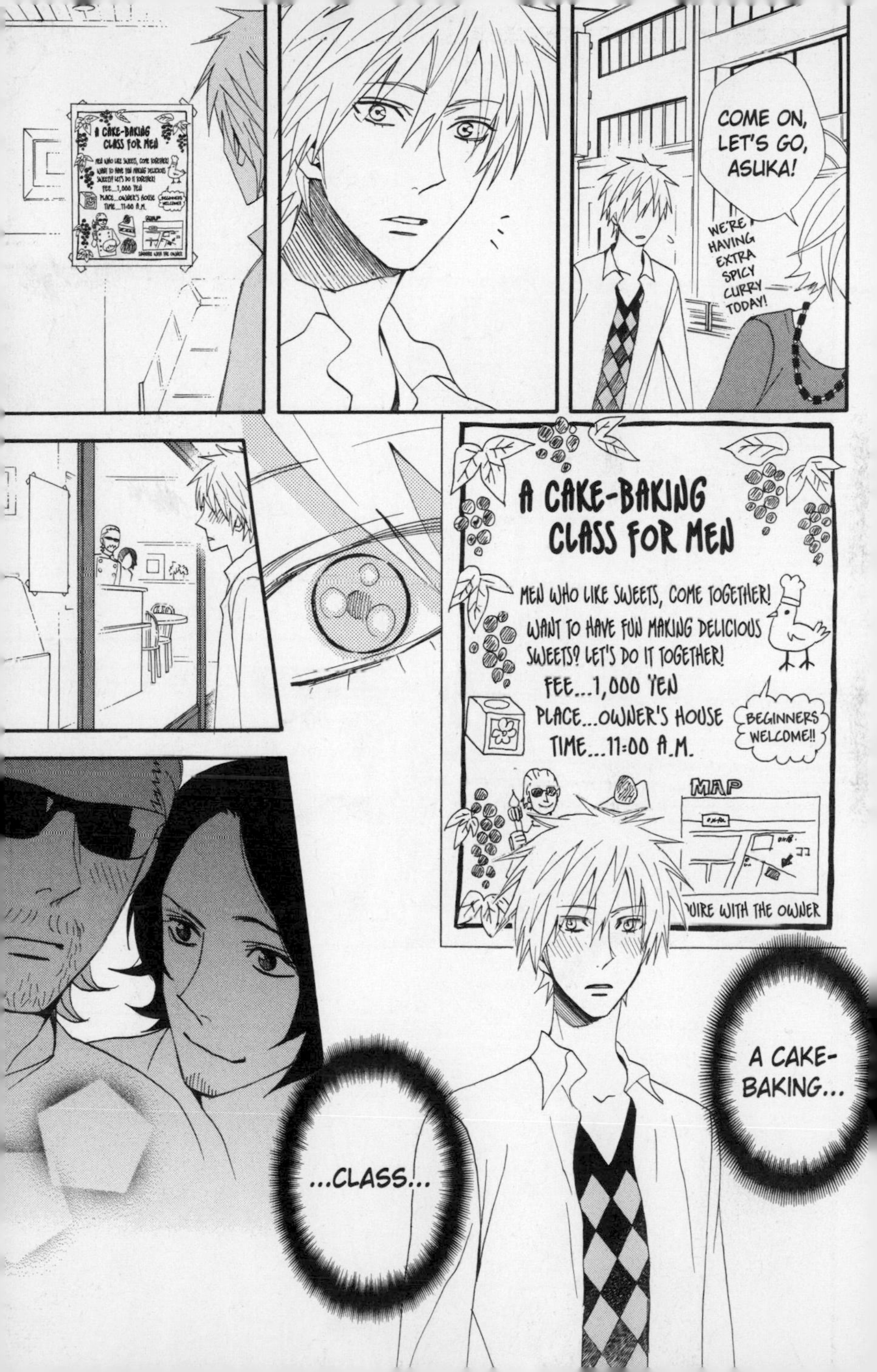
COME ON, LET'S GO, ASUKA!
WE'RE HAVING EXTRA SPICY CURRY TODAY!
A CAKE-BAKING CLASS FOR MEN
MEN WHO LIKE SWEETS, COME TOGETHER!
WANT TO HAVE FUN MAKING DELICIOUS SWEETS? LET'S DO IT TOGETHER!
FEE...1,000 YEN
PLACE...OWNER'S HOUSE
TIME...11:00 A.M.
BEGINNERS WELCOME!!
MAP
UIRE WITH THE OWNER
A CAKE-BAKING...
...CLASS...

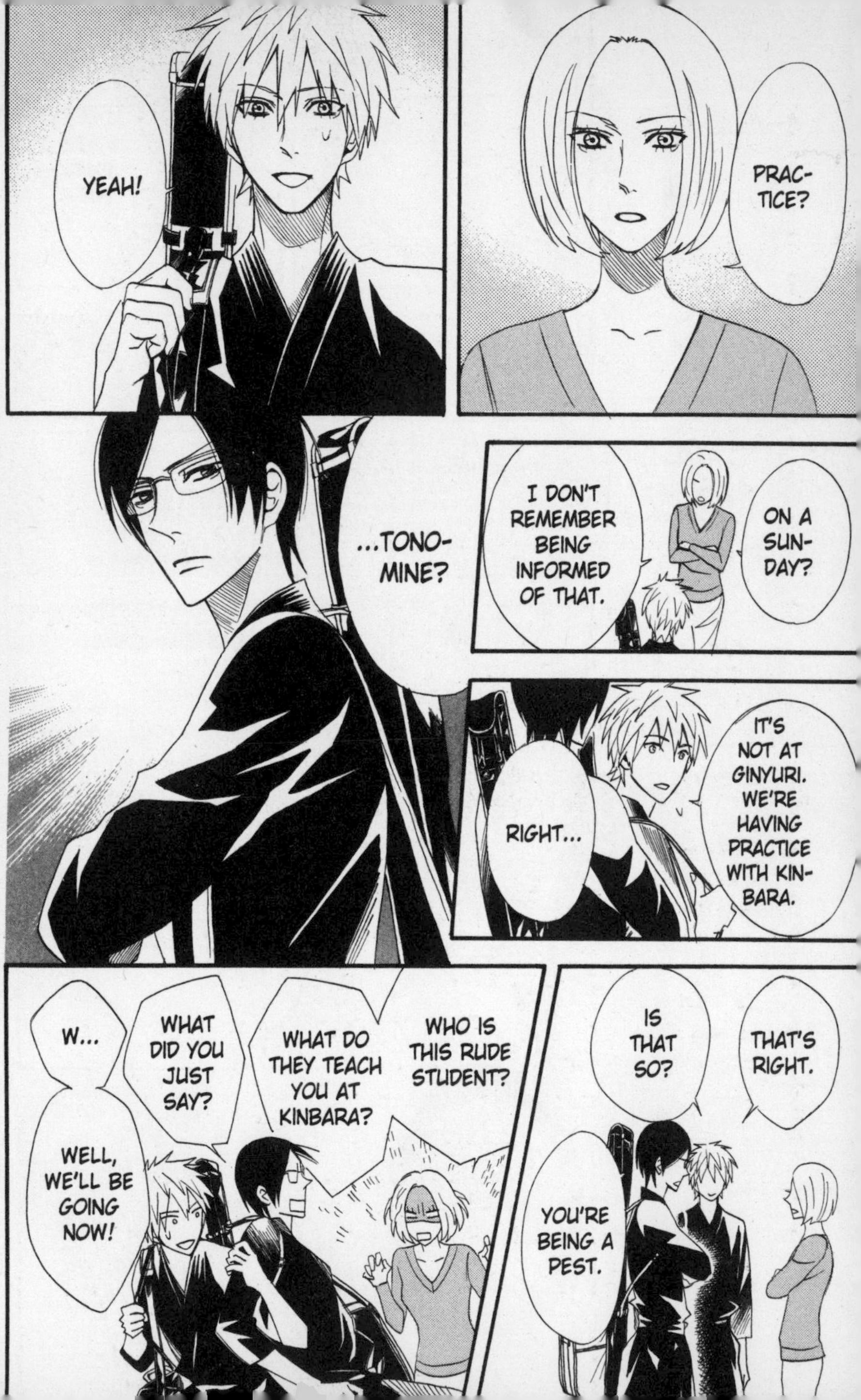
PRAC-TICE?
YEAH!
ON A SUN-DAY?
I DON'T REMEMBER BEING INFORMED OF THAT.
IT'S NOT AT GINYURI. WE'RE HAVING PRACTICE WITH KIN-BARA.
RIGHT...
...TONO-MINE?
THAT'S RIGHT.
IS THAT SO?
YOU'RE BEING A PEST.
WHO IS THIS RUDE STUDENT?
WHAT DO THEY TEACH YOU AT KINBARA?
WHAT DID YOU JUST SAY?
W...
WELL, WE'LL BE GOING NOW!

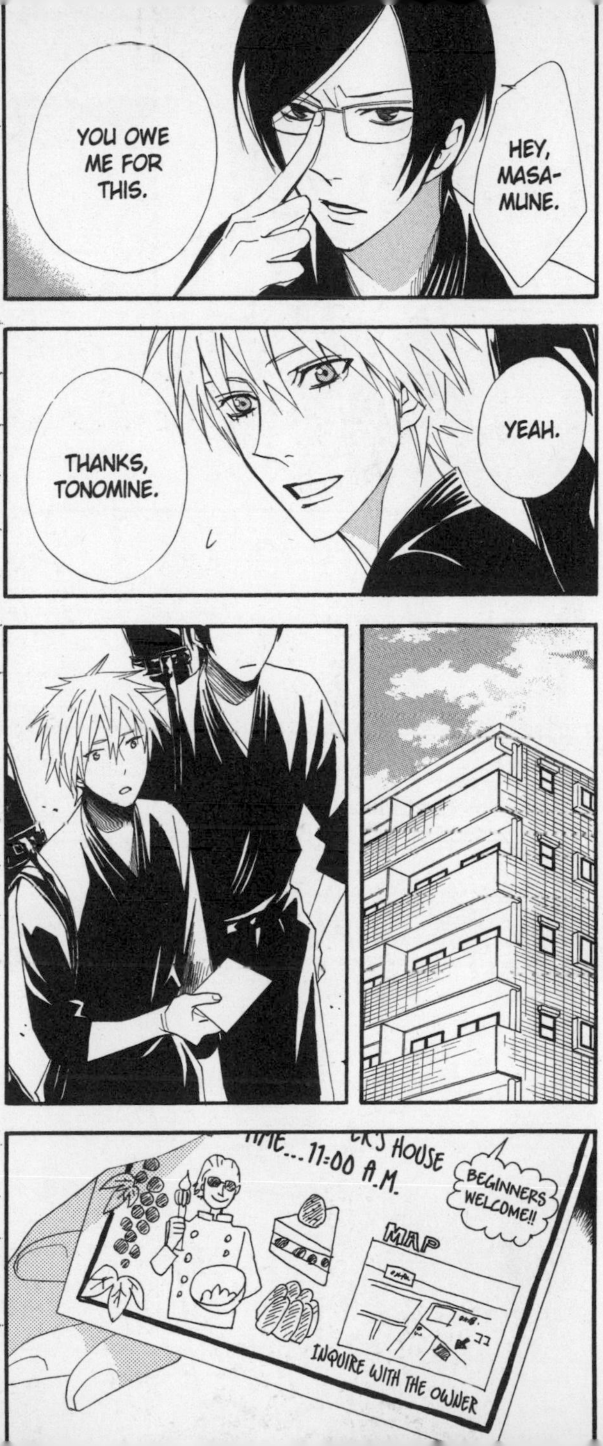
HEY, MASAMUNE.
YOU OWE ME FOR THIS.
YEAH.
THANKS, TONOMINE.
...11:00 A.M.
HOUSE
BEGINNERS WELCOME!!
MAP
INQUIRE WITH THE OWNER

Production Assistance:

Shimada-san
Takowa-san
Kuwana-san
Kaneko-san
Sakurai-san
Nakazawa-san
Tanaka-san
Kawashima-san
Sayaka-san
Yone-yan
Nishizawa-san

Special Thanks:

Abe-san
All My Readers
Mai's Family

Did you enjoy this volume? I hope to see you again next time.

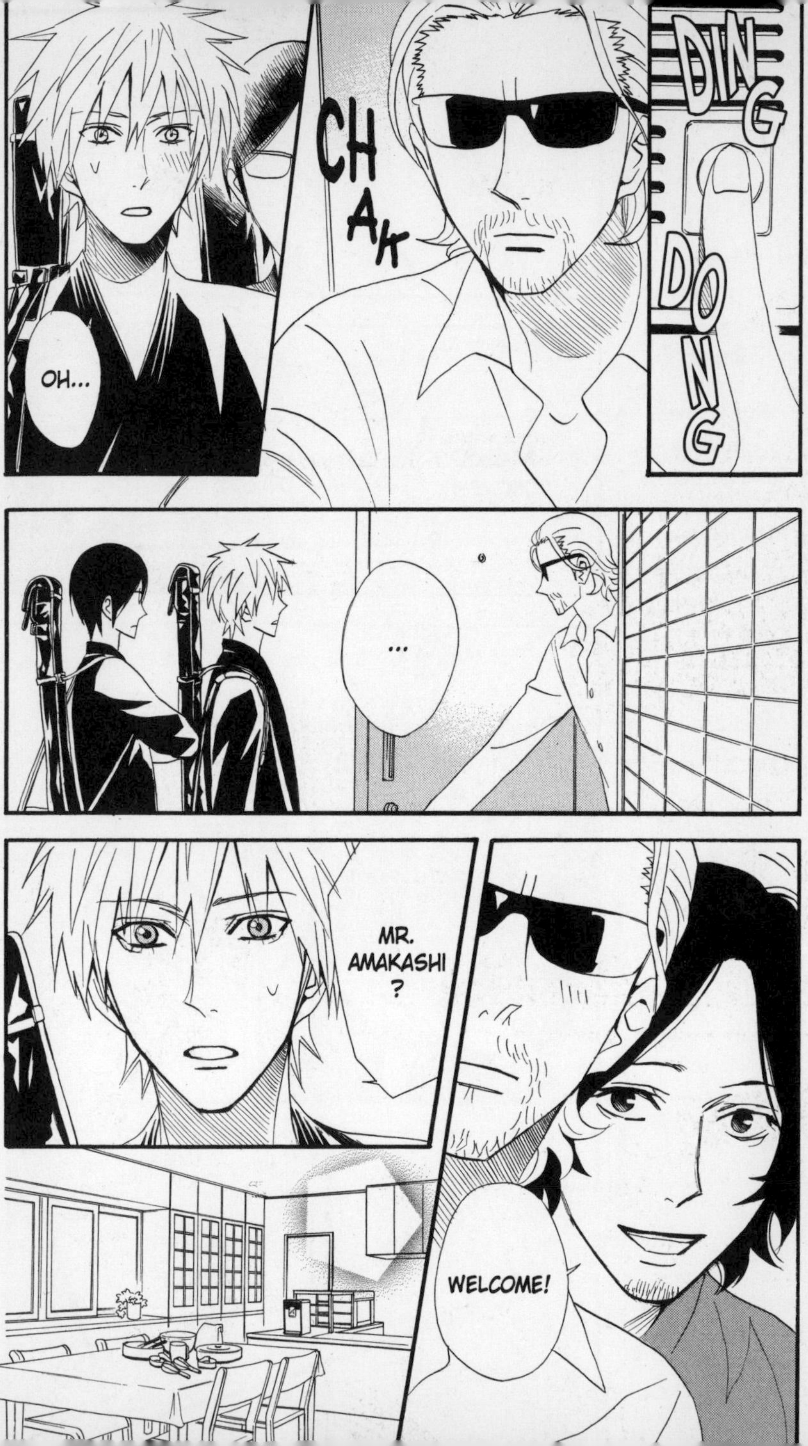
DING DONG
CHAK
OH...
...
WELCOME!
MR. AMAKASHI ?

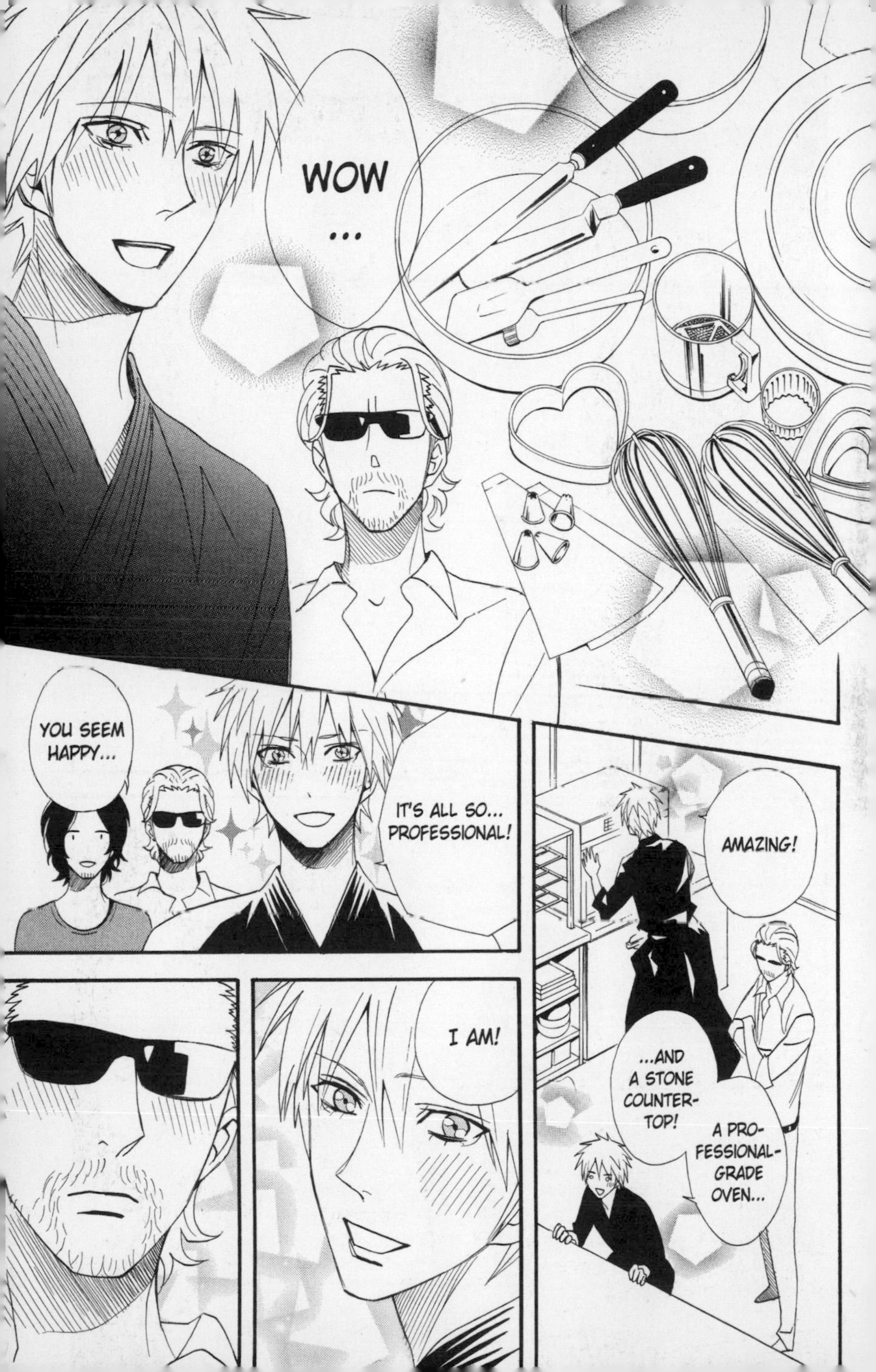
WOW
...
AMAZING!
A PRO-FESSIONAL-GRADE OVEN...
...AND A STONE COUNTER-TOP!
IT'S ALL SO... PROFESSIONAL!
YOU SEEM HAPPY...
I AM!

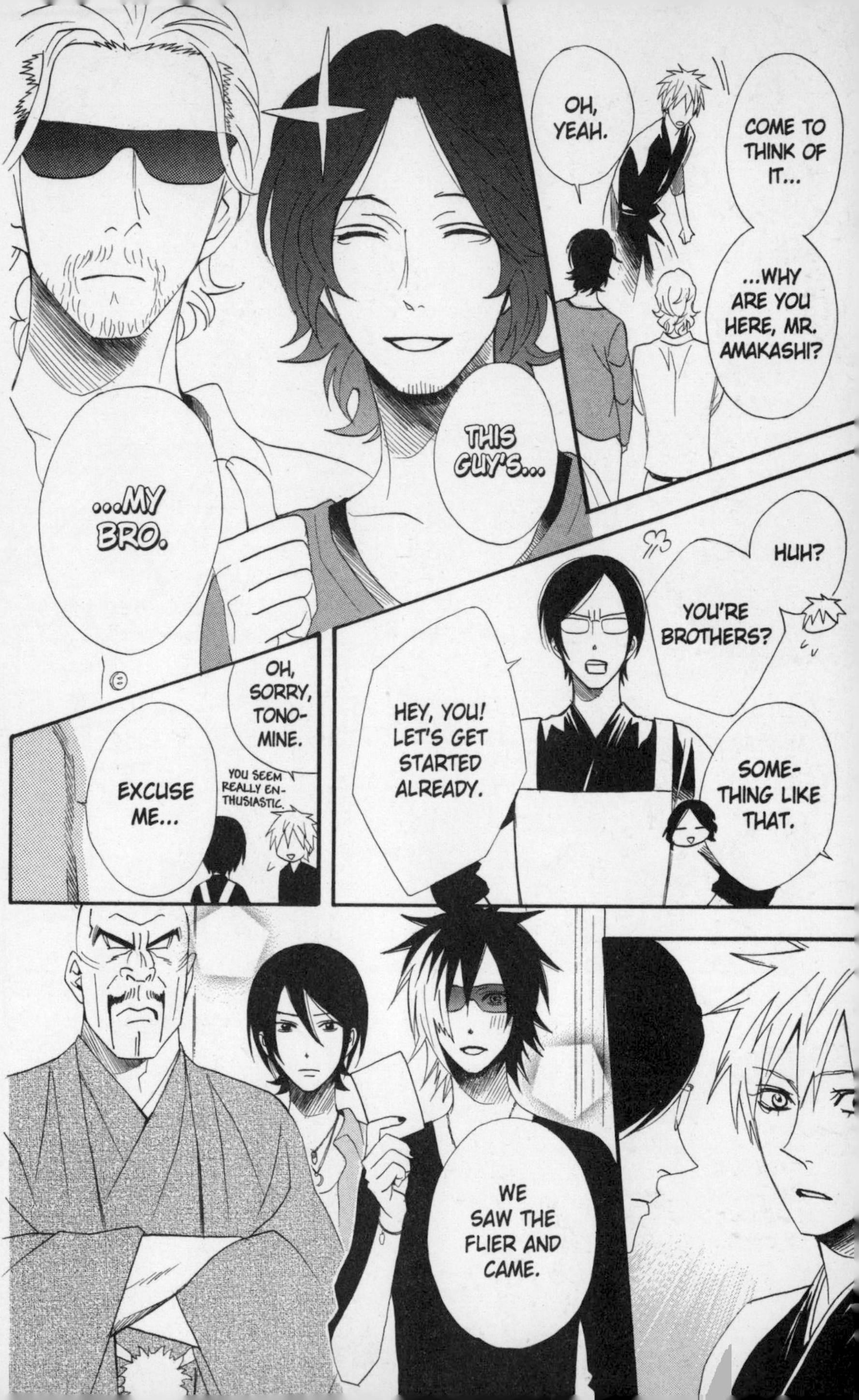
COME TO THINK OF IT...
OH, YEAH.
...WHY ARE YOU HERE, MR. AMAKASHI?
HUH?
YOU'RE BROTHERS?
THIS GUY'S...
...MY BRO.
SOME-THING LIKE THAT.
HEY, YOU! LET'S GET STARTED ALREADY.
OH, SORRY, TONO-MINE.
EXCUSE ME...
YOU SEEM REALLY EN-THUSIASTIC.
WE SAW THE FLIER AND CAME.

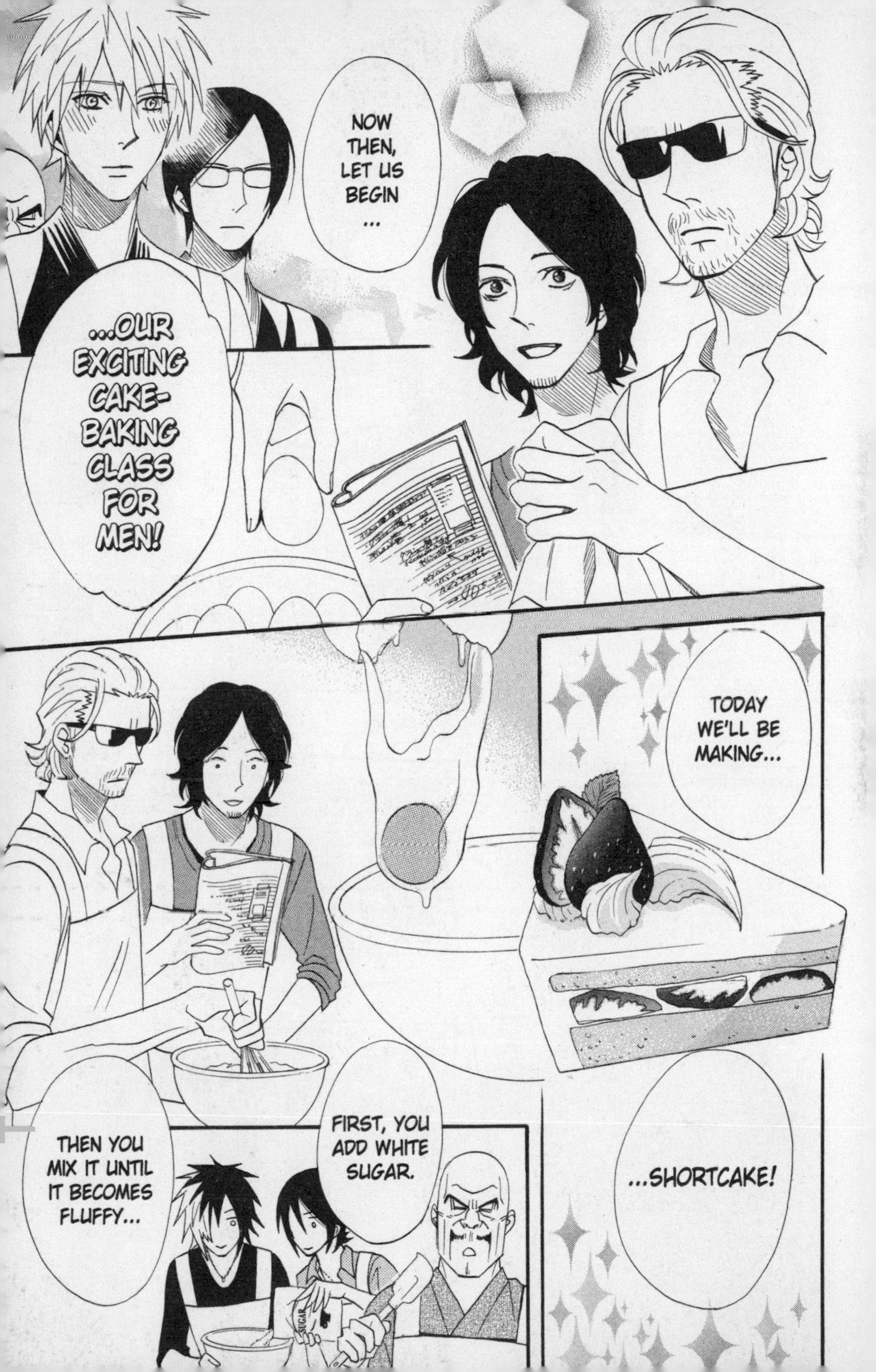
NOW THEN, LET US BEGIN ...
...OUR EXCITING CAKE-BAKING CLASS FOR MEN!
TODAY WE'LL BE MAKING...
...SHORTCAKE!
FIRST, YOU ADD WHITE SUGAR.
THEN YOU MIX IT UNTIL IT BECOMES FLUFFY...
SUGAR

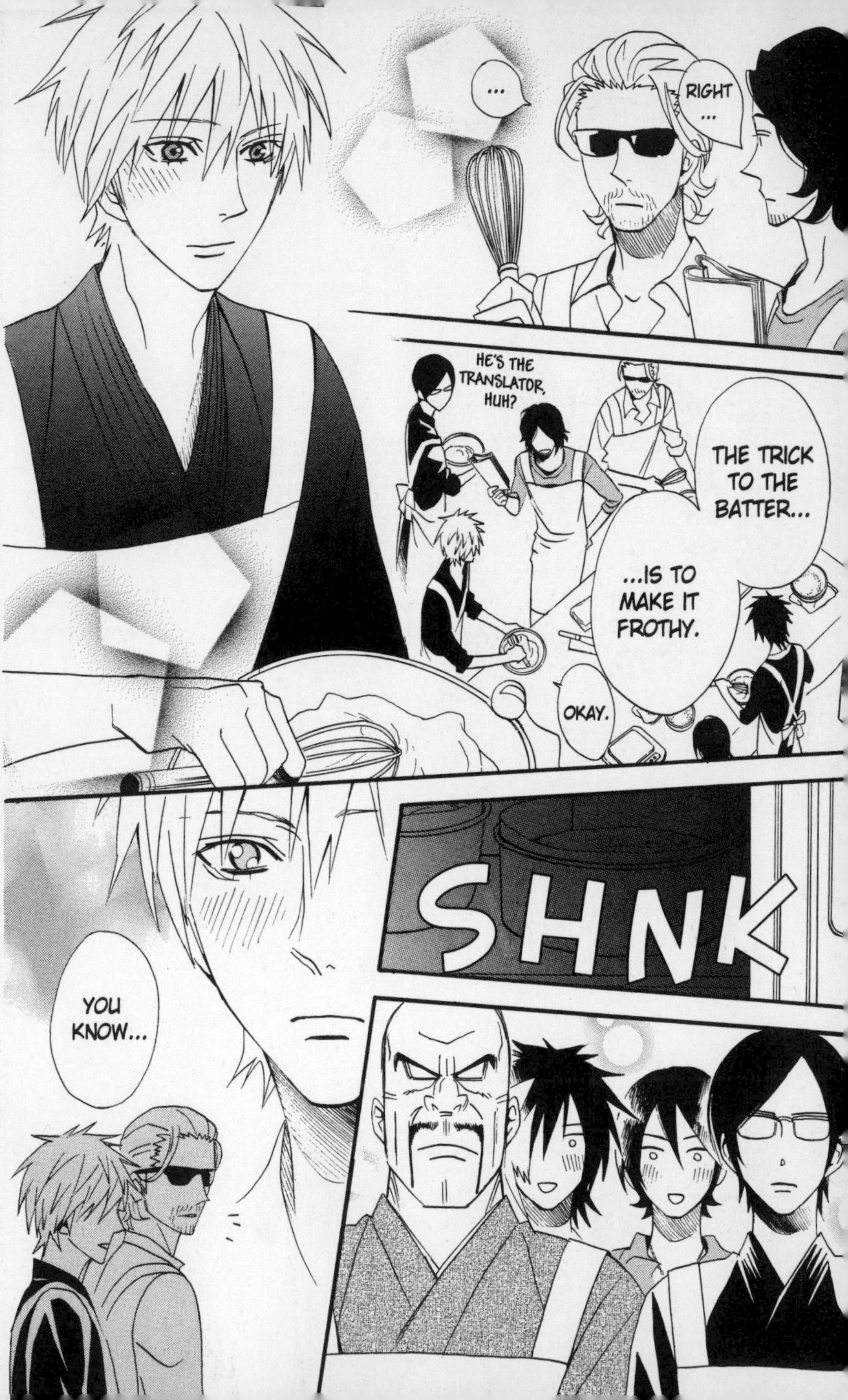
RIGHT ...
...
THE TRICK TO THE BATTER...
...IS TO MAKE IT FROTHY.
HE'S THE TRANSLATOR, HUH?
OKAY.
SHNK
YOU KNOW...

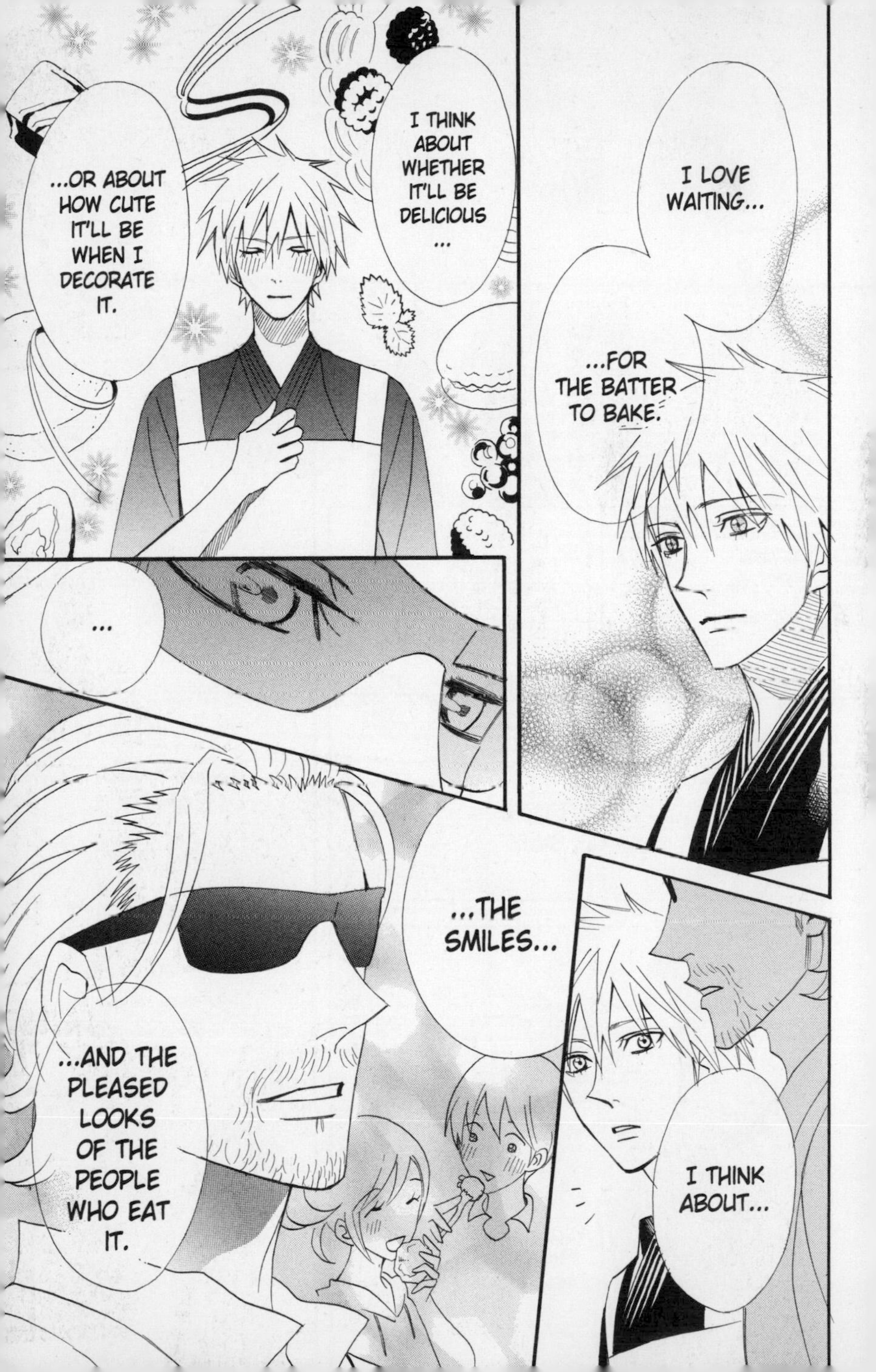
I LOVE WAITING...
...FOR THE BATTER TO BAKE.
I THINK ABOUT WHETHER IT'LL BE DELICIOUS...
...OR ABOUT HOW CUTE IT'LL BE WHEN I DECORATE IT.
...
I THINK ABOUT...
...THE SMILES...
...AND THE PLEASED LOOKS OF THE PEOPLE WHO EAT IT.

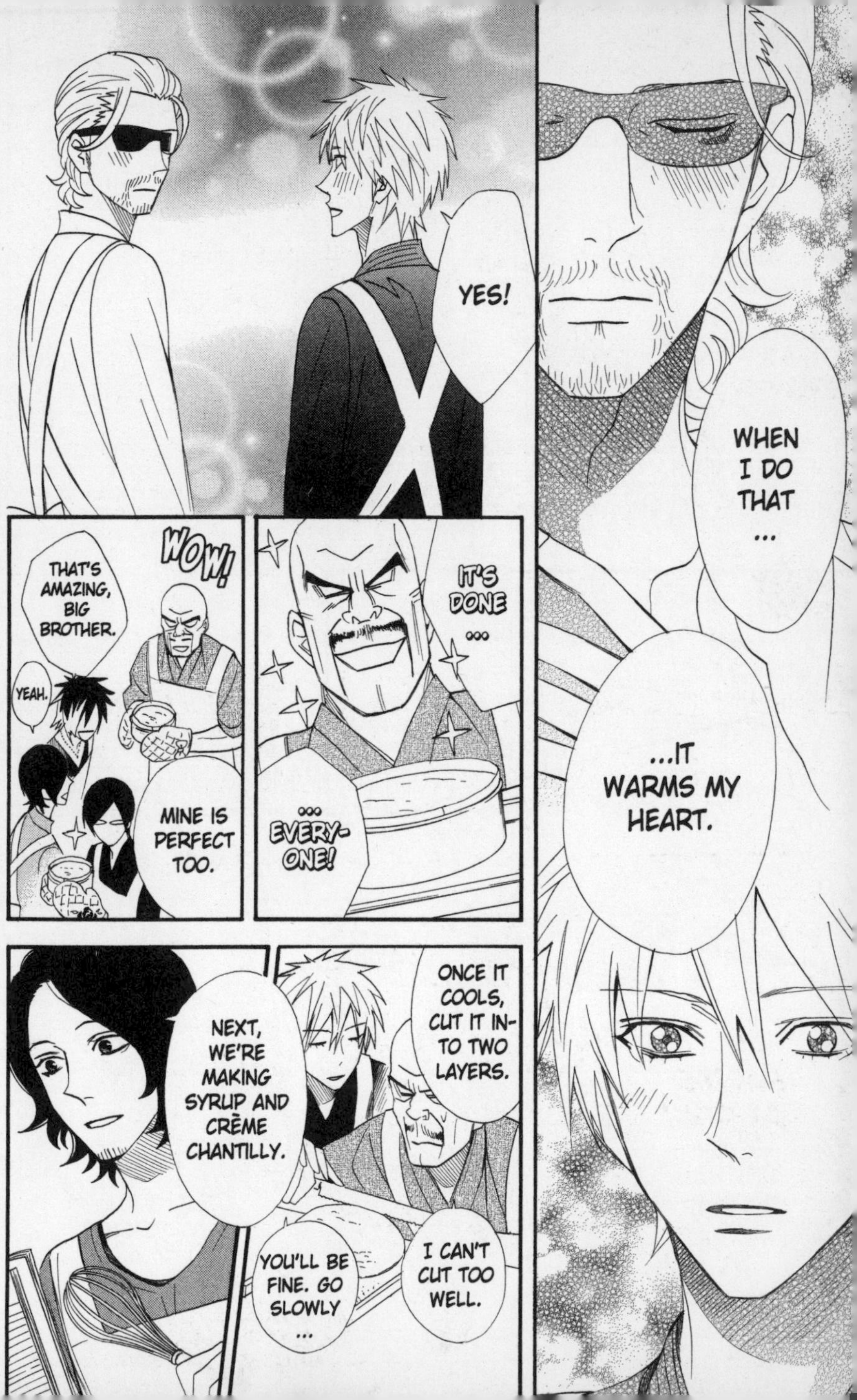
WHEN I DO THAT ...
...IT WARMS MY HEART.
YES!
IT'S DONE ...
... EVERY-ONE!
WOW!
THAT'S AMAZING, BIG BROTHER.
YEAH.
MINE IS PERFECT TOO.
ONCE IT COOLS, CUT IT IN-TO TWO LAYERS.
I CAN'T CUT TOO WELL.
YOU'LL BE FINE. GO SLOWLY ...
NEXT, WE'RE MAKING SYRUP AND CRÈME CHANTILLY.

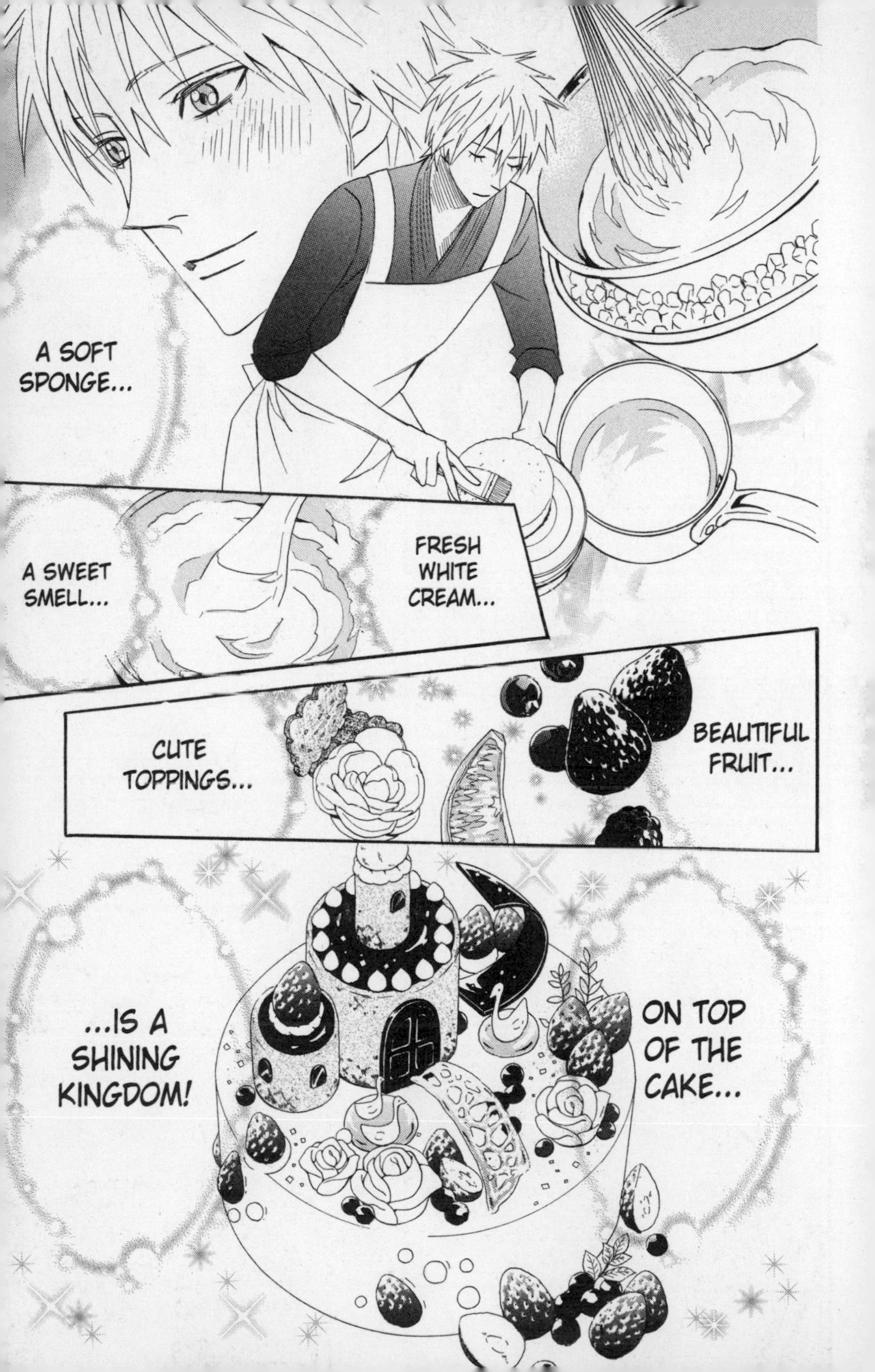
A SOFT SPONGE...
FRESH WHITE CREAM...
A SWEET SMELL...
BEAUTIFUL FRUIT...
CUTE TOPPINGS...
ON TOP OF THE CAKE...
...IS A SHINING KINGDOM!

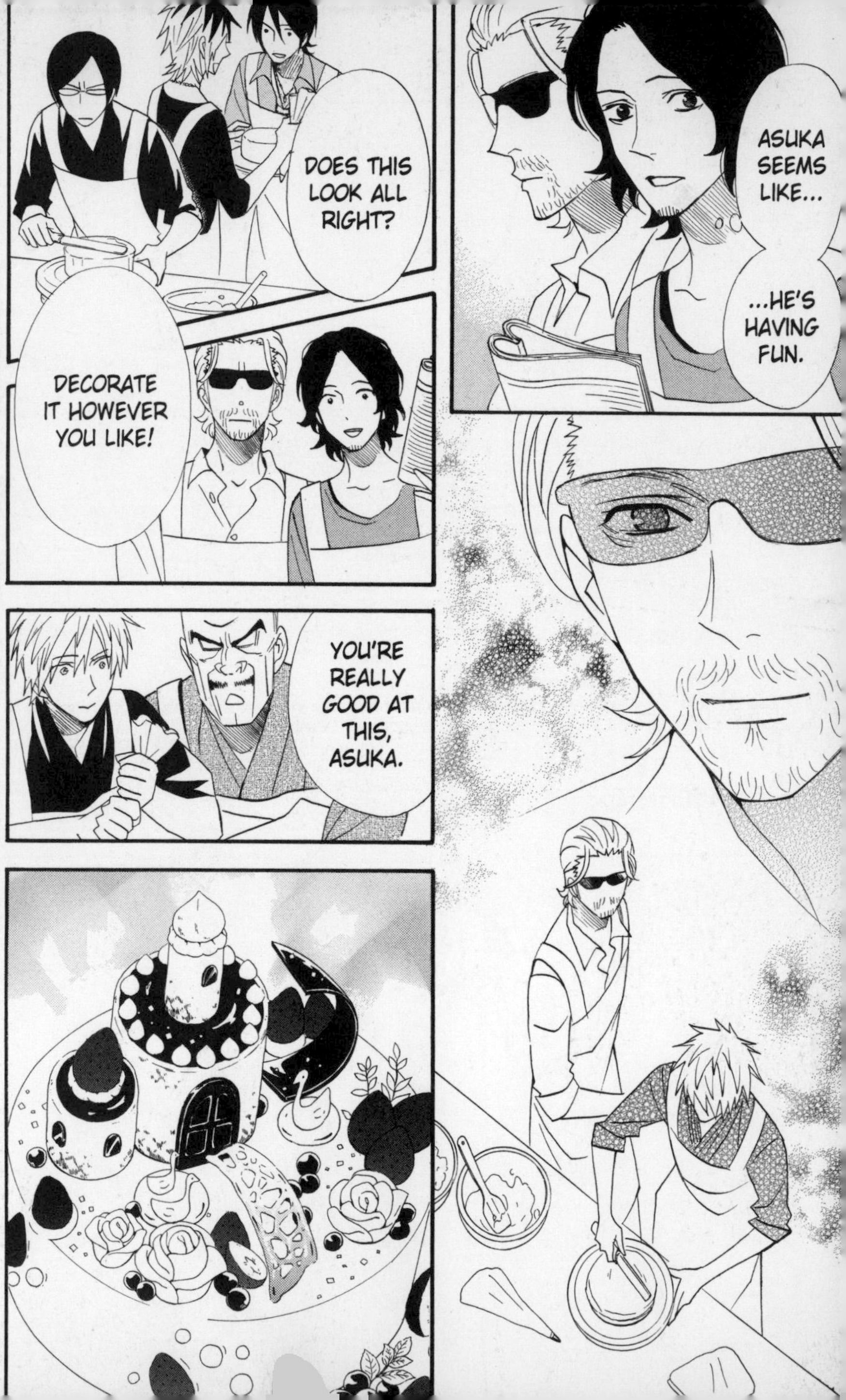
ASUKA SEEMS LIKE...
...HE'S HAVING FUN.
DOES THIS LOOK ALL RIGHT?
DECORATE IT HOWEVER YOU LIKE!
YOU'RE REALLY GOOD AT THIS, ASUKA.

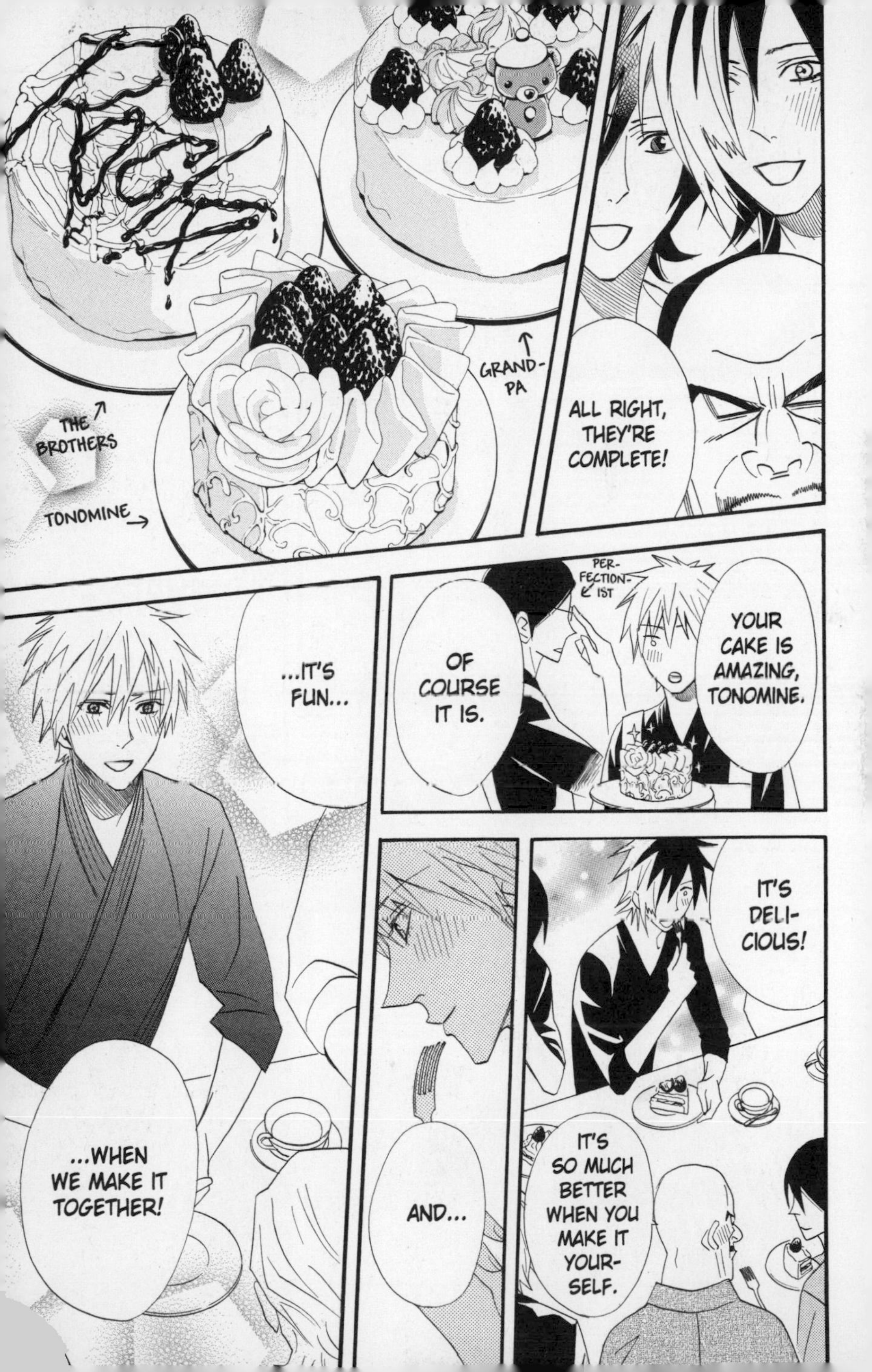
ALL RIGHT, THEY'RE COMPLETE!
GRAND-PA
THE BROTHERS
TONOMINE
YOUR CAKE IS AMAZING, TONOMINE.
PER-FECTION-IST
OF COURSE IT IS.
IT'S DELI-CIOUS!
IT'S SO MUCH BETTER WHEN YOU MAKE IT YOUR-SELF.
AND...
...IT'S FUN...
...WHEN WE MAKE IT TOGETHER!

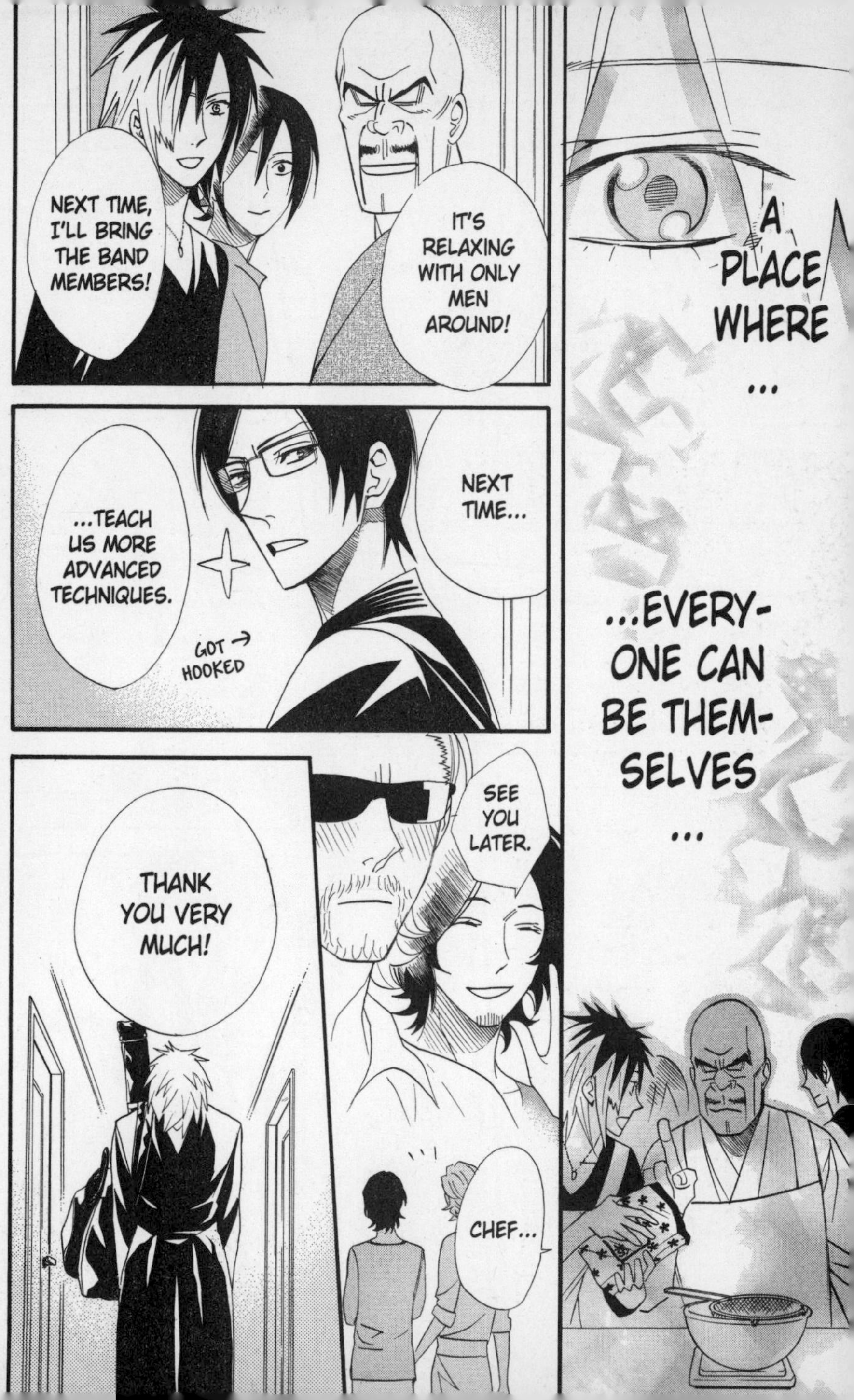
A PLACE WHERE ...
...EVERY-ONE CAN BE THEM-SELVES ...
IT'S RELAXING WITH ONLY MEN AROUND!
NEXT TIME, I'LL BRING THE BAND MEMBERS!
NEXT TIME...
...TEACH US MORE ADVANCED TECHNIQUES.
GOT → HOOKED
SEE YOU LATER.
THANK YOU VERY MUCH!
CHEF...

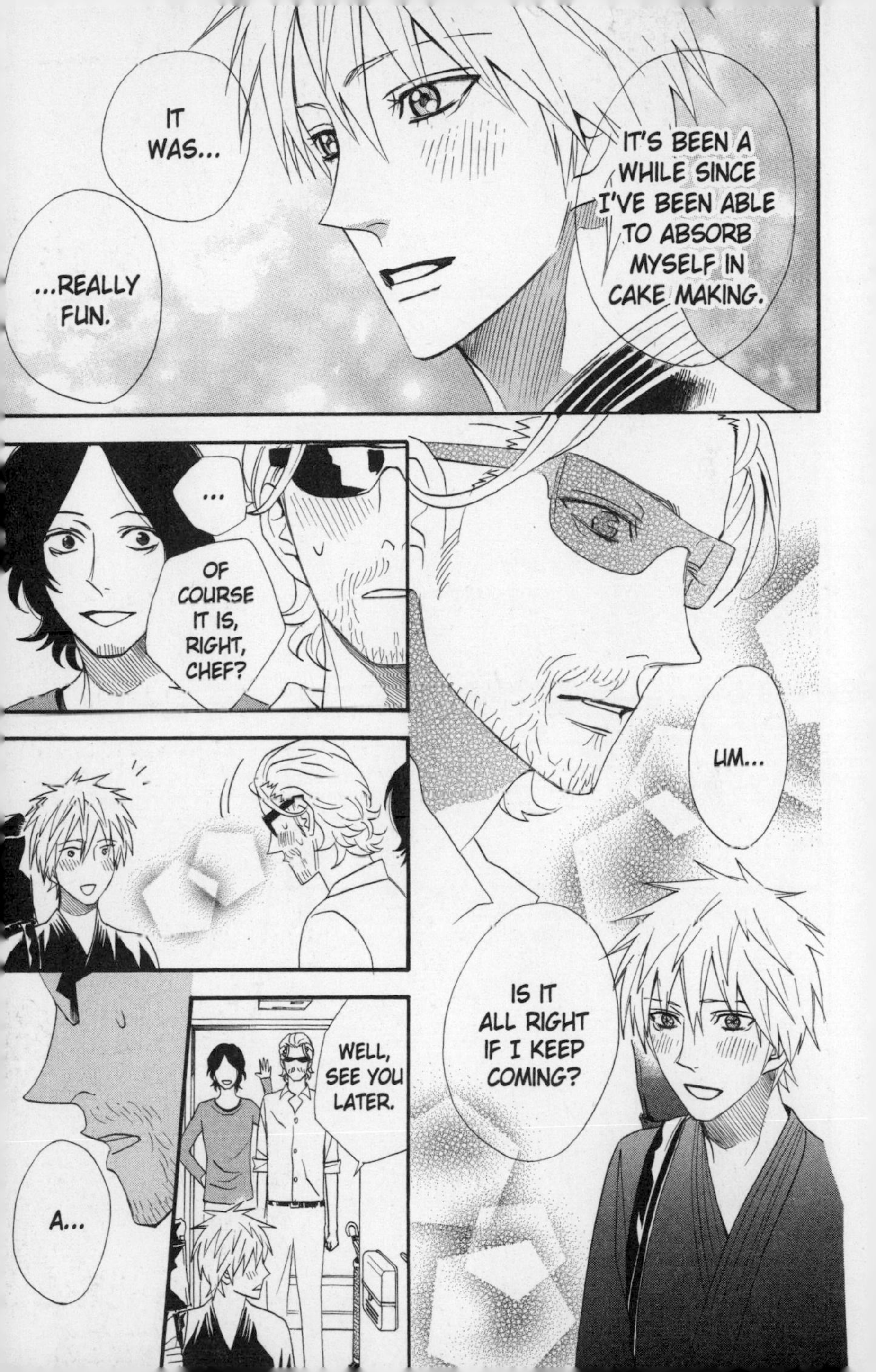
IT'S BEEN A WHILE SINCE I'VE BEEN ABLE TO ABSORB MYSELF IN CAKE MAKING.
IT WAS...
...REALLY FUN.
UM...
IS IT ALL RIGHT IF I KEEP COMING?
...
OF COURSE IT IS, RIGHT, CHEF?
WELL, SEE YOU LATER.
A...

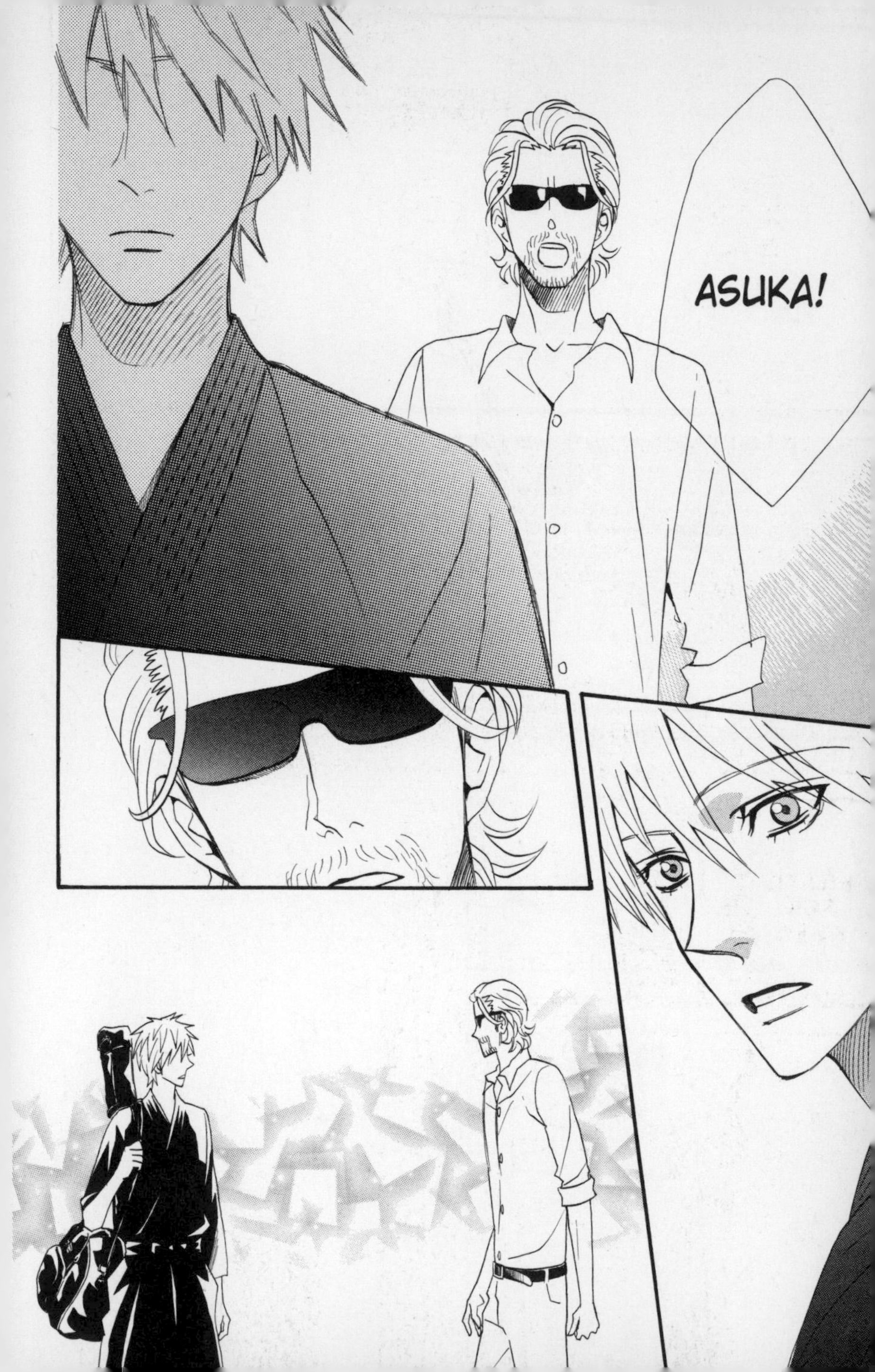
ASUKA!

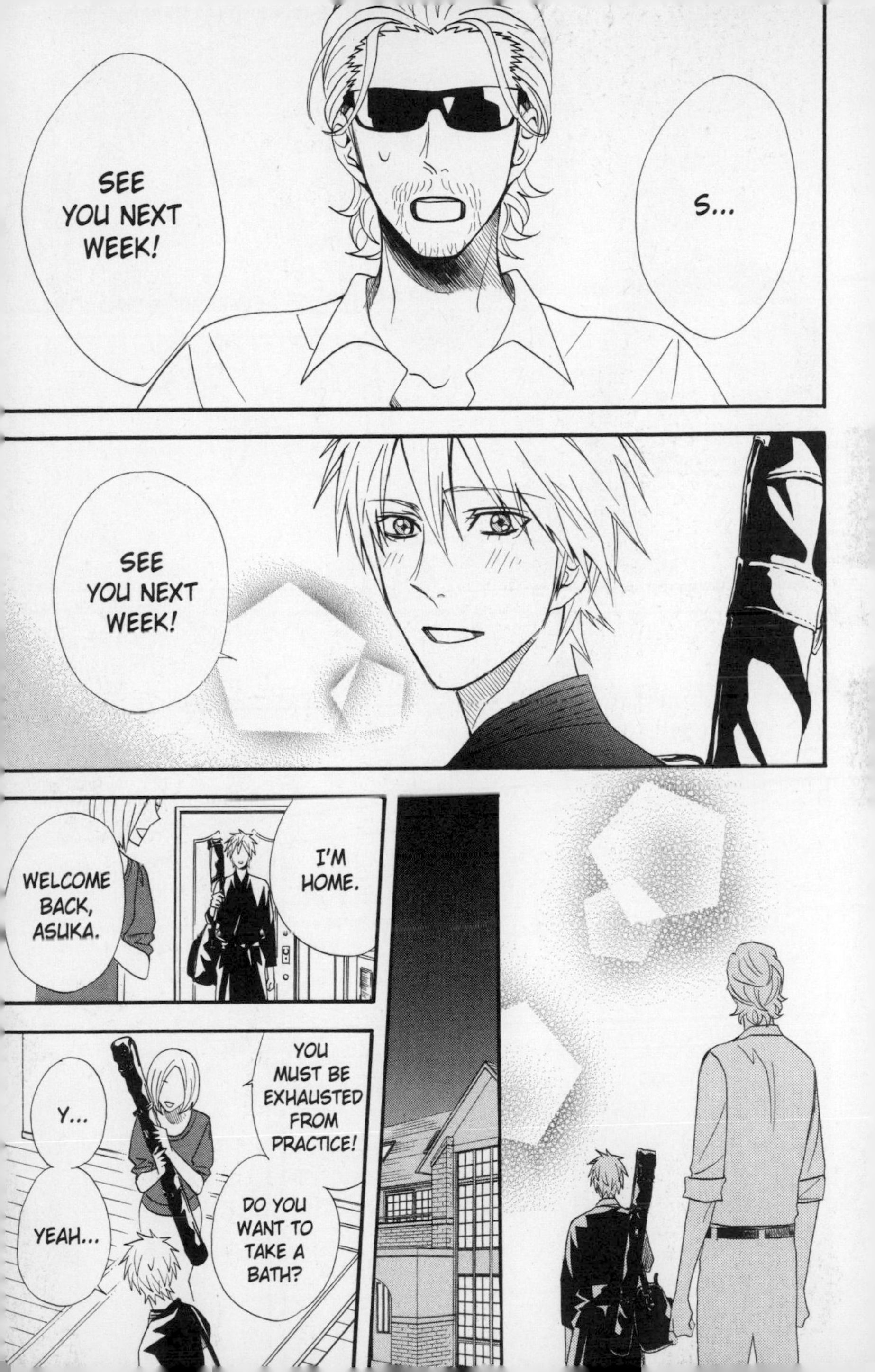
S...
SEE YOU NEXT WEEK!
SEE YOU NEXT WEEK!
I'M HOME.
WELCOME BACK, ASUKA.
YOU MUST BE EXHAUSTED FROM PRACTICE!
DO YOU WANT TO TAKE A BATH?
Y...
YEAH...

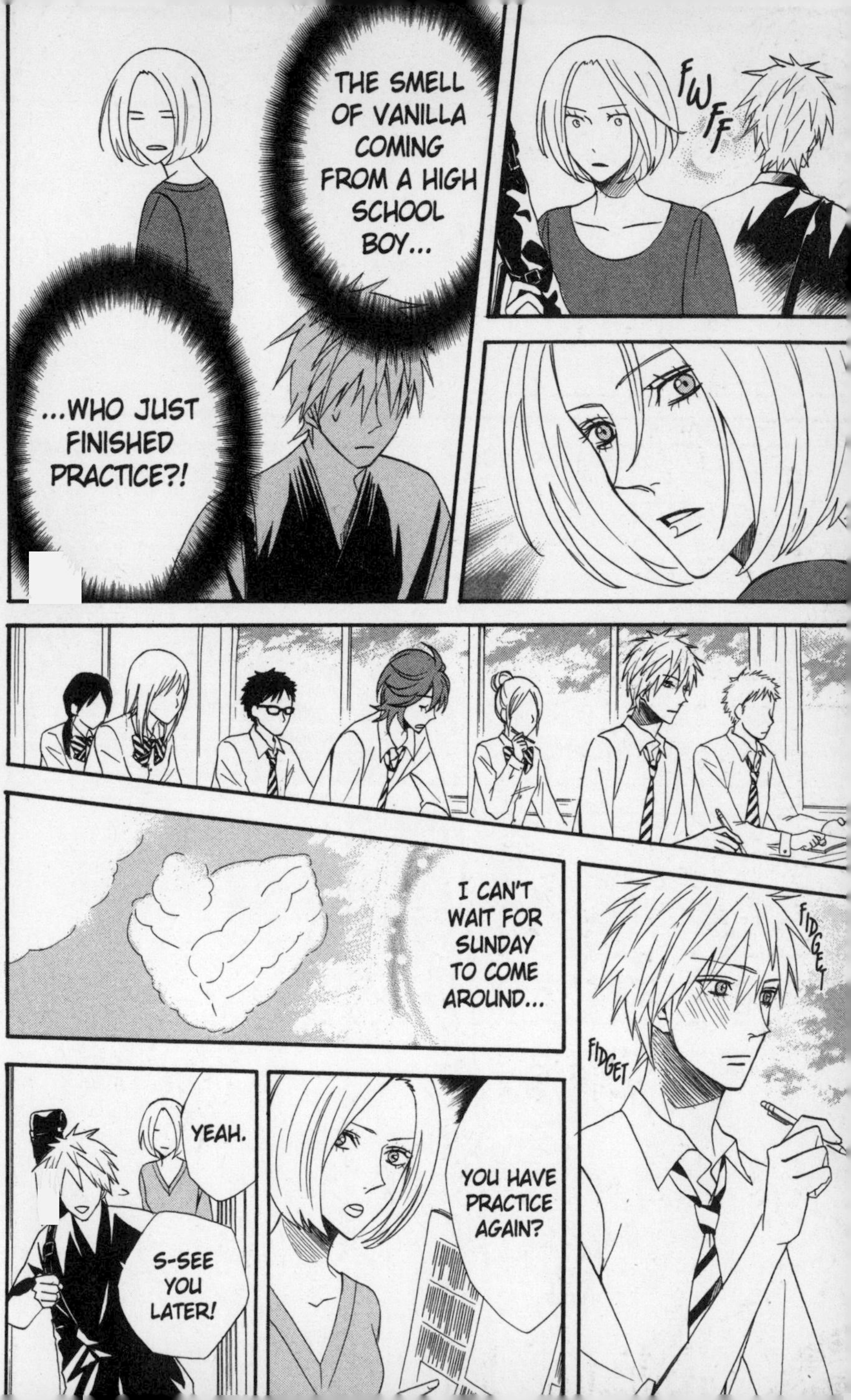
FWFF
THE SMELL OF VANILLA COMING FROM A HIGH SCHOOL BOY...
...WHO JUST FINISHED PRACTICE?!
FIDGET
FIDGET
I CAN'T WAIT FOR SUNDAY TO COME AROUND...
YOU HAVE PRACTICE AGAIN?
YEAH.
S-SEE YOU LATER!

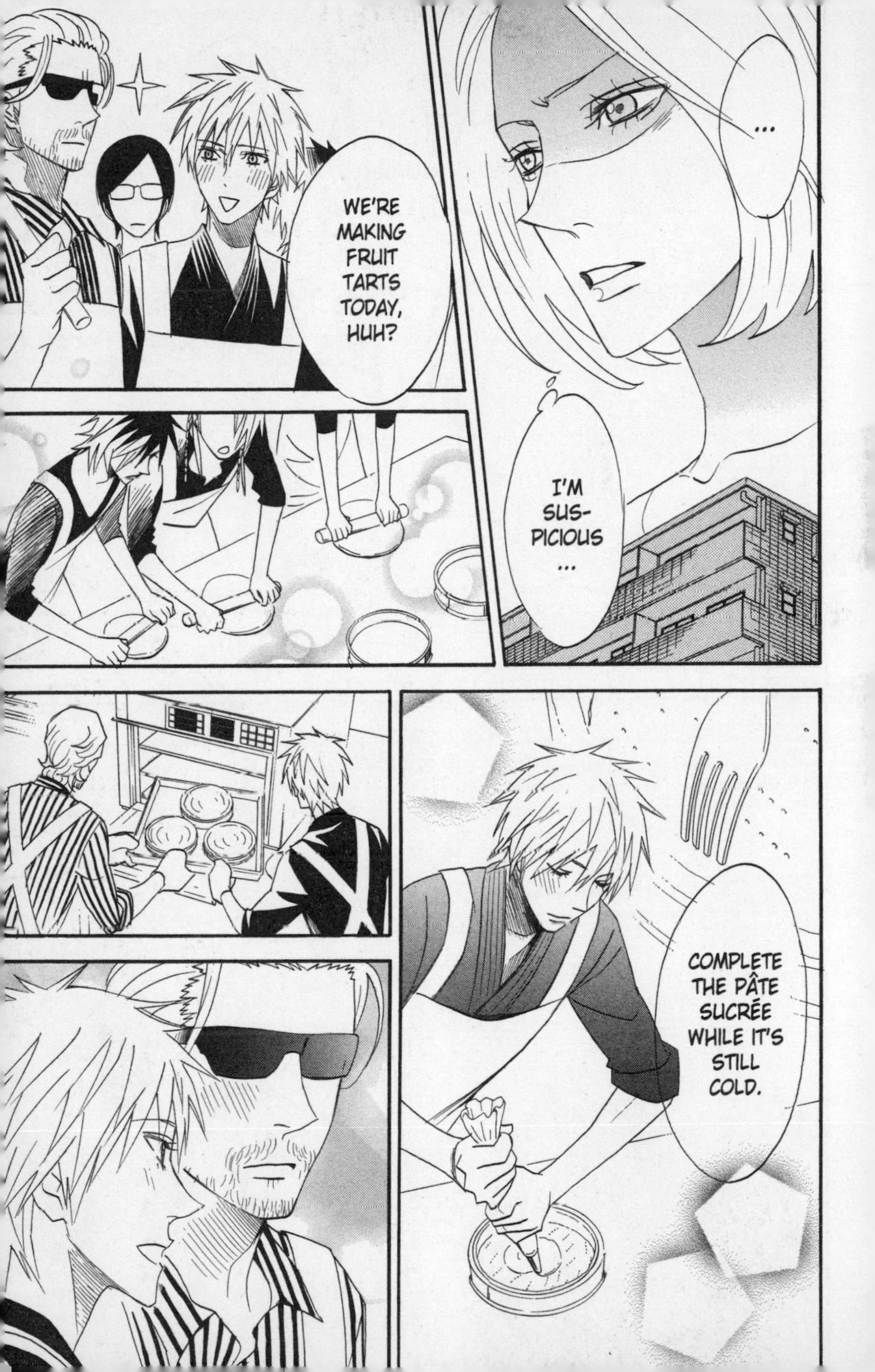
...
I'M SUSPICIOUS...
WE'RE MAKING FRUIT TARTS TODAY, HUH?
COMPLETE THE PÂTE SUCRÉE WHILE IT'S STILL COLD.

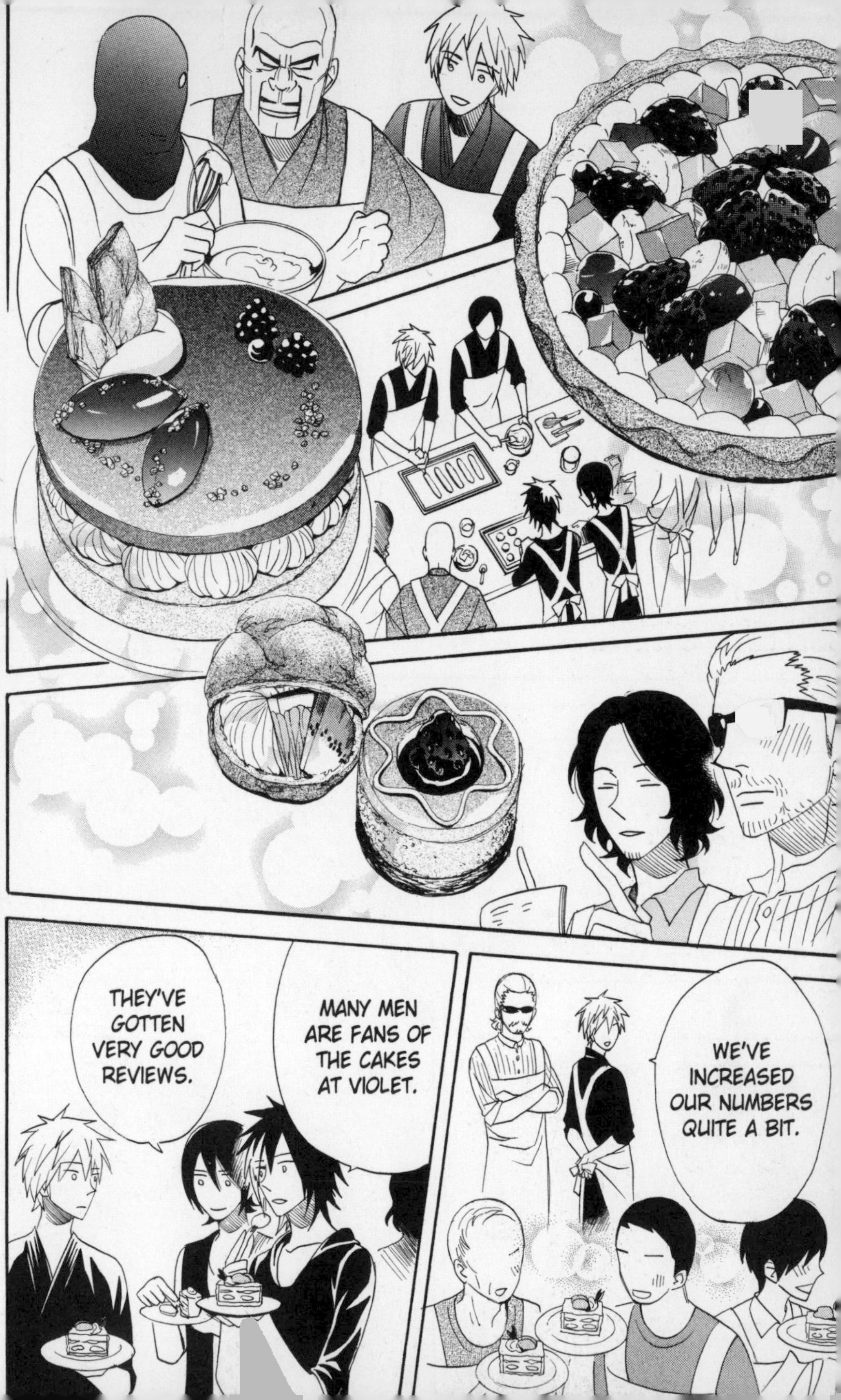
WE'VE INCREASED OUR NUMBERS QUITE A BIT.
MANY MEN ARE FANS OF THE CAKES AT VIOLET.
THEY'VE GOTTEN VERY GOOD REVIEWS.

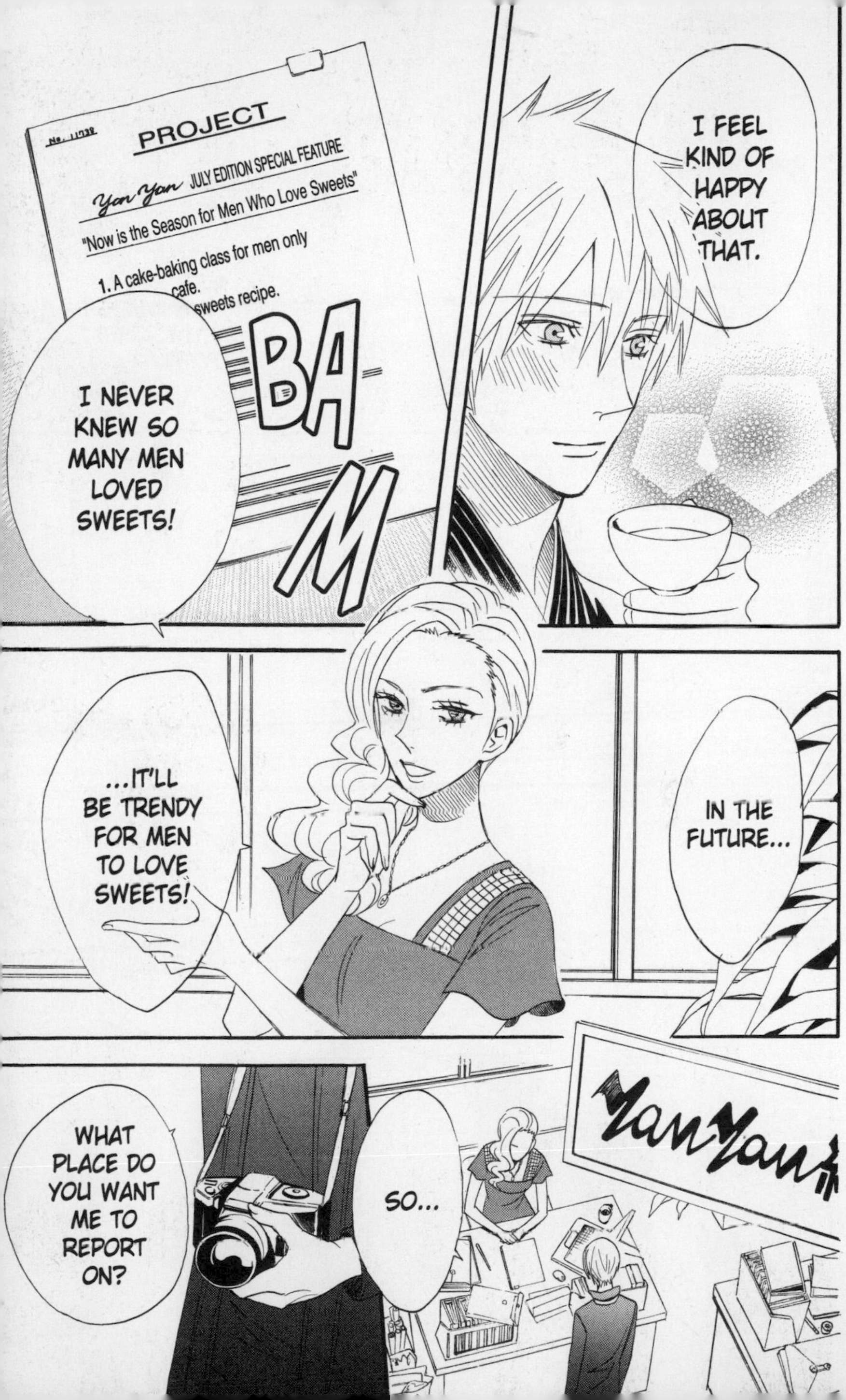
I FEEL KIND OF HAPPY ABOUT THAT.
PROJECT
Yan Yan JULY EDITION SPECIAL FEATURE
"Now is the Season for Men Who Love Sweets"
1. A cake-baking class for men only
cafe.
sweets recipe.
BAM
I NEVER KNEW SO MANY MEN LOVED SWEETS!
IN THE FUTURE...
...IT'LL BE TRENDY FOR MEN TO LOVE SWEETS!
YanYan
SO...
WHAT PLACE DO YOU WANT ME TO REPORT ON?

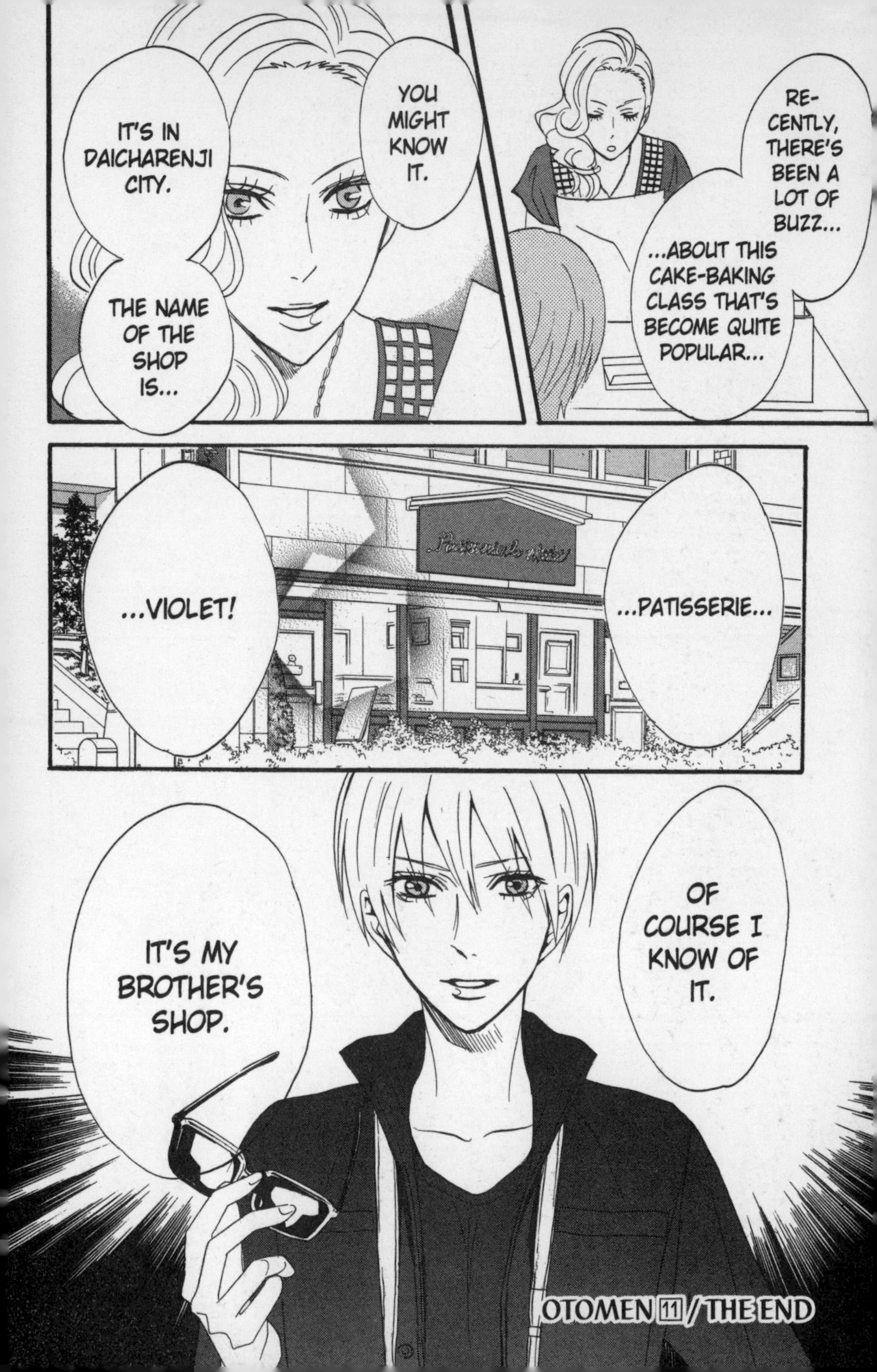
RE-CENTLY, THERE'S BEEN A LOT OF BUZZ...
...ABOUT THIS CAKE-BAKING CLASS THAT'S BECOME QUITE POPULAR...
YOU MIGHT KNOW IT.
IT'S IN DAICHARENJI CITY.
THE NAME OF THE SHOP IS...
...PATISSERIE...
...VIOLET!
OF COURSE I KNOW OF IT.
IT'S MY BROTHER'S SHOP.
OTOMEN 11 / THE END

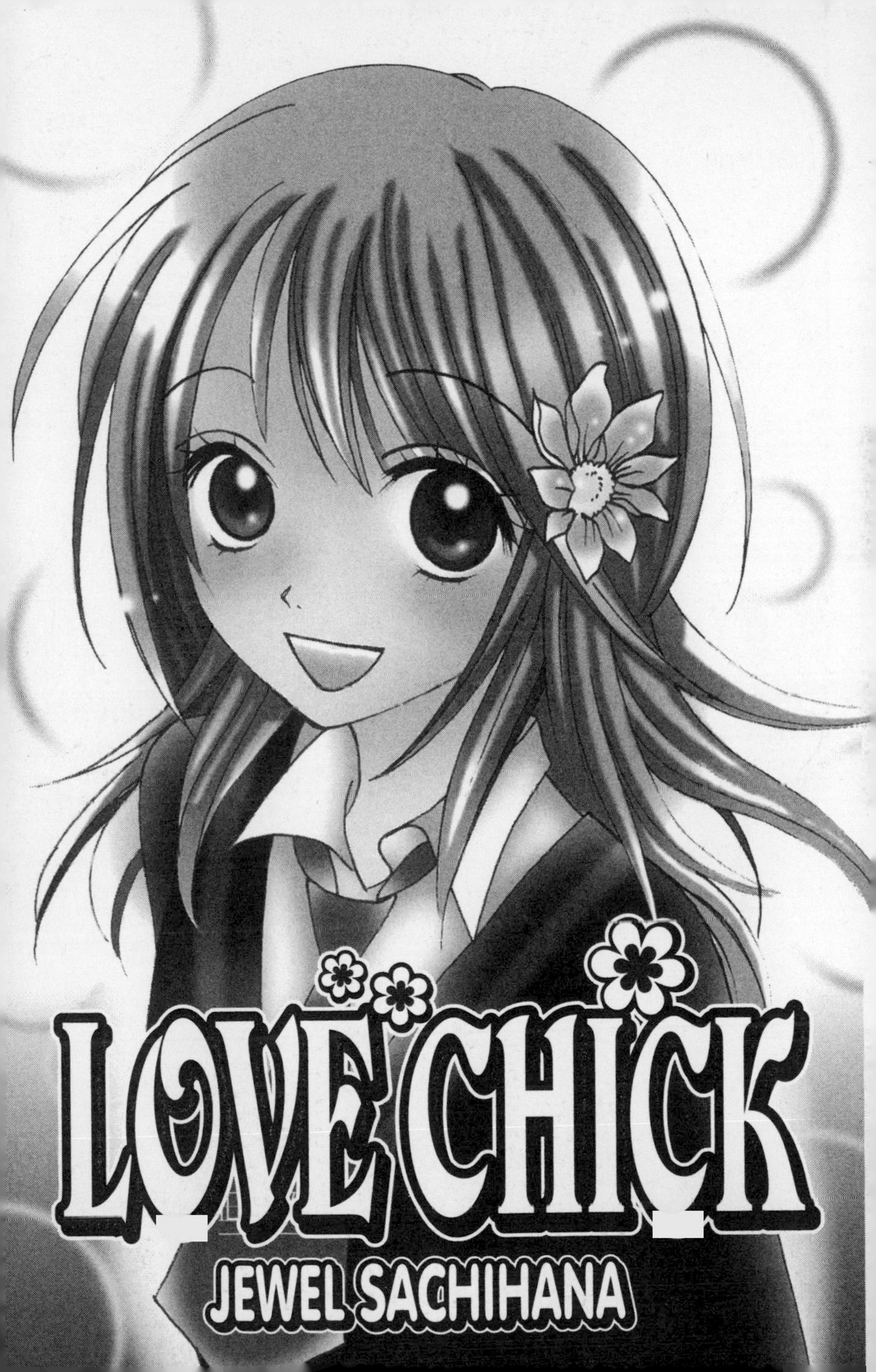
LOVE CHICK
JEWEL SACHIHANA

OTOMEN

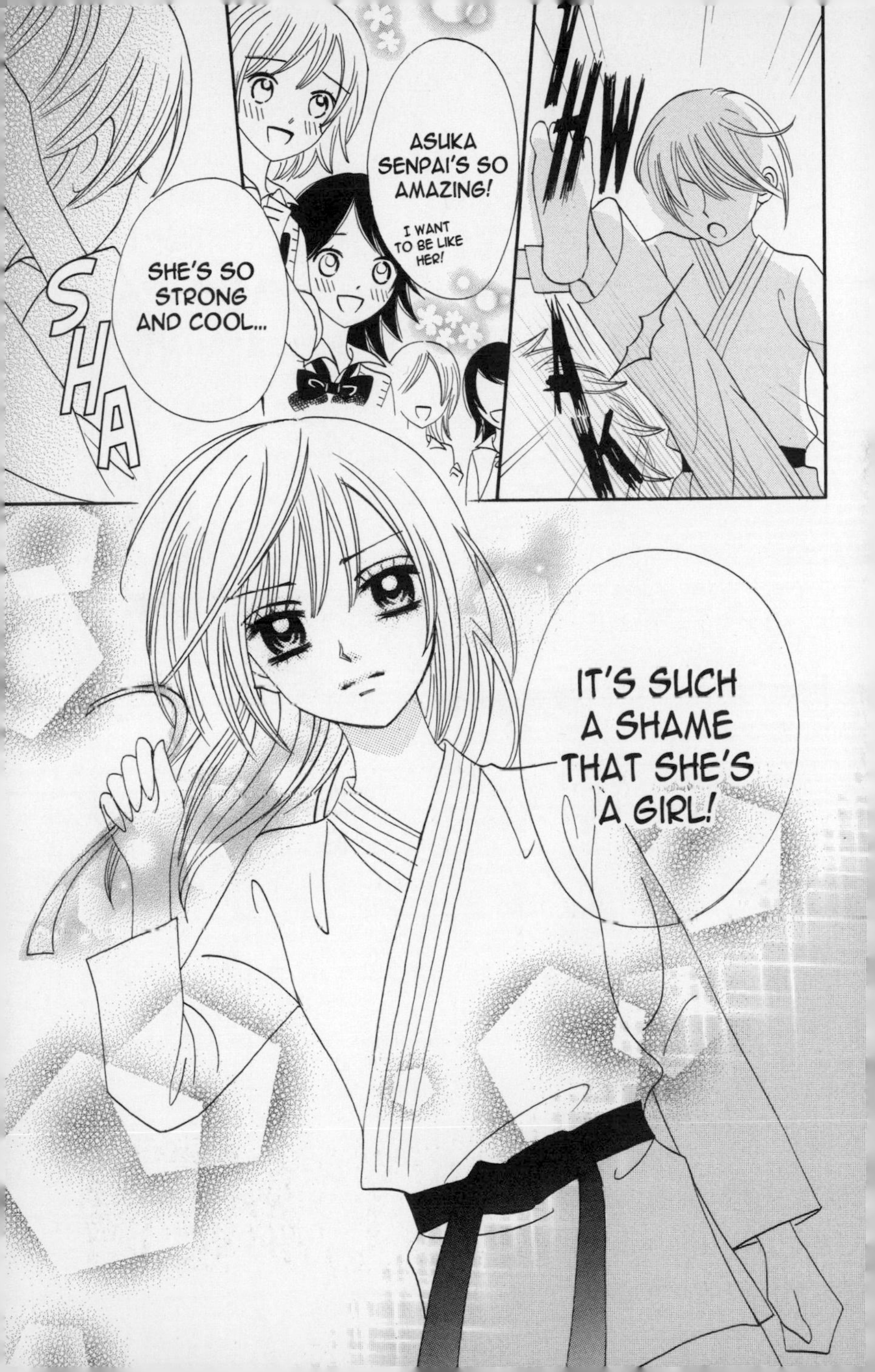
THWAK
ASUKA SENPAI'S SO AMAZING!
I WANT TO BE LIKE HER!
SHE'S SO STRONG AND COOL...
SHA
IT'S SUCH A SHAME THAT SHE'S A GIRL!

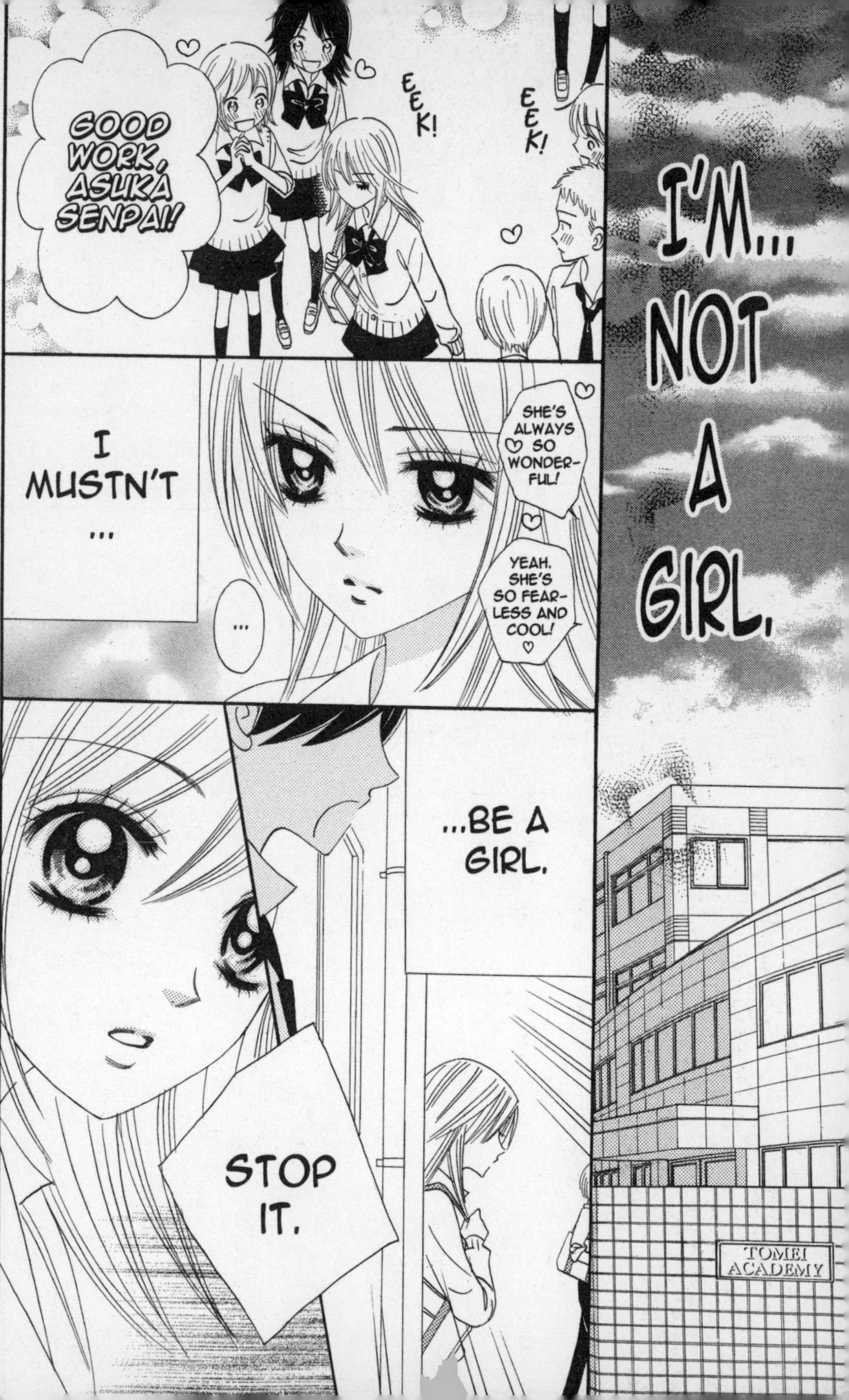
I'M... NOT A GIRL.
TOMEI ACADEMY
EEK!
EEK!
GOOD WORK, ASUKA SENPAI!
SHE'S ALWAYS SO WONDERFUL!
YEAH. SHE'S SO FEARLESS AND COOL!
...
I MUSTN'T ...
...BE A GIRL.
STOP IT.

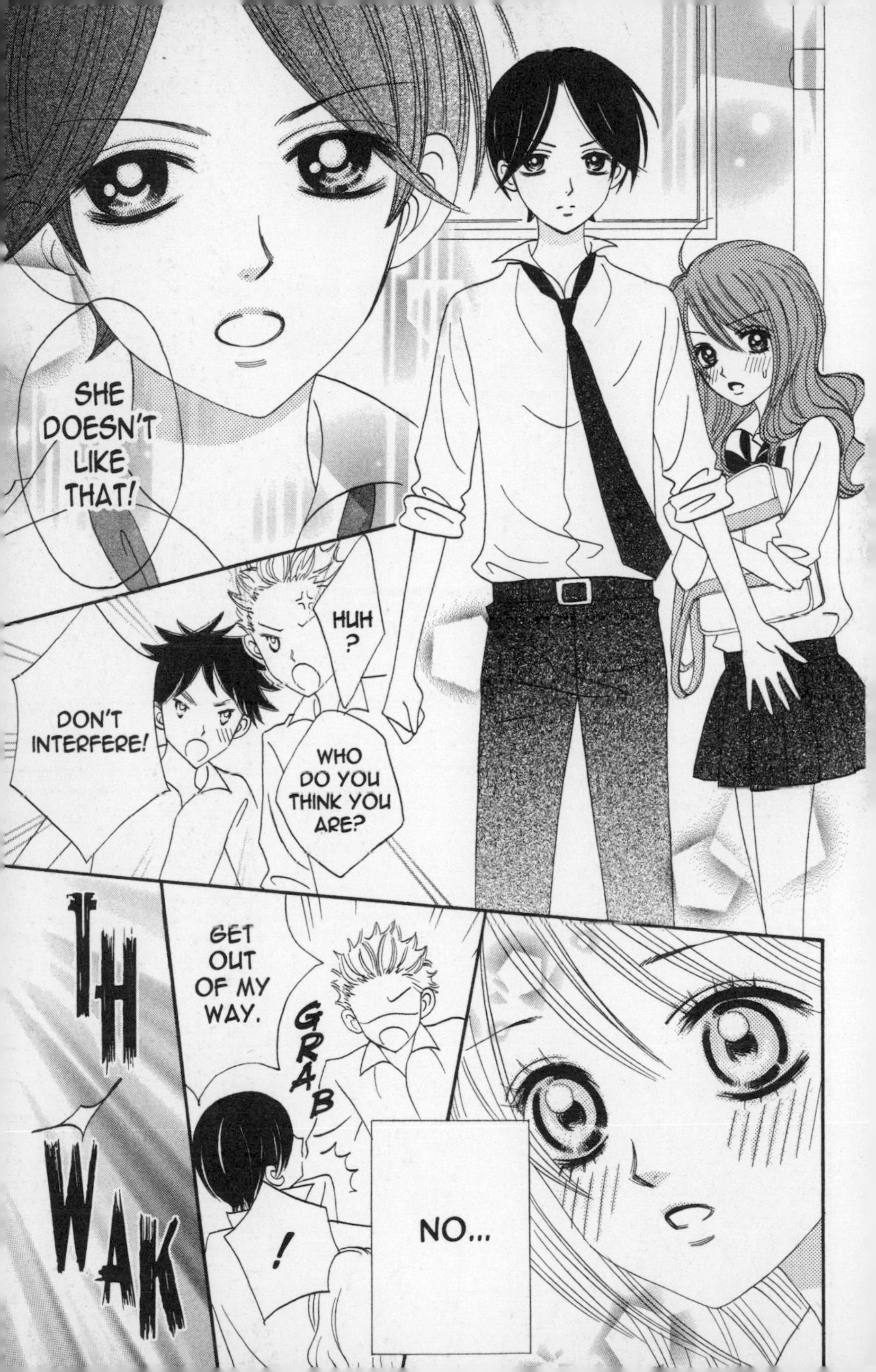
SHE DOESN'T LIKE THAT!
HUH?
WHO DO YOU THINK YOU ARE?
DON'T INTERFERE!
NO...
GET OUT OF MY WAY.
GRAB
!
THWAK

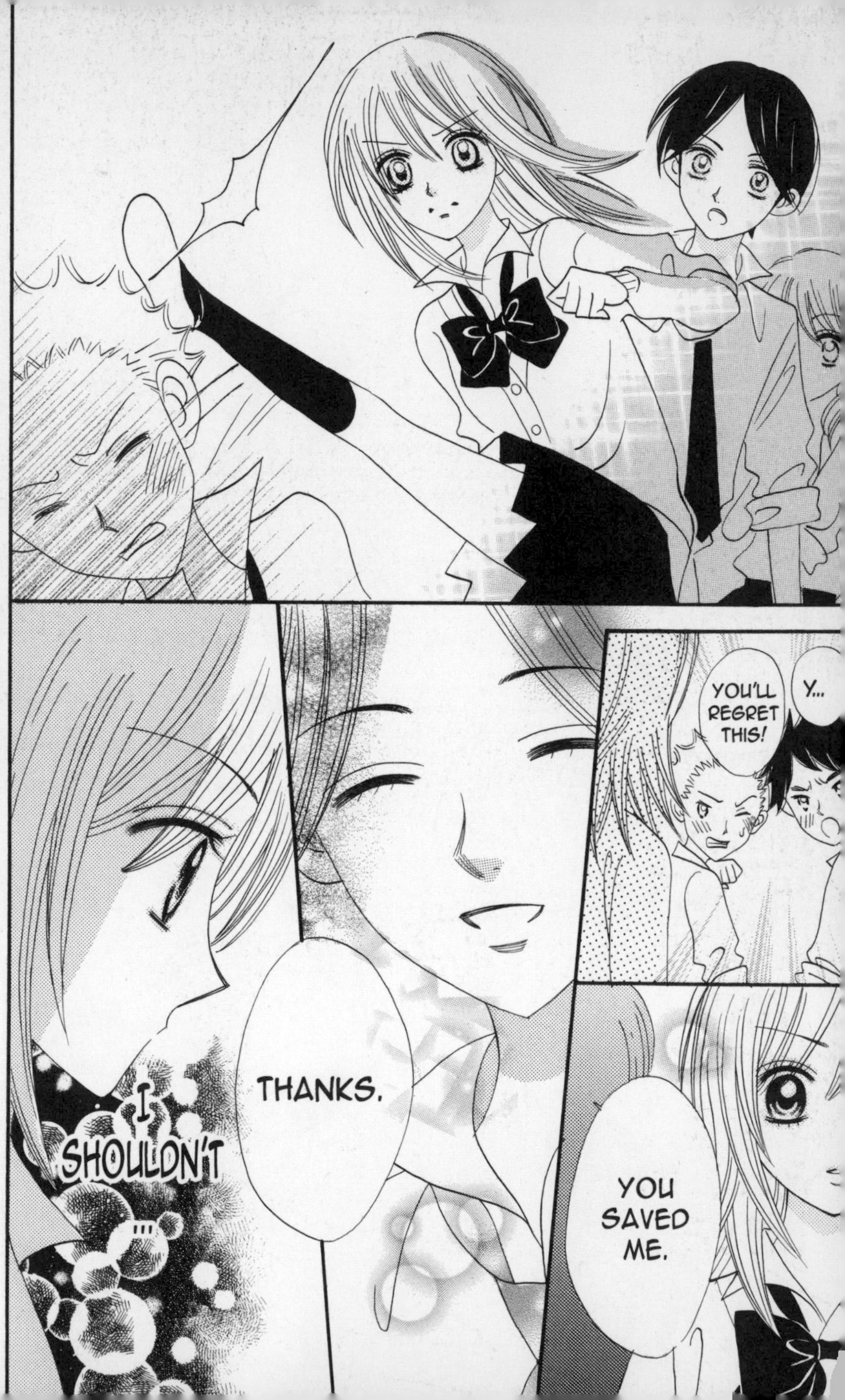
Y...
YOU'LL REGRET THIS!
YOU SAVED ME.
THANKS.
I SHOULDN'T ...

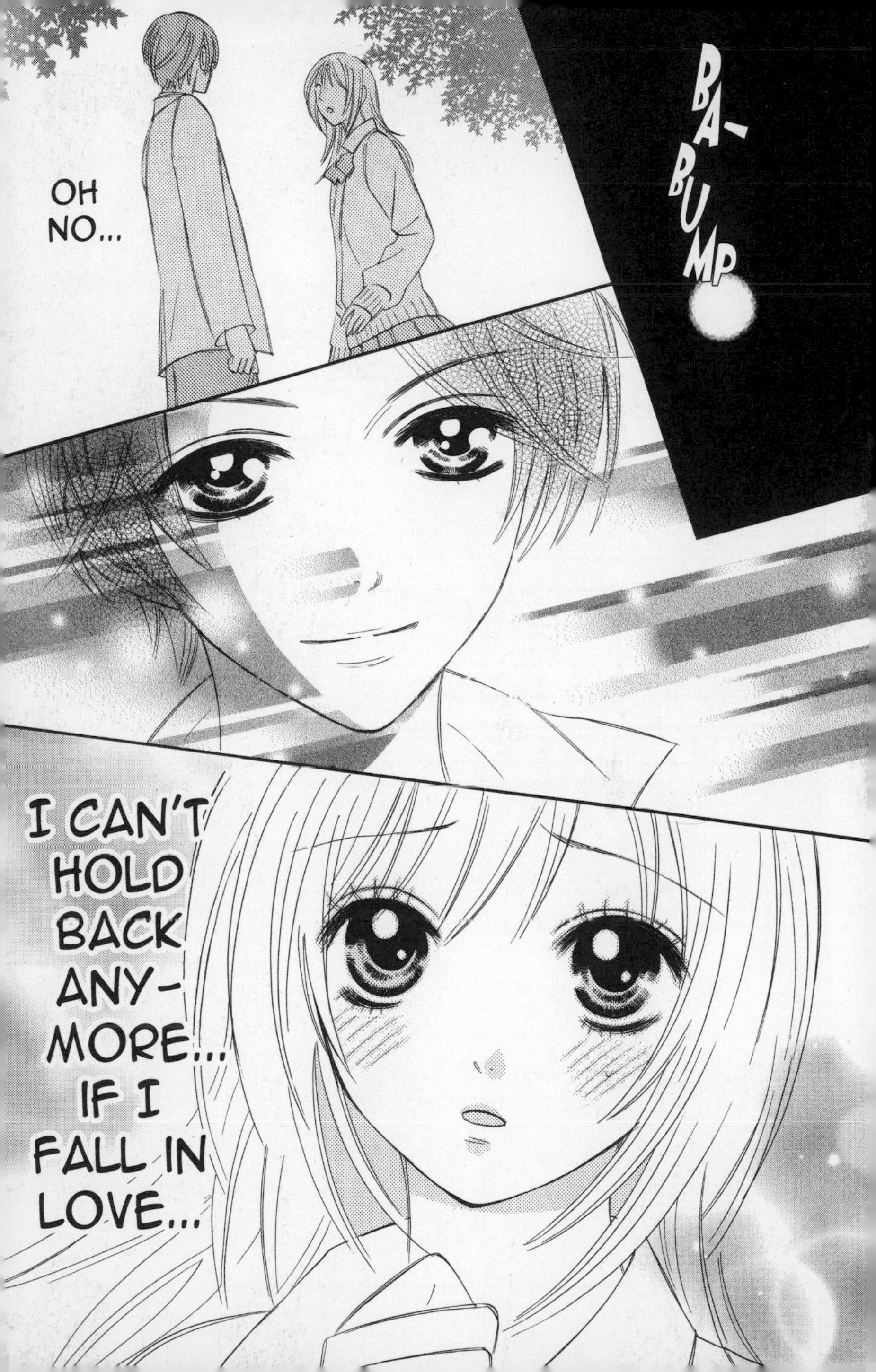
BA-BUMP
OH NO...
I CAN'T HOLD BACK ANY-MORE... IF I FALL IN LOVE...

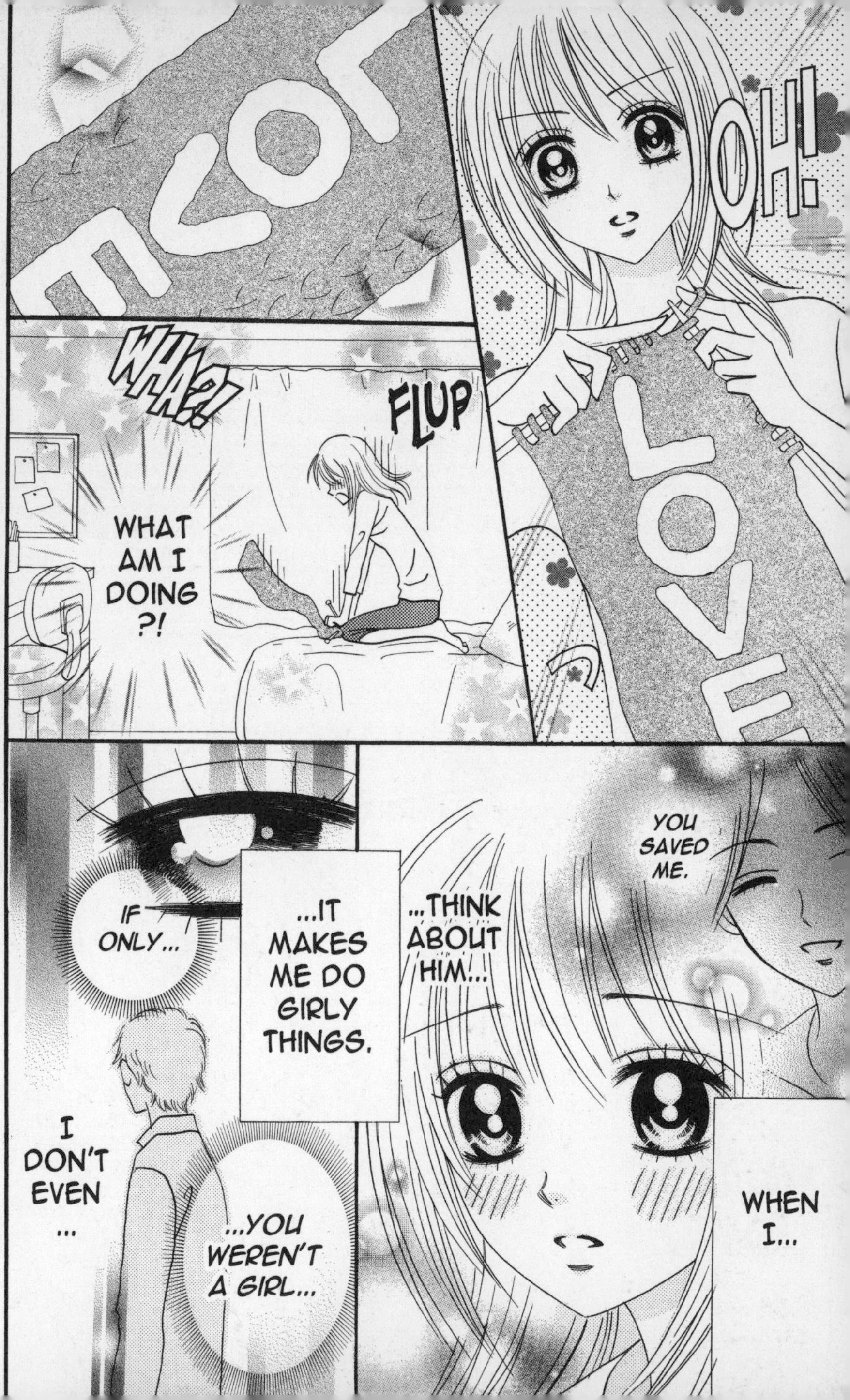
OH!
WHA?!
FLUP
WHAT AM I DOING ?!
YOU SAVED ME.
WHEN I...
...THINK ABOUT HIM...
...IT MAKES ME DO GIRLY THINGS.
IF ONLY...
...YOU WEREN'T A GIRL...
I DON'T EVEN ...

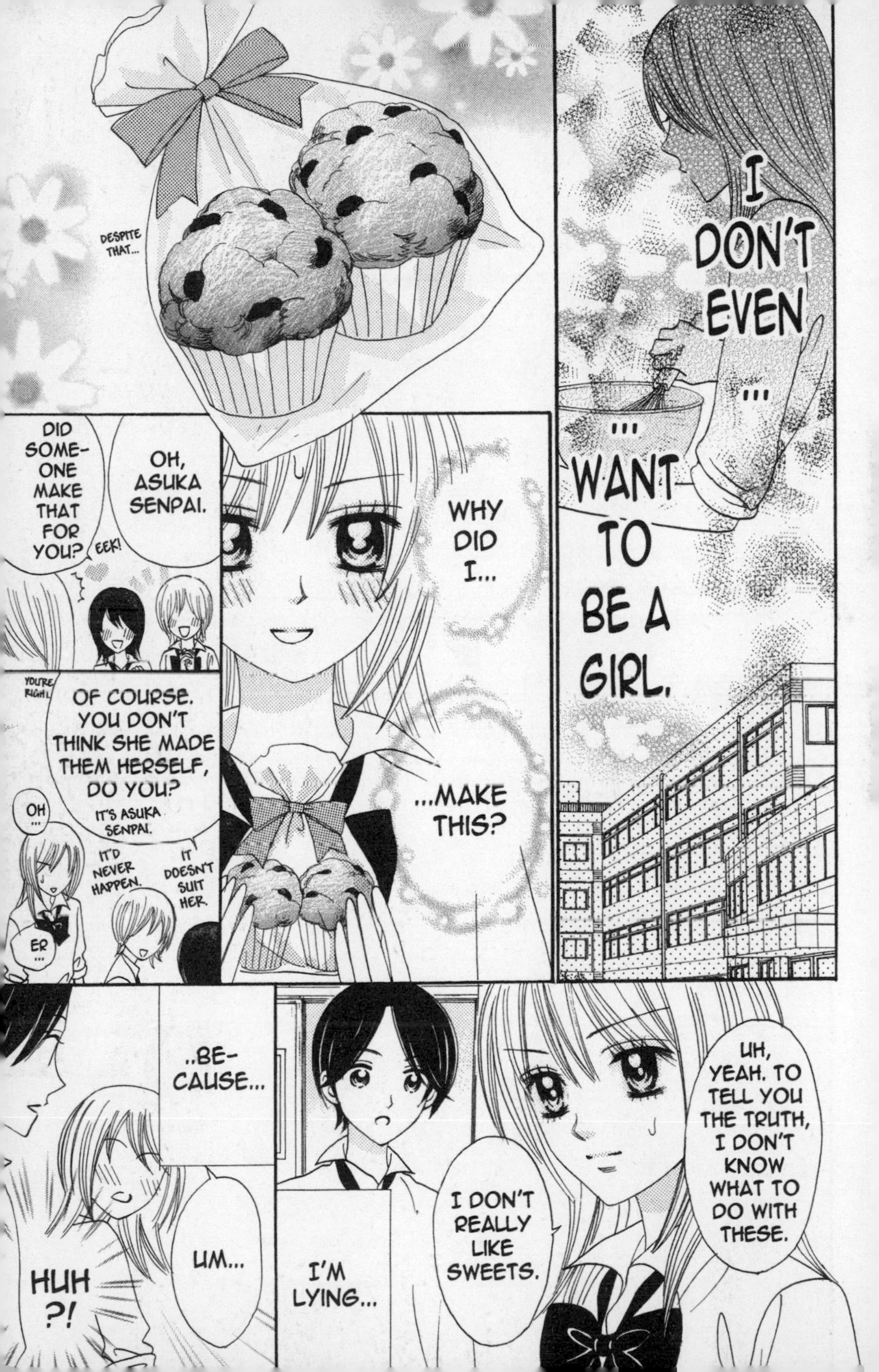
I DON'T EVEN ...
... WANT TO BE A GIRL.
DESPITE THAT...
WHY DID I...
...MAKE THIS?
OH, ASUKA SENPAI.
DID SOME-ONE MAKE THAT FOR YOU?
EEK!
OF COURSE. YOU DON'T THINK SHE MADE THEM HERSELF, DO YOU?
YOU'RE RIGHT.
IT'S ASUKA SENPAI.
IT DOESN'T SUIT HER.
IT'D NEVER HAPPEN.
OH ...
ER ...
UH, YEAH. TO TELL YOU THE TRUTH, I DON'T KNOW WHAT TO DO WITH THESE.
I DON'T REALLY LIKE SWEETS.
I'M LYING...
..BE-CAUSE...
UM...
HUH ?!

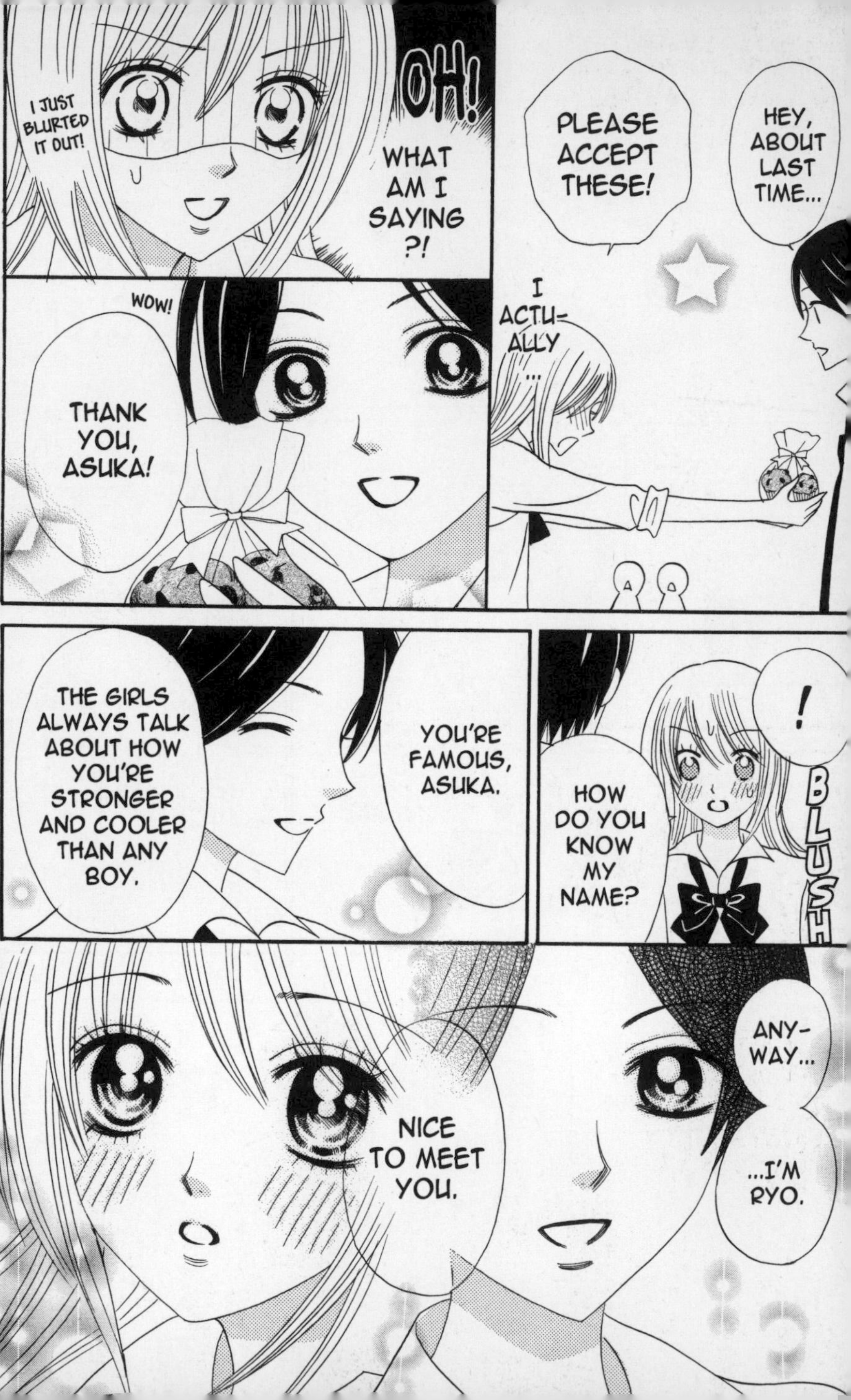
HEY, ABOUT LAST TIME...
PLEASE ACCEPT THESE!
I ACTU-ALLY...
OH!
WHAT AM I SAYING?!
I JUST BLURTED IT OUT!
WOW!
THANK YOU, ASUKA!
!
HOW DO YOU KNOW MY NAME?
BLUSH
YOU'RE FAMOUS, ASUKA.
THE GIRLS ALWAYS TALK ABOUT HOW YOU'RE STRONGER AND COOLER THAN ANY BOY.
ANY-WAY...
...I'M RYO.
NICE TO MEET YOU.

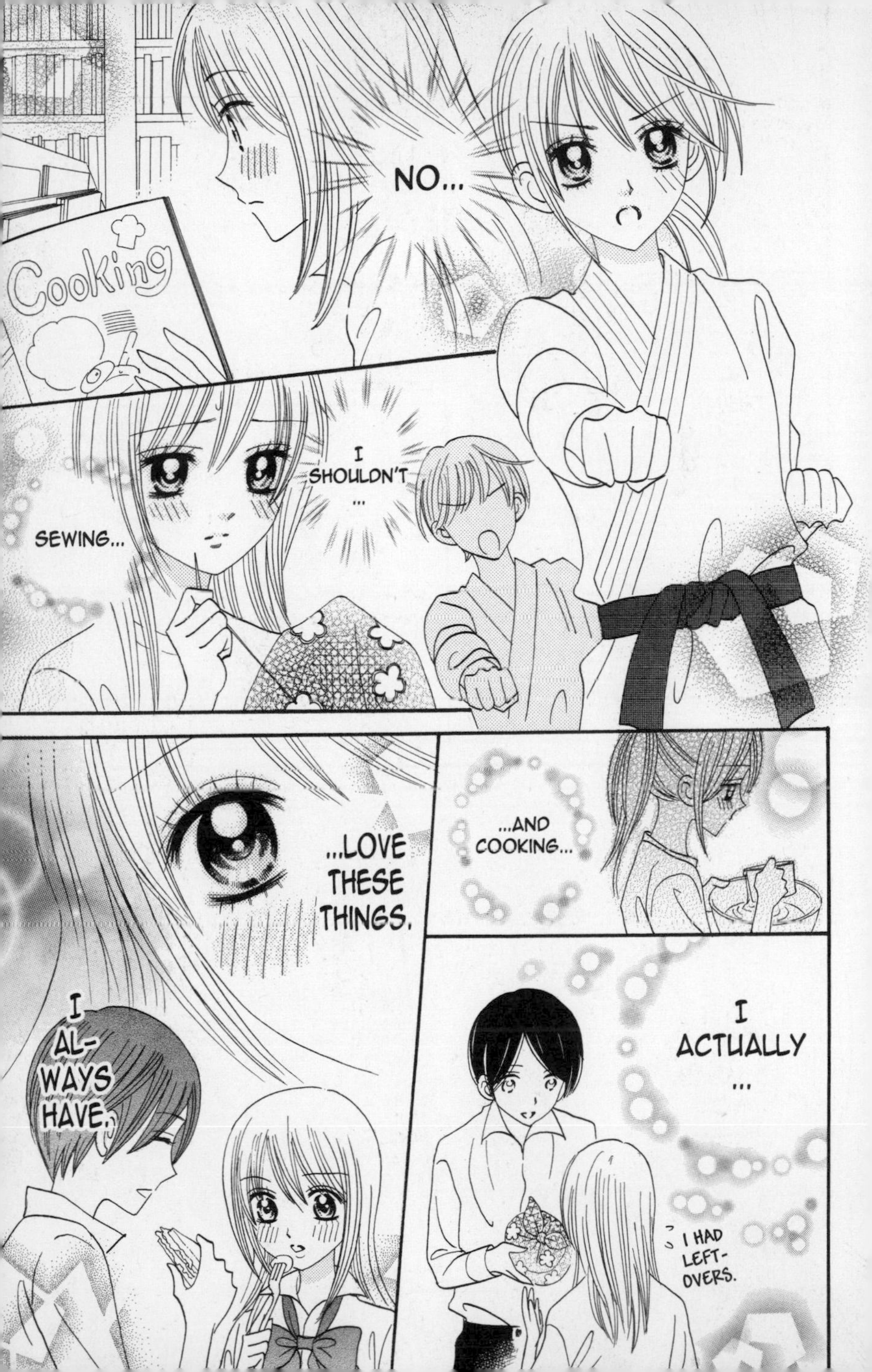
NO...
Cooking
I SHOULDN'T ...
SEWING...
...AND COOKING...
I ACTUALLY ...
I HAD LEFT-OVERS.
...LOVE THESE THINGS.
I AL-WAYS HAVE.

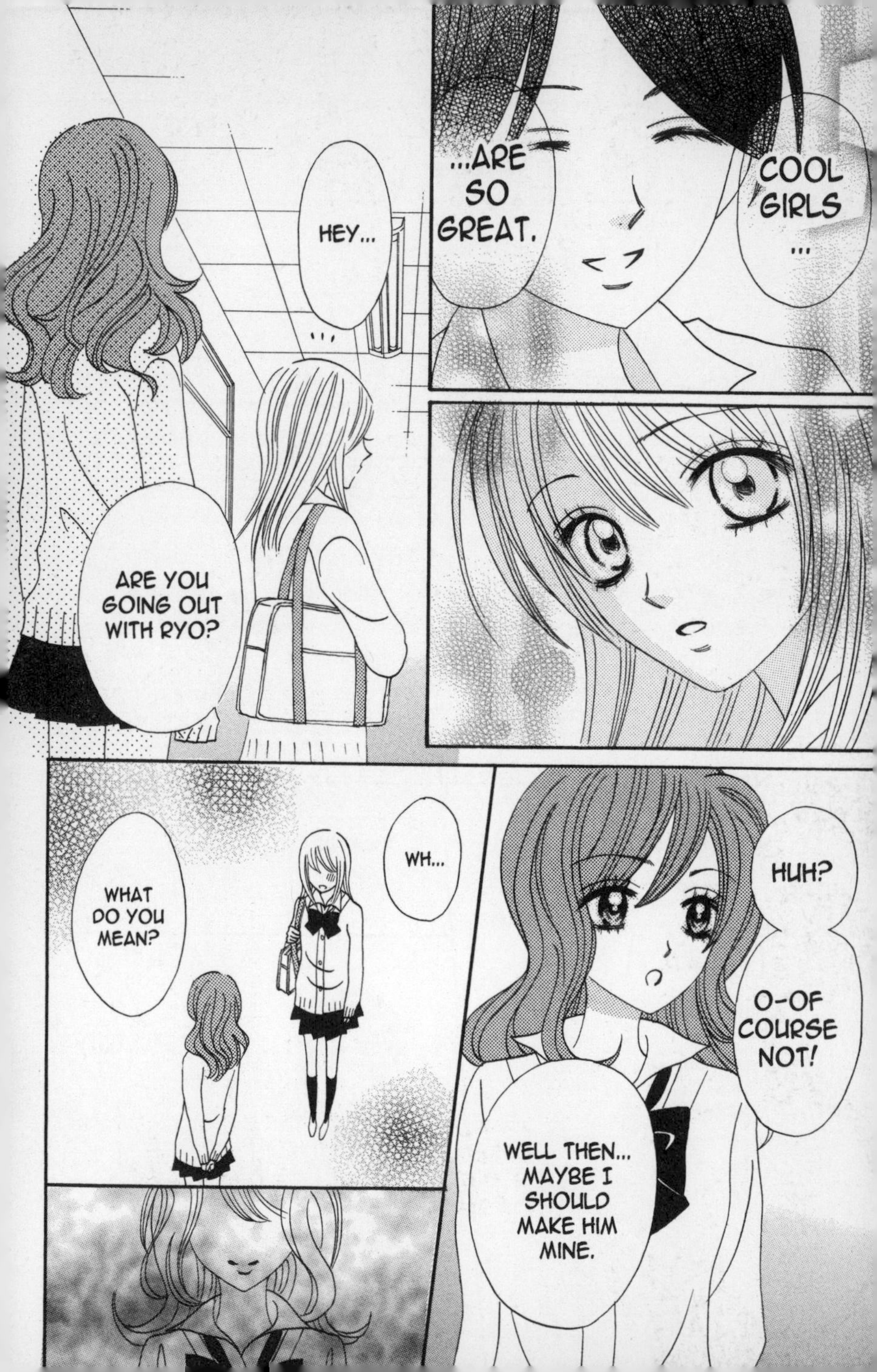
COOL GIRLS ...
...ARE SO GREAT.
HEY...
ARE YOU GOING OUT WITH RYO?
HUH?
O-OF COURSE NOT!
WELL THEN... MAYBE I SHOULD MAKE HIM MINE.
WH...
WHAT DO YOU MEAN?

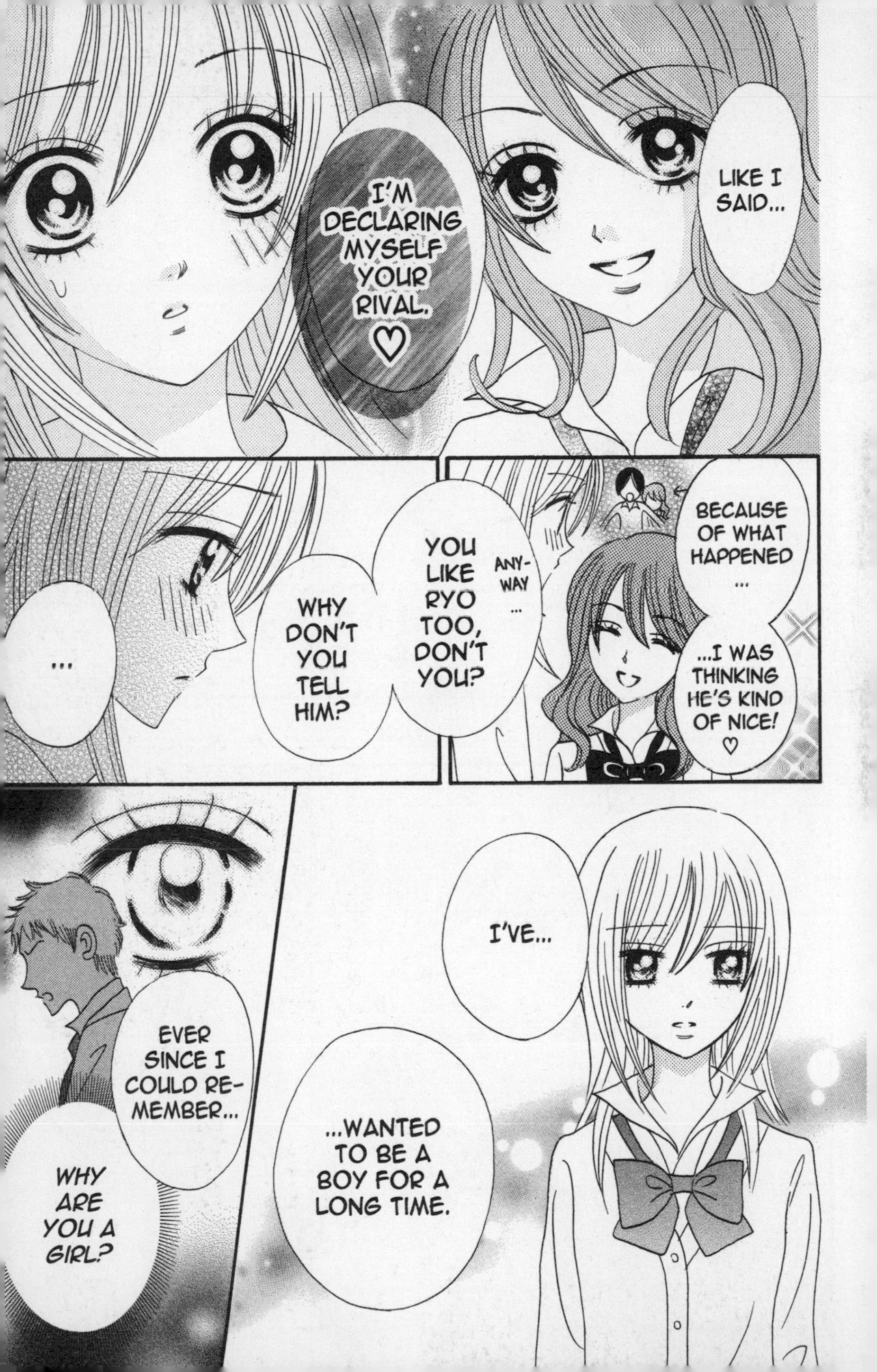
LIKE I SAID...
I'M DECLARING MYSELF YOUR RIVAL. ♡
BECAUSE OF WHAT HAPPENED ...
...I WAS THINKING HE'S KIND OF NICE! ♡
ANY-WAY ...
YOU LIKE RYO TOO, DON'T YOU?
WHY DON'T YOU TELL HIM?
...
I'VE...
...WANTED TO BE A BOY FOR A LONG TIME.
EVER SINCE I COULD RE-MEMBER...
WHY ARE YOU A GIRL?

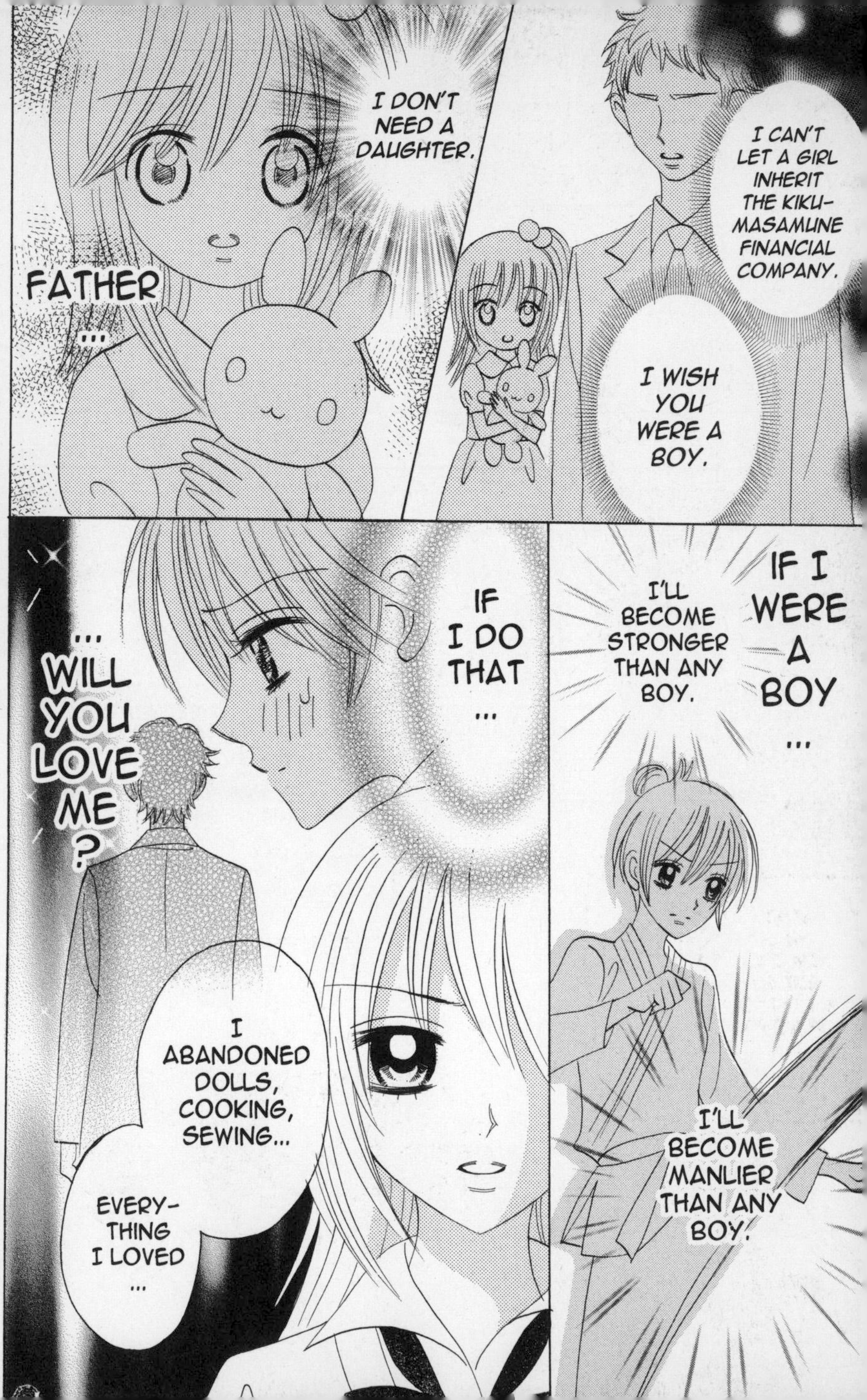
I CAN'T LET A GIRL INHERIT THE KIKU-MASAMUNE FINANCIAL COMPANY.
I WISH YOU WERE A BOY.
I DON'T NEED A DAUGHTER.
FATHER ...
IF I WERE A BOY ...
I'LL BECOME STRONGER THAN ANY BOY.
I'LL BECOME MANLIER THAN ANY BOY.
IF I DO THAT ...
... WILL YOU LOVE ME?
I ABANDONED DOLLS, COOKING, SEWING...
EVERY-THING I LOVED ...

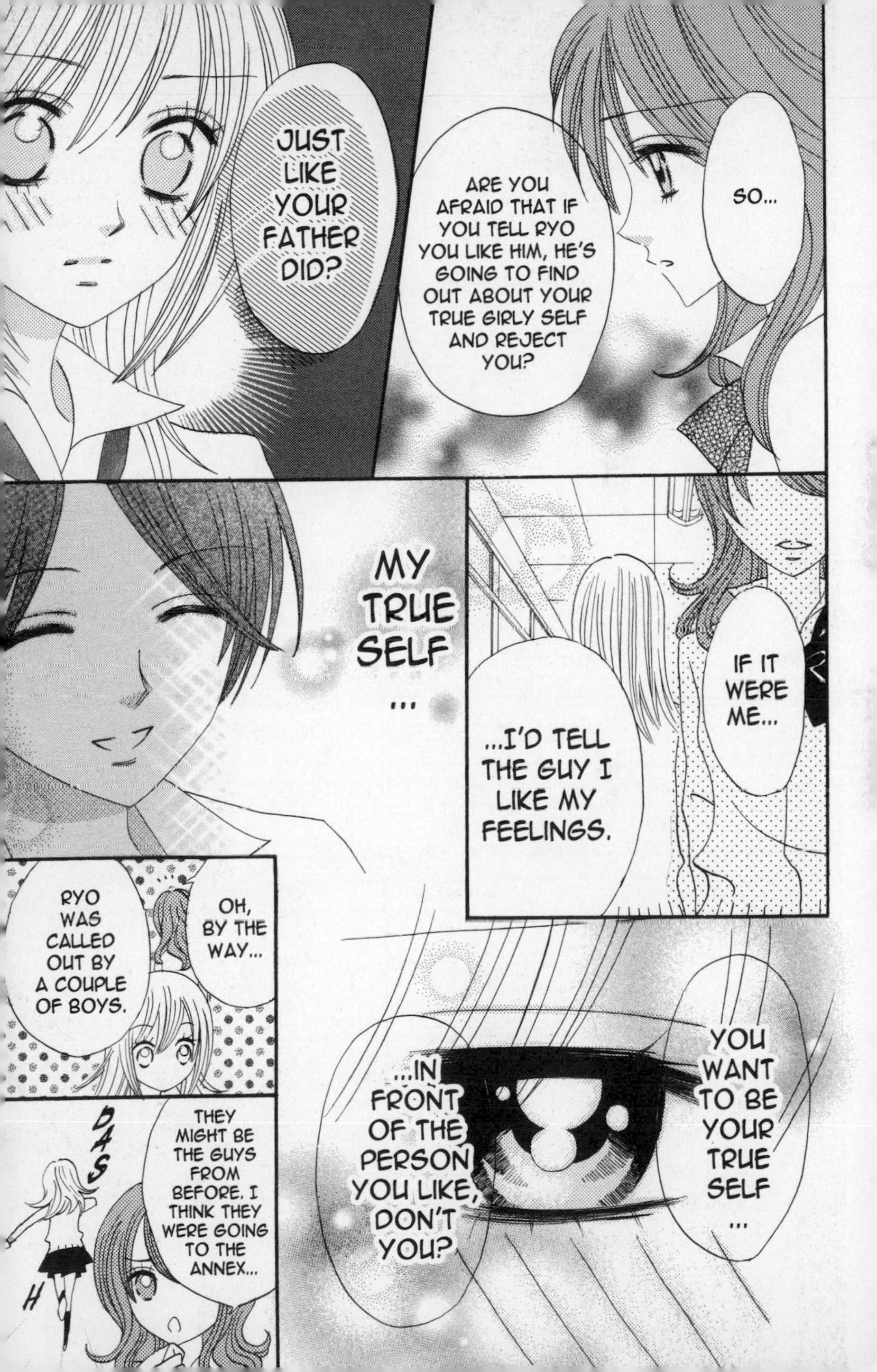
SO...
ARE YOU AFRAID THAT IF YOU TELL RYO YOU LIKE HIM, HE'S GOING TO FIND OUT ABOUT YOUR TRUE GIRLY SELF AND REJECT YOU?
JUST LIKE YOUR FATHER DID?
IF IT WERE ME...
...I'D TELL THE GUY I LIKE MY FEELINGS.
MY TRUE SELF ...
YOU WANT TO BE YOUR TRUE SELF ...
...IN FRONT OF THE PERSON YOU LIKE, DON'T YOU?
OH, BY THE WAY...
RYO WAS CALLED OUT BY A COUPLE OF BOYS.
THEY MIGHT BE THE GUYS FROM BEFORE. I THINK THEY WERE GOING TO THE ANNEX...
DASH

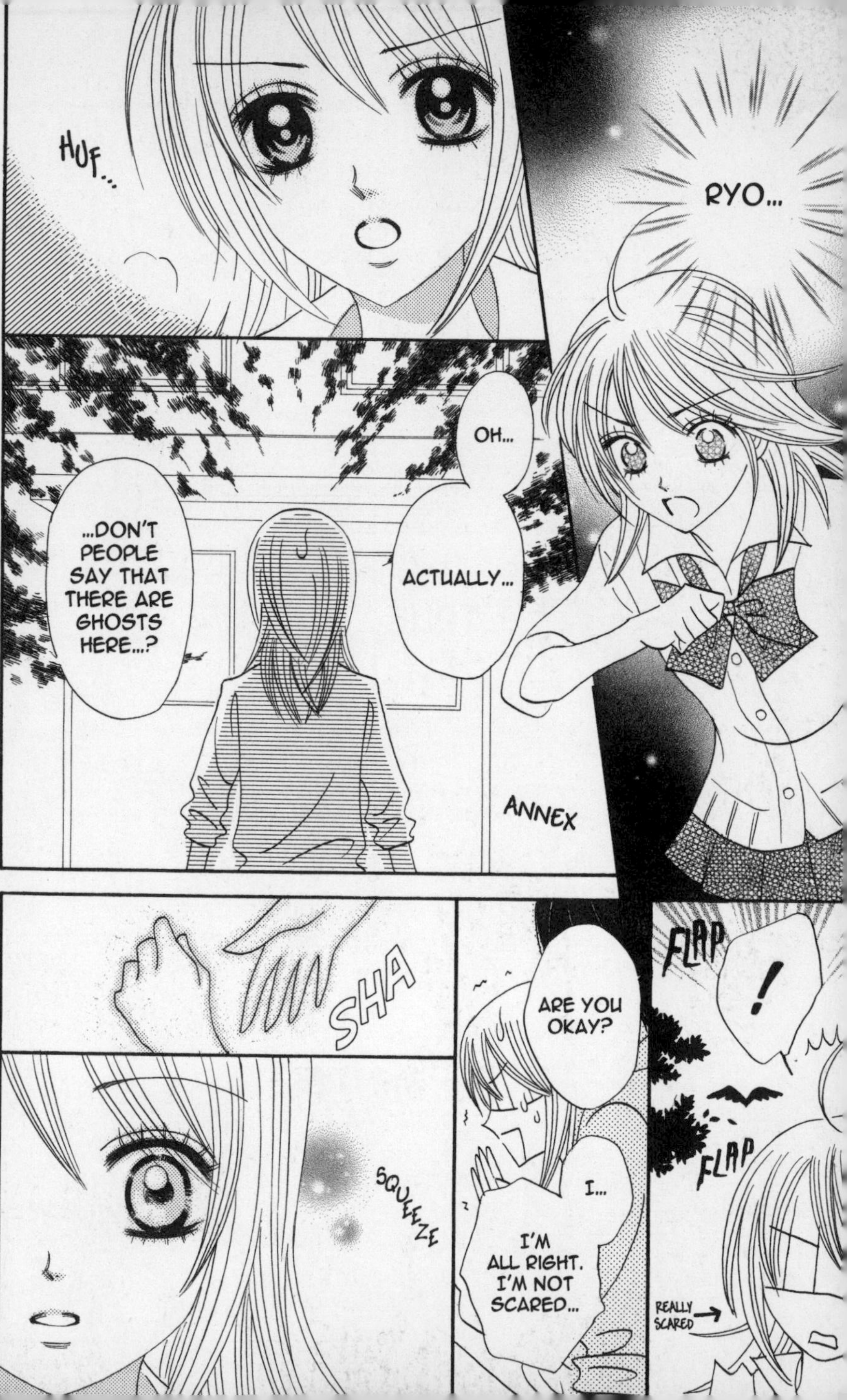
RYO...
HUF...
OH...
ACTUALLY...
...DON'T PEOPLE SAY THAT THERE ARE GHOSTS HERE...?
ANNEX
FLAP
!
FLAP
REALLY SCARED
ARE YOU OKAY?
I...
I'M ALL RIGHT. I'M NOT SCARED...
SHA
SQUEEZE

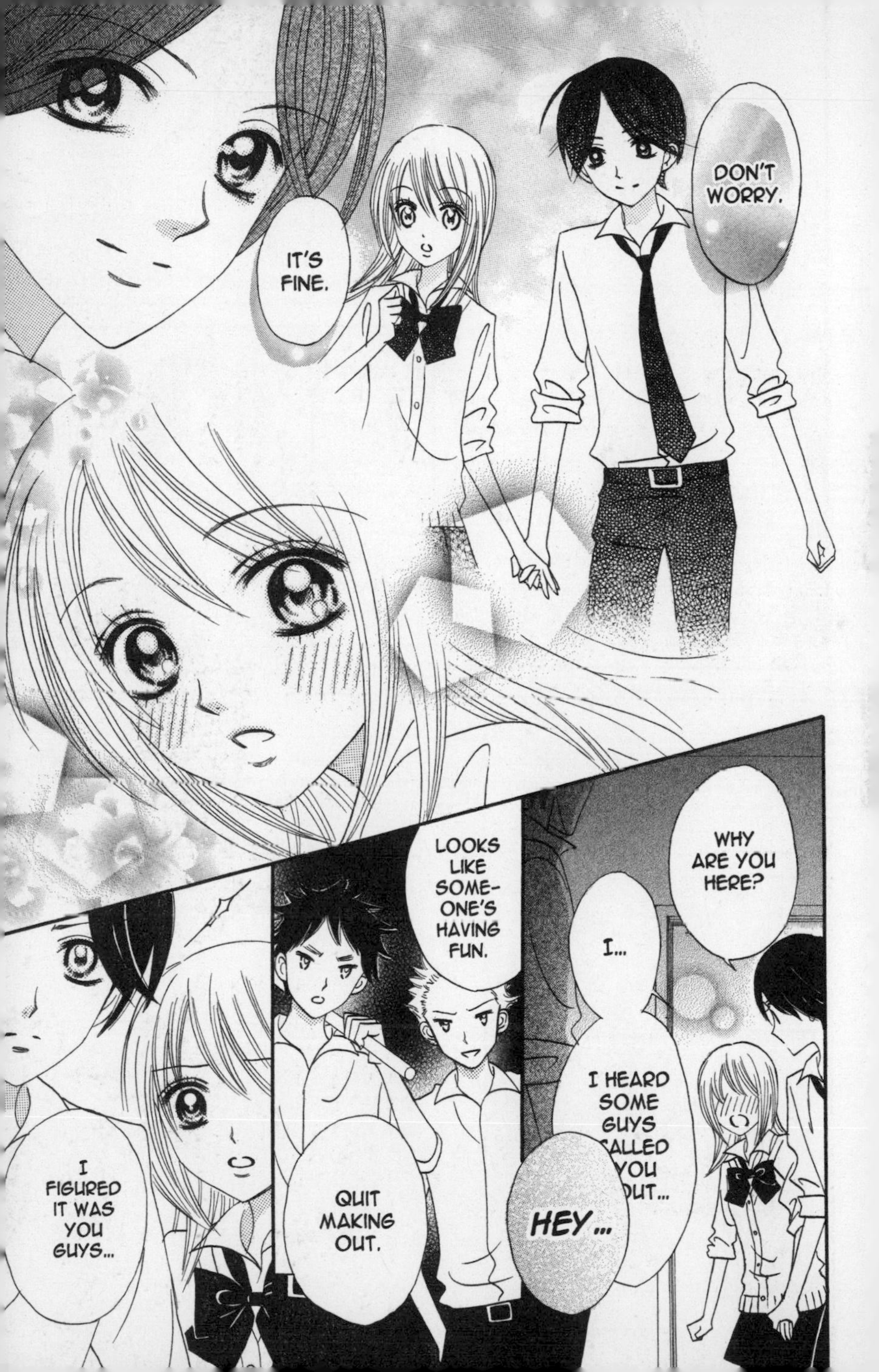
DON'T WORRY.
IT'S FINE.
WHY ARE YOU HERE?
I...
I HEARD SOME GUYS CALLED YOU OUT...
HEY...
LOOKS LIKE SOME-ONE'S HAVING FUN.
QUIT MAKING OUT.
I FIGURED IT WAS YOU GUYS...

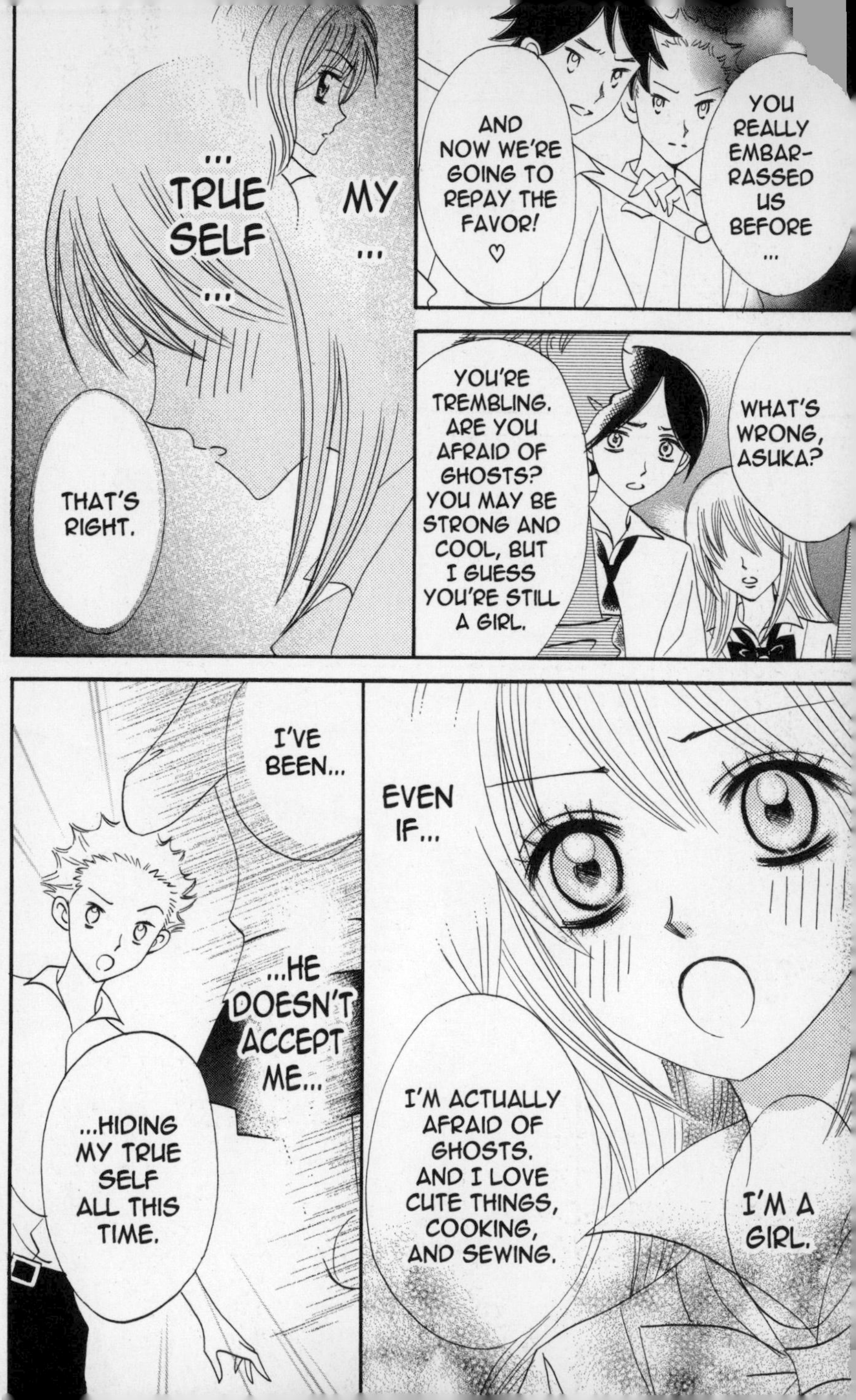
YOU REALLY EMBARRASSED US BEFORE...
AND NOW WE'RE GOING TO REPAY THE FAVOR! ♡
WHAT'S WRONG, ASUKA?
YOU'RE TREMBLING. ARE YOU AFRAID OF GHOSTS? YOU MAY BE STRONG AND COOL, BUT I GUESS YOU'RE STILL A GIRL.
MY ...
... TRUE SELF ...
THAT'S RIGHT.
I'M ACTUALLY AFRAID OF GHOSTS. AND I LOVE CUTE THINGS, COOKING, AND SEWING.
I'M A GIRL.
EVEN IF...
...HE DOESN'T ACCEPT ME...
I'VE BEEN...
...HIDING MY TRUE SELF ALL THIS TIME.

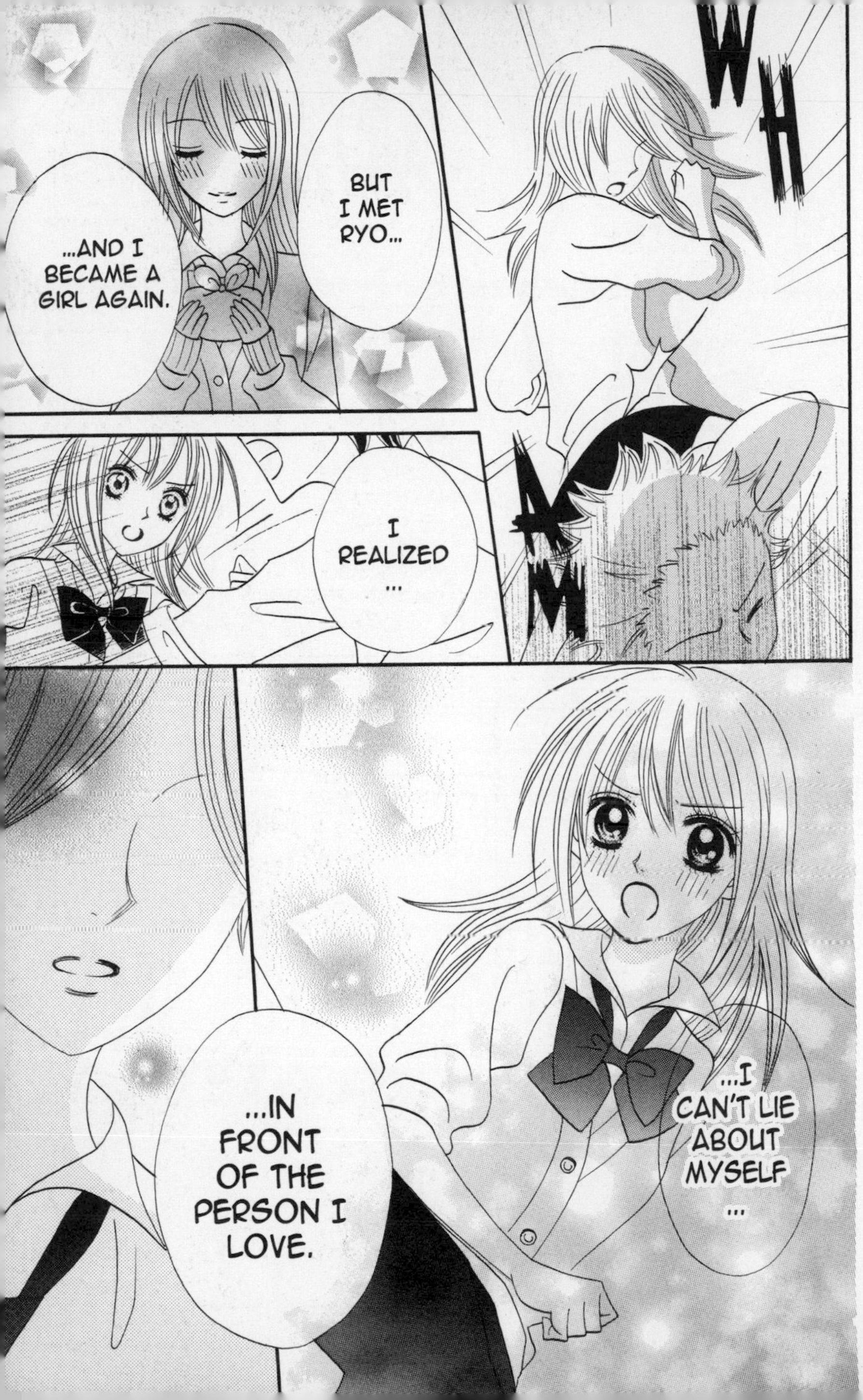
WHAM
BUT I MET RYO...
...AND I BECAME A GIRL AGAIN.
I REALIZED ...
...I CAN'T LIE ABOUT MYSELF ...
...IN FRONT OF THE PERSON I LOVE.

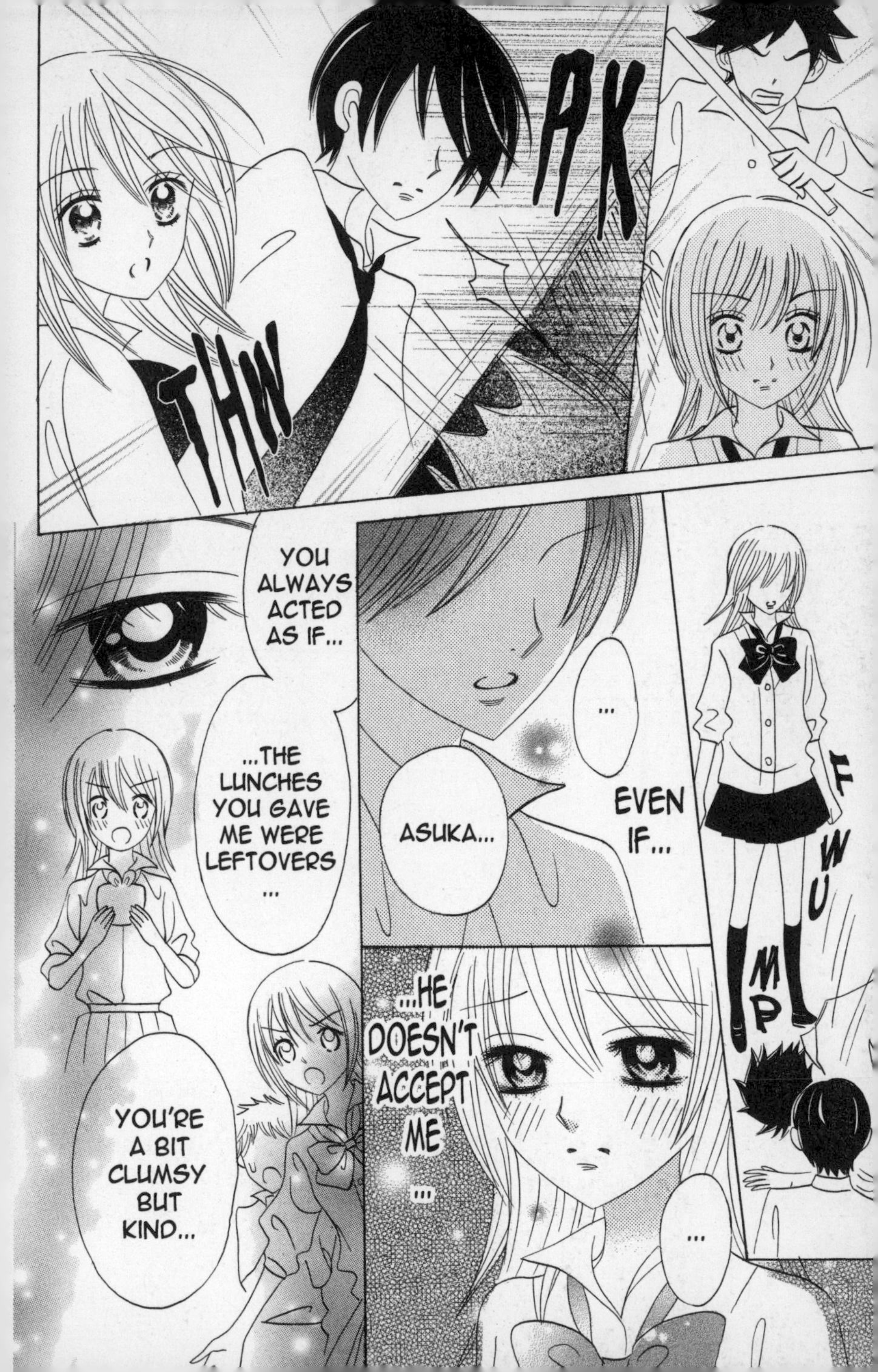

THW AK
FWUMP
...
EVEN IF...
ASUKA...
...HE DOESN'T ACCEPT ME ...
...
YOU ALWAYS ACTED AS IF...
...THE LUNCHES YOU GAVE ME WERE LEFTOVERS ...
YOU'RE A BIT CLUMSY BUT KIND...

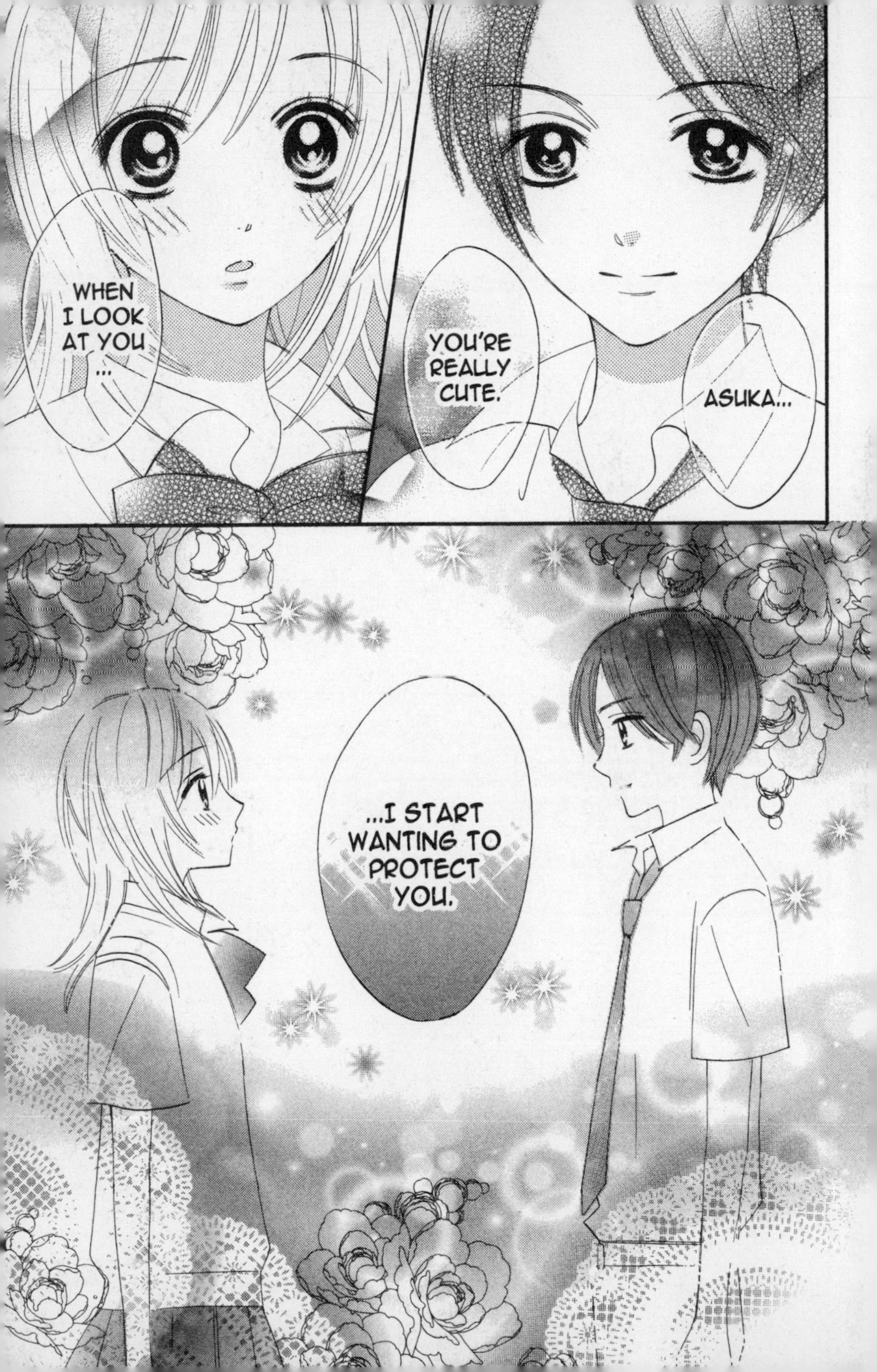
ASUKA...
YOU'RE REALLY CUTE.
WHEN I LOOK AT YOU ...
...I START WANTING TO PROTECT YOU.

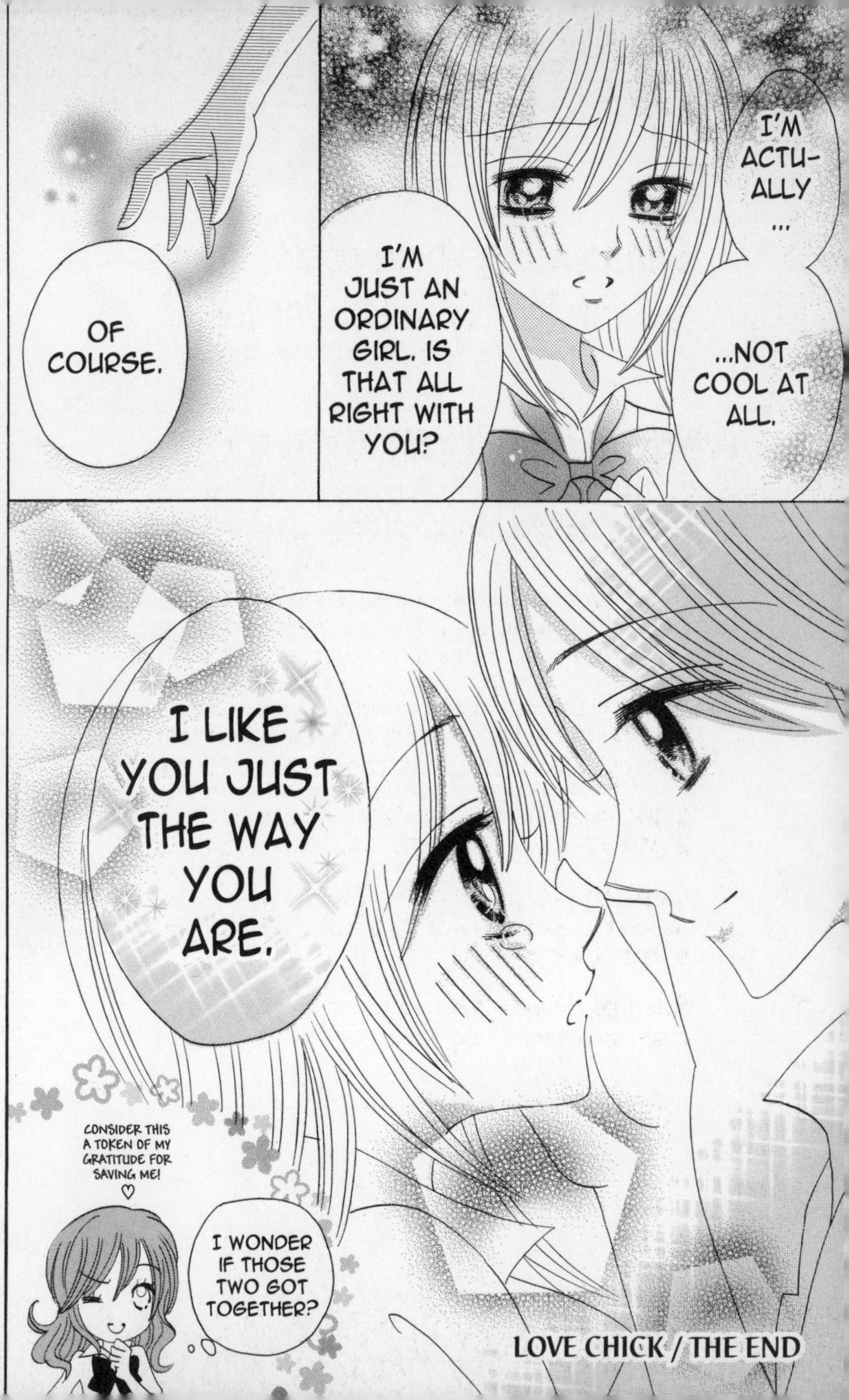
I'M ACTUALLY ...
...NOT COOL AT ALL.
I'M JUST AN ORDINARY GIRL. IS THAT ALL RIGHT WITH YOU?
OF COURSE.
I LIKE YOU JUST THE WAY YOU ARE.
CONSIDER THIS A TOKEN OF MY GRATITUDE FOR SAVING ME! ♡
I WONDER IF THOSE TWO GOT TOGETHER?
LOVE CHICK / THE END

Confused by some of the terms, but too MANLY to ask for help?

Here are some **cultural notes** to assist you!

Chan – an informal honorific used to address children and females. *Chan* can also be used toward animals, lovers, intimate friends and people whom one has known since childhood.

Kun – an informal honorific used primarily toward males; it can be used by people of more senior status addressing those junior to them or by anyone addressing male children.

San – the most common honorific title. It is used to address people outside one's immediate family and close circle of friends.

Senpai – used to address one's senior colleagues or mentor figures; it is used when students refer to or address more senior students in their school.

Sensei – honorific title used to address teachers as well as professionals such as doctors, lawyers and artists.

NOTES

Page 22, panel 4 | Bon Dance
A type of dance that is done during the Bon Festival (a Japanese Buddhist festivity where people pay their respects to the dead).

Page 102, panel 5 | Friendship Chocolate
In Japan, it's traditional for women to give chocolates to men on Valentine's Day (and men reciprocate the following month on White Day, 3/14). However, women can also give *tomo choco* (friendship chocolate) to female friends as well.

Page 153, panel 3 | Bento
A lunch box that may contain rice, meat, pickles and an assortment of side dishes. Sometimes the food is arranged in such a way as to resemble objects like animals, flowers, leaves, and so forth.

Page 155, panels 2–4 | Tale of Genji
Asuka is reading an excerpt from *Tale of Genji*, a classic work of literature written by Murasaki Shikibu.

Aya Kanno was born in Tokyo, Japan.
She is the creator of *Soul Rescue* and *Blank Slate*
(originally published as *Akusaga* in Japan's
BetsuHana magazine). Her latest work, *Otomen*,
is currently being serialized in *BetsuHana*.

OTOMEN

Vol. 11
Shojo Beat Edition

Story and Art by | **AYA KANNO**

Translation & Adaptation | **JN Productions**
Touch-up Art & Lettering | **Mark McMurray**
Design | **Fawn Lau**
Editor | **Amy Yu**

Otomen by Aya Kanno © Aya Kanno 2010
All rights reserved. First published in Japan in 2010 by HAKUSENSHA, Inc., Tokyo.
English language translation rights arranged with HAKUSENSHA, Inc., Tokyo.

The rights of the author(s) of the work(s) in this publication to be so identified
have been asserted in accordance with the Copyright, Designs and Patents Act 1988.
A CIP catalogue record for this book is available from the British Library.

Printed in the U.S.A.

Published by VIZ Media, LLC
P.O. Box 77010
San Francisco, CA 94107

10 9 8 7 6 5 4 3 2 1
First printing, August 2011

PARENTAL ADVISORY
OTOMEN is rated T for Teen and is
recommended for ages 13 and up. This
volume contains suggestive themes.
ratings.viz.com

www.viz.com

www.shojobeat.com

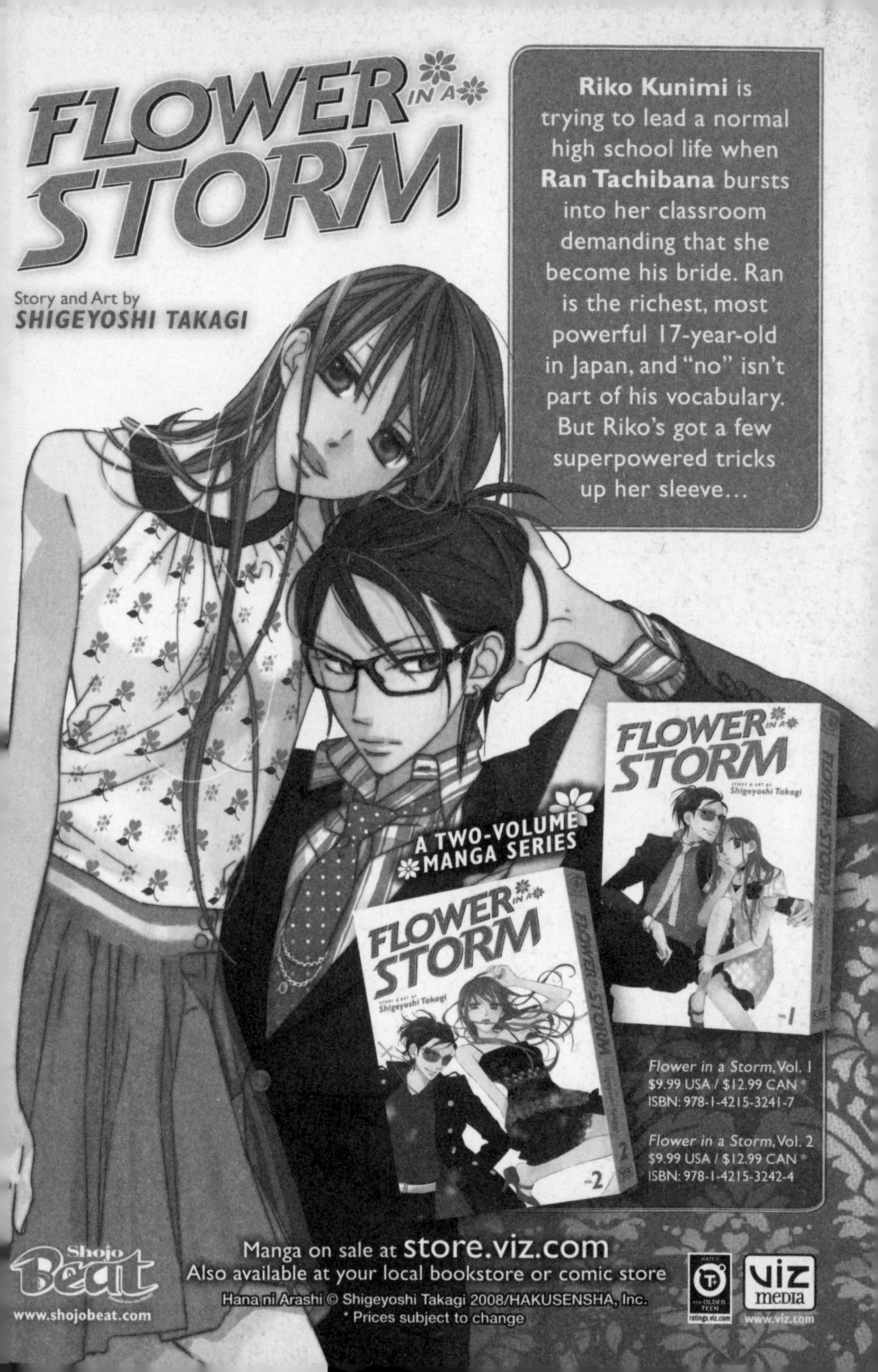
FLOWER IN A STORM
Story and Art by
SHIGEYOSHI TAKAGI
Riko Kunimi is trying to lead a normal high school life when Ran Tachibana bursts into her classroom demanding that she become his bride. Ran is the richest, most powerful 17-year-old in Japan, and "no" isn't part of his vocabulary. But Riko's got a few superpowered tricks up her sleeve...
A TWO-VOLUME MANGA SERIES
FLOWER IN A STORM
Story & Art by Shigeyoshi Takagi
Vol. 1
FLOWER IN A STORM
Story & Art by Shigeyoshi Takagi
Vol. 2
Flower in a Storm, Vol. 1
$9.99 USA / $12.99 CAN *
ISBN: 978-1-4215-3241-7
Flower in a Storm, Vol. 2
$9.99 USA / $12.99 CAN *
ISBN: 978-1-4215-3242-4
Manga on sale at store.viz.com
Also available at your local bookstore or comic store
Hana ni Arashi © Shigeyoshi Takagi 2008/HAKUSENSHA, Inc.
* Prices subject to change
Shojo Beat
www.shojobeat.com
RATED T+ FOR OLDER TEEN
ratings.viz.com
VIZ media
www.viz.com

library wars
Love & War

STORY & ART BY Kiiro Yumi ORIGINAL CONCEPT BY Hiro Arikawa

Winning the war on information, one book at a time

When the federal government tries to rid society of "unsuitable" books, an underground group of librarians and bibliophiles vows to fight back.

They are the Library Forces. And this is their story.

library
wars
1
Love & War

$9.99 USA / $12.99 CAN *
ISBN: 978-1-4215-3488-6

Manga on sale at **store.viz.com**
Also available at your local bookstore or comic store

Shojo Beat
www.shojobeat.com

RATED T+ FOR OLDER TEEN ratings.viz.com

VIZ media
www.viz.com

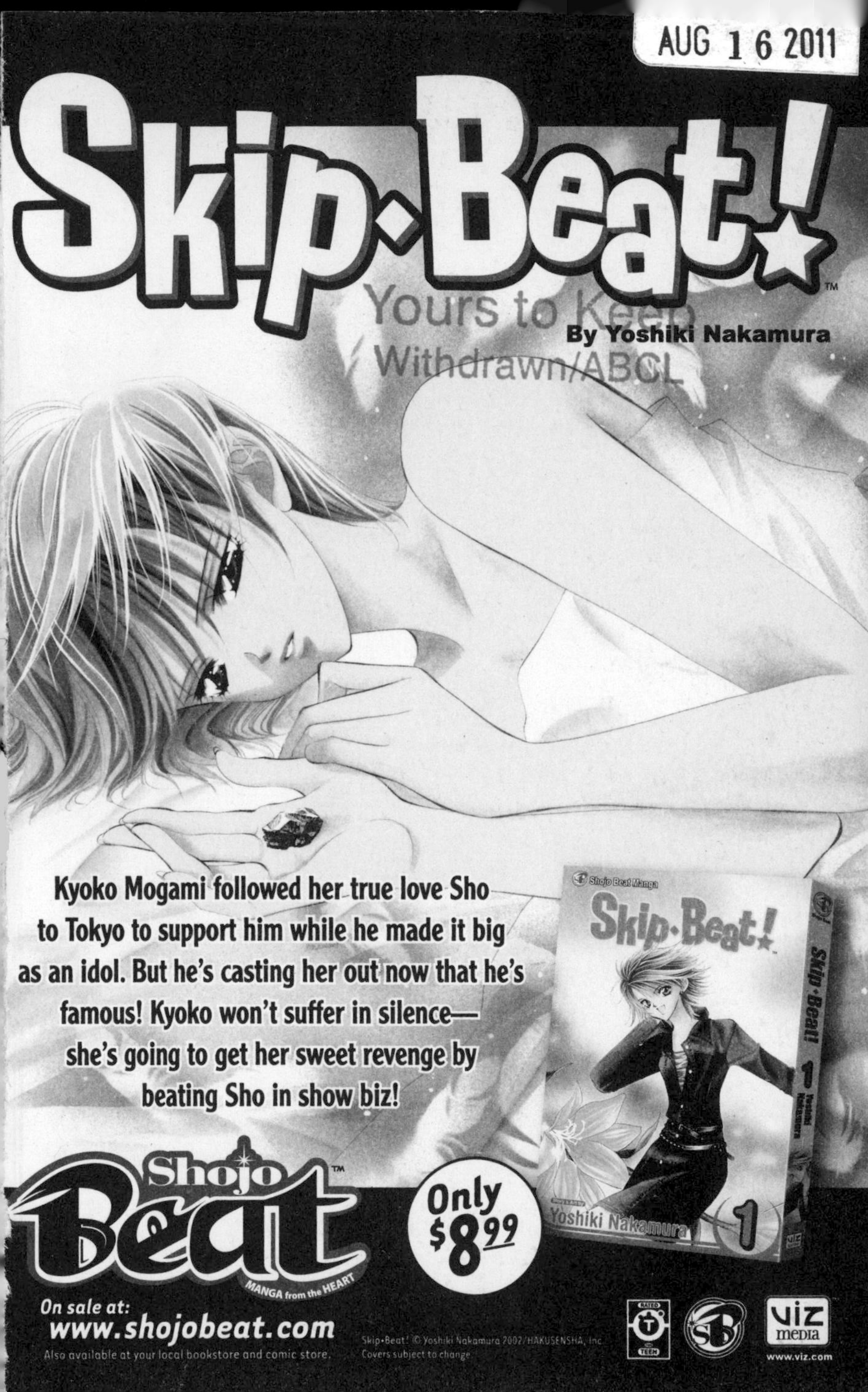
Skip·Beat!
By Yoshiki Nakamura
Kyoko Mogami followed her true love Sho to Tokyo to support him while he made it big as an idol. But he's casting her out now that he's famous! Kyoko won't suffer in silence—she's going to get her sweet revenge by beating Sho in show biz!
Shojo Beat Manga
Skip·Beat!
Yoshiki Nakamura
1
Shojo Beat
MANGA from the HEART
Only $8.99
On sale at:
www.shojobeat.com
Also available at your local bookstore and comic store.
Skip•Beat! © Yoshiki Nakamura 2002/HAKUSENSHA, Inc.
Covers subject to change.
RATED T TEEN
VIZ media
www.viz.com